Ex Libris
Terry J. Wall

Ex Libris
Terry J. Wall

"David Dockery has done it again. *Theology, Church, and Ministry: A Handbook for Theological Education* is an invaluable resource for the academy, the church, and all who care about theological education. It's both instructive and inspiring. I highly recommend it."
  —**Jason K. Allen**, president, Midwestern Baptist Theological Seminary

"Christian leaders recognize that formal theological education is in a state of change. A great deal of reshaping is already taking place in seminary education. But as new wineskins are created and old ones are refreshed, what are the indispensable and foundational elements that need to be established and strengthened? David Dockery, a highly respected Christian educator and leader, has assembled an excellent team of leaders and thinkers to address this question. The book presents an integrated and holistic vision for theological education. The application of this vision will lead to a greatly strengthened local church ministry that is both biblically rooted and culturally relevant."
  —**Clinton E. Arnold**, dean and professor of New Testament language and literature, Talbot School of Theology, Biola University

"In this impressive volume, David Dockery and a cadre of established scholars grapple with how to reintegrate the theological and ministerial disciplines that have been bifurcated over the past several centuries. I recommend it highly, not only for professors, but for pastors, seminary students, and theologically-minded Christians."
  —**Bruce Riley Ashford**, provost and professor of theology and culture, Southeastern Baptist Theological Seminary

"What a treasure! In an era where many people question the value and contribution of formal theological study, as well as its practicality and relevance, here is a book that not only makes the case but also shows it from virtually every angle possible. The book comes with both substance and heart, beating with a commitment to the pastor, the church, the hearts of believers, and the world. It reveals the value of theological reflection in its myriad ways of thinking about topics textually, theologically, historically, ethically, and transformatively, all with a view to edifying both the minister and the church. Simply well done."
  —**Darrell L. Bock**, senior research professor of New Testament studies and executive director of cultural engagement, Hendricks Center, Dallas Theological Seminary

"David Dockery is one of the most highly regarded leaders in Christian higher education. Thus it comes as no surprise that in *Theology, Church, and Ministry* he has enlisted a first-class group of scholars to serve as guides through the central issues related to theological education. In a time when ministerial training is often characterized by sharp divisions between disciplines as well as pedagogies aimed at passing on skills and information, the contributors refreshingly lead readers to a vision for theological integration aimed at spiritual formation. This is an important read for all of those involved in theological education."

—**Joshua D. Chatraw**, associate professor of theology and apologetics and executive director, The Center for Apologetics and Cultural Engagement, Liberty University

"The collection of essays by eminent seminarians and educators sheds light on all the foundational areas of theological education that we in the evangelical tradition value. *Theology, Church, and Ministry* establishes and emphasizes the synergistic connection between seminary and church, between theological education and ministry. Readers of this book whether in the West or in the Two-Thirds World, will not only appreciate the holistic view of theological education presented, but will be compelled to devote themselves to its high calling."

—**Choon Sam Fong**, dean of academic studies, Baptist Theological Seminary, Singapore

"Among theological educators in the non-western world, there have been ongoing discussions about how we should make our theological education more relevant and responsive to our own situations without compromising any biblical and historical content. Scholars are often confined to their own discipline without properly thinking about the holistic nature of theological education. To overcome such limitations I found this book extremely helpful. It is carefully crafted to prepare theological educators to be more well informed and integrally involved so that evangelical theological education becomes more missional and applicable while firmly rooted in the biblical and historical teachings. I greatly appreciate David Dockery and the many other writers for not only sharing their wisdom and experiences, but also for pushing their boundaries to be more global and futuristic."

—**Jung-Sook Lee**, president and professor of church history, Torch Trinity Graduate University, Seoul, South Korea

"*Theology, Church, and Ministry: A Handbook for Theological Education* reminds us of the essential kingdom partnership that is needed between the church and the academy in the preparation of God-called ministers of the gospel. This

important work will serve as an essential resource for those asking why we need theological education in the 21st century."
—**Ed Stetzer**, Billy Graham Professor of Church, Mission, and Evangelism, and executive director, The Billy Graham Center for Evangelism, Wheaton College

"At last, a book that strikes a compelling balance between the rigor of deep theological thought and the development of ministerial skill rooted in the fertile soil of biblical conviction. Hats off to our friend David Dockery for assembling an impressive list of contributors who are the kind of scholar-mentors that you wish you could spend an hour with. Thankfully, in this book, you can! *Theology, Church, and Ministry: A Handbook for Theological Education* is a must read for those of us who care about pleasing our Lord with our work and blessing his flock with our gifts."
—**Joseph Stowell**, president, Cornerstone University/Grand Rapids Theological Seminary

"*Theology, Church, and Ministry* is a most timely book. In a rapidly changing world where new challenges to remain faithful to the call of Christ present themselves to the church on what seems like a weekly basis, this book proves invaluable. The church today cannot afford to create silos that divide theological study and ministry practice. Just like theologians need to rethink, or refocus, their study to be directly helpful for ministry efforts, churches and ministers must re-ignite their interest in deep theological reflection on their practice to ensure faithfulness in their witness to Christ. This collection of essays is a rich and fruitful read for gospel ministers who are serious about their calling in times like these."
—**Preben Vang**, professor of Christian Scriptures and director, Doctor of Ministry Program, George W. Truett Theological Seminary, Baylor University

"This is a superlative, long awaited reference volume for those who are leaders or supporters of theological education. Under the expert guidance of Dr. David Dockery, a galaxy of highly regarded scholars and leaders has made this valuable resource available. It clarifies the role of theological education in preparing students for the pastorate and other ministries, explains its historical development, and offers guidance for further study. I wish such an outstanding volume had been available to me many years ago when I became involved in theological education."
—**Luder G. Whitlock Jr.**, president emeritus, Reformed Theological Seminary

THEOLOGY, CHURCH, AND MINISTRY

A HANDBOOK FOR
THEOLOGICAL EDUCATION

DAVID S. DOCKERY

EDITOR

NASHVILLE, TENNESSEE

Theology, Church, and Ministry
Copyright © 2017 David S. Dockery

Published by B&H Academic
Nashville, Tennessee

All rights reserved.

ISBN: 978-1-4336-4583-9

Dewey Decimal Classification: 230.071
Subject Heading: THEOLOGY—STUDY AND TEACHING \ RELIGIOUS EDUCATION \ CLERGY—EDUCATION

Unless otherwise noted, all Scripture quotations are taken from the Christian Standard Bible®, Copyright © 2017 by Holman Bible Publishers. Used by permission. Christian Standard Bible® and CSB® are federally registered trademarks of Holman Bible Publishers.

All Scripture marked ESV is taken from The ESV® Bible (The Holy Bible, English Standard Version®). ESV® Permanent Text Edition® (2016). Copyright © 2001 by Crossway, a publishing ministry of Good News Publishers. The ESV® text has been reproduced in cooperation with and by permission of Good News Publishers. Unauthorized reproduction of this publication is prohibited. All rights reserved.

All Scripture marked KJV is taken from the King James Version, which is in the public domain.

All Scripture marked NASB is taken from the New American Standard Bible®, Copyright © 1960,1962,1963,1968,1971,1972,1973,1975,1977,1995 by The Lockman Foundation. Used by permission.

All Scripture marked NIV is taken from The Holy Bible, New International Version®, NIV® Copyright © 1973, 1978, 1984, 2011 by Biblica, Inc.® Used by permission. All rights reserved worldwide.

All Scripture marked NLT is taken from the Holy Bible, New Living Translation copyright © 1996, 2004, 2007, 2013 by Tyndale House Foundation. Used by permission of Tyndale House Publishers Inc., Carol Stream, Illinois 60188. All rights reserved.

Victor Beuren | Astound US Inc
We have rights to use this illustration for the book,
ebook, and promotion of the book/ebook.
Any use for an unrelated product, or by a party outside of LifeWay
will need to be negotiated with Astound US.
(Our rep: Emily Coggins <emily@astound.us>)

Printed in the United States of America

1 2 3 4 5 6 7 8 9 10 VP 22 21 20 19 18 17

WITH GRATITUDE TO GOD FOR
Abigail, Emma, Hazel, Fisher, Colin, Annie, and Wesley

AND IN LOVING MEMORY OF
Harper

~ **PROVERBS 17:6** ~

Contents

Foreword xi
    Timothy George
Preface xv
Contributors xvii

SECTION ONE
THEOLOGICAL EDUCATION: AN INTRODUCTION

Theological Education: An Introduction 3
    David S. Dockery

Chapter One: The Foundation and Shape of Theological Education 23
    Mark L. Bailey

Chapter Two: Intellectual Discipleship
and the Value of Theological Education 43
    Sarah P. Sumner

Chapter Three: Theological Education and Ministry Calling 59
    Michael Duduit

Chapter Four: Theological Education and Spiritual Formation 74
    Dana M. Harris

SECTION TWO
THEOLOGICAL EDUCATION:
SHAPE OF MINISTRY PREPARATION

Chapter Five: Biblical Inspiration, Authority, and Canonicity 93
    D. Jeffrey Bingham

Chapter Six: The Languages of the Old Testament 115
    Kenneth A. Mathews

Chapter Seven: The Study of the Language of the New Testament 133
    Constantine R. Campbell

Chapter Eight: Introduction to the Old Testament 153
    Eric J. Tully

Chapter Nine: Introduction to the New Testament *Ray Van Neste*	174
Chapter Ten: Theology of the Old Testament *Daniel I. Block*	192
Chapter Eleven: Theology of the New Testament *Christopher W. Morgan*	217
Chapter Twelve: From Bible to Theology *Kevin J. Vanhoozer*	233
Chapter Thirteen: Systematic Theology *Malcolm B. Yarnell III*	257
Chapter Fourteen: Church History and Historical Theology *Gregory A. Wills*	281
Chapter Fifteen: Apologetics *R. Alan Streett*	299
Chapter Sixteen: Theological Ethics *Graham A. Cole*	316

SECTION THREE
THEOLOGICAL EDUCATION: CHURCH AND MINISTRY

Chapter Seventeen: Theology, Preaching, and Pastoral Ministry *Robert R. Smith*	335
Chapter Eighteen: Theology, Evangelism, and Missions *Charles (Chuck) E. Lawless*	355
Chapter Nineteen: Theology, Worldview Formation, and Cultural Engagement *Owen Strachan*	373
Chapter Twenty: Theology for Church, Worship, and Ministry *Daniel L. Akin*	389
Chapter Twenty-One: Theology and the Global Church *Timothy C. Tennent*	411
Scripture Index	429
Name Index	437
Subject Index	444

Foreword

TIMOTHY GEORGE

During the seven years I spent as a student at Harvard Divinity School, I frequently passed through Johnson Gate as I walked across Harvard Yard on my way to Widener Library. A plaque on the northern side of Johnson Gate contains a quotation from *New England's First Fruits* (1640), an early history of the Puritan beginnings of Massachusetts Bay Colony:

> After God had carried us safe to New England, and we had built our houses, provided necessaries for our livelihood, reared convenient places for God's worship, and settled the civil government: One of the next things we longed for, and looked after, was to advance learning and perpetuate it to posterity; dreading to leave an illiterate ministry to the churches, when our present ministers shall lie in the dust.

Harvard's Puritan forebears determined to establish what they called "a seminary in the wilderness" in order to train ministers of the gospel for the service of the church. Building on the Protestant heritage they had brought with them from the Old World, they wanted to pass on the faith intact to the rising generation. They assumed as something inherent in the nature of civil and humane society itself that *education* and *reformation* belonged invariably together.

The scholars who have contributed to this handbook represent evangelical theological schools and denominations which, at their best, have also stressed the coinherence of intellect and piety. But the fact is, we evangelicals have not always been at our best. We have often been contrarians and reactionaries. We have found it difficult to hold intellectual rigor and spiritual nurture in equipoise. Cotton Mather once reported that when his famous grandfather, John Cotton, was a student back in England, at Cambridge, he was worried that "if he became a godly man, t'would spoil him in being a *learned* one." But, of course, the opposite is also true. We can all think of students we have known who, in the process of becoming learned, have forgotten to be godly.

One of the themes that courses through this volume is the deadliness of such a dichotomy. Not so many years ago, few if any Protestant or evangelical seminaries paid much attention to spiritual formation. That was something the Catholics did! Now our accreditation standards hold us all accountable for the spiritual nurture of our students. Genuine theological education should aim for transformation, not the mere transfer of cognitive data from one mind to another. We can be satisfied with neither rigid intellectualism on the one hand nor unreflective sentimentalism on the other. Our aim ought to be rather head and heart together, puritanism and pietism, both together at their best. As Thomas Aquinas, echoing Augustine, put it, "Theology is taught by God, teaches God, and takes us to God."

But how to do this in a school that cultivates at once the life of the mind and the flourishing of the soul? It has now been more than two hundred years since Friedrich Schleiermacher published his *Brief Outline on the Study of Theology* (1811), establishing thereby a *ratio studiorum* for the various disciplines within a theological faculty. This well-tested fourfold schema (biblical, historical, systematic, practical) has served many generations of theological students and, with some modifications, remains intact in most seminaries to this day. But this pedagogical pattern has brought more disparity than clarity to the task of theological education. As Kevin Vanhoozer puts it, Schleiermacher's model "draws and quarters the body of theology into different members, distinct areas of specialization that, like the fallen Humpty Dumpty, cannot easily be put back together." This has resulted in the loss of a coherent theological vision, as more and more theological teachers seek a sense of *primary* identification with a professional guild of like-minded scholars. Add to this a disjointed cafeteria-styled curricula, and the graduation of typical (stereotypical?) seminary "products" who are not theologians in any serious sense of the word. This problem is not unique to evangelical theological schools, but neither are they exempt from it. Some of the essays in this volume define and defend traditional disciplines within the body of divinity, seeking to show connections across the curriculum. Others suggest ways of addressing and overcoming fragmentation itself.

Max Stackhouse once defined the task of theological education as the shaping of ministers formed by the "warranted wisdom" and "grounded *scientia*" of the Christian tradition. For evangelicals, the precise *warranting* and *grounding* of this work must be defined both in terms of a specific doctrinal content and a foundation of *praxis*. Cardinal Newman wrote that "nothing is easier than to use the word 'God' and mean nothing by it." Theological seminaries exist to serve the mission of God—the covenantal God of the Bible, the one, true, eternal, living, triune God of holiness and love—and this means prayer and worship are not ancillary but central to their core identity.

A theological seminary is not a church, but it is a school of the church, and all who study, work, and teach in such a school share a sacred calling. Lesslie Newbigin reminded us that the church of Jesus Christ is the embodiment of gospel truth made alive in the power of the Holy Spirit. The church is not only the most effective apologetic for the Christian message in our increasingly fragile and fragmented world, but it is also the only one likely to get a hearing in such a world. The ecclesial vocation of theological education requires all of us to pray and work for healthier churches, for our theological schools will not flourish without faithful communities of God's people to join them in partnerships of prayer and mutual support.

Theological education over the next decades of the twenty-first century will need to be increasingly personal, incarnational, global, and gospel centered. It will also need to take the longer view and remember the summons to humility found in these words by Reinhold Niebuhr:

> Nothing that is worth doing can be achieved in a life time; therefore we must be saved by hope. Nothing which is true or beautiful or good makes complete sense in any immediate context of history; therefore we must be saved by faith. Nothing we do, however virtuous, can be accomplished alone. Therefore we are saved by love.

Preface

Theology, Church, and Ministry: A Handbook for Theological Education has been designed to introduce readers to the place that theological education plays in preparing God-called ministers for service in the church of the Lord Jesus Christ. The initial section seeks to help readers understand what theological education is, how it has developed, and the role it has in providing formation and preparation for ministry. The second section surveys the heart of a theological education curriculum including the study of biblical languages; the introduction to the Old and New Testaments; the importance of biblical inspiration and hermeneutics; the place of biblical, systematic, and historical theology; along with the significant areas of ethics and apologetics. The final section of this volume aims to help readers see the connection between theology, church, and ministry with an eye toward preaching, pastoral ministry, worship, evangelism, missions, and worldview formation. The final chapters help readers connect theological education to the church, and to the ever-expanding need to understand the importance of the global church.

There has been no effort to conform the chapters to a uniform approach. Each author, dealing with his or her subject, has been given the freedom to shape the chapter in light of an overall purpose, which is to show the importance of theological education for the church, and the importance of each subject for the work of theological education. Because the study of languages differs from the study of theology, which differs from preaching, we believe readers will get a better sense of the various subject matters and approaches to the overall work of theological education by allowing each chapter to be so developed.

A volume of this kind cannot address every discipline that is taught at seminaries and divinity schools. A second volume would be needed to include chapters on church music, Christian education, pastoral counseling, psychology of religion, world religions, sociology of religion, church leadership, church recreation, demographically based ministries (such as ministry to singles, youth, children, and seniors), as well as other topics. The chapters that are included primarily focus on preparation for pastoral ministry and those areas that are foundational for all types of ministry.

Each chapter provides a broad survey and introduction of the field, helping the readers understand why these areas of study are important for theological education, while also pointing to some initial steps that indicate how the subject of the chapter relates to the larger field of theological education. This handbook is an introductory study that has been prepared for prospective theological students, interested donors and friends, as well as board members who guide and direct institutions across this country and around the world. The goal of this volume is to help all of us involved in the work of theological education better understand its importance for the life of the church. Each chapter points readers beyond what is found therein with helpful questions ("Questions for Further Reflection") and a list of books or key articles ("Sources for Further Study").

I want to thank each contributor for participating in this collaborative effort. Each brings significant experience and expertise to this work. Hopefully the various perspectives representing numerous institutional and denominational backgrounds will produce a pleasing symphonic harmony for our readers. In addition, I want to offer a word of appreciation to Chris Thompson and Jim Baird for their guidance for this volume. I am grateful for the encouragement offered by Jean Myers and the conscientious assistance provided by Lisa Weathers. Lisa's careful attention to each step of this project has been a true gift. Finally, I want to say a big "thank you" to my wife, Lanese, who has provided prayer support for yet another writing project. Our prayer is that many will be helped by this volume, that the church will be strengthened, and that our great God will be glorified.

Soli Deo Gloria
David S. Dockery

Contributors

Daniel L. Akin, president, Ed Young Sr. Chair of Expository Preaching, and professor of preaching and theology, Southeastern Baptist Theological Seminary

Mark L. Bailey, president and senior professor of Bible exposition, Dallas Theological Seminary

D. Jeffrey Bingham, dean, School of Theology, and professor of theology, Southwestern Baptist Theological Seminary

Daniel I. Block, Gunther H. Knoedler professor of Old Testament, Wheaton College

Constantine R. Campbell, associate professor of New Testament, Trinity Evangelical Divinity School

Graham A. Cole, dean and professor of biblical and systematic theology, Trinity Evangelical Divinity School

David S. Dockery, president, Trinity International University / Trinity Evangelical Divinity School

Michael Duduit, founding dean, College of Christian Studies and the Clamp Divinity School, professor of Christian ministry, Anderson University

Dana M. Harris, associate professor of New Testament, Trinity Evangelical Divinity School and editor, *Trinity Journal*

Charles E. (Chuck) Lawless, dean and vice president of graduate studies and ministry centers and professor of evangelism and missions, Southeastern Baptist Theological Seminary

Kenneth A. Mathews, professor of Old Testament, Beeson Divinity School

Christopher W. Morgan, dean of the School of Christian Ministries and professor of theology, California Baptist University

CONTRIBUTORS

Robert R. Smith Jr., Charles T. Carter Baptist Chair of Divinity, Beeson Divinity School

Owen Strachan, associate professor of Christian theology and director, The Center for Theological and Cultural Engagement, Midwestern Baptist Theological Seminary

R. Alan Streett, senior research professor of biblical theology, Criswell College

Sarah P. Sumner, founder and president, Right On Mission Academy

Timothy C. Tennent, president and professor of world Christianity, Asbury Theological Seminary

Eric J. Tully, assistant professor of Old Testament and Semitic languages, Trinity Evangelical Divinity School

Kevin J. Vanhoozer, research professor of systematic theology, Trinity Evangelical Divinity School

Ray Van Neste, professor of biblical studies and director, Ryan Center for Biblical Studies, Union University

Gregory A. Wills, dean, School of Theology, and David T. Porter Professor of Church History, The Southern Baptist Theological Seminary

Malcolm B. Yarnell III, research professor of systematic theology, director of the Oxford Study Program, and director of the Center for Theological Research, Southwestern Baptist Theological Seminary

Section One
Theological Education: An Introduction

Theological Education: An Introduction

DAVID S. DOCKERY

*"Make disciples of all nations . . .
teaching them to observe everything I have commanded you."*
—MATTHEW 28:19–20

"You heard about him and were taught by him, as the truth is in Jesus."
—EPHESIANS 4:21

"Holding to the faithful message as taught."
—TITUS 1:9

Theological education in the twenty-first century must carry out the essential teaching task commissioned by the risen Christ (Matt 28:19–20). Based on Paul's teaching in Eph 4:11–16, the church has attempted to carry out this charge since the first century. The goals of this teaching ministry are threefold: to build up the church, to lead it to maturity in faith, and to lead it to unity.[1] Those goals continue to be the focus of the teaching arm of the church, which is a function that belongs to institutions of theological education. Theological education must be academically sound; it must be grounded in the Scriptures; it must be Christ centered; and it must be

---

1. See Robert L. Saucy, "Doing Theology for the Church," in *The Necessity of Systematic Theology*, ed. John Jefferson Davis (Grand Rapids: Baker, 1978), 61–74.

ministry and mission focused. Theological educators need to be sensitive to the changes in the churches and in society. They also need courage to lead and a listening ear to respond to the churches; indeed, it is a two-way street.[2]

Theological institutions have a responsibility to prepare ministers for the issues they will encounter in the churches while remaining focused on the classical disciplines of theology.[3] Theological education at its best focuses on head, heart, and hands. If those involved in the work of theological education focus only on the head, we will have ministers who are well informed but not Christianly formed. Theological education in the twenty-first century must help people develop (1) a theologically informed way of seeing the world (the head), (2) Christian responses to life (the heart), and (3) Christian strategies and motivations for ministry (hands). We believe this full-orbed understanding can only be addressed when we understand that theology and theological understanding find their focus in the church.[4] The history of the church has been intertwined with this important work, even though most historians locate the first freestanding seminary in the early nineteenth century.[5] Let us turn our attention to a brief look at these key developments throughout the history of the church.[6]

From the New Testament Period to the Time of Augustine

Little difference can be discerned between the theological preparation provided for church members and that designed for church leaders in the apostolic and postapostolic periods. Pastors and church leaders were called to ongoing study (2 Tim 2:15) in order to provide oversight for the ministry of the Word of God in the midst of worship services, as well as to train and disciple new converts (2 Tim 2:2; Titus 1:9).

---

2. See David S. Dockery, "Ministry and Seminary in a New Century," *Southern Seminary Magazine* 62:2 (1994): 20–22.

3. See David S. Dockery, "A Theology for the Church," *Midwestern Journal of Theology* 1, no. 1 (2003): 10–20.

4. See John Frame, "Studying Theology as a Servant of Jesus," *Reformation and Renewal* 11, no. 1 (Winter 2002): 45–69; and Craig S. Keener, *The Mind of the Spirit* (Grand Rapids: Baker, 2016), 257–66.

5. See George M. Marsden, *The Soul of the American University: From Protestant Establishment to Established Nonbelief* (New York: Oxford University Press, 1994), 74.

6. See Michael Reeves, *Theologians You Should Know. An Introduction: From the Apostolic Fathers to the 21st Century* (Wheaton: Crossway, 2016), for an introduction to the thinkers who have shaped theological education through the years.

Apostolic Period

The apostle Paul, writing to the church at Thessalonica, urged followers of Jesus Christ to "stand firm and hold to the traditions you were taught, whether by what we said or what we wrote" (2 Thess 2:15). Similarly the apostle exhorted Timothy, his apostolic legate, to "hold on to the pattern of sound teaching" (2 Tim 1:13). The history of Christianity is best understood as a chain of memory.[7]

Wherever the Christian faith has been found, there has been close association with the written Word of God, with books, education, and learning. Studying and interpreting the Bible became natural for members of the early Christian community, having inherited the practice from late Judaism.[8]

The tradition that would eventually shape more formal approaches to theological education locates its roots in the interpretation of Holy Scripture. From the earliest days of Christian history, Christians have used the Bible in various ways.[9] The rich heritage has shaped the Christian tradition on both individual and corporate practices. Some of these include (1) the Bible as a source for information and understanding of life, (2) the Bible as a guide for worship, (3) the Bible as a wellspring to formulate Christian liturgy, (4) the Bible as a primary source for the formulation of theology, (5) the Bible as a text for preaching or teaching, (6) the Bible as a guide for pastoral care, (7) the Bible as a foundation for spiritual formation, and (8) the Bible as the model for literary and aesthetic enjoyment.

Postapostolic Tradition

Beginning in the second century, some of these uses of the Bible started to shape the early stages of theological education in the church, which was shaped by a shared faith in the uniqueness and significance of Jesus of Nazareth. Formal training by the time of the second century, during

---

7. See Gregg R. Allison, *Historical Theology: An Introduction to Christian Doctrine* (Grand Rapids: Zondervan, 2011); David S. Dockery and Timothy George, *The Great Tradition of Christian Thinking* (Grand Rapids: Crossway, 2012); and John Rogerson, Christopher Rowland, and Barnabas Lindars, *The History of Christian Theology* (Grand Rapids: Eerdmans, 1988).

8. See Virginia Stem Owens, "Fiction and the Bible," *Reformed Journal* 38 (July 1988): 12–13; and Richard N. Longenecker, *Biblical Exegesis in the Apostolic Period* (Grand Rapids: Eerdmans, 1975).

9. See Karfried Froehlich, *Biblical Interpretation in the Early Church* (Philadelphia: Fortress, 1984); and Gerald Bray, *Biblical Interpretation: Past and Present* (Downers Grove: InterVarsity, 1996).

the time of Justin Martyr (100–165), Irenaeus (125–202), and Tertullian (150–225), tended to focus in areas of philosophy and rhetoric.[10]

The authority of the church, the canon, and efforts toward theological formation had reached new heights by the beginning of the third century, which saw the rise of schools, intertwined with classical learning, science, philosophy, and centers of art. Steps toward serious biblical interpretation and theological education began to develop and mature in the schools of Alexandria and Antioch.[11] During this time Origen (185–254) and Clement (150–215) provided creative leadership for the Alexandrians, while John Chrysostom (349–407) and Theodore of Mopsuestia (350–428) greatly influenced developments in Antioch. The Alexandrians looked to the rule of faith and mystical interpretation as key sources for shaping theological education for the people of God. The Antiochenes looked to reason and the historical development of Scripture as the foci for understanding Christian thought.

Athanasius (296–371), more than anyone else during the fourth century, shaped the church's understanding of the expanding rule of faith, which became the framework for theological understanding and catechesis. The brilliant fourth-century theologian greatly influenced the three great Cappadocian fathers: Basil of Caesarea (ca. 329–379), his brother Gregory of Nyssa (ca. 330–395), and his friend Gregory of Nazianzus (ca. 330–389). In this splendid trio the subject matters for theological education with the orthodox statements about Jesus Christ and the trinitarian God reached their climax. Because of the Christological debates in the fourth and fifth centuries, church leaders became more theologically oriented in their approach to reading Scripture. The consistent articulation of the church's orthodox faith, coupled with pastoral concerns for the edification of the faithful, provided norms for the shaping and advancement of the work of theological instruction.[12]

---

10. See Henry Chadwick, *Early Christian Thought and Classical Tradition* (Oxford: Clarendon, 1966); Robert M. Grant, *Greek Apologists of the Second Century* (Philadelphia: Westminster, 1988); and J. N. D. Kelly, *Early Christian Doctrines* (San Francisco: Harper and Row, 1978).

11. See Alloys Grillmeier, *Christ in the Christian Tradition*, vol. I, *From the Apostolic Age to Chalcedon* (451), trans. by John Bowden, 2nd ed. (Atlanta: John Knox, 1974); R. V. Sellers, *Two Ancient Christologies: A Study in the Christological Thought of the Schools of Alexandria and Antioch in the Early History of Christian Doctrine* (London: SPCK, 1954); and Jaroslav Pelikan, *The Preaching of Chrysostom* (Philadelphia: Fortress Press, 1967).

12. See Craig A. Blaising, *Athanasius* (Lanham, MD: University Press, 1992); Gerald L. Bray, *Creeds, Councils and Christ* (Downers Grove: InterVarsity, 1984), 92–171.

The Influence of Augustine

The father of the Christian intellectual tradition and the most influential shaper of Christian theology during the first thousand years of church history was Augustine (351–430).[13] He gladly upheld the authority of the rule of faith, thus shaping the confessional tradition, as had no one before him. Augustine's brilliance could hold together creativity and creed; author, text, and interpreter; the historical and the figurative/allegorical; as well as faith and reason.[14]

In holding together faith and reason, Augustine paved the way for future theologians and theological educators. He provided a model for thinking Christianly about the world, stressing the priority of faith for understanding God's revelation to humanity in creation, experience, and ultimately in Jesus Christ and Holy Scripture.[15] In doing so Augustine always stressed that biblical interpretation and Christian thinking about all aspects of life should encourage love for God, for the church, and for neighbor. Augustine's influence on the shape of the Christian intellectual tradition and theological education has been, in many ways, incalculable. Some even suggest that the work of shaping the theological tradition over the past fifteen hundred years is best understood as a footnote to the work of Augustine. Augustine left for following generations the legacy of a monastic life committed to study, evidenced by his prolific writings.[16]

Justo González has noted that during this time the practice also arose of employing monastic life as an opportunity to study. The monastic schools began to occupy a central place in European intellectual life as well as for those preparing for ministry. While what can be called theological education greatly advanced during this period, we must recognize that there were still no formal schools for the preparation of ministers. Personal mentoring, guidance, and teaching from pastors and bishops, including Augustine himself, remained the primary model for theological education.[17]

---

13. See Matthew Levering, *The Theology of Augustine* (Grand Rapids: Baker, 2013).
14. See Robert E. Cushman, "Faith and Reason," in *A Companion to the Study of St. Augustine*, ed. Roy W. Battenhouse (New York: Oxford, 1955), 290–94.
15. See Beryl Smalley, *The Study of the Bible in the Early Middle Ages*, 2nd ed. (Oxford: Blackwell, 1952).
16. See Peter Brown, *Augustine of Hippo: A Biography* (Berkeley: University of California Press, 2013).
17. See Justo L. González, *The History of Theological Education* (Nashville: Abingdon, 2015), 19–23.

The Medieval and Reformation Periods

These important centuries were shaped and introduced by the ecumenical councils of the church (325–787).[18] As the church expanded and matured, it also faced new and greater challenges concerning the church's beliefs. How should the Trinity be believed and proclaimed? If Jesus Christ is fully God, how can he simultaneously be fully human? If Jesus Christ is one person, how do we understand his two natures and two wills? What is meant by the phrase, "the Holy Spirit, the life giver"? Questions regarding the Trinity, the incarnation of Jesus Christ, and the nature and sinfulness of humanity ushered in and characterized the years known as the medieval period. This was a time when the church's understandings of its leadership and organization were developing into their hierarchical form. The theological tradition during this time was challenged, expanded, and strengthened, particularly through the efforts of Anselm (1033–1109), Bernard of Clairvaux (1090–1153), and Thomas Aquinas (1225–1274).[19]

Medieval Education

The students of these outstanding thinkers for the most part became pastors, but these teachers of the church did not perceive of their role as primarily preparing people for ministry. In seeking to prioritize and advance the Christian intellectual tradition, they helped provide a prominent place for the developing universities birthed during these years. While early Christian education emphasized catechetical purposes, medieval universities were largely shaped for the purpose of professional education, with some general education for the elite. Of the seventy-nine universities in existence in Europe during this time, Salerno was best known for medicine, Bologna for law, and Paris for theology.[20] Thus the aim of most medieval institutions was not focused on ministerial education so much as philosophical and contemplative inquiries.[21]

---

18. See Gerald Bray, *Creeds, Councils and Christ: Did the Early Christians Misrepresent Jesus?* (Dublin: Mentor, 2009).
19. See William C. Placher, *A History of Christian Theology* (Philadelphia: Westminster, 1983), 146.
20. See Jonathan Hill, *The History of Christian Thought* (Downers Grove: InterVarsity, 2003), 131–60.
21. See Mark Noll, "Reconsidering Christendom," in *The Future of Christian Learning*, ed. Thomas A. Howard (Grand Rapids: Brazos, 2008), 23–70; and Alister McGrath, *The Intellectual Origins of the European Reformation* (Oxford: Blackwell, 2004), 11–117.

Nowhere was this kind of serious Christian engagement better seen in this medieval context than in the work of Thomas Aquinas. Aquinas carried on a multisided conversation with the biblical text, the church fathers, and Aristotle. Simultaneously, he invested in both dialogical and apologetical responses to Muslim and Jewish thinkers such as Averroes and Maimonides. Before and after the Reformation, the work of Aquinas greatly influenced Roman Catholic thinkers as well as Protestant philosophers.[22]

Aquinas and other medieval thinkers flourished in a context where the Christian faith provided shape and illumination for the intellectual landscape and the central mission of the university generally focused on inquiry in pursuit of truth. Faith in the context of medieval Christendom was understood to be an indispensable ally, not an enemy, of reason and intellectual exploration. Since the medieval period, Christian universities which arose *ex corde ecclesia*, "from the heart of the church," have been one of the primary places where the Christian faith has been advanced and from which formal ministerial education began to take shape.[23]

The Renaissance

The Renaissance envisioned the revival of Greek and Roman literature while newer subjects were developing during the medieval periods such as arithmetic, geometry, and music. The Reformation period placed education within the context of a Christian worldview. While Martin Luther (1483–1546) is widely recognized as the father of the Reformation, in reality he, in many ways, carried forward the work of Peter Waldo (1140–1218), John Wycliffe (1330–1384), Jon Hus (1373–1415), Girolamo Savonarola (1452–1498), and even Desiderius Erasmus (1466–1536). All of these prioritized the Scriptures in bold ways, but Erasmus (even more so than Luther), through the influence of John Colet (1466–1519), rediscovered the priority of the historical sense of biblical interpretation.[24]

---

22. See E. Gilson, *The Christian Philosophy of St. Thomas Aquinas*, trans. L. K. Shook (London: Victor Gollancz, 1957).

23. John J. Piderit, "The University at the Heart of the Church," *First Things* 94 (June/July 1999): 22–25; see also David C. Steinmetz, "The Superiority of Pre-critical Exegesis, *Theology Today* 27 (1980): 31–32.

24. See David S. Dockery, "The History of Pre-critical Interpretation," *Faith and Mission* 10 (1992): 3–33; and David S. Dockery, "Foundations for Reformation Hermeneutics: A Fresh Look at Erasmus," in *Evangelical Hermeneutics*, ed. M. Bauman and D. Hall (Camp Hill, PA: Christian Publications, 1995), 53–76.

Erasmus exemplified the finest in Renaissance scholarship, which emphasized the priority of the original sources (*ad fontes*). The ultimate source to which Erasmus turned was the Greek New Testament.[25] Coupled with his emphasis on the sources was a truly historical understanding of ancient texts, yet he also desired for the biblical texts to bring edification to the readers through the spiritual sense. As significant and as innovative was the work of Erasmus, the pivotal and shaping figures of the Reformation were Martin Luther (1483–1546) and John Calvin (1509–1564).

Reformation Initiatives

Luther, reclaiming the key aspects of the Augustinian tradition, also insisted that the Bible itself is its own best interpreter. This commitment rested on the foundation of a complete trust in the Bible's truthfulness and authority. Believing that the God of truth had spoken in Scripture, Luther likewise believed humans must stand under the authority of the Bible. Scripture provided the framework for seeing all of life and for understanding all human thinking because, for Luther, the Bible was the Word of God itself. Luther thought deeply about the relationship between faith and reason, demanding that the human intellect adjust itself to the teachings of Holy Scripture.[26] Luther's bold advances have influenced Christian thinkers and the works of theological education for five centuries, yet John Calvin in a sense "out-Luthered" Luther to shape aspects of the Christian intellectual tradition that have developed since the sixteenth century.

John Calvin was the finest interpreter of Scripture and the most precise Christian thinker of this period. Even a rival such as Jacob Arminius claimed that Calvin's work was incomparable, saying, "He stands above others, above most, indeed, above all."[27] Calvin stressed education, providing a catechetical system that has been carried all over the world. Calvin's theology, best seen in the final edition of his *Institutes*

---

25. See J. H. Bentley, *Humanist and the Holy Writ* (Princeton: Princeton University Press, 1983), 115–26; and A. Rabil, *Erasmus and the New Testament: The Mind of a Christian Humanist* (San Antonio: Trinity University Press, 1972), 43–45.
26. See David S. Dockery, "Martin Luther's Christological Hermeneutics," *Grace Theological Journal* 2 (1983): 189–203.
27. Cited by C. Bangs, *Arminius: A Study in the Dutch Reformation* (Nashville: Abingdon, 1971), 287–88.

of the Christian Religion (1559), influenced large sectors of Europe, Old and New England.[28]

Yet Philip Melanchthon (1497–1560) more than anyone else in the Reformation period advanced theological education initiatives. More than fifty cities sought his help in his role as educator and theologian.[29] His *Loci Communes* (1521), the first systematic expression of Lutheran ideas, gained widespread influence due to its clear and irenic approach. He helped to reform eight universities and to found four others. From his chair of Greek literature at Wittenberg, Melanchthon penned numerous textbooks for use in many academies, schools, and institutions. These things earned him the title of "Preceptor of Germany."[30]

Melanchthon proposed a new theological curriculum that emphasized the study of Scripture in the original languages. He proposed beginning with the study of Romans, then moving to the rest of the New Testament, then to the Old Testament, and concluding with the study of the Gospel of John. The study of theology began with the study of God, moving to the doctrines of creation, sin, redemption, law, and gospel, and concluding with eschatology. Hundreds flocked to the University of Wittenberg to prepare themselves for faithful services in churches and schools. From this period came the threefold aspects of the curriculum that have influenced the shape of theological education for nearly five centuries: (1) the study of the Bible and its interpretation, (2) the study of doctrinal theology, and (3) the application of these subjects with special attention to the practical administration of churches, preaching, worshipping, and ministry. Formal theological studies became a requirement for ministerial ordination during the sixteenth century. Prior to this time such requirements had not been put in place, but this practice has continued to be the expectation in most traditions up to the present time.[31]

---

28. P. A. Verhoef, "Luther and Calvin's Exegetical Library," *Concordia Theological Journal* 3 (1968): 5–20; B. A. Gerrish, *The Old Protestantism and the New: Essays on the Reformation Heritage* (Chicago: University of Chicago Press, 1982); see Timothy George, *Theology of the Reformers* (Nashville: B&H, 2013), 171–265.

29. See Gregory B. Graybill, *The Honeycomb Scroll: Philip Melanchthon at the Dawn of the Reformation* (Minneapolis: Fortress, 2015), 145–337.

30. González, *The History of Theological Education*, 70–77; see also Thomas A. Howard, *Protestant Theology and the Making of the Modern German University* (Oxford: Oxford University Press, 2006), 60–79.

31. Ibid.

Roman Catholic Education

A brief note about Roman Catholic theological education during these years seems important to add. Monastic schools, characteristic of the medieval years, merged with the newer humanistic approaches. The Council of Trent (1545–1563) provided a careful and detailed response to the Lutheran Reformation, particularly related to the role of tradition in relationship to Scripture, as well as the meaning, role, and importance of the sacraments in the life of the church.[32] The decrees of Trent restricted theological education to the context of seminary, which was understood as a quasi-monastic institution influenced by the University of Paris, that provided a spiritual community for the purposes of theological and ministerial formation. A central place was given to the reading of patristic and classical texts in their original languages. This approach to theological education continued with minimal changes until the Second Vatican Council in the 1960s.[33]

The Post-Reformation and Modern Periods

Tracking the streams that influenced the practice and shape of theological education during the church's first sixteen centuries has led us through the work of the second-century apologists, the Alexandrian and Antiochene schools, Augustine, the medieval thinkers and monastic, and the Reformers and reform movements. By the seventeenth century these streams proliferated, resulting in both fragmentation and greater variety of the expressions of the Christian movement.[34]

The Enlightenment

Many aspects of the expansion were good and helpful as the Christian message began to circle the globe. On the other hand, the vast influence of Enlightenment and post-Enlightenment thought challenged the very heart of the Christian faith, raising questions about authority, tradition, and the role of reason. The Enlightenment, which blossomed in the eighteenth

---

32. See John W. O'Malley, *Trent: What Happened at the Council* (Cambridge, MA: Harvard University Press, 2013).

33. González, *The History of Theological Education*, 79–85; see John L. Elias, *A History of Christian Education: Protestant, Catholic, and Orthodox Perspectives* (Malabar, FL: Krieger, 2002), 191–222. For additional discussion of Orthodox education beyond our treatment in this chapter, see 223–53.

34. See David S. Dockery, "Denominationalism: Historical Developments, Contemporary Challenges, and Global Opportunities," in *Why We Belong: Evangelical Unity and Denominational Diversity* (Wheaton: Crossway, 2013) 177–209.

century, was a watershed in the history of Western civilization. The Christian consensus that had existed from the fourth through the sixteenth centuries was hampered, if not broken, by a radical secular spirit. Enlightenment philosophy could be characterized by its stress on the primacy of nature and reason over special revelation. Along with this elevated view of reason, the movement reflected a low view of sin, an antisupernatural bias, and an ongoing questioning of the place of authority and tradition.[35]

The Contribution of Friedrich Schleiermacher

Friedrich Schleiermacher (1768–1834) led the way with his efforts to synthesize the Christian faith with Enlightenment ideas. With his book *On Religion: Speeches to Its Cultured Despisers* (1799), Schleiermacher called for a way in which the Christian faith could be heard afresh in a rapidly changing culture, attempting to adapt the Christian faith to a new mode of thinking. Such efforts to translate the Christian faith to the changing times were not just attempts to make the Christian faith relevant or to bring Christianity to a place where it could be heard afresh. This new movement, known as liberalism, transformed the Christian faith into something quite different. Accompanying these trends, Schleiermacher brought new approaches to theological education.[36] Schleiermacher's thinking was formed in a pietistic context, yet he rejected the core of pietism. This vision for theological education can be followed in his 1811 publication, *Brief Outline of Theological Studies*. Here he proposed three curricular categories: philosophical theology, dogmatic theology, and pastoral theology, which evidenced some continuity but mostly discontinuity with Melanchthon's approach.

Philosophical theology attempted to study and articulate a particular form of the feeling of dependence on God and its place and context of other religious feelings, which included philosophy of religion and comparative religions. Dogmatic theology was the study of the teachings of the church at a given moment and particularly in the present. Schleiermacher contended that theology should be radically Christocentric in order to

---

35. See G. R. Evans, *History of Heresy* (London: Blackwell, 2003); and Colin Brown, *Christianity and Western Thought: A History of Philosophers, Ideas, and Movements* (Downers Grove: InterVarsity, 1990) 173–340.

36. See C. W. Christian, *Friedrich Schleiermacher* (Waco: Word, 1979); Gary Dorrien, *The Making of American Liberal Theology: Imagining Progressive Religion: 1805–1900* (Louisville: WJK, 2001), xiii–xxv; and Howard, *Protestant Theology and the Making of the Modern German University*, 178–211.

serve the church as a concrete community of faith. Dogmatic theology also included the critical study of the Bible and historical theology, while pastoral theology included all that is necessary to function as a minister in the church.[37] Schleiermacher initiated a trajectory that emphasized critical studies which, contrary to Schleiermacher's intention, tended to separate the study of theology from the life of the church, creating a tension between the academy and the congregations. One of the purposes of this volume is to show and underscore the importance of carrying out the work of theological education for the sake of the church by developing pastor-theologians, biblical expositors, and faithful ministers.

American Theological Education

Early American colleges governed by trustees from related religious groups provided education within the context of faith and grounded in the pursuit of truth for Christ and his church.[38] The schools, by the early nineteenth century, faced similar challenges to those associated with Schleiermacher and the University of Berlin. The German model espousing research and academic freedom began to influence American theological education in the nineteenth century. For formal ministerial education, college graduates remained for at least one additional year to study the body of divinity with the president and a professor of theology, while working in an intern-like role with a pastor or by serving as a tutor for other students.

Andover

The first freestanding seminary, Andover in Massachusetts, was birthed in 1808 as an expression of protest against the drift toward liberalism and Unitarianism in the New England colleges, especially at Harvard. Other seminaries followed, including Princeton (1812), Union of Virginia (1824), Newton (1825), Mercersburg (1836), Union of New York (1836), and Southern Baptist Seminary (1859). Seminary enrollment expanded

---

37. See James C. Livingston, *Modern Christian Thought: From the Enlightenment to Vatican II* (New York: MacMillan, 1971), 96–114; and Roger E. Olson, *The Journey of Modern Theology: From Reconstruction to Deconstruction* (Downers Grove: InterVarsity, 2013), 130–46. A contrary vision to Schleiermacher's was developed by Dietrich Bonhoeffer. See his *Theological Education Underground: 1937–1940*, ed. Dirk Schulz and Victoria J. Barnett (Minneapolis: Fortress, 2012).

38. See E. Brooks Holifield, *Theology in America: Christian Thought from the Age of the Puritans to the Civil War* (New Haven: Yale University Press, 2003).

rapidly during the first half of the nineteenth century. Most of the seminaries started during this century had strong denominational ties with the Presbyterian, Congregational, Lutheran, Episcopal, and Baptist denominations.[39] Three examples of different visions for theological institutions illustrate the streams and trajectories for theological education that developed during the nineteenth century.

Princeton

Andover and Princeton offered a curricular trajectory, in continuity with Melanchthon's efforts in the sixteenth century, that has shaped American theological education for two hundred years. The three-year program included biblical studies, theological studies, and studies in the practice of ministry, which remain the areas of focus for the volume. Both institutions, based on their institutional charters, were established to advance orthodox and scholarly Calvinism.[40] Princeton, in particular, under the leadership of Charles Hodge (1797–1878), A. A. Hodge (1823–1886), and B. B. Warfield (1851–1921), pushed against the Schleiermachian approach to theology with its developing liberalism and critical approach to biblical studies.[41] The impact of Princeton Seminary lives on at numerous Presbyterian and evangelical institutions today.[42]

Mercersburg

The Mercersburg theological tradition was led by John Williamson Nevin (1803–1886) and Philip Schaff (1819–1893). Mercersburg advanced a Christocentric theological approach emphasizing the consensus of the early church councils, the best of Lutheran and Reformed scholarship, warm-hearted piety, a commitment to formal worship patterns and practices, and an appreciation of early church traditions to counter the shallow revivalism

---

39. See Glenn T. Miller, *Piety and Intellect: The Aims and Purpose of Ante-Bellum Theological Education* (Atlanta: Scholars' Press, 1990).
40. Marsden, *The Soul of the American University*, 74–197.
41. See Mark A. Noll, ed., *The Princeton Theology 1812–1921: Scripture, Science and Theological Method from Archibald Alexander to Benjamin Breckinridge Warfield* (Grand Rapids: Baker, 2001); Paul Helseth, *Right Reason and the Princeton Mind* (Phillipsburg: P&R, 2010); and Bradley J. Gundlach, *Process and Providence: The Evolution Question at Princeton, 1845–1929* (Grand Rapids: Eerdmans, 2013).
42. See W. Andrew Hoffecker, *Piety and the Princeton Theologians: Archibald Alexander, Charles Hodge, and Benjamin Warfield* (Phillipsburg: P&R, 1981).

of the day as well as the progressive drift taking place in other schools and churches.[43]

Southern Baptist Theological Seminary

In many ways The Southern Baptist Theological Seminary, founded in 1859, has been the pioneer in theological education. Beginning with the threefold vision of the founding president, James P. Boyce (1827–1888), Southern Seminary emphasized confessional and orthodox theology, stressed serious scholarship in service to the church, and opened the doors for those lacking educational privilege through the study of the English Bible. This vision provided a distinctive Baptist and congregationalist approach to theological education in the nineteenth century.[44]

Southern was one of the first seminaries to develop a research doctoral program at the end of the nineteenth century. With the development of a university model for seminary education with separate schools within the institution, Southern advanced curriculum programs for world religions and missions, Christian education, pastoral counseling and psychology of religion, church music, social work, and church growth.[45] These initiatives provided opportunity for enlargement in the subject matter to be taught, increased the number of electives for students, addressed developing needs in multistaff churches, and opened doors for advanced graduate study for Southern graduates.[46]

The struggle within denominations, the expansion of nondenominational churches and parachurch movements, and the doctrinal tensions growing out of the modernist-fundamentalist divide in the first half of the twentieth century have created both creative opportunities and new challenges for theological education in the twentieth and twenty-first

---

43. See Luigi Giussani, *American Protestant Theology* (Montreal: McGill-Queen's University Press, 2013), 48–51.
44. Gregory A. Wills, *Southern Baptist Theological Seminary 1859–2009* (Oxford: Oxford University Press, 2009), 1–52; see Thomas J. Nettles, *James Petigru Boyce: A Southern Baptist Statesman* (Phillipsburg: P&R, 2009), 106–35; and Timothy George, *James Petigru Boyce: Selected Writings* (Nashville: Broadman, 1989), 30–59.
45. See David S. Dockery, "Southern Seminary and the Theological Heritage of Southern Baptists," *Southern Seminary Magazine* 63:2 (1995): 2–5.
46. See Glenn T. Miller, *Piety and Profession: American Protestant Theological Education, 1870–1970* (Grand Rapids: Eerdmans, 2007), 499–506; and William Brackney, *Congregation and Campus* (Macon, GA: Mercer, 2008).

centuries.[47] The Association of Theological Schools noted that by 2016 there were more than 270 accredited institutions representing a wide range of Protestant, Evangelical, Roman Catholic, and Orthodox institutions of theological education reflecting a broad spectrum of doctrinal, ecclesiastical, and theological perspectives. One of the purposes of this volume is to enhance theological education grounded in the message of the gospel in service to the church, the academy, and the public square for the present day in light of the various themes addressed in this chapter.[48]

Theology, Theological Education, and the Church

At the heart of a theological seminary is the study of theology.[49] For too many people, however, the province of theology is not the church but is limited to the realm of the specialist in the academic world. Christian theology should be at the heart of theological education and should engage the broader academic world as well as society at large; there is a rightful place for a public theology. Ultimately, however, theology is for the church.[50]

Theology

Theology is certainly not the whole of church life, but there must be a place for the true intellectual love of God, for Jesus has commanded his followers to love God with heart, soul, strength, and mind, and to love one's neighbor as well (Matt 22:37–39). Certainly this should not lead to some cold intellectual approach to the faith unaccompanied by affection. For too many people, theology is a kind of intellectual aloofness or uncommitted intellectual curiosity.[51]

---

47. See Miller, *Piety and Profession*, 404–50; and Miller, *Piety and Plurality: Theological Education Since 1960* (Eugene, OR: Cascade, 2014).

48. See other proposals for the life and work of theological education: David H. Kelsey, *To Understand God Truly: What's Theological About a Theological School* (Louisville: WJKP, 1992); Robert J. Banks, *Reenvisioning Theological Education: Exploring a Missional Alternative to Current Models* (Grand Rapids: Eerdmans, 1999); David H. Kelsey, *Between Athens and Berlin: The Theological Education Debate* (Grand Rapids: Eerdmans, 1993); Daniel O. Aleshire, *Earthen Vessels: Hopeful Reflections on the Work and Future of Theological Schools* (Grand Rapids: Eerdmans, 2008); and Perry Shaw, *Transforming Theological Education* (Columbia, CA; Langham Global Library, 2014).

49. See Kevin J. Vanhoozer and Owen Strachan, *The Pastor as Public Theologian* (Grand Rapids: Baker, 2015), 183–88; and R. Albert Mohler, "The Pastor as Theologian" in Daniel L. Akin, ed., *A Theology for the Church* (Nashville: B&H, 2014*)*, 723–28.

50. See Akin, *Theology for the Church*; and John S. Hammett, *Biblical Foundations for Baptist Churches* (Grand Rapids: Kregel, 2005), 67–80.

51. Ibid.

Theology renders service to the church in many ways. It satisfies the mind so that we can know God (Jer 9:23–24) and know the living Christ (Phil 3:10–14). Theology is necessary for the church's teaching and apologetic tasks (1 Pet 3:15). Theology is important as a touchstone for understanding what the church believes and for recognizing the principles by which the allegiance of its members will be judged. Such beliefs and practices come from serious theological reflection. Theology also points to ethics. If the church is to live in the world with a lifestyle that brings glory to God, then we must learn to think deeply—to deal not only with issues of personal ethics but also with the implications of the biblical faith for social, economic, and political ethics.[52]

Theology is more than God's words for me as an individual; theology is God's words for the church, the community of faith. It is important that we understand theology in both individual and community perspectives. If the church is central to God's plan, then we cannot push to the edge what is central for God.[53] Theological education is an effort to equip ministers and church leaders for the building up of the church (Eph 4:13–16). Equipping involves moving believers toward the unity of the faith and a maturity of the faith that has the full knowledge of God's Son. The kind of maturity described in Ephesians 4 needs a carefully articulated theological foundation that will lead the church away from instability and gullibility toward wisdom, trust, and discernment.[54]

Theological Education

Likewise, the building up of the people of God results in the advancement of the gospel mission. In actualizing that mission, the church is called to be faithful, to discern, to interpret, and to proclaim the gospel of Jesus Christ as the transforming power for the world. The responsibility for making theology applicable for the church rests with theological educators. The work of serious scholarship by theological educators remains essential, but we must seek to eliminate the academy-versus-church or scholar-versus-practitioner dichotomy that tends to magnify specialization, leading to fragmentation of mission and disconnection from the

---

52. See Millard J. Erickson, *Christian Theology* (Grand Rapids: Baker, 1998), 18–38.
53. See Stanley J. Grenz, *Theology for the Community of God* (Nashville: B&H, 1994), 1–34.
54. See the discussion of theological education in David S. Dockery, *Southern Baptist Consensus and Renewal* (Nashville: B&H, 2008), 134–63.

church.⁵⁵ We need theological educators who can write and communicate in ways that are both accessible to, and engaging of, the church and the culture. Church leaders and theologians throughout history have frequently commended the biblical writers for their clarity, simplicity, and brevity. Theological educators would be wise to emulate and prioritize these characteristics for the days ahead. Theological educators have the responsibility to help the church articulate what it believes, practices, and proclaims primarily for the good of believers, as well as for a watching world.⁵⁶

Theology and healthy theological education provide the backbone for the church. The work of theological education, done well, helps develop mature believers, strengthening heart, head, and hands, and resulting in the praise and exaltation of God. Healthy theological education, founded on good theology, should always lead to doxology. Theological education needs to be seen as an extension of the work of the church, similar in importance to evangelism and worship.⁵⁷

The Church

Hopefully this volume will enable readers to understand that church practice based on unsound theology will itself be unsound and even dangerous. Church leaders who have been well prepared will help church members better understand the Christian faith. Believers desire to share their evangelistic efforts, and, moreover, can help lead Christ followers to an awareness and worship of the grandeur, the greatness, and goodness of the one true and wise God. Theological education can also provide resources for God's people to recover a true understanding of human life. In this sense God's people can once again gain a sense of the greatness of the soul. In doing so, the people of God can recover an awareness that God is more important than we are, that the future life is more important than this one, and that a

---

55. See Miroslav Volf, ed., *Practicing Theology: Beliefs and Practices in the Christian Life* (Grand Rapids: Eerdmans, 2002).

56. See Robert L. Saucy, "Doing Theology for the Church" in John Jefferson David, ed., *The Necessity of Systematic Theology* (Grand Rapids: Baker, 1978).

57. See Kevin J. Vanhoozer, *Pictures at a Theological Exposition: Scenes of the Church's Worship, Witness, and Wisdom* (Downers Grove: InterVarsity, 2016).

right view of God provides genuine significance and security for the living of these days.[58]

The church can better understand what it believes and why these things should be believed. When the church carries out this theological task, and when theological education is church centered and church focused, the true content of the faith, the whole counsel of God (Acts 20:27), can be preserved and proclaimed in churches in the United States and around the globe.[59] The future of theological education must prioritize commitments to intercultural and international initiatives. Faithful theological education affirms for the churches that the Bible is the living Word of God written. Christ is the living Word of God revealed in it, and the Holy Spirit is the voice of God in it revealing Christ to the church. Understanding these truths in the context of Christian history offers insight for today and guidance for the future, preserving the church from wrongheaded fads. Knowledge of the past keeps the church from confusing what is merely a contemporary expression from that which is enduringly relevant.[60] We pray that these understandings and commitments will help ensure the faithful work of theological educators as they prepare the next generation of ministers for the church of the Lord Jesus Christ.

A Hopeful Future

We need institutions of theological education to recommit themselves to academic excellence in teaching and scholarship, in research and service, as well as in personal discipleship and churchmanship. At the same time, we must lay hold of the best of the Christian theological tradition and carry it forward to engage the culture and the academy. Service on behalf of faithful evangelical education is a distinctive calling.[61] Those of us who have

---

58. See Kevin J. Vanhoozer and Daniel J. Trier, *Theology and the Mirror of Scripture: A Mere Evangelical Account* (Downers Grove: InterVarsity, 2015); and J. I. Packer, *Concise Theology* (Wheaton: Tyndale, 1993).

59. See Timothy C. Tennent, *Theology in the Context of World Christianity* (Grand Rapids: Zondervan, 2007); and Michael F. Bird, *What Christians Ought to Believe: An Introduction to Christian Doctrine Through the Apostles' Creed* (Grand Rapids: Zondervan, 2016).

60. See Gerald Bray, *God Has Spoken: A History of Christian Theology* (Wheaton: Crossway, 2014); and John D. Hannah, *Our Legacy: The History of Christian Doctrine* (Colorado Springs: NavPress, 2001).

61. See Donald G. Bloesch, *Essentials of Evangelical Theology* (San Francisco: Harper and Row, 1978), 7–20; and David S. Dockery, "Evangelicalism: Past, Present, and Future," *Trinity Journal* 36NS (2015): 3–21. A vision for an evangelical ecumenism has been carefully articulated by Timothy George, "The Reformation and the New Ecumenism," in *Protestantism After 500 Years*, ed. Thomas A. Howard and Mark A. Noll (Oxford: Oxford University Press, 2016), 319–32.

contributed to this volume desire to join hands in order to pray and serve together to advance the work of theological education for the good of all concerned and for the glory of our great God.[62]

Questions for Further Reflection

1. What are some key lessons to be learned from the history of theological education that will be helpful for the work of theological educators in the twenty-first century?
2. What difference does context make for the delivery of theological education?
3. How can churches and denominations work together with theological institutions to strengthen efforts related to the preparation of ministers and those called to serve the people of God?

Sources for Further Study

Anthony, Michael J. and Warren S. Benson. *Exploring the History and Philosophy of Christian Education*. Grand Rapids: Kregel, 2003.

Dockery, David S., ed. *Faith and Learning: A Handbook for Christian Higher Education*. Nashville: B&H, 2011.

Elias, John L. *A History of Christian Education: Protestant, Catholic, and Orthodox Perspectives*. Malabar, FL: Krieger, 2002.

Forest, Benjamin K. and Elmer L. Towns, ed. *A Legacy of Religious Educators: Historical and Theological Introductions*. Lynchburg: Liberty University Press, 2017.

González, Justo L. *The History of Theological Education*. Nashville: Abingdon, 2015.

Howard, Thomas Albert. *Protestant Theology and the Making of the Modern German University*. Oxford: Oxford University Press, 2006.

Marsden, George M. *The Soul of the American University: From Protestant Establishment to Established Nonbelief*. Oxford: Oxford University Press, 1994.

---

62. Several themes in this chapter have been previously published and developed in David S. Dockery, *Biblical Interpretation Then and Now* (Grand Rapids: Baker, 1992); David S. Dockery, *Renewing Minds: Serving Church and Society in Christian Higher Education* (Nashville: B&H, 2008); Dockery, *Southern Baptist Consensus and Renewal*; and Dockery and George, *The Great Tradition of Christian Thinking*.

Miller, Glenn T. *Piety and Intellect: The Aims and Purposes of Ante-Bellum Theological Education*. Atlanta: Scholars Press, 1990.

_____. *Piety and Plurality: Theological Education Since 1960*. Eugene, OR: Cascade, 2014.

_____. *Piety and Profession: American Protestant Theological Education 1870–1970*. Grand Rapids: Eerdmans, 2007.

Noll, Mark A. *Jesus Christ and the Life of the Mind*. Grand Rapids: Eerdmans, 2011.

Chapter One

THE FOUNDATION AND SHAPE OF THEOLOGICAL EDUCATION

MARK L. BAILEY

Diememe Noelliste has voiced the broad vision for theological education as "the formation of the people of God in the truth and wisdom of God for the purpose of personal renewal and meaningful participation in the fulfillment of the purpose of God in the Church and the world."[1] Embedded in that statement is a set of components that can be viewed as either complementary or competing, depending on the philosophy of seminary education one affirms. Arguments have been advanced for the primacy of theological training as knowledge, formation, leadership, or mission.[2] In reality all four are important as evidenced by the defining statement for theological curriculum for those schools that are a part of the Association of Theological Schools (ATS) of North America: in a theological school the overarching goal is the development of theological understanding, that is, aptitude for theological reflection and wisdom pertaining to a responsible life in faith. Comprehended in this overarching goal are others such as deepening spiritual awareness, growing in moral sensibility and character, gaining an intellectual grasp of the tradition of a faith community, and acquiring the abilities requisite to the exercise of ministry in that community.[3]

---

1. Diememe Noelliste, "Towards a Theology of Theological Education," *Evangelical Review of Theology* 19, no. 3 (July 1995): 299.
2. See Brian Edgar, "The Theology of Theological Education," *Evangelical Review of Theology* 29, no. 3 (July 2005): 208–217.
3. Commission on Accrediting, *General Institutional Standards* (Pittsburgh: Association of Theological Schools, 2010), 5, http://www.ats.edu/uploads/accrediting/documents/general-institutional-standards.pdf.

In order to remain faithful to God and his Word, a few mission-critical questions must be answered for those involved in theological education. What does it look like for a consistent theology to be fleshed out in the educational endeavor of a seminary or graduate school of theology? How will men and women be equipped to have both the character and capability to serve the church of Jesus Christ? Above all, and within all that it endeavors, theological education must demonstrate its affirmation of the authentic faith of the first century on the one hand and be able to articulate that biblical faith to the twenty-first century audience on the other. The purpose of this chapter is to set forth some foundational principles and surface some of the contemporary challenges shaping the cultural landscape of those who would give themselves to the privilege and responsibility of theological education.

✻ Foundational Principles ✻

Biblical in Authority

The commitment to the priority and the authority of Scripture is an integral element of the evangelical tradition. Such a commitment to the Word of God seems foolish to many in an increasingly secular culture, even among the so-called Christians who get unwittingly enamored with that culture. The Bible, as the Word of God, is the supreme authority for sound theology; and a sound theology is foundational for effective ministry preparation. Foundational to the Christian faith is that God really exists and has acted and spoken in history.

The authority of Scripture is rooted in the ultimate Author of Scripture. The Bible itself testifies to the origin, process, character, and reception of Holy Scripture. Second Peter 1:20–21 reveal that the Bible is the result of neither human reasoning nor initiative but owes its origination to the superintending work of the Holy Spirit. "Above all, you know this: No prophecy of Scripture comes from the prophet's own interpretation, because no prophecy ever came by the will of man; instead, men spoke from God as they were carried along by the Holy Spirit."

Inspiration is that process by which an omnipotent God so guided the human authors of Scripture in the recording of God's revelation that the end product was the exact Word of God exactly as God wanted to communicate it in the words of the original manuscripts. Men spoke from God being moved (lit. "carried along") by the Holy Spirit. According to Paul in 2 Timothy 3:16, the resultant character of that process is that every portion of Scripture is said to be *theopneustos*, the result of the breath or (better yet, in light of Peter's statement above) the Spirit of God. While God used human authors in the process, only the Bible itself is said to be "inspired."

First Corinthians 2:9–16 describes the process of the revelation, inspiration, and illumination of the Scriptures. The critical agency of the Holy Spirit is emphasized in all three stages. What humanity would never have otherwise known about the deep truths of God, the Spirit revealed (1 Cor 2:10). By that same Spirit, through the superintended process of inspiration, the thoughts of God have been put into the words of human language (1 Cor 2:11). In addition, the Holy Spirit was not only the Encoder of God's revelation; he is also the necessary Decoder of that truth. The Bible asserts that without the work of the Spirit, humanity could never receive or comprehend the thoughts of God (1 Cor 2:12). Paul also confirms that only those who possess and are walking by the Spirit can receive and profit from the revealed mind of God though Christ (1 Cor 2:14–16). Neither the unsaved, who are devoid of the Spirit, nor the believer who is living according to the flesh, can adequately comprehend or correctly apply God's truth to their lives (1 Cor 2:14; 3:1–3).

The Bible as the Word of God is the inspired revelation of the person, work, and revealed will of God. Therefore it must be held as the superior and evaluating authority over human reason, personal experience, or ecclesiastical tradition. Michael Horton contends, "The Church must be reminded that, when the text of Scripture is no longer regulating her doctrine, life, and worship, her authority and power, which is grounded in the Gospel of Christ revealed in Scripture, will soon be lost."[4] The church speaks with authority only when it gives proper voice to the revealed Word of God. Jesus never lost sight of this in his own life and ministry, telling his disciples, "For I have not spoken on my own, but the Father himself who sent me has given me a command to say everything I have said. I know that his command is eternal life. So the things that I speak, I speak just as the Father has told me" (John 12:49–50).

---

4. Michael S. Horton, "Recovering the Plumb Line," in *The Coming Evangelical Crisis: Current Challenges to the Authority of Scripture and the Gospel*, John H. Armstrong, ed. (Chicago: Moody Press, 1996), 246.

What has been called the "formal principle of the Reformation" summarized in the phrase, *Sola Scriptura*, affirms that only those beliefs and practices that rest firmly on scriptural foundations can be regarded as binding on Christians.[5] Alister McGrath aptly echoes this sentiment: "The only way Christianity can free itself from the subservience to cultural fashion is to ensure that it is firmly grounded in a resource that is independent of that culture. . . . Evangelicalism thus addresses today's culture without needing to become trapped within that culture."[6]

The two most significant roles of Scripture are to reveal truth and refute error. The first speaks of the ability of Scripture to convey the truth God intended with divine objectivity. The second provides the correction to the ever-present tendencies of subjectivity on the part of its interpreters. The Bible is foundational for both objective truth and personal relevance. Everything is changing, and seminaries must change to stay effective—not change for the sake of changing but for the sake of fulfilling their missions. But what must not change is the commitment to the truth of the inerrant Scriptures.

If the authority of the Bible is sourced in its ultimate Author, then the *whole* of what God has said is the necessary foundation for all theological education. Few are the schools who teach their students the whole Bible. Robert Jensen states, "Scripture's story is not part of some larger narrative, it is itself the larger narrative of which all other true narratives are parts. And so do not, when reading Scripture, try to figure out how what you are reading fits some larger story, for there is no larger story."[7] The compelling benefits of equipping students with a working comprehension of the whole Bible are many. A few of the more prominent ones will suffice for this occasion.

First, it allows for the whole story of the Bible and all of the grand themes of the Scriptures to be understood. Second, individual passages within a book will make more sense when one understands the context of the whole book, thus reducing the tendency to misinterpret a text by taking it out of context. Third, it demonstrates a response of faith in the truth that

---

5. Alister McGrath, *Evangelism and the Future of Christianity* (Downers Grove: InterVarsity, 1995), 59.
6. Ibid., 63.
7. Robert Jensen, "Scripture's Authority in the Church" in *The Art of Reading Scripture*, ed. Ellen F. Davis and Richard B. Hays (Grand Rapids: Eerdmans, 2003), 34.

every passage is inspired by God (πᾶσα γραφὴ θεόπνευστος) and therefore profitable (ὠφέλιμος) for life change and the preparation for ministries of good works (2 Tim 3:16–17). Fourth, there will be less risk to skip difficult or controversial issues if they are taught or preached at their appropriate juncture within a sermon series or passage sequence. Fifth, it shows allegiance to the statement of Jesus, who said that man should live "on every word that comes from the mouth of God" (Matt 4:4). Sixth, handling the whole Bible promotes the continual growth of the expositor for a lifetime of ministry. And seventh, it allows for both biblical and systematic theology to be done with quality and clarity, granting appropriate attention to the whole council of God. As Thomas Long writes, "Preachers need to give congregations their Bibles back, to rebuild their theological vocabulary, one brick, one word, one concept, one text at a time."[8]

Theological in Foundation

If the Bible is foundational to theology, and theology is foundational to effective ministry, then a good theological education must demonstrate its commitment to the "faith once delivered" and be able to articulate that biblical faith to the contemporary setting. John Hannah contends that "theology is a call to the church to return to God and make him the center of its priorities and life."[9] The kind of commitment that should shape theological education should be framed by an orthodox view of Scripture and a Christ-centered trinitarian faith as derived from the Bible and summarized by the historical councils of the church. Michael Svigel has recently advanced an approach along these lines, locating an evangelical understanding of theology in historic Christian orthodoxy. For him orthodoxy reflects those "tried and true interpretations of the Bible's major themes, its overarching story, and its fundamental truths."[10] He organizes what he considers to be the core three terms: the *center*, the *story*, and the *markers*.

The Center: Orthodoxy continuously points us to the
person and work of Jesus Christ in his first and second coming

---

8. Thomas G. Long, "The Witness of Preaching," *Ministry* 74, no. 7 (July 2001): 9.

9. John Hannah, "The Place of Theology in the Postmodern World: Is the Study of Theology and History an Antiquated Discipline?" *Reformation and Revival* 11, no. 1 (Winter 2002): 13.

10. Michael J. Svigel, *Retro-Christianity* (Wheaton: Crossway, 2012), 88.

as the central theme of the Bible, theology, the Christian life, and all reality.

The Story: Orthodoxy reminds us of the overarching biblical narrative of creation, redemption, and ultimate restoration effected by the harmonious work of the triune God: *from* the Father, *through* the Son, and *by* the Holy Spirit.

The Markers: Orthodoxy provides specific and memorable markers that help determine when our doctrine is out of bounds while providing a fenced field in which the Christian can think and act (emphasis in the original).[11]

For Svigel the content of orthodoxy includes seven basic doctrines derived from Scripture and clarified through the church councils. They include: (1) the doctrine of God: the triune God as Creator and Redeemer; (2) humanity and sin: the fall and resulting depravity; (3) the gospel of God the Son: the person and work of Christ; (4) the doctrine of salvation: salvation by grace through faith; (5) the Bible: inspiration and authority; (6) the church: redeemed humanity incorporated into Christ; and (7) the future: the restoration of humanity and creation.[12] Theology that is faithful to the historic Christian faith should be trinitarian framed, Christ centered, and doxologically focused.

Trinitarian Framed

The doctrine of the Trinity is at the heart of the Christian faith. As Timothy George writes, "The doctrine of the Trinity belongs to the pattern of Christian truth because without it we cannot really understand the narrative of Jesus as the story of God, and if the story of Jesus is anything other than the story of God, there is no Gospel. The doctrine of the Trinity is necessary for understanding the Bible's overarching account of what God has said and done in history."[13] Likewise David Dockery writes, "Thus a thoughtful Christian will focus on the Trinitarian shape of the Christian faith: (1) in

---

11. Ibid.
12. Ibid., 98–105. See Alister McGrath for a list of six distinctives to evangelicalism in *Evangelism and the Future of Christianity*, 55–56. Leith Anderson and Ed Stetzer summarized four distinguishing tenants as a set of markers for contemporary evangelicalism in "Defining Evangelicals in an Election Year" in *Christianity Today* 60, no. 3 (2016): 52, accessed February 22, 2017, http://www.christianitytoday.com/ct/2016/april/defining-evangelicals-in-election-year.html.
13. Timothy George, "The Pattern of Christian Truth," *First Things* 154 (June/July 2005): 23.

the initiative of the creator God *revealing* Himself; (2) in the love of Christ in *redeeming* us from our sins; and (3) in the Holy Spirit in *regenerating* us and facilitating every aspect of thinking and living Christianly" (emphasis in original).[14]

Three great ecumenical creeds—the Apostles' Creed, the Nicene Creed, and the Athanasian Creed—are structured around the relationship of "God in three Persons," underlying the essential importance of trinitarian theology. Rowan Williams advances: "Trinitarian theology, in so far as it is concerned with what 'kind' of God Christians worship, is far from being a luxury indulged in solely by remote and ineffectual dons; it is of cardinal importance for spirituality and liturgy, for ethics, for the whole of Christian self-understanding."[15] An informed understanding of the Trinity rooted in the biblical texts and articulated in the historic creeds of the church is an indispensable frame of reference for a theology that is distinctly Christian.

Christ Centered

The central doctrines of the Christian faith concern the person and work of Jesus Christ, the core essence of the gospel. Without Jesus Christ there is no gospel and no Christian faith. Alister McGrath affirms, "Scripture is, for evangelicals, the central legitimizing resource of Christian faith and theology, the clearest window through which the face of Christ may be seen."[16] Jesus is indeed the center of the Scriptures. As Revelation 19:10 concludes, "The testimony of Jesus is the spirit of prophecy." Thomas Oden explains the necessity of connecting the historical Christ with contemporary ministry. "If ministry cannot be clearly established as the continuation of Jesus's own intentions and practice, we lose its central theological premise."[17] The promise by Jesus of his accompanying presence continues to sustain, nourish, and direct present ministry. His pattern of servanthood continues to set a model and tone for leadership and ministry for the body of Christ.

---

14. David S. Dockery, "Introduction—Faith and Learning: Foundational Commitments" in *Faith and Learning: A Handbook of Christian Higher Education*, ed. David S. Dockery (Nashville: B&H, 2012), 9–10.

15. Rowan Williams, *Wrestling with Angels: Conversations in Modern Theology* (London: SCM Press, 2007), 142.

16. McGrath, *Evangelicalism and the Future of Christianity*, 61.

17. Thomas C. Oden, *Pastoral Theology: Essentials for Ministry* (San Francisco: Harper and Row, 1983), 59–60.

Not only central to the gospel and Christian ministry, Jesus is central to the whole biblical narrative. Along this angle John Stackhouse Jr. writes, "The person and work of Christ do not merely crown God's work of revelation and redemption as a sort of splendid ornament or even as the best example of God's activity in the world. The person and work of Christ constitute the defining chapter of the whole narrative, the hinge of history, the basis upon which everything else in creation makes sense."[18] Symbolically stated, between creation on the one end and the crown on the other rises the cross of Jesus Christ.

Doxologically Focused

The climax of theological studies should be doxology. All theological study is a means to a greater end, and that end is worship. Ron Allen, in his book *The Wonder of Worship,* writes, "God's glorious work in redemption of fallen humanity is not an end in itself; it is part of the larger picture of God's work in eternity, which centers in the display of his transcendent glory."[19] Nowhere is this more obvious than in the doxologies of the opening of the letter to the Ephesians where each stanza of the trinitarian work of God climaxes with the phrase "bring praise to his glory" or "to the praise of his glory." John Frame also correlates these twin themes: "Redemption is the means; worship is the goal. In one sense worship is the whole point of everything. It is the purpose of history, the goal of the whole Christian story. Worship is not one segment of the Christian life among others. Worship is the entire Christian life, seen as a priestly offering to God."[20]

By *doxology* is meant that the focus of the Christian experience should be to know God better than we know anyone else and to love God more than we love anything or anyone else. *Worship* is more to be defined by subject than style as Gordon Borror wrote in *Worship: Rediscovering the Missing Jewel*: "The lesson which seems to require constant rediscovery is the fact that worship is not primarily a state of art but rather a state of the heart. By state of the heart we mean the driving desire behind the worship

---

18. John G. Stackhouse Jr., *Evangelical Landscapes: Facing Critical Issues of the Day* (Grand Rapids: Baker Book House, 2002), 106.
19. Ronald B. Allen, *The Wonder of Worship* (Nashville: Thomas Nelson, 2001), 21.
20. John Frame, *Worship in Spirit and Truth* (Phillipsburg, NJ: P&R, 1996), 11.

life of the believer."[21] The focus of all study and service should be directed toward God for his honor and glory!

Spiritual in Its Nature

Tony Sargent states, "The basic, overriding goal of evangelical theological education is spiritual formation with a view to communicating with clarity and power the historic faith."[22] The New Testament is replete with references to the work of the Spirit in the life of the believer. Theological education must always have the spiritual formation of its students as a high priority. Ephesians 3:16–17 records the opening of Paul's prayer for the Ephesian church: "I pray that he may grant you, according to the riches of his glory, to be strengthened with power in your inner being through his Spirit, and that Christ may dwell in your hearts through faith." The development of the inner life of the student must be a high priority in theological education. "The test of Christian spirituality is conformity of heart and life to the confession and character of Jesus as Lord."[23] While a host of passages could be marshaled to this point, a few seem appropriately central.

According to Romans 12:2 and 2 Corinthians 3:18, the term Paul uses for the renewal and growth of the Christian into Christlike conformity is *transformation*. The word *transformed* is used four times in three contexts in the New Testament. In the Gospels (Matt 17:2; Mark 9:2) the term is used of the transfiguration of Jesus on a mountain in northern Galilee. In the Epistles, Paul uses the term in Romans 12:2 and in 2 Corinthians 3:18 for the catalytic transformational change that is encouraged in the life of the believer. According to Romans 12:2, if people in general and seminary students in particular are going to discover and fulfill the will of God, they must *dedicate* themselves to God, *separate* themselves from the world, and allow the Word of God to effectively *permeate* their lives.

The only other time the word *transform* is mentioned with reference to the believer is in 2 Corinthians 3:18, and that passage specifies the components needed to see a life transformed. Second Corinthians 3:18 reads,

---

21. Ronald B. Allen and Gordon Borror, *Worship: Rediscovering the Missing Jewel* (Portland: Multnomah Press, 1982), 23.
22. Tony Sargent, "The Value of Theological Education for Ministry and Service," address to the Baptist Union Assembly, Scotland, October 24, 2001 (unpublished).
23. T. R. Albin, "Spirituality," *The New Dictionary of Theology*, ed. Sinclair B. Ferguson and David F. Wright (Leicester, UK: InterVarsity Press, 1988), 657.

"We all, with unveiled faces, are looking as in a mirror at the glory of the Lord and are being transformed into the same image from glory to glory; this is from the Lord who is the Spirit." "We all" speaks of the Christian community whether the local church or even the seminary community. "With unveiled faces" is defined in the context as those who have turned to the Lord through faith in Jesus Christ. The reference to "looking as in a mirror" may be to the Word of God as the place of revelation and reflection where "the glory of the Lord"—the life of Christ—can be seen. The catalytic action, "are being transformed (μεταμορφόω) into the same image," is the miraculous process of life-change into Christlikeness: "the same image." The growth is characterized as moving in stages "from glory to glory"—literally from (*apo*) glory, into (*eis*) glory. The power behind the transformation is "from the Lord who is the Spirit." To put it succinctly, a dynamic Christian experience is God's transformation of the life of the believer into the image of Christ, through the Word of God, by the power of the Spirit of God, in fellowship with the people of God. To borrow from the four-stage metamorphosis that happens in the growth of a butterfly, we can trace what it could look like for a biblically rooted theology to be fleshed out in the theological educational endeavor such as a seminary. Theological education that transforms is a dynamic process of taking students from saving *grace* through healthy *growth* to discovering their *giftedness* to reflecting God's *glory* in all facets and phases of their lives. What begins with *reconciliation* moves through *renewal* to *reproduction* and culminates in *reflection*.

If spiritual transformation is God's goal for everyone in the church, then it is the role of the seminary to equip and encourage transformed students to serve in transformed churches that will transform the world for the name and fame of Jesus Christ. *The Manifesto on the Renewal of Evangelical Theological Education* advocates, "Our educational programmes must deliberately foster the spiritual formation of the student. We must look for a spiritual development centered in total commitment to the lordship of Christ, progressively worked outward by the power of the Spirit and into every department of life. We must devote as much time and care and structural designing to facilitate this type of growth as we readily and rightly provide for cognitive growth."[24]

---

24. "Manifesto on the Renewal of Evangelical Theological Education," *Evangelical Review of Theology* 19, no. 3 (July 1995): 312.

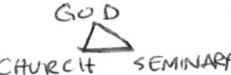

Missional in Vision

Since he is the appreciated editor of this volume, it is only fitting to cite David S. Dockery when he writes, "A distinctive theology for Christian higher education will have Christ as its center, the church as its focus, and the influencing of culture as a key element of its vision."[25] "Missional" is the connectedness of theological education to the evangelistic task in the world. The triangulation of God, the church, and the seminary has been well stated in the Lausanne Movement's *Cape Town Commitment* of 2011: "The mission of the Church on earth is to serve the mission of God, and the mission of theological education is to strengthen and accompany the mission of the church."[26] Gnana Robinson identifies a two-level purpose for theological education: "[I]n a broader sense it is for preparing the people of God for doing God's will in this world; and in a narrower sense it is for preparing candidates for doing the ministry of the Church."[27] Accordingly, theological education must stay connected to the church for its validation while staying focused on the world for its vision.

Church Connected

The church is God's appointed agent for the fulfillment of his purposes in this period of God's work in history. Therefore, the task of accomplishing theological education is to fulfill the mission of God (*missio Dei*) by equipping the church in its mission to reach the world. The seminary should be a servant to the church. Kristine Stache highlights this partnership in the following statement:

> Somewhere in the middle (of all church or all seminary) is a place where institutions and congregations listen to one another. Somewhere in the midst of it all churches well need to rely on the wisdom and vision of academic institutions for pedagogy, curricular outcomes, and processes. Seminaries will need to enter into deep listening with congregations, learning

---

25. David S. Dockery, "Developing a Theology for Christian Higher Education" in *Renewing Minds* (Nashville: B&H, 2008), 125.
26. Lausanne Movement, *Cape Town Commitment*, part II.VI.4, accessed February 22, 2017, https://www.lausanne.org/content/ctc/ctcommitment.
27. G. Robinson, *Theological Education in India: The Journey Continues* (Chennai: Christian Literature Society, 2000), 32.

through them and with them to determine the needs and resources of the church at large.[28]

Too often seminary education can create inflated minds and deflated hearts. Through Peter God called for a balanced growth and development in grace and knowledge (2 Pet 3:18). The benefits the church brings to the seminary include the context in which biblical truth can be applied, the ministry skills developed and deployed, and a protection from being too theoretical and esoteric. The benefits the seminary can bring to the church consist of the richness of theological resources, not the least of which is "to keep the flame of understanding the religious tradition burning."[29] Theological education develops graduates to strengthen the church in order to reach the world through the gospel of Jesus Christ and thereby glorify God.

Globally Focused

The work of missions is the activity of the church throughout the entire world. A relatively new term, *missio Dei*, Latin for "the sending of God," comprehensively describes "everything God does in relation to the kingdom and everything the church is sent to do."[30] There can be no question the Great Commission to disciple the nations is the heart of the disciples' mission in the world (Matt 28:19–20). Jesus took the lead to command a worldwide vision with every ethnicity in mind. To stay globally focused, theological educators must partner with ministries of Bible translation, reaching the unreached people groups, and the apologists, all of whom labor seeking a hearing for the gospel of Jesus Christ. On the local level, ties need to be formed to reach the marginalized and the underprivileged as settings for internships and effective mentoring. Such experiences develop the heart and soft skills of ministry so necessary for effective future ministries.

Purposeful in Goal

There is always the perennial danger of mistaking the means for the end. Educational activity is no guarantee for accomplishing ultimate purposes.

---

28. Kristine Stache, "Formation for the Whole Church: A New/Old Vision of Theological Education in the 21st Century," *Dialog: A Journal of Theology* 53, no. 4 (Winter 2014): 291.
29. Daniel O. Aleshire, *Earthen Vessels* (Grand Rapids: Eerdmans, 2008), 132.
30. A. Scott Moreau, Gary R. Corwin, and Gary B. McGee, *Introducing World Missions: A Biblical, Historical and Practical Survey* (Grand Rapids, MI: Baker, 2004), 73.

A series of passages come to mind that articulate the end goals (teleology) for theological education—clearly defined goals for both an individual Christian and for the church.

Individual Goals

First, for the individual Paul states the goal (*telos*) of all biblical instruction is love qualified by a transformed life (1 Tim 1:5). This echoes Jesus's response to the challenge of the Pharisees as to which law was most prominent. The love Jesus intends is an unsegmented love for God and a self-sacrificing love for others. Paul, however, qualifies the kind of love God intends. Love for God and others should flow from a life of purity, integrity, and sincerity. To Timothy, Paul writes, "Now the goal of our instruction is love that comes from a pure heart, a good conscience, and a sincere faith" (1 Tim 1:5). Purity is the result of a cleansed heart. Integrity is the overall description of life that stems from a good conscience. Sincerity reflects a faith that is both objective and subjective. Objectively, faith is the body of truth to believe; subjectively, it is personal belief in that body of truth. Both are to be held without hypocrisy (the literal meaning of *sincere* in this passage). As it relates to the task of theological education, Parker Palmer rightly asks, "How can the places where we learn to know become the places where we also learn to love?"[31]

Second, Colossians 1:28–29 state, "We proclaim him, warning and teaching everyone with all wisdom, so that we may present everyone mature in Christ. I labor for this, striving with his strength that works powerfully in me." Hence, the spiritual maturity of everyone in the church is the goal of the ministry. In Galatians 4:19 Paul specifies such maturity is really Christlikeness: "My children, I am again suffering labor pains for you until Christ is formed in you." Theological education must be more about the transformation of the student than the mere transference of the subject matter.

Corporate Goals

The difference between the means and the ends for the church is also identifiable in such passages as Ephesians 4:10–13. The means are the gifted

---

31. Parker Palmer, *To Know as We Are Known: A Spirituality of Education* (San Francisco: Harper and Row, 1983), 9.

people God has given as gifts to the church, and the ends relate to the spiritual health and ministries of the saints. Theological education should remain focused on effective ministry as the evidence of successful equipping. And that ministry will be successful if, and only if, it results in the interpersonal unity, intrapersonal maturity, and doctrinal purity of the church. With the teaching, preaching, counseling, and all that is entailed in church leadership, of utmost importance are the matters of life-change objectives for both the individual and the church as a whole. In the educational environment of outcome assessments theological educators must never forget the biblically defined ends God expects and will no doubt one day assess for success.

Contemporary Challenges

Mary Hess states the current challenge of theological education well when she writes, "Absent any imagination, the work of many theological educators has become an ever more shrill and anxious attempt to transfer the rich content of our disciplinary fields into the increasingly distracted heads of an ever more diverse student body."[32] The distractions that accompany educating theological students today are myriad. Daniel O. Aleshire, in his role as executive director of the Association of Theological Schools (ATS), has often spoken to that community about the changes taking place in the church and the changes taking place in the academy. His book, *Earthen Vessels*, is a masterful case for theological schools even in the midst of those changes. He states the current challenge for theological schools is to "articulate a sufficiently compelling reason to invite a new generation of board members, contributors, students, and faculty to sustain and improve these schools and take them into the future that they are called to serve."[33] Since his work was published, unprecedented cultural convulsions and moral land mines have only exacerbated the situation facing seminaries and theological graduate schools.

---

32. Mary Hess, "Learning Amidst Transforming Traditions," *Theological Education* 49, no. 1 (2014): 10.

33. Daniel O. Aleshire, *Earthen Vessels*, 6.

Changing Face of American Christianity

The loss of denominational identities and the devaluation of doctrine have created a new challenge for theological educators. Douglas Jacobson notes, "In the United States, . . . conservative congregations pulling out of mainline denominations are part of a broader issue relating to the loss of denominational identity and coherence generally. Both liberal and conservative denominations across the board don't have the kind of loyalty or connectiveness with their congregations that they had 20 or 30 years ago."[34] This is evidenced by the renaming of existing churches and the planting of "community" churches, even if those congregations identify privately with a particular denomination or movement. The loss of theological identity also reflects increasing levels of biblical illiteracy.

Shifts in Global Christianity

While it may appear at times that Christianity is grasping for air in America, response to the gospel witness seems to be flourishing in other centers of the world. For some time researchers have chronicled the continuing shift of the Christian epicenter from the West to the "global South" of Africa, Asia, and Central and Latin America.[35] The mission of Christianity can no longer be characterized as the "West for the Rest." In fact, the consensus is that the models of westernized theological training are inadequate for the majority world. Graham Cheesman points out that "Two Thirds of the world Christians are radically rethinking the structure and context of theological education as they have received it at the hands of the missionary enterprise."[36] The resulting challenge is the need to avoid both compromise due to contextualization and the importing of the worst of westernized and commercialized Christianity.

---

34. "Are People Losing Denominational Identity?" Fellowship of Confessing Anglicans, accessed May 19, 2016, https://fcasa.wordpress.com/2011/08/07/are-people-losing-denominational-identity.

35. See especially Philip Jenkins, *The Next Christendom: The Coming of Global Christianity* (New York: Oxford University Press, 2011); and Miriam Adeney, *Kingdom Without Borders: The Untold Story of Global Christianity* (Downers Grove: IVP Books, 2009). See also Wes Granberg-Michaelson, "Think Christianity Is Dying? No, Christianity Is Shifting Dramatically," *Washington Post*, May 20, 2015, accessed May 19, 2016, https://www.washingtonpost.com/news/acts-of-faith/wp/2015/05/20/think-christianity-is-dying-no-christianity-is-shifting-dramatically.

36. Graham Cheesman, "Competing Paradigms in Theological Education Today," *Evangelical Review of Theology* 17, no. 4 (October 1993): 484.

The Rise of Niche Ministries

Forty years ago seminaries trained mostly men for ministries as pastors, Christian education directors, or foreign missionaries. Such traditional roles are no longer standard fare. Most schools have multiple degrees and various tracks with niche ministries for both men and women. This has been balanced with the declining interest in professional ministry and the recent phenomenon of the rise of professionals who want biblical and theological training to equip them for the church and community opportunities of leadership.

Cultural Pluralism and Secularism

America has become the playground of the new tolerance, which in reality is a tolerance for anything but the exclusive message of the gospel of Jesus Christ and the Christian faith. The relativizing of opinion to individual preference and the loss of an external objective standard for truth and morality have paved the pathway for both secularism and pluralism. Ironically, while both are politically correct, they are mutually contradictory.

Along with an increased interest in spirituality is a declining interest in Christianity. The increase of the "nones" is reflective of the trend. This term refers "to people who self-identify as atheists or agnostics, as well as those who say their religion is 'nothing in particular'—[it now makes] up roughly 23 percent of the U.S. adult population. This is a stark increase from 2007, the last time a similar Pew Research study was conducted, when 16 percent of Americans were 'nones.'"[37] In addition, one cannot help but notice the aggressive migration of Islam. What was once geographically confined to the East has now come to the countries and cities of the West.

J. I. Packer verbalizes the difficult environment for doing theological education today: "Thus whole post-Christianity shouts loud, syncretism rides high, calling on us to affirm a transcendental unity of religions in some form and to mute our witness to the Trinity, the incarnation, the atonement, the resurrection, the reign and future return of the Lord Jesus

---

37. Michael Lipka, "A Closer Look at America's Rapidly Growing Religious 'Nones,'" Pew Research Center, May 13, 2015, accessed February 22, 2017, http://www.pewresearch.org/fact-tank/2015/05/13/a-closer-look-at-americas-rapidly-growing-religious-nones.

Christ—in other words, to eliminate the Christian essentials altogether."[38] Further he writes, "The ideal of Christian education for which we stand is being left high and dry in the secular build-up of our self-styled post-Christian world, with its worship of technique, its vacuum of values, and its materialism and pessimism lurking just below the surface."[39]

Shifting Student Demographics

With the advent of distance education, alternative scheduling, and online distribution, the average age of the seminary student is increasing. In addition, many imbedded staff members already serving in ministry are enrolling in theological studies. More and more opportunities for women in ministry positions have changed the demographics of most seminaries as well. The perception of a traditional seminary of predominately young male college graduates is no longer the reality.

Paralysis of Student Debt

Challenges for the contemporary seminary student revolve around the issues of time, place, and cost. The issue of time is the difficulty of the *availability* of classes for students seeking to balance their obligations of school, jobs, church, and family. The question of place is that of *accessibility*. Residency requirements are of necessity changing from a definition of location to that of professor-student interaction. Classes can be taken on campus, at extension sites, or online. Many times it is a hybrid of two or three. Cost reflects the challenge of *affordability*. Both the cost of the education and the baggage of college debt are major obstacles to matriculation and graduation from seminary.[40] The fact that the government will lend a student an unlimited amount for life expenses even beyond tuition and fees encourages even more indebtedness. Without counsel and realistic

---

38. J. I. Packer, "Kingdom Education: Today's Task," in *Thinking Christianly: Christian Higher Education and a Vigorous Life of the Mind*, Paul R. Corts, ed. (Birmingham, AL: Sherman Oaks Books, 2011), 215.

39. Ibid., 224.

40. "National data from the Center for the Study of Theological Education at Auburn Theological Seminary indicates both the number of students entering seminary with debt and the amounts they have to pay back upon entering the workforce are increasing substantially. 'It is no longer unusual for seminary graduates to leave school with $70,000 to $80,000 in debt,' says Sharon Miller, associate director of the center." David Briggs, "The High Cost of Service: Student Debt Burdens Religious Workers," Association of Religious Data Archives, accessed February 22, 2017, http://blogs.thearda.com/trend/featured/the-high-cost-of-service-student-debt-burdens-religious-workers.

planning for the future, many seminary graduates could find themselves unable to assume ministry positions with modest remuneration or achieve appointment to the mission field.

Explosion of Technology

Technology has been a game changer for education in general and theological education in particular. There are four aspects to consider. The *upside* of technology is increased capabilities of access and organization of content. The *downside* is the increasing cost to stay current. The *flipside* is the changes technology has meant for how one learns, teaches, and worships in the contemporary ministry settings. The *outside* is the challenge and opportunities technology affords for accessibility and distribution of theological education both nationally and globally.

Economic Uncertainty

International economic uncertainty has everyone nervous and creates a hesitancy for many to take risks. Seven years after the financial crisis of 2008 and 2009, recovery is still weak in most parts of the global economy. Global debt has grown by $57 trillion, raising the ratio of debt to GDP by 17 percentage points.[41] Donor bases for most ministries are older and shrinking as they pass away. Added to this is the rising cost of tuition required from students as denominational support and government funding become more and more scarce. The challenge will be to cultivate a new generation of donors from those for whom charitable giving has not necessarily been a strong suit.

Conclusion

Vernon Davis insightfully states, "The call in academia is for freedom; the cry in the church is for faith. At stake for new ventures in theological education is whether the process of education in the academy can demonstrate outcomes that are consonant with their confessional foundations."[42] In the steeplechase of the culture with its increasing hurdles and deepening water hazards, the task of theological education can be daunting to many and

---

41. Uuriintuya Batsaikhan and Pia Hüttl, "The Global Debt Overhang," (blog), *Bruegel*, October 26, 2015, accessed May 19, 2016, http://bruegel.org/2015/10/the-global-debt-overhang.

42. Vernon Davis, "The Unsettled Landscape of Theological Education," *Review and Expositor* 95 (1998): 2.

downright off-putting to others. However, we remember that if Christianity, by God's design, could be birthed and flourish in the first century with all its political tyranny, we have every reason to work with a tenacious conviction to biblical truth, a compassion shaped by God's grace, and a courage forged from a faith in the One who is both the designer of all reality and the definer of all that has meaning.

Questions for Further Reflection

1. What are the primary purposes for theological education?
2. What are the essential components of an evangelical theology?
3. In light of the history of theological drift in schools originally founded to train ministers, how can a school help protect doctrinal fidelity for future generations?
4. What does it mean for a school to be Christ centered in its mission and curriculum?
5. What are some practical ways to keep doxology as the rightful end of theology?
6. In what ways should the church and the seminary be mutually supportive and mutually dependent?
7. What are the most challenging trends in the culture or the church that threaten the survival of graduate theological education?

Sources for Further Study

Aleshire, Daniel O. *Earthen Vessels*. Grand Rapids: Eerdmans, 2008.

Anderson, Leith. *The Church for the Twenty-first Century*. Minneapolis: Bethany House, 1992.

Banks, Robert J. *Reenvisioning Theological Education: Exploring a Missional Alternative to Current Models*. Grand Rapids: Eerdmans, 1999.

Calian, Carnegie Samuel. *The Ideal Seminary: Pursuing Excellence in Theological Education*. Louisville: Westminster John Knox, 2002.

Cannel, Linda. *Theological Education Matters: Leadership Education for the Church*. Newburg, IN: Edcot Press, 2006.

Cheesman, Graham. "Competing Paradigms in Theological Education Today." *Evangelical Review of Theology* 17, no. 4 (October 1993): 484–99.

Davis, Vernon. "The Unsettled Landscape of Theological Education." *Review and Expositor* 95, no. 4 (Fall 1998): 485–90.

Dockery, David S. "Introduction—Faith and Learning: Foundational Commitments," in *Faith and Learning: A Handbook of Christian Higher Education*. Edited by David S. Dockery. Nashville: B&H, 2012. Pages 9–10.

Edgar, Brian. "The Theology of Theological Education." *Evangelical Review of Theology* 29, no. 3 (July 2005): 208–17.

Farley, Edward. *The Fragmentation and Unity of Theological Education.* Philadelphia: Fortress, 1983.

Hess, Mary. "Learning Amidst Transforming Traditions." *Theological Education* 49, no. 1 (2014): 9–16.

Kelsey, David. *To Understand God Truly: What's Theological About a Theological School.* Louisville: Westminster John Knox, 1992.

Litfin, Duane A. *Conceiving the Christian College: A College President Shares His Vision of Christian Higher Education.* Grand Rapids: Eerdmans, 2004.

"Manifesto on the Renewal of Evangelical Theological Education." *Evangelical Review of Theology* 19, no. 3 (July 1995): 307–13.

Shaw, Perry. *Transforming Theological Education: A Practical Handbook for Integrative Learning.* Carlisle, Cumbria: Langham Global Library, 2014.

Stache, Kristine. "Formation for the Whole Church: A New/Old Vision of Theological Education in the 21st Century." *Dialog: A Journal of Theology* 53, no. 4 (Winter 2014): 286–92.

Stackhouse, John G., Jr. *Evangelical Landscapes: Facing Critical Issues of the Day.* Grand Rapids: Baker Book House, 2002. Page 106.

Svigel, Michael J. *RetroChristianity: Reclaiming the Forgotten Faith.* Wheaton: Crossway, 2012.

———. *Theological Education in the Evangelical Tradition.* Edited by D. G. Hart and R. Albert Mohler Jr. Grand Rapids: Baker, 1996.

Chapter Two

Intellectual Discipleship and the Value of Theological Education

SARAH P. SUMNER

Why should anyone invest in theological education? What purpose does it have? What value does it bring? Does it enhance the Christian life or diminish it by requiring so much study? Why should anyone sign up for theological schooling when the Bible seems to say that believers have "no need" to be taught by "anyone" since our "anointing" from the Lord "teaches" us about "all things" (1 John 2:27 NASB)?[1] Is it wise for students to risk being confronted and bombarded by academic complexities that have distracted seminarians from "the simplicity and purity of devotion to Christ" (2 Cor 11:3)? Is it true, as sometimes said, that going to "seminary" amounts to going to "cemetery"? Is seminary a burial ground where students' faith dies? Given all the spiritual fallout that happens in seminaries, what compelling reasons are there for Christians to support the enterprise and exercise of formal theological learning?

Welcome to the morass of theological education! This realm, so to speak, is a land where land mines lay because this is where the battle of the truth about God is fought and waged at the highest conceptual level. No doubt, it is daunting to enter into the fray where theological truths and lies are sometimes difficult to distinguish. Nevertheless, it is our responsibility

---

1. All excerpts from Scripture in this chapter come from the New American Standard Bible (NASB), Nashville: Holman Bible Publishers, 1977.

to "contend earnestly for the faith which was once for all handed down to the saints" (Jude 3).

How, though, will we learn to fight with the sword of the Spirit, which is the Word of God, unless we are trained to know the difference between interpreting and misinterpreting Scripture? Moreover, how will we manage to stand up against all of the convincing, yet mistaken, academic arguments that seep into the churches and lead God's people astray? How will we even pray unless we understand the difference between praying honest prayers and saying public prayers of propriety?[2]

The church needs spiritual guardians—pastors and church elders along with prophets and professors—to be Spirit-filled, logic-skilled, intellectual warriors who equip the flock of God to "see to it" that "no one" with credentials subtly takes us "captive" through "philosophy and empty deception" and that no one *untrained* steeps us in beliefs that accord with "tradition" and "the elementary principles of the world" rather than "according to Christ" (Col 2:8). The church needs guardians to take full notice that while 1 John 2:27 says, "You have no need for anyone to teach you," this statement is in a context that is talking about false teachers.[3] A careful reading shows that the prior verse, 1 John 2:26, says, "These things I have written to you concerning those who are trying to deceive you."

It hits the naïve hard when suddenly they find that seemingly nice people have deceived them. How slow believers are to accept the grievous truth that when Jesus says, "Behold, I send you out as sheep in the midst of wolves" (Matt 10:16), some of those "wolves" are crouching in the church congregation. Unless we are prepared theologically, we may willfully refuse to recognize that "wolves" are sometimes cloaked in ecclesiastical garb. Yet all of us should be warned and apprised ahead of time that it is not safe to entrust our souls to anyone but God. Scripture tells us plainly in 2 Cor 11:13–14 that some in the church of Corinth were "false apostles, deceitful workers, disguising themselves as apostles of Christ. No wonder, for even Satan disguises himself as an angel of light."

---

2. In the context of a good theological education, there are important questions to ask about prayer: What does it mean to pray "in the Spirit" (Eph 6:18)? What does it mean to pray "in the name" of Jesus (John 14:13–14; 15:16; 16:23–24, 26)? What does it mean to "watch and pray" (Matt 26:41; Luke 21:36)?

3. See 1 John 2:4, 9, 11, 18–19, 22.

People need proper theological education to tell the difference between sheepskin-covered wolves and real sheep. Because of this, I have long made it a habit as a professor of theology, when testing my seminary students, to write tricky theological questions because dangerous theology is out there, and often it looks so good. Never does it come with a label on it that says, "Danger: This is wolf theology." Nor does it come framed in a neon sign that flashes the words, "Look out! This is a heresy!" *Heresy*, simply defined, is "wrong theology." Heresy often seems quite sensible. But if taken far enough, heresy redefines Christianity.

There is a reason the Lord has given "some" as "teachers" in the church (Eph 4:11), and that is because young and old alike need to be taught theologically. Even Jesus had to be taught. The Bible says that Jesus "kept increasing in wisdom and stature" (Luke 2:52; cf. Isa 7:14–16). Jesus's growth implies that he had to learn theologically to "let no one deceive" him "with empty words" (Eph 5:6). Jesus soaked himself in truth and enveloped himself in prayer so that he would not succumb to Satan's lies. Jesus was never deceived, and I believe the reason for that, in part, is because he was well taught. Church history, according to Protestants and Catholics and Eastern Orthodox alike, traditionally says that Mary, Jesus's mother, taught him God's Word.[4] Unless we are well taught, we are likely *not* to notice that "certain persons" have "crept in unnoticed" who "turn the grace of our God into licentiousness and deny our only Master and Lord, Jesus Christ" in ways that we excuse (Jude 4).

The church, therefore, needs teachers. In recent decades among evangelicals, the spiritual gift of leadership has garnered much more attention than has the spiritual gift of teaching. As a result, Western civilization has largely become biblically illiterate. Consequently many churchgoers have blindly succumbed to heretical thinking by deciding, for instance, there is no such thing as a real location called hell. Taking seriously the truth of what Scripture says about hell does not comport with "politically correct" thinking that has watered down the doctrine of God's judgment. Divine judgment does not sound "loving" to those who have never been taught theologically what love is.

---

4. Mary's Magnificat proves that she was a learned woman who had treasured truth in her heart. See Luke 1:46–55. For further reading on Jesus's mother, Mary, see Scot McKnight's easy-to-read volume, *The Real Mary: Why Evangelicals Can Embrace the Mother of Jesus* (Brewster, MA: Paraclete Press, 2007).

When the spiritual gift of teaching is neglected or downplayed, so is theological education (Rom 12:6–7; 1 Cor 12:28). We all need to be sharpened and renewed in our minds over and over again (2 Pet 1:12) by teachers who are well equipped. With that we all need to be developed theologically to the point of becoming solid teachers ourselves.[5] The Bible says plainly, "The Lord's bond-servant must . . . be . . . able to teach" (2 Tim 2:24).

Someone has to teach the church leaders and teachers who, in turn, teach everyone else. Many in our day seem to have blind spots in this. Despite the biblical fact that church elders, in particular, are required to be "able to teach" (1 Tim 3:2), rarely do church elders obtain formal theological training. According to the Scriptures, church elders are responsible to "be able both to exhort in sound doctrine and to refute those who contradict," yet few church elders (regardless of how sincere and sacrificial they may be), know how to "hold fast" to God's Word and understand it theologically as sound doctrine (Titus 1:9).

Do we fear that theological education would make church elders arrogant? Do we assume that seminary training really does nothing more than puff students up with head knowledge? The best theological training steers students toward repentance. A rigorous, robust program of theological studies should produce stalwart saints, not "scribes and Pharisees" (Matt 23:13). Yes, the Bible says that "knowledge makes arrogant" (1 Cor 8:1), but the Bible also says that knowledge fears the Lord (Prov 1:7).

In the Old Testament book of Hosea, the Lord God laments, "My people are destroyed for lack of knowledge. Because you have rejected knowledge" (Hos 4:6). Rejecting knowledge is not a Christian thing to do. We are deceived if we think having knowledge automatically works to our disadvantage—and also to our church leaders' disadvantages. Consider Jesus, who had more knowledge than anyone else in world history, yet Jesus was the most humble person ever.

The key to having right knowledge lies in learning theologically how to know *in the way* we "ought to know" (1 Cor 8:2). Here it is instructive to learn the Hebrew word for knowledge: *da'at*. The word *da'at* refers to "relational knowledge." Relational knowledge allows us to know God

---

5. To be clear, this does not count those who are incapacitated. This caveat illustrates the theological principle that Christianity is reasonable, not unreasonable.

personally. Only when we know God personally can we know as we ought to know.

The unquestioned aim of contemporary academic scholarship is mastery, dominance, power, and control. Knowledge (information) selfishly meant for dominance "makes arrogant" (1 Cor 8:1). Thus, when pastors and teachers take in theological education in order to use it selfishly for the purpose of dominating others, they do not have *da'at*. But when students take in Scripture and every form of truth as *da'at*, they thereby enhance their relationship with God, other people, nature, and themselves. Reverence for God lies at the base of true knowledge. Hence, the writer of Proverbs says, "The fear of the LORD is the beginning of *da'at*" (Prov 1:7).

Right knowledge is both relational and intellectual. Never is it purely academic. Whereas the word *academic* generally refers to the worldly institutions of academia, the word *intellectual* refers to the human mind, and certainly God calls Christians to be "renewed" in the spirit of our "mind" (Eph 4:23). One of the main aims of good theological education is to renew the "born again" mind (John 3:1–7).

Time and again the Bible emphasizes the importance of the renewal of our minds (Ps 51:6; Eph 4:23; Phil 4:8). How will we learn to love God with "all our mind" (Matt 22:37)? Loving God foremost is an all-encompassing task. Thus in Romans 12:2, we are commanded *not* to be "conformed" to the world (by way of academia) but rather to be "transformed" by the renewal of our minds (through rigorous theological education dispensed not only in school but also in the churches and in our homes). Intellectual renewal based on knowing God personally is totally different from academic conformity to the godless innovations of the world.

The world embraces academic truth. The world knows how to parse Greek verbs found in the New Testament. The world knows the history of the town of Nazareth. The world knows that Jesus lived in Nazareth. The world even knows that Jesus is alleged to be the promised Messiah who fulfilled the Old Testament prophesies. What the world does *not* know is the love of the Father. The world is like the Pharisees whom Jesus said did "not have the love of God" within themselves (John 5:42). They were loveless because they rejected God's love in pursuit of worldliness.

To make a similar point, the world knows much about worldliness, yet the world knows little about godliness. Only those who know God are set up to understand what godliness truly is. We need *da'at* in our seminaries in order to teach believers how to have the right kind of knowledge.

Good theological education joyfully imparts the right kind of knowledge by issuing it to students in the form of relational teaching. Every seminary professor ought to be required to relate to students lovingly as a spiritual father or spiritual mother who engages students' character as well as students' homework. True theological education is virtually synonymous with discipleship.

All this is to say that theological education is enormously beneficial when it is truly theological and truly educational. Often it is neither. In this fallen world many churchgoers and many seminarians are miseducated in churches and schools. To *miseducate* means "to mislead and misinform." Since all of us are in process—either becoming more like Christ or becoming less like Christ—we have to be careful to educate, not miseducate, other people.

Etymologically, the English word *education* derives from the Latin words *ex* (meaning "out") and *ducare* (meaning "to lead"). To educate literally means to "lead out" in the sense of leading students out of naïveté, ignorance, arrogance, deception, fear, and confusion. *Nota bene*: The sense of the word *educate* does not at all mean to lead students away from the truth about God. On the contrary it means just the opposite. Education, by definition, has everything to do with leading people toward truth.

Theological education has to do with leading people toward capital-*T* Truth. Jesus said, "I am . . . the truth" (John 14:6). Theology itself is essentially the study of Truth. Yes, the word *theology* literally means "the study (*ology*) of God (*theos*)." But since God is not an object to be studied (given that God is the Creator, not an aspect of creation), it is technically inaccurate to define theology in terms of the literal meaning of the word.

It is considerably more accurate to understand theology as the study of the truth about all God has revealed. Because the study of Truth is vast, theology is vast. Theology is by far the most expansive subject in the cosmos. How could it not be? Theology has to do with everything about God, including all that God has revealed.

In order to do more justice to the subject of theology, the next section will explain it in more detail. The final section then will give a truncated description—a little teaser—of the value of theological education in terms of how it helps us understand our own baptism and fulfill the Great Commission and the Great Commandment.

What Is Theology?

What is theology? Before answering that question, allow me to explain what theology is not. First, theology is not the formal study of world religions. It is not a social science that introduces people to the manifold variety of spiritualities in world cultures and society. Nor is it a branch of sociology. Second, theology is not an impractical, heady exercise for brainy academics who have no common sense. Theology is not sheer speculation. Although theology deals with mysteries, these mysteries are revealed to us at least to the extent that we can realize that these mysteries exist. Third, theology is not chicanery. Albeit some theologians are caught up academically in sophistry, theology itself has nothing to do with conjured-up machinations, verbal manipulations, spiritual abuse, or hoity-toity pretentiousness. As I said before, theology has to do with humbly seeking truth.

Theology is actually classified as a science and traditionally as the queen of sciences. Theology is scientific on account of three main things: (1) its aim is to find truth; (2) it has a distinctive means of apprehending its subject matter; and (3) it has a disciplined procedure. In other words, like every other science, theology seeks truth, not by randomly making guesses or presumptuously labeling mysteries as "truth" but rather by discovering identifiable truth in a disciplined, methodical way. Every science *qua* science has a method that entails both a means (of apprehending what it studies) and a procedure (for investigating what it apprehends). Theology's method of accessing what it studies is to use faith as its means.

At first blush, it may sound silly to hear that faith is a valid means for accessing truth about God, but let us here acknowledge that every science uses faith to believe the scientific method truly does accord with reality. As I will soon explain, faith is indispensable for all knowledge.

All sciences have scientific means for apprehending their fields of investigative study. For example, astrophysicists use telescopes to study constellations. How else is there to access the truth about stars and other heavenly bodies without having the proper tools to access outer space? Likewise, for their means, geologists use seismographs to do direct research on earthquakes. Without a seismograph it is difficult to measure the intensity of tremors or find the epicenter of an earthquake. Analogously, just as geologists and astrophysicists have their own special means of getting at the objects they are studying, so theology has its own means too.

On this point we must have unequivocal clarity: there is no alternative means of accessing what is studied in theology because God has made it such that no one can apprehend the truth about God, except by way of faith (Heb 11:6). Faith is the only means of getting at the stuff that theology formally studies: that which God has revealed.

The great theologian, Saint Anselm (AD 1033–1109), thus famously said in his *Proslogion,* "*Credo ut intelligam.*" That's Latin for "I believe; therefore I understand." Knowledge is gained by faith seeking understanding (*fides quaerens intellectum*), not the other way around. We do not believe because we understand; rather, we understand because we believe (John 7:14–18). The principle applies to every subject. No one can understand math without believing first in the existence and validity of numbers.

Again, theology is the study of that which God has revealed.[6] What God has revealed is known as *divine revelation.* Thus theology, in essence, is the study of divine revelation. With regard to theology's method, we use the means of faith; that is, we access the reality of divine revelation by believing in God (whose image within each of us makes "evident" God's existence; see Rom 1:19). Then with our God-given capacity to reason, we get on with the procedure of doing theology by thinking with the logic of humanity known as *common sense.*[7]

Lest anyone object and claim that logic is too worldly to be used for finding truth, let us recognize what Scripture says about reason. The first chapter of the Gospel of John (vv. 1, 14) reveals this eye-opening truth: "In the beginning was the Word, and the Word was with God, and the Word was God . . . and the Word became flesh, and dwelt among us." The surprise of this truth is found in the Greek word *Logos* which is translated in English as "Word." In the beginning was the Word, the Logic, the Reason,

---

6. I am indebted to my teacher, the late H. O. J. Brown, for his clear teachings on this. See H. O. J. Brown, *Heresies* (Peabody, MA: Hendrickson, 1998).

7. Not every theologian agrees with the notion of Scottish Common Sense Realism that bequeathed to evangelicals a belief in the reliability of common sense as a tool that helps connect us to reality. For instance, some theologians argue instead that all spiritual knowledge is mystical. To pursue more knowledge about common sense realism, see the philosophical teachings of Thomas Reid. For an introduction to Thomas Reid, see Nicholas Wolterstorff, *Thomas Reid and the Story of Epistemology (Modern European Philosophy)* (New York: Cambridge University Press, 2004).

the Meaning (John 1:1); and the Word, the Logic, the Reason, the Meaning was *with* God (John 1:1); and the Word, the Logic, the Reason, the Meaning *was* God (John 1:1); and the Word *became flesh* and dwelt among us (John 1:14). God in the flesh was named Jesus. Jesus really is the Reason, not only "for the season" but also for the meaning of life.

Theologically we can see why people fall into despair without Jesus. Think about it. If Jesus is the meaning, we should not be surprised that when people encounter meaninglessness, they despair—feel like dying. John 1:1 implicitly reveals to us that meaninglessness amounts to Jesus-lessness. Without Jesus, who is "the life" (John 14:6), we feel lifeless.

We can take this line of thought a step further. God has revealed that the meaningfulness of meaning is virtually the same thing as the reasonableness of reason and the logicality of logic. Thus when human beings see that there is no good reason for something, we usually call it stupid. Innately we all know life cannot be meaningful unless it is somehow reasonable and logical.

The main theological point revealed by implication in John 1:1 and John 1:14 is that God himself is reasonable. Christianity itself, therefore, is quintessentially reasonable. Christianity, unlike Hinduism, does not accept blatant contradictions that are nonsensical. We do not say, for instance, that "A = not A" because claiming that is patently illogical. It is absurd, likewise, to say that "8 = not 8" or that "God is not God" or that "truth is not truth." While our lives may seem absurd on account of the meaningless and unreasonableness and irrationality we encounter, the good news of theology is that God is not irrational or absurd. God has more wisdom and more sanity than we can begin to fathom (Job 28). His ways are not lower than our ways; on the contrary, they are "higher than [our] ways" (Isa 55:9). It is logical to believe, therefore, that God is entirely trustworthy (1 Cor 1:9; Jas 1:17).

The Value of Theological Education

Multiple volumes of books could be written to explain the far-reaching value of good theological education. The benefits of studying divine revelation (what God has revealed about himself and everything else) are way too many to count. This section, therefore, is limited in scope to focusing on these two things: (1) the little-known fact in evangelical circles that the purpose of theology, historically speaking, is to teach believers the meaning of their own baptism; and (2) the reality that both the Great Commission and the Great Commandment call for theological education.

Understanding Your Own Baptism

According to the learned theologian, Thomas Oden, Christians have both "the right and the responsibility" to know the meaning of their baptism.[8] Reflecting on church history, Oden says the purpose of theology traditionally has been to explain "the ancient ecumenical faith" into which believers are baptized.[9] The baptismal formula, "in the name of the Father and the Son and the Holy Spirit," revealed to us by Jesus in the Great Commission (Matt 28:19) beckons us to question what our baptism means. What does it mean to be baptized in the name of the Father and the Son and the Holy Spirit? Who is the Father? Who is the Son? Who is the Holy Spirit? These three questions are the most fundamental questions of theology.

Although theology is a multifaceted subject, primarily it is the study of God's revelation of God's self. Theology wants to know the nature of God's self. Does God have a self? Is God three selves? What does it mean to be baptized into three different names—the name of the Father, and the Son, and the Holy Spirit? Are the Father and the Son both male? Is the Holy Spirit female? Is the Holy Spirit the heavenly mother of the Son? Is God the Father married to the Holy Spirit? How can God the Father have a Son?

Theology investigates and ponders all of this because "what comes into our minds when we think about God is the most important thing about us."[10] A. W. Tozer rightly states, "The history of mankind will probably show that no people has ever risen above its religion, and man's spiritual history will positively demonstrate that no religion has been greater than its idea of God."[11] What we think about God inevitably determines what we think about everything else.

What, then, are we to think about the meaning of baptism? In answer to this question, Christians have historically written baptismal confessions called creeds. A *creed* is a brief summary or formal statement of the biblical

---

8. See Thomas Oden, *The Living God*, vol. 1 of *Systematic Theology* (San Francisco: HarperOne, 1987), 11.
9. Ibid.
10. See A. W. Tozer, *Knowledge of the Holy* (San Francisco: Harper, 1961), 1.
11. Ibid.

faith that traces back to apostolic teaching. The word derives from the Latin verb *credo*, "I believe." The Apostles' Creed is the most common baptismal confession. Reasonably, it was organized in a three-part way to teach believers what it means to be baptized in three Persons: Father, Son, and Spirit.[12]

The Apostles' Creed

I believe in God, the Father Almighty, Creator of heaven and earth.
I believe in Jesus Christ, his only Son, our Lord,
who was conceived by the Holy Spirit, born of the virgin Mary,
suffered under Pontius Pilate, was crucified, died, and was buried.
He descended into hell; the third day he rose again from the dead.
He ascended into heaven; he is seated at the right hand of the Father,
and he will come to judge the living and the dead.
I believe in the Holy Spirit,
the holy, catholic, apostolic Church,
the communion of saints,
the forgiveness of sins,
the resurrection of the body, and the life everlasting.
Amen.

The theology in the Apostles' Creed provides believers with deep truths that powerfully inform our identities. We are baptized into the name of the highest authority, God, who authored (created) heaven and earth. Logically we can deduce that the Author of the cosmos has authority over all that he created. If every baptized believer understood (at the level of his or her conscious sense of identity) the dignity we have as children of our Father, God, and as forgiven friends of Jesus, God's Son, and as empowered ministers of God's Spirit; then we would surely "walk in newness of life" (Rom 6:4). Our baptism announces this "in the name of the Father, and the Son, and the Holy Spirit."

Yet many churchgoers today see baptism as optional, as if it were a meaningless ceremony. The Apostles' Creed, however, publicly declares that our baptism informs us of who we truly are. The Greek word *baptizo*

---

12. Other early ecumenical creeds such as the Nicene Creed (AD 325), the Constantinopolitan Creed (AD 351), and the Athanasian Creed (AD 500) were similarly structured in accordance with this threefold pattern.

literally means "to immerse, to submerge, to wash."[13] To be *immersed* "in the name" of the Father, and the Son, and the Holy Spirit is to take on the highest name and wear it as if you had just married God on high and had your name legally changed to match his. To be *submerged* in the name of the Father, Son, and Spirit is symbolically to be "buried" into death with Jesus Christ and raised up with him again in victory. To be *washed* by the baptismal waters is to be holistically saved, not by "the removal of dirt from the flesh," but rather by Christ's "appeal to God" that gives us clear consciences by cleansing us from all sin on account of his death (1 Pet 3:18–21).

Baptism not only tells us who we are, but it also covers who we are. The waters of baptism physically encase us as a tomb would. Baptism is a picture of our deaths, that is, of our dying to our "old" selves (Eph 4:22). Yet it also is a picture of our rising from the dead so that "Christ" becomes "our life" (Gal 2:20; Col 3:3–4). Baptism announces that we have been made "new" (Eph 4:24). With the waters of baptism, God graciously covers us so that we no longer have to feel ashamed (Gen 2:25–3:11).

Who among us would know, apart from having a teacher to educate us theologically, that baptism pertains to God's compassionate desire to heal us from our shame? Good theological education offers so much more, and when it is *da'at*, it makes us want to sing.

Can you imagine how redemptive it would be for anxious high schoolers in youth groups, and troubled spouses in marriages, and lonely divorcees, and all who are unhappily unmarried, and addicts, and worriers, and those who suffer daily from disabilities, and for isolated pastors, and angry pastors' kids, and orphans, and all frightened children, and poor people who are destitute, and rich people who feel empty, and those who are sick, and all the remaining souls whom I have not mentioned truly understood—in a *da'at* way—what it means to be baptized in the name of the Father (who created them and loves them), and the Son (who died for them), and the Holy Spirit (who comforts them and unites them to other believers)?

How many problems would instantly be fixed, and how many relationships would suddenly be restored if people would think theologically (i.e., truthfully) about their own baptisms?

---

13. To learn more about baptism, see G. R. Beasley-Murray *Baptism in the New Testament* (Grand Rapids: Eerdmans, 1962).

Notice that in the formula of the Apostles' Creed, there is no explicit mention of the baptism of the Spirit that refers to the spiritual gift of speaking in tongues. For sure, the *charismata* ("spiritual gifts") detailed in Scripture are verified, biblical realities (Rom 12; 1 Cor 12; Eph 4). Yet the Creed points instead to the church, and the communion of saints, and the forgiveness of sins, and the resurrection of the body, and the life everlasting; and it links all of these to the Holy Spirit.

Theology interprets your baptism; it unpacks the spiritual message of your baptism. Among thousands of other things, your baptism tells you that the Spirit of the living God wants you to rest in your belongingness in the Christ (Eph 4:4–6). It says that you are not alone (1 Cor 12:14). You are not an outcast (1 Cor 1:26–29). Rather, you are personally invited to commune with the saints of God (1 John 1:3). Your baptism, further, says that the Holy Spirit of God longs for you to let go of all the bitterness in your heart that keeps you from the joy that should be yours (Eph 4:31; John 15:11). God's Spirit seeks to comfort you (John 14:26) and convince you that you have no need to strive or prove yourself (Ps 46:10). God wants *you* to partake of his divine nature (2 Pet 1:4) and dwell in the love of the Father, Son, and Spirit (Ps 23:6). Baptism says all this and much more, yet without theological education most people's baptisms seem silent.

Fulfilling the Great Commission

Have you ever paused to consider that both the Great Commission and the Great Commandment necessitate theological education? The Great Commission refers to Jesus's words in Matt 28:18–20: "All authority has been given to Me in heaven and on earth. Go therefore and make disciples of all the nations, baptizing them in the name of the Father and the Son and the Holy Spirit, teaching them to observe all that I commanded you; and lo, I am with you always, even to the end of the age." The Great Commandment refers to Jesus's answer to a lawyer's question, "Teacher, which is the great commandment in the Law?" (Matt 22:35–36). Jesus said to him, "You shall love the Lord your God with all your heart, and with all your soul, and with all your mind" (Matt 22:37).

Jesus's mandate to us is clear. We are to love the Lord our God foremost by loving people enough to make disciples of them (Matt 22:37–39; 28:19). Yet how can we make disciples who are baptized in the name of the

Father, Son, and Spirit unless we teach them who God is? And how can we follow through with Jesus's commissioning us to "teach them to obey all that I commanded you," unless we are taught what obedience means in our context?

Bear in mind, it is possible to misinterpret the commandments of Christ. For example, when Jesus says, "If your right eye makes you stumble, tear it out and throw it from you . . . if your right hand makes you stumble, cut it off and throw it from you" (Matt 5:29–30), he is speaking hyperbolically in order to make a theological point. To understand Jesus's words so literally as to think we can sanctify ourselves by maiming ourselves is to misunderstand Jesus's message.

Logic sheds light on the matter. Why pluck out one eye when you still have another eye left? Whatever sin can be committed with one eye can likewise be committed with the other. So then, what is Jesus saying in this passage? Is he magnifying the absurdity of self-righteous religiosity? Is he simply saying that it is possible to become so legalistic that you would maim yourself for naught? Or is he also telling us in the form of a disturbing, gruesome picture that dismembering ourselves is better than being banished to hell?

The need for theological education becomes practical as soon as we begin to take seriously the need to fulfill the Great Commission by obeying Jesus's commands. How can we "make disciples" by teaching them "to observe all that [Jesus] commanded" if we do not understand what Jesus told us to do or if we are flat-out unwilling to obey him? Admittedly, no one knows entirely how to understand Jesus's words with perfect accuracy. But there are degrees of inaccuracy that we can together avoid if we will discipline ourselves to study and pray and be teachable and learn how to think theologically.

Conclusion

This chapter provides guidance to potential students, trustees, and donors who are grappling with real tensions and trying to figure out if theological education is worthwhile. The conclusion here is, yes, it is worthwhile for those who are determined to love God with all their minds, gain the knowledge of *da'at*, understand their own baptisms, and fulfill the Great Commission.

Questions for Further Reflection

1. Have you ever pondered the meaning of your own baptism? How does it affect your sense of identity to know that you have been baptized into the name of the Father and the Son and the Holy Spirit? Have you ever been baptized? Why is baptism important? Should people be baptized as infants or adults? Should they be sprinkled or immersed? What does Scripture say?
2. What comes into your mind when you think about God? What do you think Tozer means when he says this is the most important thing about you?
3. How reasonable do you believe Christianity is? Is there any logic to the gospel? In what sense is Jesus Christ the meaning of life? In what specific ways does Jesus give meaning to your life?
4. Now that you have read this chapter, what theological questions do you have?
5. What is your own conclusion: Is theological education worthwhile? What are the spiritual risks involved in having church leaders who are not trained theologically?

Sources for Further Study

Farley, Edward. *Theologia: The Fragmentation and Unity of Theological Education.* Eugene, OR: Wipf and Stock, 2001.

Hancock, Curtis L., and Brendan Sweetman, ed. *Faith and the Life of the Intellect.* Washington D.C.: Catholic University of America Press, 2003.

Hauerwas, Stanley. *The State of the University: Academic Knowledges and the Knowledge of God.* Oxford, UK: Blackwell Publishing, 2007.

Kelsey, David H. *To Understand God Truly: What's Theological About a Theological School?* Louisville: Westminster/John Knox, 1992.

Marsden, George M. *The Outrageous Idea of Christian Scholarship.* Oxford, UK: Oxford University Press, 1997.

McGrath, Alister. *The Passionate Intellect: Christian Faith and the Discipleship of the Mind.* Downers Grove: InterVarsity Press, 2010.

Noll, Mark. *Jesus Christ and the Life of the Mind.* Grand Rapids: Eerdmans, 2011.

_____. *The Scandal of the Evangelical Mind.* Grand Rapids: Eerdmans, 1994.

Oden, Thomas. *Systematic Theology.* 3 vols. San Francisco: HarperOne, 1987-94.

Reeves, Michael. *Delighting in the Trinity: An Introduction to the Christian Faith.* Downers Grove: InterVarsity Press, 2012.

Tozer, A. W. *Knowledge of the Holy.* San Francisco: Harper, 1961.

Chapter Three

THEOLOGICAL EDUCATION AND MINISTRY CALLING

MICHAEL DUDUIT

Then I heard the voice of the Lord asking:
Who should I send? Who will go for us?
I said: Here I am. Send me.
—ISAIAH 6:8

Theological education is the task of equipping those whom God has called for lives of mission and ministry. But what does it mean when we refer to God's "call" in the life of a man or woman? What does it mean when someone says he or she has been "called to ministry"? The call of God, in one sense, is extended to every believer. God calls each Christian to salvation—something that would not be available apart from the work of the Holy Spirit in our lives. And each believer is called to serve Christ—to fulfill some function within the body of Christ—as Paul observes in 1 Corinthians 12. As Kristopher Barnett writes, "All believers are under the general call of God. They are called to follow and obey. This call demands humility and holiness. In addition, each and every believer is invited to join God in His redemptive activity in the world. They are called to make disciples and be witnesses. This is a broad call that applies to any who claim the name of Christ."¹ Yet in addition to this general call to every believer, there is also a more specific call to a unique role of leadership and service within the church.

---

1. Kristopher Barnett, "What Is a Call to Ministry," *Now That You've Been Called to Ministry* (Anderson, SC: AUMinistry Press, 2013), 15.

Years ago it was common to hear a reference to someone being "called to full-time Christian service," but that wording is questionable; at what point does God call anyone to part-time service in the kingdom? No matter how we serve the kingdom—as pastor of a great urban congregation or as nursery assistant in a tiny country church—we are called to full-time faithfulness and commitment to Christ.

Other times we may hear a reference to "vocational Christian service." Yet in many instances of a bi-vocational pastor, who has a full-time vocation and serves in a ministerial role unrelated to that vocation, the calling to service may not be one's primary vocation but nevertheless reflects a clear and powerful call of God to some area of ministry leadership. Perhaps it is best to use the simple phrase "call to ministry" to reflect the reality of a God-given summons to carry out a special place of leadership or service within the body of Christ. As we will see, that calling may take different forms and lead to a variety of ministry roles within the church.

The Biblical Foundation for a Call to Ministry

There is no one verse to which we can turn and say, "Here is what the Bible says about how someone is called to ministry." The Scriptures do not give us guidelines for a "license to preach," ordination, or creating a pastor search committee. Yet the Bible is filled with illustrations of individuals who were called by God to serve some significant task in the story of redemption.

Abraham was set apart (or called) by God to leave his home, journey to a new land, and become the father of a new people who would become God's chosen people and the launching pad of the church (Gen 12:1–3). The call of Abraham was, in one sense, a model of other biblical call experiences: he was chosen purely by God's grace, not because of any inherent merit or qualities he possessed, and was given a task to perform that God would use to accomplish his eternal purpose.

As a murderer and fugitive from justice, Moses was certainly not who one would consider a prime candidate for God's call. But while tending sheep in the middle of nowhere, Moses heard God speak out of a burning bush to summon him to the challenging task of leading the Hebrew people out of slavery and into the Promised Land (Exod 3:1–4:17). At the death of Moses, God called Joshua to lead the people in crossing the Jordan and claiming the land God had promised them (Josh 1:1–9).

During the period of the judges, God called Gideon to lead the people in overthrowing the Midianites. The description of that call includes an ironic twist, as the angelic messenger proclaims him to be a "mighty warrior" even as he is in hiding from the Midianites! Despite Gideon's frequent and strenuous objections, God reinforces the call with the assurance that he would be with Gideon in leading the people to victory (Judges 6).

God sent Samuel to the house of Jesse to find a king, and he evaluated the sons one by one to find "the LORD's anointed one" (1 Sam 16:6). When the youngest son, David, finally appeared, the Lord told Samuel, "Anoint him, for he is the one" (1 Sam 16:12).

The story of Israel's great prophets is a story of men who experienced a unique call of God to become his messengers. The sixth chapter of Isaiah is the best-known prophetic call, as Isaiah's prophetic vision ushers him into the presence of God, surrounded by the angelic host. There is a cleansing of the prophet, as the angel touches his lips with a burning coal taken from the altar, saying, "Now that this has touched your lips, your iniquity is removed and your sin is atoned for" (vv. 6–7). And then the voice of the Lord is heard posing the question, "Who should I send? Who will go for us?" and Isaiah responds, "Here I am. Send me" (v. 8). Isaiah's call and his positive response are followed by the Lord's specific commission to take his message of judgment to an unfaithful people.

The call of Jeremiah reached into the womb, as God tells his prophet, "I chose you before I formed you in the womb; I set you apart before you were born. I appointed you a prophet to the nations" (Jer 1:4–5). Like Moses, Jeremiah sought to avoid God's call by insisting on his own inadequacy: "I don't know how to speak since I am only a youth" (v. 6). But God swept aside his objections, insisting that Jeremiah would go where he was sent and speak what God told him, "for I will be with you to rescue you" (vv. 7–8). God's call is not only a call to serve but also a promise of God's presence and provision.

As we move into the New Testament, one of the most obvious examples of divine calling is Jesus's calling of his disciples. As Matthew describes the scene, Jesus is walking along the shore of the Sea of Galilee when he sees Simon Peter and Andrew fishing: "'Follow me,' he told them, 'and I will make you fish for people'" (Matt 4:19). Immediately after that he saw James and John, the sons of Zebedee, and Matthew tells us, "He called them. Immediately they left the boat and their father and followed him" (vv. 21–22). Some chapters later, Matthew describes his own call to become a disciple: Jesus calls him from the tax office where he was working, and Matthew begins to follow Jesus (Matt 9:9).

One of the most dramatic examples of God's call is found in Acts 9, as Jesus interrupts Saul on his way to terrorize Christians in Damascus and turns the persecutor's life upside down. As Saul sits blind and waiting in Damascus, God sends Ananias to meet with him. God reveals his call on Saul's life to Ananias before he reveals it to Saul (soon to be Paul): "The Lord said to him, 'Go, for this man is my chosen instrument to take my name to Gentiles, kings, and Israelites'" (Acts 9:15).

As he ministered to the young churches as part of his own calling, Paul helps them understand more about God's call to individuals to take on special roles of kingdom service. Describing the unity and diversity to be found in the body of Christ, the church, Paul explains, "Now grace was given to each one of us according to the measure of Christ's gift. . . . And he himself gave some to be apostles, some prophets, some evangelists, some pastors and teachers, equipping the saints for the work of ministry, to build up the body of Christ, until we reach unity in the faith and in the knowledge of God's Son, growing into maturity with a stature measured by Christ's fullness" (Eph 4:7, 11–13). Within this passage we learn several critical truths about what it means to be called to ministry.

Our Call Is by Grace

You are not called to serve because of any inherent worth in you; indeed, any value you have is there by divine gift. Paul wants us to understand that God's call is accompanied by his gift of the capability to fulfill that calling. Referring to Eph 4:7, R. Kent Hughes explains, "Grace" here means "the ability to perform the task God has called us to." In Rom 12:6, he similarly explains, "We have different gifts, according to the grace given us. And likewise in 3:7–8 Paul says that his apostleship came with the gift of God's grace. The point for us is: *each of us has received this enabling grace in the exact proportion Christ gave it.*"[2]

---

2. R. Kent Hughes, *Ephesians: The Mystery of the Body of Christ* (Wheaton: Crossway Books, 1990), 131.

Theological Education and Ministry Calling

God Calls Us Personally
Paul writes, "And he himself gave some to be apostles, some prophets, some evangelists, some pastors and teachers" (Eph 4:11). God chooses individuals to serve in specific roles of ministry. (In the Pastoral Epistles, Paul expands on this discussion.) God does not call groups; he calls people. You are not called because your father was called, or your family was called, or your tribe was called; you are called to ministry because God selected you personally to be an instrument of his grace in service.

God Calls Us to Various Roles
God does not call you to a generic version of ministry. He calls you to serve in a specific role, such as evangelist or pastor-teacher. That does not mean you may not serve in different roles over a lifetime of ministry; Paul himself told his protégé Timothy that he has been "appointed a herald, apostle, and teacher" (2 Tim 1:11). God can use each experience of service to equip and prepare you for a different role at a different season of your life.

Though God calls us to specific roles of ministry and gifts us to carry out those roles, he may also call us to one role for one season of life, then to a different role at a new phase of life and ministry. For example, often new ministers will serve for a time ministering to young people in the church; then, as he matures, the minister may be called to a different role, as a pastor, missionary, or some other part within the body of Christ. Even those who serve as pastors find that their roles change as their churches change; the pastor of a congregation of fifty has a different type of service than the one who leads a congregation of five thousand, but both are called to serve faithfully within the specific places God has put them.

Our Calling Is to Serve the Church
Why does God call individuals to serve the church in these various roles? The purpose of those in "the work of ministry" is to "build up the body of Christ" (Eph 4:12). Our calls to ministry are not for our own sakes but for the church. We are to serve in such a way that we equip the saints for their own kingdom service, which will produce unity within the body of Christ. The ultimate result of faithful ministry is seen in the lives of mature believers "with a stature measured by Christ's fullness" (v. 13). When those whom God has called are able to provide Spirit-anointed service to the church, the

result is congregations that display unity and are active in sharing the gospel and proclaiming the kingdom to a lost world.

Scripture reflects both a general calling to all believers to serve the kingdom and a more specific calling to certain individuals to carry out unique roles of leadership and ministry within the church. While some today discount the idea of "calling" and consider ministry more a career and an opportunity one discovers, the Bible seems to emphasize that God calls out certain men and women to serve the church in ways that go beyond the more general calling of all believers. In analyzing examples of calls to individuals in the Bible, Gordon MacDonald writes,

> Each biblical call was unique. No call seems like any other. The circumstances, the nature, the expectations of the call: all customized. When God wanted a word said or a people led, he mandated a person to make it happen in an unprecedented way. Calls were not classified ads so that anyone could volunteer. Persons, sometimes strange persons, were selected while others, seemingly more worthy and capable, were not. There was only one Esther, one John the Baptizer. There was only *one* Moses in spite of what Miriam and Aaron dared to think the day they asked, "Hasn't he also spoken through us?" These not-so-novel observations are worth repeating. For they form a foundation for authoritative ministry in the twenty-first century. If we have lost our faith in the idea that such calls continue today, then perhaps we have lost touch with the supernatural element that ministry desperately needs.[3]

Understanding Your Call to Ministry

The young man entered his pastor's office and settled into a chair across the desk from the veteran minister. He began the conversation: "Pastor, I wanted to talk to you about something. I think God may be calling me into the ministry."

---

3. Gordon MacDonald, "God's Calling Plan," *Leadership Journal 24:4* (Fall 2003), accessed January 13, 2017, http://www.christianitytoday.com/le/2003/fall/3.35.html?.

Expecting his pastor to express delight at this revelation, the young man was shocked when his pastor replied, "Son, the first thing I would say is that if you can do anything else besides enter the ministry, then you should."

That was hardly the answer he had been expecting, so the young visitor asked, "Are you telling me I should not go into the ministry?"

The older pastor smiled and said, "No, son. What I am saying is that if God is not calling you, then you'll never be happy in ministry. If this is your mom calling you, or a Sunday school teacher encouraging you, or anything else other than the call of God on your life, then don't do it." Then he added, "But if God is calling you and is placing his hand on your life in this way, you won't be happy doing anything else."

That pastor was not making an original observation. Many years ago, in his *Lectures to My Students*, London pastor Charles Spurgeon said, "If any student . . . could be content to be a newspaper editor, or a grocer, or a farmer, or a doctor, or a lawyer, or a senator, or a king, in the name of heaven and earth let him go his way; he is not the man in whom dwells the Spirit of God in its fullness, for a man so filled with God would utterly weary of any pursuit but that for which his inmost soul pants."[4]

Ministry is not for the faint of heart; it is challenging, rigorous, often looked down upon. For every celebrity pastor living an affluent lifestyle, there are thousands living on modest incomes, wondering how they will put their kids through college. The pastor of a hundred-member church often has a hundred supervisors, each expecting the pastor to serve his or her individual needs and live up to sometimes-unreasonable expectations. Ministry is not for those seeking wealth and comfort, and unless one senses the clear call of God in their lives, it will be easy to cast aside such a role in search of something easier.

Longtime pastor Erwin Lutzer writes, "I don't see how anyone could survive in the ministry if he felt it was just his own choice. Some ministers scarcely have two good days back to back. They are sustained by the knowledge that God has placed them where they are. Ministers without such conviction often lack courage and carry their resignation letter in their coat pocket. At the slightest hint of difficulty, they're gone."[5]

---

4. Charles Haddon Spurgeon, *Lectures to My Students: Complete and Unabridged* (reprint, Grand Rapids: Zondervan, 1954), 26.

5. Erwin W. Lutzer, "Still Called to the Ministry," *Moody Monthly* 83, no. 7 (March 1983): 133.

So how does one know if he or she is being called to ministry? How do you determine if the call you are sensing is from God or from family and friends? There are three major factors to consider as you evaluate whether God is calling you to serve in this way.

You Will Sense an Inner Compulsion

Most of those who sense God's call do not have an Isaiah 6 experience, complete with angels, burning coals, and a vision of God on his throne. But whether a dramatic sense of call or a "still, small voice," the call to ministry always involves an inner sense of God's presence and a sense of God's calling to some special service. When God calls, he provides an inner compulsion to serve. The prophet Jeremiah felt this compulsion to proclaim God's truth to the people. He said, "I say: I won't mention him or speak any longer in his name. But his message becomes a fire burning in my heart, shut up in my bones. I become tired of holding it in, and I cannot prevail" (Jer 20:9).

Centuries later the apostle Paul had much the same feeling about the mandate God had given him to preach the gospel. Writing to the believers at Corinth, Paul insisted, "For if I preach the gospel, I have no reason to boast, because I am compelled to preach—and woe to me if I do not preach the gospel!" (1 Cor 9:16). In the following verse Paul refers to his own sense of calling as a "commission," a responsibility given to him by God.

When God is authentically extending a call to ministry, such an inner compulsion will not be momentary; it will be ongoing, persistent. Sometimes ministers recall sensing God's call for an extended time—sometimes even years—before they finally relented and accepted God's unique purpose for their lives. As Chuck Fuller observes, "This internal compulsion to enter ministry, though, must not be merely impulsive or reactionary. A fleeting thought, a single pondering, a convicting encounter, or a 'what if' moment does not constitute a call to gospel work. Compulsion has roots."[6] When God is calling, he places an inner sense of his direction within our minds and hearts, a hunger to respond to that call.

---

6. Chuck Fuller, "How Do You Know If You Are Called to Ministry?," *Now That You've Been Called to Ministry* (Anderson, SC: AUMinistry Press, 2013), 25.

You Will Receive External Confirmation

A call to ministry is rarely a secret known only to the recipient of such a call. Indeed, it is often the case that the person's pastor and fellow church members begin recognizing that call before the individual does.

For example, a young Christian woman demonstrates a hunger to learn more about God's Word and begins to share the gospel with friends and family. When her church announces an outreach effort or ministry project in the community, her name is usually the first one on the sign-up list. She works a part-time job and saves her money faithfully to enable her to go on several mission trips with members of her church.

One Sunday in the worship service, she walks down the aisle at the time of invitation to announce that she is sensing God's call to become a missionary, only to find that many in the church come to celebrate with her and to indicate they have been sensing her call for a long time and have been praying for her. That affirmation from others who know her provided further confirmation to solidify the inner compulsion she already felt that God had a special calling for her life.

If an individual feels he or she may be experiencing a call to ministry, but that calling is not receiving confirmation from others, it may be a caution flag. It could be that the sense of call is momentary and will pass, or it could be that the individual is receiving an authentic call but needs to be mentored and equipped. As the pastor and others spend time teaching, and as the hunger for God's Word grows and matures, the individual's newfound desire for and participation in kingdom service will demonstrate the reality of the call and result in external confirmation from the congregation.

How should a church respond when someone testifies to a call to ministry? Chuck Fuller notes that "the membership and leadership of a local church should help a person discern and refine a call to ministry in each of the following ways: identifying specific flaws in character that, if not purged, would subvert ministry; detecting spiritual maturity and overall readiness for service; discerning what gifts for ministry a person possesses, and what types of ministries those particular gifts would best serve; refining skills in leadership and working with people; developing skills in preaching and public communication; gaining experience in teaching and pastoral ministries."[7]

---

7. Ibid.

Does it matter which comes first, the inner compulsion or external confirmation? No, but it does matter that both ultimately become a reality. George W. Truett became longtime pastor of the First Baptist Church in Dallas, Texas, and one of America's greatest preachers, but he had no sense of God's call in his life until the congregation declared their own recognition that God was calling Truett. Gordon MacDonald tells the story:

> Young Truett was studying law and, occasionally, preaching for a congregation when the pulpit needed filling. One night in a church business meeting, an older man arose and, in part, said, "This church has a duty to perform, and we have waited late and long to get about it. I move, therefore, that this church call a presbytery to ordain George W. Truett to the full work of the gospel ministry." This motion was made and seconded without consulting Truett. Truett was thunderstruck. He rose to his feet and said, "You have me appalled; you simply have me appalled." But one person after another stood up and said, "Brother George, we have a deep conviction that you ought to be preaching." He begged them to hold off for six months. They said, "We won't wait six hours. We are called to do this thing now . . . we dare not wait . . . we must follow our convictions." Truett recalled, "There I was, against a whole church, against a church profoundly moved. There was not a dry eye in the house—one of the supreme solemn hours in the church's life. I was thrown into the stream, and just had to swim." I would dare to say—realizing there have been extraordinary exceptions—that a call to ministry is not a call until a portion of the body of Christ has said it is a call.[8]

Whichever comes first, when God calls you to ministry, he will reveal that to you and to the body of Christ. But that is not where it ends.

You Will Demonstrate a Desire to Serve

When God calls you to ministry, he calls you to serve and gives you a desire to be involved in his kingdom work. No matter what area of ministry God

---

8. MacDonald, "God's Calling Plan."

is calling you to, you will hunger to be involved in ministry. I recall being surprised many years ago when I was attending seminary that a number of seminary students did not actively participate in a local church while they were studying for ministry. These were individuals who said God had called them to serve the church in some way, but on Sunday morning they preferred to sleep in or sit on the porch enjoying a cup of joe and the Sunday newspaper rather than joining the people of God in worship. My guess is that most of those one-time seminarians didn't last long in ministry and moved on to other pursuits because if your life does not demonstrate a desire to serve the kingdom and be a functioning part of the body of Christ, there is little evidence you have experienced an authentic call of God to ministry.

If you have been called to ministry, then you have been called to serve. And if you aren't willing to serve faithfully at the launching point of your ministry, then you aren't likely to serve faithfully in the years ahead. In addition to a desire to serve, however, you will also have a desire to prepare for such service.

Preparing to Fulfill God's Call in Your Life

A call to ministry is a call to prepare. Just as you would expect your physician to have preparation, just as you would expect an attorney or a teacher to prepare to carry out their work, so it is important for a person in ministry to have a solid preparation so that he or she will be able to present the truths of God's Word accurately and effectively.

In a letter encouraging his young coworker Timothy, Paul wrote, "Be diligent to present yourself to God as one approved, a worker who doesn't need to be ashamed, correctly teaching the word of truth" (2 Tim 2:15). As Thomas Lea notes, "Paul was urging his Christian friend to work with such diligence that he would have no fear of shame for poor quality work . . . (and) to be accurate in delivering the message of truth."[9]

An effective minister is a faithful student. That does not mean every minister will be able to take advantage of all educational opportunities. There are God-called pastors in less-developed parts of the world who may never have an opportunity to take a college or seminary class. But they are

---

9. Thomas D. Lea and Hayne P. Griffin Jr., *1, 2 Tim; Titus*, vol. 34 of *The New American Commentary* (Nashville: Broadman, 1992), 215.

still students as they spend hours prayerfully learning more of God's Word so they can be workers who don't "need to be ashamed, correctly teaching the word of truth."

However, a man or woman called by God to minister in other parts of the world has an obligation to take advantage of every educational opportunity the Lord grants to gain the knowledge and preparation required for effective ministry in the twenty-first century. Certainly there is a sense of urgency in the hearts of many who have experienced God's call and a hunger to move beyond preparation and to practice. Yet taking shortcuts in preparation may limit what God does in a particular ministry. Bryan Cribb writes, "I have a question that I ask my students, many of whom are young and eager to get on the field as quickly as possible (particularly those called to the mission field). Let's say they have 60 years of ministry ahead of them. Would they rather have 50–55 years of substantive ministry or 60 years of ministry that may not be as fruitful as it could have been with proper study and practice first?"[10]

An important part of ministry preparation is typically a formal education, which may include an undergraduate degree from a college or university, plus graduate study in ministry. Such education provides a foundation for a lifelong learning experience as a minister of the gospel. Such an education includes general studies to provide broad-based historical and cultural knowledge, then study in specific areas relating to ministry service, including biblical studies and languages, spiritual formation, evangelism and missions, preaching and teaching, leadership and church administration, Christian ethics and worldview, church history, theology and philosophy.

Ministers who have not yet started a college education should consider their options carefully when planning for college. As you prepare for years of vital ministry service, you want the best foundation possible—one that equips you to learn well, to think critically, and to communicate effectively.

Many students preparing for ministry naturally choose to attend a Christian college or university. Such students should be aware that just because a school has a church or denominational relationship does not mean students receive Christ-centered higher educations. At some schools, that church relationship means little more than weekly chapel services.

---

10. Bryan H. Cribb, "What the Bible Says About the Call to Ministry," *Now That You've Been Called to Ministry* (Anderson, SC: AUMinistry Press, 2013), 36.

At an authentically Christ-centered college or university, that commitment impacts every element of life—from the residence hall to the classroom. Such schools have Christian scholars in the classroom, integrating insights from a Christian worldview into their academic disciplines. The application of Christian thinking into varied fields offers an excellent model for young ministers as they prepare for the same challenge in their own ministries.

As a future pastor or church leader, one of the other benefits of a Christian college or university is the relationships you establish that stay with you for the rest of your life and ministry. The friend you make in New Testament class or in the ministerial association may become a trusted friend and colleague with whom your life intersects for decades to come.

Following a baccalaureate degree at a college or university, the typical pattern is for the new minister to begin a seminary or divinity school degree with an intensive focus on biblical studies, theology, practical ministry, and related subjects. (A seminary is usually a freestanding institution for theological study, while a divinity school is typically part of a larger university.) For many years the traditional seminary degree has been the master of divinity, which generally requires around ninety credit hours of study (although the actual number varies from seventy-two to more than a hundred hours at different seminaries). The MDiv provides a range of study, which typically includes Bible (including biblical languages Greek and Hebrew), theology, preaching, pastoral care, and church administration.

In recent years seminaries and divinity schools have begun to offer alternative degrees to the MDiv, usually with a smaller number of credit hours required and a less comprehensive range of subjects. Such degrees are often designed for the minister who is older and wishes to receive an enhanced level of ministry training but without the years required to complete the MDiv (which is usually three years or more).

Another trend is the development of online courses and degree programs by many seminaries and divinity schools. Such programs allow ministers to receive additional training without leaving their places of service and moving to the seminary campus.

One question many students ask is, "If I am going on to seminary, do I need to major in religion or Christian studies in my bachelor's degree?" While some students do opt for other majors—such as history or English—there are real benefits to doing an undergraduate major in college as well. One benefit is that it provides a solid basis for later excellence in graduate or seminary programs. In fact, many students take advanced courses in seminary in place of more basic courses they did in a strong Christian studies program as an undergraduate. A benefit for those who may delay graduate study is that undergraduate programs provide the majority of preparation for ministry service as they graduate and move into church or other ministry roles.

A recent trend is the development of blended programs that allow students to begin their MDiv studies while still finishing their baccalaureate degrees. Such programs may allow diligent students to complete both the BA and MDiv in as little as five years, as compared to the more traditional pattern of four years in college and three years in seminary.

A solid ministry education at a quality Christian college or university, followed by a master's degree (such as the MDiv) at a seminary or divinity school, provides a valuable foundation for the man or woman seeking to serve the church and the kingdom in response to God's call. No matter what the level or quality of education, however, there is no substitute for the call of God in one's life. Ministry begins with and is built on the call of God.

Questions for Further Reflection

1. Are there examples of a "call to ministry" found in Scripture? Are there similarities in these examples that give us guidance for today?
2. How does the call to ministry differ from the more general call to kingdom service for all believers?
3. If you have sensed a call to ministry, in what way have the factors involved in calling influenced your own understanding of your call?
4. Why is theological education such an important step to take in response to God's call?

Sources for Further Study

Allen, Jason. *Discovering Your Call to Ministry.* Chicago: Moody, 2016.
Clowney, Edmund P. *Called to the Ministry.* Phillipsburg: P&R, 1976.
Guinness, Os. *The Call: Finding and Fulfilling the Central Purpose of Your Life.* Nashville: Thomas Nelson, 2003.

Harvey, Dave. *Am I Called?: The Summons to Pastoral Ministry.* Wheaton: Crossway, 2012.

Iorg, Jeff. *Is God Calling Me?* Nashville: B&H, 2008.

Chapter Four

THEOLOGICAL EDUCATION AND SPIRITUAL FORMATION

DANA M. HARRIS

In the early centuries of the church, great attention was paid to the character formation and spiritual maturity of new converts as evidenced in the emphasis placed on catechesis.¹ Instruction in the faith and spiritual formation were integrally connected. Ordination focused on the candidate's spiritual fervor and desire for God.² Two millennia later, however, the relationship between theological education and spiritual formation is often unclear or uneasy.³

The aim of this chapter is to show how theological education and spiritual formation are organically related and how spiritual formation is an essential aspect of theological education. The nature of both theological education and spiritual formation are considered first. Then challenges and promises of spiritual formation are outlined. Finally, some possibilities for spiritual formation in theological education are offered.

---

1. See esp. Andrew B. McGowan, *Ancient Christian Worship: Early Church Practices in Social, Historical, and Theological Perspective* (Grand Rapids: Baker Academic, 2014), 95–98, 135–82. See also George Kalantzis, "From the Porch to the Cross: Ancient Christian Approaches to Spiritual Formation," in *Life in the Spirit: Spiritual Formation in Theological Perspective*, ed. Jeffrey P. Greenman and George Kalantzis (Downers Grove: InterVarsity, 2010), 63–81.

2. Carl Volz, "Seminaries: The Love of Learning or the Desire for God?" *Dialog* 28, no. 2 (1989): 104.

3. This disjuncture was not always the case. See, for example, Jean LeClercq, *The Love of Learning and the Desire for God: A Study of Monastic Culture*, trans. Catharine Misrahi (New York: Fordham University Press, 1961). He traces the development of scholastic (focused on learning) and monastic (focused on spirituality) methods, and he discusses how theology and spirituality were integral aspects of clerical education.

The Nature of Theological Education

Theological education "broadly defined . . . is preparation—intellectual, experiential and spiritual—for serving and leading a church or community of faith."[4] This preparation often leads to a professional degree, such as the master of divinity. Ideally, however, the goal of theological education is not limited to degree acquisition but also includes some spiritual formation.

Two approaches to theological education are particularly helpful when considering spiritual formation. The first is a personalist approach, outlined by Graham A. Cole, which offers a vision of human flourishing that begins with an understanding of the personal, triune God and the reality of humans created in his image.[5] Human flourishing is oriented vertically in relation to God and horizontally in relation to others. The outcome for theological education on a personalist view is to teach students how "to think theologically and how to live Christianly *coram Deo* [before God]."[6] Another helpful approach, put forth by Ellen T. Charry, understands the goal of theology to be wisdom. Drawing upon Augustine, she maintains that *scientia* (the study of theology and Scripture) serves *sapientia* (wisdom). Thus, "theological endeavor is a spiritual exercise for the sake of a wise and happy life in God."[7]

Both approaches stress the integral connection between thinking and living, between the acquisition of knowledge and the formation of character. Regrettably this connection is not always appreciated, especially when spiritual formation is seen as a desirable but ultimately nonessential aspect of theological education.[8]

---

4. As quoted in "The FTE Guide to Theological Education," available online at fteleaders.org/fteguide. See also Daniel O. Aleshire and Barbara G. Wheeler, "Theological Education: Concepts of," *Cambridge Dictionary of Christianity*, ed. Daniel Patte (Cambridge: Cambridge University Press, 2010), 1219–21. They note that theological education divides into three prevalent patterns: religious formation, which focuses on the intellectual, spiritual, and pastoral formation of candidates; rational, philosophically focused approaches; and practical, skills-based approaches.

5. Graham Cole refers to biblical personalism "as a vision of life, paying particular attention to the personalist purpose of the Triune God, the flourishing of persons in relation," in "Theological Education: A Personalist Perspective," *Journal of Christian Education* 44, no. 3 (2001): 21.

6. Cole, "Theological Education," 24.

7. Ellen T. Charry, "Educating for Wisdom: Theological Studies as a Spiritual Exercise," *Theology Today* 66, no. 3 (2009): 298.

8. For a discussion of the formative aspect of education, especially as a means of directing one's desire toward God, see James K. A. Smith, *Desiring the Kingdom: Worship, Worldview, and Cultural Formation* (Grand Rapids: Baker Academic, 2009).

The Nature of Spiritual Formation

Spiritual formation concerns the transformation of a believer into Christ-likeness.[9] This transformation involves renewing the mind (Rom 12:2) and conformity to the image of Christ (Rom 8:29; 2 Cor 3:18). Paul likens this formation to childbirth (Gal 4:19) and to attaining maturity in Christ (Eph 4:13). Such maturity is the goal of Christian proclamation, exhortation, and instruction (Col 1:28–29). Spiritual transformation depends on the indwelling Spirit (Rom 8:11) and the grace of God (cf. 2 Pet 3:18).

At its core, spiritual formation is ultimately restorative—restoring to those who bear the image of God (Gen 1:26–27) the glory that was originally intended for them (Heb 2:10; cf. Ps 8:5–6) but is now revealed in the image of Christ (1 Cor 15:49; 2 Cor 3:18).[10] Spiritual formation recalls the garden of Eden—in which human beings were rightly related with God, with each other, within themselves, and to the rest of creation—and is a means of grace used by God to restore these ruptured relationships in his redeemed people. Thus, spiritual formation is holistic in nature, involving the mind, spirit, and body[11] and concerns both the individual and the community of the redeemed.[12] Finally, spiritual formation recalls God's original purposes for humanity (to image him and to extend his rule

---

9. Spiritual formation has a long history. Richard Foster surveys six spiritual traditions, including the contemplative, holiness, charismatic, social justice, evangelical, and incarnational, in *Streams of Living Water: Essential Practices from the Six Great Traditions of Christian Faith* (New York: HarperCollins, 2001). See also Richard F. Lovelace, *Dynamics of Spiritual Life: An Evangelical Theology of Renewal* (Downers Grove: InterVarsity, 1979). For a stimulating discussion of Dietrich Bonhoeffer's views on theological education and spiritual formation, see Paul R. House, *Bonhoeffer's Seminary Vision: A Case for Costly Discipleship and Life Together* (Wheaton: Crossway, 2015); and Stephen Plant, "Theological Education and Christian Formation in Conversation with Dietrich Bonhoeffer's *Life Together*" *Colloquium* 47, no. 2 (2015): 180–94.

10. Cf. Mel Lawrenz, *Dynamics of Spiritual Formation* (Grand Rapids: Baker, 2000), 145–46: "This is the heart of spiritual formation—the intentional, sustained repatterning of a person's life after the pattern set out by God when he created human beings in his image, but made possible only by divine transforming power."

11. "Spiritual formation works with the whole person, not only a soul to be saved or a mind to be taught" (John M. Dettoni, "What Is Spiritual Formation?" in *Christian Educator's Handbook on Spiritual Formation*, ed. Kenneth O. Gangel and James C. Wilhoit [Wheaton: Victor, 1994], 13). Cole talks about a holistic Christian spirituality that includes orthodoxy (right beliefs), orthopraxis (right practices), and orthokardia (right attitudes). Graham A. Cole, "At the Heart of a Christian Spirituality," *Reformed Theological Review* 52 (1993): 50–55. Thus spiritual formation, properly understood, counters any type of functional gnosticism that fails to understand the organic interaction between the body and the spirit. This is discussed further below.

12. Graham Cole also indicates the need for "orthokoinonia"—"relating rightly to one another in the community of faith" ("Theological Education," 27).

throughout the world; the "cultural mandate") and points to God's mission to reconcile the world back to himself through the redemptive work of Christ (Col 1:20).[13]

Spiritual formation follows from the Spirit's work of regeneration, or "new birth," in the believer based on the completed work of Christ. Whereas a believer is justified upon conversion, sanctification is an ongoing process in the believer's life. Although spiritual transformation is ultimately possible only through the Spirit, God provides various means (prayer, Scripture reading and mediation, confession, etc.) that nurture and foster this transformation.[14] Thus spiritual formation is the intentional appropriation of these means for the ongoing work of maturity in the believer's life. Intentionality, however, must not be misunderstood as legalism (attempting to earn God's favor), formalism (stressing the efficacy of certain techniques), or Pelagianism (denying the necessity of the Spirit's work in transforming an individual).[15]

The Challenges of Spiritual Formation and Theological Education

It would seem obvious that the aims of theological education and spiritual formation are complementary, not contradictory. Even so, the relationship between the two in actual practice often faces numerous challenges.[16] These

---

13. For a helpful biblical overview of spiritual formation and a brief historical survey, see M. Robert Mulholland Jr., "Spirituality and Transformation," in *Dictionary of Christian Spirituality*, ed. Glen G. Scorgie (Grand Rapids: Zondervan, 2011), 216–21.

14. Traditionally spiritual disciplines have focused on prayer, Scripture reading, solitude, confession, meditation, worship, and service. Richard Foster presents a tripartite grouping of spiritual disciplines: inward disciplines (meditation, prayer, fasting, study); outward disciplines (simplicity, solitude, submission, service); and corporate disciplines (confession, worship, guidance, celebration). See Richard J. Foster, *Celebration of Discipline: The Path to Spiritual Growth* (San Francisco: Harper and Row, 1978). Dallas Willard distinguishes between disciplines of abstinence (solitude, silence, fasting, frugality, chastity, secrecy, sacrifice) and disciplines of engagement (study, worship, celebration, service, prayer, fellowship, confession, submission). See Dallas Willard, *The Spirit of the Disciplines: Understanding How God Changes Lives* (San Francisco: Harper and Row, 1988). See also Donald S. Whitney, *Spiritual Disciplines for the Christian Life* (Colorado Springs: Navpress, 1991); and M. Robert Mulholland Jr., *Invitation to a Journey: A Road Map for Spiritual Formation* (Downers Grove: InterVarsity, 1993).

15. Spiritual formation is ultimately about the imitation of Christ (*imitatio Christi*); thus it is not a program of self-actualization or self-improvement but rather the formation of Christ within the believer.

16. Discussions about the gap between theological education and spiritual formation have been ongoing for decades. For a helpful summary, see Walter L. Liefeld and Linda M. Cannell, "Spiritual Formation and Theological Education," in *Alive to God: Studies in Spirituality Presented to James Houston*, ed. J. I. Packer and Loren Wilkerson (Downers Grove: InterVarsity, 1992), 239–52.

challenges occur both at the institutional level and at the personal levels of students and professors.

One of the most common obstacles for spiritual formation in divinity schools and seminaries is a lack of structured education. Whereas academic curricula and professional programs are explicitly outlined in course catalogs, spiritual formation is often an assumed aspect of theological education, implicit within some course offerings or left to the (often informal) mentoring of students by professors.[17] This can be exacerbated by trends toward increasing specialization within disciplines as well as an artificial separation of the theoretical and practical aspects of theological education.[18] In the extreme this can lead to the conclusion that spiritual formation has no formal place in theological education. Moreover, many seminaries and divinity schools face an increasing number of administrative and financial challenges such as issues with accreditation, legal compliance, and ongoing pressures to make theological education more accessible and affordable.[19] In many cases there is pressure for programs with fewer degree hours and for more diverse delivery systems including (but not limited to) online courses and programs.[20] In view of such pressures, as well as perceived difficulties of assessment and quantifiable outcomes, spiritual formation can be perceived as optional or impractical even when its desirability is acknowledged.[21]

Another challenge occurs when a false dichotomy is created between theological education and spiritual formation. There can be an assumption

---

17. Traditionally, divinity schools have been one of many schools comprising a single university, whereas seminaries have typically been associated with a particular denomination and may or may not be part of a university. These distinctions, however, have become increasingly blurred. The terms are used interchangeably here.

18. These problems are well documented. See, for example, Edward Farley, *Theologia: The Fragmentation and Unity of Theological Education* (Philadelphia: Fortress, 1983); David H. Kelsey, *Between Athens and Berlin: The Theological Education Debate* (Grand Rapids: Eerdmans, 1993); and George Lindbeck, "Spiritual Formation and Theological Education," *Theological Education* 24 (1988): 10–32. For a recent critique, see Linda M. Cannell, "Theology, Spiritual Formation and Theological Education," in *Life in the Spirit: Spiritual Formation in Theological Perspective*, 229–49.

19. See, for example, John M. Palka, "The Impact of Societal and Educational Trends on Theological Education in the Lutheran Church–Missouri Synod," *Concordia Journal* 30 (2004): 217–37; and Kristine Stache, "Formation for the Whole Church: A New/Old Vision of Theological Education in the 21st Century," *Dialog* 53 (2014): 286–92.

20. The possibilities for online spiritual formation are discussed below.

21. Related to assessment is the question of who determines acceptable outcomes for spiritual formation and how these are quantified. See, for example, H. Frederick Reisz, "Assessing Spiritual Formation in Christian Seminary Communities," *Theological Education* 39 (2003): 29–40; and John Harris, "Assessment of Ministry Preparation to Increase Understanding," *Theological Education* 39 (2003): 117–36.

(rarely articulated) on the part of both faculty and students that one must choose between academic excellence and spiritual growth. Implicit within this assumption is the belief that academic study cannot simultaneously nourish one's spirit. Related to this are pressures from the academy or professional societies that maintain that academic rigor and objectivity preclude the possibility of a personal faith commitment on the part of the researcher.

Still another challenge is presented by the ever-increasing demands placed on both faculty and students. The roles professors play in the spiritual formation of students are essential. The organic nature of spiritual formation is such that it is better "caught than taught," thus the spiritual formation of those who will be forming (professors) others (students) is paramount. Yet faculty face various pressures including course preparation, teaching, supervising (especially if PhD programs are involved), publishing, speaking, and commitments to local churches. Factoring in spiritual formation raises legitimate questions of compensation, whether in terms of course reduction or financial remuneration.[22] Similarly, students are equally fragmented as they face tremendous challenges, often juggling school, families, part-time jobs, and ministry commitments. For many students, spiritual formation, although desired, is one of the first things to be cut when they are pressed for time.[23]

Related to the issues of overload and fragmentation is the prevalence of "gnostic" thinking that denies the reality of an embodied existence. The culture of graduate-level theological education often rewards all-nighters, joking that caffeine and sugar are legitimate sleep substitutes, and views good eating habits and physical exercise as either unrealistic or unnecessary.[24] Unfortunately this ethos and these habits often continue and shape

---

22. This is particularly true when spiritual formation is an implicit part of the curriculum. Although faculty may be personally committed to the spiritual formation of their students, institutional structures often reward publication and teaching for tenure and promotion against time devoted to implicit, uncompensated elements of a curriculum.

23. Thus, it may be wise for institutions to consider carefully the workload and other expectations of their students and faculty. This could include evaluating assignments, identifying overlap in the curriculum, exploring opportunities for faculty collaboration, etc.

24. The failure to understand the integration of the body and spirit also has implications for the community: "[T]he flight toward disembodiment can be seen as a flight from relationality, a desire to negate our basic need for God and others" (M. Elizabeth Lewis Hall and Erik Thoennes, "At Home in Our Bodies: Implications of the Incarnation for Embodiment and Christian Higher Education," *Christian Scholar's Review* 36 [2006]: 34).

students' future ministries in which they try to do everything (and are often expected to do so) at the expense of their spiritual, emotional, relational, physical, and sometimes moral well-being.

Finally, by the time many students make it to graduate school, they have been formed by an individualistic culture that rewards intense competition and fosters a false sense of self that believes worth and identity depend on one's accomplishments and grade-point average.[25] Thus it is not surprising that many students begin their theological education with little or no awareness of their spiritual needs or the value of spiritual formation.[26] Related to this can be a failure to see the value of spiritual formation for students on the part of administrators and faculty within theological institutions.

Such challenges can appear insurmountable, but they are not. Theological institutions committed to spiritual formation have the opportunity to think creatively and holistically about spiritual formation, but they have to do so with intent. The increasing pressures and challenges facing seminaries and divinity schools suggest that reliance on implicit, informal, or individual approaches to spiritual formation increases the likelihood that spiritual formation ends up unaddressed in theological education. Indeed, it may even be desirable for theological institutions to identify and address specific detriments to spiritual formation within their institutions. With thought and planning, however, spiritual formation can make significant contributions to theological education.

The Potential of Spiritual Formation and Theological Education

The challenges of incorporating spiritual formation into theological education can seem overwhelming, but the potential of spiritual formation to enhance the overall aims of theological education are tremendous. Two

---

25. The same is often the case for professors who have been shaped by the same culture.
26. This is likely to increase in light of trends away from denominational, or indeed any religious, affiliation among millennials. See Marilyn Naidoo, "Spiritual Formation in Protestant Theological Institutions," in *Handbook of Theological Education in World Christianity: Theological Perspectives—Regional Surveys—Ecumenical Trends*, ed. Dietrich Werner, David Esterline, Namsoon Kim, and Joshva Raja (Oxford: Regnum, 2010), 189–91. The lack of spiritual formation in matriculating students is discussed by Virginia Samuel Cetuk, *What to Expect in Seminary: Theological Education as Spiritual Formation* (Nashville: Abingdon, 1998).

such potentials include greater self-awareness and a more global understanding of the church.

Spiritual Formation and Self-Awareness: A Holistic View of God, Self, and Community

A healthy understanding of oneself includes an awareness of one's own limitations as a created being. As Graham Cole states, "We are creatures before we are Christians."[27] Spiritual formation is one aspect of self-care that recognizes the need to nourish one's soul and to set healthy boundaries.[28] Burnout among ministers is a real issue; thus cultivating ongoing disciplines such as rest (Sabbath), prayer and confession, and Scripture reading (just to mention a few) during seminary counters the functional gnosticism (such as poor sleeping and eating habits) so prevalent in graduate-level studies. Such practices foster an appreciation of one's embodied existence and an acceptance of one's limitations.[29]

Spiritual formation affords the opportunity to explore one's gifting and calling through intentional times of reflection and sharing. Such practices in the context of the seminary community also foster an appreciation of others' gifts and callings. Awareness of one's uniqueness encourages both grateful confidence (of what can be offered to others) and humble appreciation (of what is needed from others). Intentional reflection also provides opportunities to consider and clarify one's calling.

Increasing self-awareness also facilitates the integration of the mind and spirit. A holistic recognition of oneself can begin to address the perceived dichotomy between the intellectual and the spiritual. As Gordon Smith writes, "Rigorous intellectual exercise is good for the soul.... A lecture on justification by faith... is part of spiritual formation. A study of the nature and character of evil can be a vital aspect of one's complete spiritual character development."[30] Thus the academically rigorous pursuit of theology can

---

27. Cole, "Theological Education," 25.
28. Bob Burns, Tasha D. Chapman, and Donald G. Guthrie list five elements that are necessary for long-term flourishing in ministry: spiritual formation, self-care, emotional/cultural intelligence, prioritizing one's marriage and family, and understanding leadership and management. See Bob Burns, Tasha D. Chapman, and Donald G. Guthrie, *Resilient Ministry: What Pastors Told Us About Surviving and Thriving* (Downers Grove: InterVarsity, 2013).
29. As Hall and Thoennes rightly comment, "Our limitations are not sinful, but our pride in not acknowledging our limitations is indeed sinful" ("At Home in Our Bodies," 44).
30. Gordon T. Smith, "Spiritual Formation in the Academy: A Unifying Model," *Theological Education* 33 (1996): 84.

be a powerful means of spiritual formation.[31] Stephanie Paulsell suggests, "[a] spirituality of intellectual work would help us claim the contemplative dimension of our vocation as something that relates us to our community rather than something that separates us from it."[32]

Awareness and appreciation of one's strengths, limitations, gifts, and calling begin with the individual, but this self-understanding can only be fully actualized in community.[33] Thus the role of the community is an essential element of spiritual formation. Yet that community must be cultivated, and attitudes that damage it need to be addressed. Such attitudes include competition, insecurity, and fear. Recognizing one's unique gifts and calling begins to mitigate the need to compete or compare with others. Even in the absence of time pressures, students would withdraw from seminary communities because they are not safe places. But when gratitude and humility are intentionally valued and modeled, communities become powerful places where significant spiritual formation occurs.

Spiritual Formation and Diversity: A Global View of God, Self, and Community

A healthy understanding of oneself also includes an awareness of one's own context, including denominational, socioeconomic, cultural, geographic, educational, theological, generational, gender, and ethnic contexts. The changing demographics and realities associated with globalization require increasing awareness of one's own context and appreciation of how it fits into the larger setting of God's global mission. Lack of such understanding may cause one to assume that one's own experience is universal and normative. Thus exposure to others reveals the vastness of God's world and fosters greater self-awareness.

---

31. For more on spiritual formation and intellectual rigor, see James W. Sire, *Habits of the Mind: Intellectual Life as a Christian Calling* (Downers Grove: InterVarsity, 2000); Clifford Williams, *The Life of the Mind: A Christian Perspective* (Grand Rapids: Baker Academic, 2002); and Richard J. Mouw, *Called to the Life of the Mind: Some Advice for Evangelical Scholars* (Grand Rapids: Eerdmans, 2014).

32. Stephanie Paulsell, "Theological Table Talk: Spiritual Formation and Intellectual Work in Theological Education," *Theology Today* 55 (1998): 232. See also Gordon Smith, "Spiritual Formation in the Academy: A Unifying Model," and Patricia Ann Lamoureux, "An Integrated Approach to Theological Education," *Theological Education* 36 (1999): 141–56.

33. Graham Cole is again helpful here: "In a personalist's universe the supreme values consist of persons, and those persons in proper relation to one another. Theological education that does not allow for the flourishing of persons in fellowship and which does not foster growth in Christlikeness is adrift from its biblical moorings" ("Theological Education," 23).

Exposure to diversity as a means of spiritual formation is well grounded in Scripture. The Acts of the Apostles records the advance of the gospel into increasingly diverse contexts. As the early church responded to the challenges that arose from this diversity, it experienced unprecedented growth. The goal of such expansion is captured in Revelation 7, where the great multitude from every nation, tribe, people, and language joins together in worship of the Lamb. This biblical grounding is essential. As Sandra Marie Van Opstal notes, "The primary reasons we should pursue multicultural worship . . . are neither pragmatic nor trends, but biblical community and mission."[34]

Diversity offers significant opportunities for spiritual formation and theological education. To be sure, diverse expressions of spirituality may initially be unappreciated or threatening. Yet just as one individual does not possess all the gifts and resources to be self-sufficient, so also no one culture can independently reveal the vastness of God's love and mission. Thus exposure to diverse expressions of Christian spirituality can expand the horizons of one's own spirituality. For example, many African Christians have a deep awareness of the supernatural and have experienced God's healing and guidance in ways that may not be familiar to students from a North American, white suburban context. Students from Latin or Asian contexts often understand the corporate dimensions of worship more fully than those from cultures that focus on the individual.[35] Willie James Jennings notes the "untapped . . . potential to bring various minority students along with white students into a shared project of collaborative formation that brings both their communities together."[36] Such collaborative projects could also afford opportunities for thoughtful reflection on issues of social justice and reconciliation. Like other aspects of spiritual formation, however, intentionality is required, and theological institutions need to create opportunities where diverse backgrounds and experiences are welcomed, received, and valued. As with

---

34. Sandra Maria Van Opstal, *The Next Worship: Glorifying God in a Diverse World* (Downers Grove: InterVarsity, 2016), 23.

35. For a helpful discussion of "worship cultures," see Van Opstal, *The Next Worship*, 201–6. See also Justo L. González, *Mañana: Christian Theology from a Hispanic Perspective* (Nashville: Abingdon, 1990), 157–67.

36. Willie James Jennings, "The Change We Need: Race and Ethnicity in Theological Education," *Theological Education* 49 (2014): 35–42. See also the constructive insights in Christena Cleveland, *Disunity in Christ: Uncovering the Hidden Forces That Keep Us Apart* (Downers Grove: InterVarsity, 2013).

all aspects of spiritual formation, local churches and ministries could offer significant resources here. Other options include shared curricula between seminaries reflecting different denominations and theological traditions.[37]

Some Possibilities and Practicalities of Spiritual Formation in Theological Education

Due to its holistic nature, there are many ways spiritual formation can be incorporated into theological education, including both on-campus and online possibilities, both of which are briefly explored here. This section concludes with discussion about spiritual formation and assessment.

On-Campus Spiritual Formation

One of the easiest ways to incorporate spiritual formation into theological education is through the existing curriculum.[38] Thus the significance of topics such as theological anthropology, models of sanctification, and ecclesiology for spiritual formation could be highlighted. The need for spiritual formation and self-care is a natural component of pastoral practices classes. Worship classes could explore various spiritual traditions, liturgies, and disciplines, and ways these could be integrated into the local church. Spiritual formation projects within local churches could fulfill field education and internship requirements. If possible, new classes on spiritual formation could be created or workshops that model spiritual disciplines could be offered. Classrooms also afford many opportunities to model spiritual practices, such as opening prayer, time for corporate prayer, and meditation on Scripture.[39]

Extracurricular activities also provide many opportunities for spiritual formation. Perhaps the most formative of such activities is corporate

---

37. See, for example, Elizabeth Y. Sung, "Fostering Theological Discernment and Ecumenical Formation: An Interseminary Model," *Journal of Ecumenical Studies* 49 (2014): 311–18.
38. For more practical suggestions, see Gordon Smith, "Spiritual Formation in the Academy: A Unifying Model"; Patricia Ann Lamoureux, "An Integrated Approach to Theological Education"; and H. Frederick Reisz, "Assessing Spiritual Formation."
39. For some professors this comes naturally; for others it is challenging. Faculty workshops focusing on spiritual formation and its incorporation in the classroom could be helpful. See Gordon Smith, "Spiritual Formation in the Academy: A Unifying Model."

worship in the context of regular chapel services.[40] Various practices such as confession and *lectio divina* (guided reading, meditation, and prayer on a Scripture passage) could be effectively modeled.[41] Exposure to diverse music, from various denominational traditions to different cultures, could supplement existing repertoires.[42] Public recitation and affirmation of historical creeds and written prayers could be added. Nonliturgical institutions might consider an exploration of the liturgical calendar that incorporates the historical background of various seasons (such as Advent and Lent) and days dedicated to individuals or events (such as All Souls Day or Pentecost).

Prayer is a vital aspect of spiritual formation.[43] In addition to chapel services, specific venues could include weekly faculty and student prayer, as well as regular times throughout the school year for community prayer, including opportunities for corporate confession and lament, perhaps within the context of contemporary social justice issues. Dedicated spaces (both indoor and outdoor) for prayer and solitude could also be provided. Sabbath rest is also an important element of spiritual formation. Seminaries might consider regular community meals that allow for extended fellowship or a community trip to a local retreat center or Bible camp. Finally, given the necessity of community for spiritual formation, seminaries and divinity schools should consider ways to foster community. This could include spiritual formation groups led by faculty members and prayer groups that focus on specific issues, such as renewal within the community, human trafficking, or persecuted Christians. Community service is also an effective venue for spiritual formation. Groups comprising both faculty and students could partner with local prison or refugee ministries and follow up times of outreach with reflection and prayer. Given the prevalence of commuter and/or evening students, possibilities for evening chapel or spiritual formation groups should also be explored.

---

40. The significance of worship for spiritual and theological formation cannot be overstated. See especially James K. A. Smith, *Desiring the Kingdom*.

41. See Richard Foster and James B. Smith, *Devotional Classics: Selected Readings for Individuals and Groups* (San Francisco: HarperSanFrancisco, 1993).

42. See Van Opstal, *The Next Worship*, 119–38, 195–200.

43. Helpful resources for prayer and the Psalms include Dietrich Bonhoeffer, *Psalms: The Prayer Book of the Bible* (Minneapolis: Augsburg, 1970); and Eugene Peterson, *Answering God: The Psalms as Tools for Prayer* (New York: Harper and Row, 1989).

Spiritual Formation and Online Opportunities

One of the most common objections to online theological education concerns the issue of spiritual formation. Widespread skepticism accompanies the idea that online spiritual formation is possible. Although physical presence is an extremely important aspect of embodiment, face-to-face does not always equate with personal engagement. For example, in the physical classroom, the majority of students are often silent and only the voices of a handful of students are actually heard. Thus physical presence in and of itself does not guarantee meaningful participation. Moreover, best practices in online education intentionally develop significant opportunities for interaction with professors and other students. The stereotypical image of an isolated student in a basement on a computer in the middle of the night is often far from the reality of online course cohorts where interaction and participation are integral elements of the online course design.[44]

The potential for and presence of online communities are essential for millions of individuals every day who stay connected through various social media platforms such as Facebook, Snapchat, and Twitter. This is not to argue for the superiority of online communities, but it is important to recognize that digital connection is possible.[45] This is particularly important given the realities of "digital natives," whose presence in theological institutions will only increase. Thus, the faulty understanding that online equates to individual (as opposed to community) must be challenged. Instead, it is more accurate to think of online as one type of community. As in all communities, the cohesion and flourishing of an online community requires intentional commitment on the part of its participants.

Given the reality of online education, the increasing demand for fully online degree programs, and the growing digital presence of most seminaries

---

44. The key is a cohort model with some synchronous components (e.g., chat rooms, discussion forums, Google hangouts). Spiritual formation is significantly enhanced in a hybrid model that provides for face-to-face interaction (e.g., one week a year or a weekend each semester) in conjunction with online programs.

45. "Online experiences show us that we can give and receive care for one another, value those relationships, and share with one another those dimensions that go into creating connection and community" (Mary L. Lowe and Stephen D. Lowe, "Reciprocal Ecology: A Comprehensive Model of Spiritual Formation in Theological Education," *Theological Education* 48 [2013]: 9). See also Marilyn Naidoo, "Ministerial Formation of Theological Students Through Distance Education," *HTS Theological Studies* 68, no. 2 (2012): 1–8; and John M. Palka, "The Impact of Societal and Educational Trends."

and divinity schools, it is imperative that theological institutions carefully consider and thoughtfully engage the potential for online spiritual formation.[46] Indeed, the prevalence of online social networking that already exists in theological institutions significantly blurs clear lines between on-campus and online for participation within a given community.[47]

Spiritual Formation and Assessment

The holistic nature of spiritual formation raises concerns about the issue of assessment. How does one assess what a spiritually formed person looks like? Factors such as maturity in Christlikeness, integration of oneself within a community, and yieldedness to the Spirit are nearly impossible to quantify. There are, however, effective forms of assessment involving intentional reflection and self-assessment. Karen Kangas Dwyer and Edward M. Hogan have developed a questionnaire students can take at the beginning and end of their seminary experiences that fosters self-reflection and assessment.[48] Students are asked to rank certain statements, such as "I am experiencing and understanding how to integrate prayer with my daily life" or "I understand the difference between reading Scripture and praying with Scripture." Another approach is the creation of a graduate profile that indicates specific traits and skills that are desirable for ministry, including spiritual formation, and then evaluates students through self-assessment, peer, and external reviewers.[49] A less formal option might be a final exit interview during which students are asked to describe their spiritual formation journey throughout seminary. Although spiritual formation is not easily quantifiable, assessment is possible, and intentional reflection on one's own spiritual formation is effective for raising self-awareness.

---

46. As Lowe and Lowe observe, "The community of faith in which we seek to cultivate spiritual formation or skilled ministerial practice is changing with the growing familiarity of social and digital networking. This change in how we seek to cultivate spiritual formation and teach habits of theological reflection manifests itself most clearly in the online presence that characterizes more and more of our institutions" (Lowe and Lowe, "Reciprocal Ecology," 8).

47. Indeed, many online students either live on campus or are within driving distance. Online courses enable these students to accommodate work schedules or childcare needs.

48. Karen Kangas Dwyer and Edward M. Hogan, "Assessing a Program of Spiritual Formation Using Pre and Post Self-Report Measures," *Theological Education* 48 (2013): 25–34.

49. John O. Enyinnaya, "Graduate Profile as a Tool for Enhancing Spiritual Formation in Theological Education Today," *Ogbomoso Journal of Theology* 16 (2011): 69–78.

Conclusion

It should be clear at this point that spiritual formation is essential to theological education. Indeed the two are organically related and mutually reinforcing, although they are clearly not the same. As students grow in their understandings and appropriations of theology and biblical studies, ideally they are also being shaped spiritually by this study. So also as students grow in spiritual maturity, they are more able to understand and appropriate their theological educations. For this reason spiritual formation can be readily integrated into various aspects of the curriculum and often facilitates overall theological educational goals.

Churches and ministries look for theologically grounded and spiritually mature seminary graduates who can lead others in their own spiritual formations. As is often said, no church can rise above the spiritual level of its pastor. Hence the spiritual formation begun in seminary must be an intentional, ongoing priority.

Theological institutions thus play a significant role in spiritual formation, but it is wise to acknowledge that many important sources of spiritual formation occur beyond the campus. Even so, spiritual formation is a vital aspect of theological education that must be intentionally considered and developed. The exact ways spiritual formation are integrated into theological education, however, are ultimately determined by the unique needs and aims of each theological institution.

Questions for Further Reflection

1. How is spiritual formation approached in your theological institution? Is it an implicit desire or explicit part of the curriculum?
2. What are some of the challenges or detriments to spiritual formation in your particular seminary or divinity school?
3. How might spiritual formation be incorporated into your theological institution? What outcomes would you like to see for spiritually formed graduates?

Sources for Further Study

Burns, Bob, Tasha D. Chapman, and Donald G. Guthrie. *Resilient Ministry: What Pastors Told Us About Surviving and Thriving.* Downers Grove: InterVarsity, 2013.

Calhoun, Adele Ahlberg. *Spiritual Disciplines Handbook: Practices That Transform Us.* Downers Grove: InterVarsity, 2005.

Chandler, Diane J. *Christian Spiritual Formation: An Integrated Approach for Personal and Relational Wholeness.* Downers Grove: IVP Academic, 2014.

Gangel, Kenneth O., and James C. Wilhoit. *Christian Educator's Handbook on Spiritual Formation.* Wheaton: Victor, 1994.

Greenman, Jeffrey P., and George Kalantzis. *Life in the Spirit: Spiritual Formation in Theological Perspective.* Downers Grove: IVP Academic, 2010.

House, Paul R. *Bonhoeffer's Seminary Vision: A Case for Costly Discipleship and Life Together.* Wheaton: Crossway, 2015.

Smith, James K. A. *Desiring the Kingdom: Worship, Worldview, and Cultural Formation.* Grand Rapids: Baker Academic, 2009.

Van Opstal, Sandra Maria. *The Next Worship: Glorifying God in a Diverse World.* Downers Grove: InterVarsity, 2016.

Williams, Clifford. *The Life of the Mind: A Christian Perspective.* Grand Rapids: Baker Academic, 2002.

Section Two
Theological Education: Shape of Ministry Preparation

Chapter Five

BIBLICAL INSPIRATION, AUTHORITY, AND CANONICITY

D. JEFFREY BINGHAM

The Necessity and Nature of the Word of God

Silence is paradoxical. The sages and poets sing much about the virtues of silence.

> Even a fool is considered wise when he keeps silent.[1]

> Rest in God alone, my soul, for my hope comes from him.[2]

> Good as is discourse, silence is better and shames it.[3]

> Then bid me sing of love no more,
> But let me silent be;
> For silence is the speech of love,
> The music of the spheres above,
> That suits a soul like thee.[4]

---

1. Prov 17:28.
2. Ps 62:5.
3. Ralph Waldo Emerson, "Circles," in *Ralph Waldo Emerson: Selected Essays, Lectures and Poems*, ed. Robert D. Richardson (New York: Bantam, 2007), 199.
4. Richard Henry Stoddard, "The Speech of Love," in *The Poems of Henry Richard Stoddard* (New York: Charles Scribner's Sons, 1880), 58.

Solace, Order, and Existence

Yet silence can be deceitful when it substitutes for truth. "The cruelest lies are often told in silence," wrote Robert Louis Stevenson. "A man may have sat in a room for hours and not opened his teeth, and yet come out of that room a disloyal friend or a vile calumniator."[5] Silence can be complicit if protest against evil is required. Where an ear yearns for words of love, silence can be hateful. If praise is fitting, silence is demoralizing; when guidance is needed, silence is misleading. Where the gospel is not proclaimed, silence is damning. Repeatedly in Scripture believers plead with God not to be silent. His silence terrifies those in trouble; they view it as passivity, as absence, as apathy, as indifference—or worse. Sometimes it is seen as divine favoritism for the wicked.[6]

In the case of Moses's account of creation, silence accompanied the chaos, the formlessness, emptiness, and darkness of the initial state of the heavens and earth before God ordered, formed, and filled them. Only when God's voice shatters the silence is there order and light. The association of silence with disorder and vacuity, however, is only implied in Genesis 1 by the repeated divine decrees that cause the forming and filling of the heavens and earth. Later Jewish apocalyptic interpretation, nevertheless, explicitly joins silence to the darkness of Gen 1:2: "And then the Spirit was hovering, and darkness and silence embraced everything."[7] The Genesis account begins with silence and darkness and disorder and emptiness.[8] Finally, shall we say, blessedly, into the void God speaks his word in the third verse. Nahum Sarna put it this way: "The divine word shatters the primal cosmic silence and signals the birth of a new cosmic order."[9] A. W. Tozer, noting the same implication, wrote that when God spoke forth his creative word, "Chaos heard it and became order, darkness heard it and became light."[10] The word of God replaces the empty terror

---

5. *Virginibus Puerisque* in *The Works of Robert Louis Stevenson*, Vailima Edition, vol. 2 *Virginibus Puerisque, The Amateur Emigrant, The Pacific Capitals, Silverado Squatters* (New York: Charles Scribner's Sons, 1921), 61.
6. Hab 1:13; Ps 28:1; Ps 83:1.
7. 2 Esd 6:39. The cause of the silence seems to be the absence of the voices of both God and humanity.
8. Cf. Cornelius Plantinga, *Engaging God's World: A Christian Vision of Faith, Learning and Living* (Grand Rapids: Eerdmans, 2002), 29.
9. Nahum M. Sarna, *The JPS Torah Commentary: Genesis* (Philadelphia: The Jewish Publication Society, 1989), 7.
10. A. W. Tozer, *The Pursuit of God* (Las Vegas: IAP, 2009), 50.

of silence with divine provision and crafts the cosmos into a good and beautifully arranged structure.[11] Here Moses introduces the wonderful gift God gives his creatures for the first time. With it all other gifts, all other blessings, begin. The first gift God gives to his creatures is the grace of his word whereby he breaks the cold, dark void of silence and brings light into being as the first in a grand succession of creatures that culminates in the formation of richly supplied human beings. Here we learn that we exist and remain only because of the grace of his word.[12] Here we learn that unless God speaks, we have no being. Here we learn that we are utterly reliant on God's words and commandments. Here we learn that divine speech and revelation are the foundation of all well-ordered, bountiful existence. Here we learn that God's voice gives birth to light. Not only does the word of God create, not only does it bring something from nothing, but it illuminates. Only by means of God's word are we able to see things as they really are.

Illumination

How good it was of God to speak into the emptiness and darkness and to break the silence! His voice illumines, calms, brightens, informs, and guides. The sheep always prefer the shepherd's voice to silence, and they recognize it and distinguish it from the voices of imposters.[13] Such divine benevolence certainly provides the ideal for these words of Israel's sage: "A timely word—how good that is!"[14] The Genesis text, then, inaugurates the grand biblical theme of the word of God as luminous: "Your word is a lamp for my feet and a light on my path. . . . The revelation of your words brings light and gives understanding to the inexperienced."[15] The divine act of speaking forth light is fitting for the One who "wraps himself in light as with a garment."[16]

---

11. Cf. Walther Eichrodt, *Theology of the Old Testament*, vol. 1, trans. J. A. Baker (Philadelphia: Westminster, 1967), 71.
12. Cf. Karl Barth, *Church Dogmatics*, 3.1, trans. J. W. Edwards, O. Bussey, and H. Knight (Edinburgh: T&T Clark, 1958), 110.
13. John 10:3–5, 16, 27.
14. Prov 15:23. Cf. Genesis Rabbah 3:3.
15. Ps 119:105; Ps 119:130; cf. Prov 6:23.
16. Ps 104:2 NIV; see also Hab 3:4; Isa 60:19; Rev 21:23.

Potency for Life

The Genesis account is also the primer for Scripture's teaching on the potency of God's word. Multiple times, for example, prophetic texts describe the power of God's word to control the history of both Israel and the Gentiles.[17] Two of the most lucid texts on this theme are Isa 55:10–11 and Heb 4:12. The first assures Israel that God's word always accomplishes the divine purpose. The second promises a group of early Jewish Christians that God's word is precise in judgment.

Eternal Validity

Finally, Genesis 1 introduces the doctrine of the eternality of God's word. The divine word, internal to God himself, comes forth "in the beginning" as he inaugurates his creation of the heavens, the earth, and all that fills them.[18] His word was in the beginning with him. John, the evangelist, will later take up this language and apply it to God's Son and Word, the second person of the trinity, who becomes flesh.[19] Other passages follow through on the notion begun in Genesis 1. Isaiah and Peter contrast the everlasting stability of the divine word with the temporal, transitory natures of field, flowers, and flesh while Jesus contrasts the permanence of his words with heaven and earth.[20]

Human Flourishing

Several other Old Testament texts echo the teaching of Gen 1:3 that God's word is his means of creation.[21] Such texts, along with Genesis 1, establish the word of God as the basis of created nature and, consequently, the divine word as the basis for humanity's historical existence within the created world.[22] Scripture's account of this world's genesis establishes that God exercises his sovereignty over this world and its history by means of the divine word. Therefore, *the word of God is the basis for the existence of all creatures in this world.* Again the pattern of God's speaking in Genesis 1 manifests the archetype for later, more fully developed biblical themes:

---

17. Cf. Eichrodt, *Theology of the Old Testament*, 73; cf. Jer 1:5, 9–10; Ezek 2:1–3:27.
18. Gen 1:1.
19. John 1:1–2, 14.
20. Isa 40:6–8; 1 Pet 1:24–25; cf. Jas 1:10–11; Ps 103:15–16; Matt 24:35; Mark 13:31; Luke 21:33.
21. Isa 41:4; 45:12; 48:13; Amos 9:6; Ps 33:6; 148:1–5.
22. Cf. Eichrodt, *Theology of the Old Testament*, 74–75.

Humans live "on every word that comes from the mouth of the Lord."[23] Blessed and prosperous is the one whose "delight is in the Lord's instruction."[24] The divine word contains within it divine provision.[25]

Attention to the divine word is the means by which human beings flourish. God's words normatively form the charters for the blessed life within defining moments of the history of redemption: Israel with Moses at Mount Sinai, Jesus's Sermon on the Mount, John with the Spirit on the mountain and his vision of the New Jerusalem.[26] Throughout the history of redemption, the words of God are at the root of the creation and flourishing of all redeemed communities.

When God graciously and benevolently breaks the terror and emptiness of silence by speaking his timely, eternal, omnipotent, calming, informative words, darkness is illumined, the heavens and earth are ordered and filled, communities of the redeemed are formed and given hope, and history is governed. We have just seen a few of the results and properties of God's word as they relate to the first episode of God's speech at creation. Scripture, however, records many more episodes of divine revelation. We now turn our attention to various testimonies of Scripture about the different ways in which God reveals himself and his relation to his creation.

Revelation in the Bible

General Revelation

Traditionally, divine revelation is divided into general and special revelation. General revelation is when God manifests himself in a manner that is accessible to all people everywhere at all times. For example, the heavens, the refreshing and nurturing rains, and the fruitfulness of crops seen in everyday life have been visible to everyone since the beginning. They bear witness to the benevolent Creator and his glory.[27] All of creation testifies to the Creator's eternal power and divine nature.[28] However, even though the

---

23. Deut 8:3; Luke 4:4; Matt 4:4; cf. Eichrodt, *Theology of the Old Testament*, 74. On the allusive nature of Deut 8:3 and several options for its meaning, see John Goldingay, *Old Testament Theology*, vol. 3 *Israel's Life* (Downers Grove: IVP, 2009), 668.

24. Ps 1:1–3.

25. Cf. P. C. Craigie, *The Book of Deuteronomy*, New International Commentary on the Old Testament (Grand Rapids: Eerdmans, 1976), 185.

26. Exod 19:6; Matt 5:1–3, 10, 17–20, 45; Rev 21:10–22:5, 12–13, 16, 20. Cf. Ezek 40:2.

27. Ps 19:1; Acts 14:17.

28. Rom 1:20.

physical world and its bounty reveal aspects of God, this does not mean the observer of nature comprehends the content of nature's revelation correctly or that the content available in nature is sufficient for a saving knowledge of God.

Paul spoke firmly about humanity's perverted readings of nature. Whereas creation proclaimed the glorious Creator, human observers worshipped the creature and refused to acknowledge God.[29] Humans chose not to benefit from God's self-manifestation. Instead, they reduced him to a creature among other creatures, a thing among other things. They eliminated God and occupied themselves with the foolish religious business of idolatry.[30]

Humans have an impediment when it comes to interpreting the data of nature. This impediment calls into question all attempts to form a true view of God and his creation, a natural theology, merely by natural means. Paul knows nothing of humanity's ability in and of itself to arrive at a natural union with God or a natural knowledge of God. Humans in their fallen, natural state do not willingly witness or accurately assess natural revelation.[31] Although God has been merciful in employing nature as a means of revelation, two limitations exist in construction of a natural theology: (1) nature's manifestation of God is authoritative, yet incomplete; it does not reveal, for example, the triune being of God or the redemptive work of Christ; and (2) humanity's comprehension of nature's revelation is flawed.[32]

We can see in several biblical texts, which at first glance may be called upon to justify a natural theology, that in each case, grace and special revelation are required to build a trustworthy, comprehensive theology. In a text such as Acts 14:14–18, for example, it is important to note that those in Lystra had not arrived at a true concept of the divine through general revelation. And, although Barnabas and Paul appeal to natural phenomena (vv. 16–17) in their preaching, they do so by prefacing their remarks with the Scriptures that interpret such phenomena by pointing to the living Creator

---

29. Rom 1:18–25.
30. Cf. Karl Barth, *The Epistle to the Romans*, 6th ed., trans. Edwyn C. Hoskyns (New York: Oxford University, 1933), 47–50.
31. Karl Barth, *Church Dogmatics*, 2.1, trans. T. H. L. Parker, W. B. Johnston, Harold Knight, and J. L. M. Haire (Edinburgh: T&T Clark, 1957), 121. In modern theology Barth emerges as the strongest proponent of this position.
32. John Calvin, perhaps, offers the classical Protestant analysis of the blessings and limitations of general revelation (*Institutes* 1.1–5).

God (v. 15).[33] In Athens, Paul, in Acts 17:22–31, repeatedly employs the Old Testament as he proclaims a theology of natural phenomena (vv. 24–27) and concludes his sermon with an appeal for repentance in light of the man who is the risen, eschatological judge (vv. 30–31).[34] In each case human beings had not appropriated general revelation well, and in each case general revelation required supplementation by Scripture.

Special Revelation

This apostolic pattern of recourse to Scripture in order to explain general revelation provides an important focus on the exigency of special revelation. In contrast to the former, special revelation involves God's acting in order to manifest himself to particular people at specific times. Such manifestations take a variety of forms. Some are immediate, as a person or persons, without the intervention of a mediator, receive a revelation from God. Others are mediated. In these cases human and nonhuman mediators are employed by God in order to provide revelations of himself to people.

The Bible gives evidence of several forms of immediate revelation: (1) the appearances of God in a theophany or vision; (2) the acts and works of God in history; (3) a dream or a vision in which God does not appear; (4) the propositional word of God, spoken or written; and (5) the person of Jesus Christ, the incarnate Word of God. In a theophany (or Christophany), God (or specifically the Son) manifests himself visibly so humans may see him as, for example, a man or another form not specified by the biblical author.[35] Even if the Son of God is visible in Old Testament accounts, such appearances are not incarnate appearances. That appearance awaits the nativity of Mary's son, Jesus.

Some of God's historical acts are also revelatory in a special manner. When the Lord restores Zion, all the nations of the earth will witness his redemptive power and righteousness.[36] God's magnificent inclusion of the

---

33. Ps 146:6; e.g., 1 Sam 17:26, 36.
34. Cf. 1 Kgs 8:27; Isa 66:1–2; Job 35:6, 8; Ps 16:2–3; 50:12–14; Isa 40:14–18; 1 Chr 29:14; Gen 9:4; Lev 17:11; Deut 12:23. One might also appeal to the "Nature Psalms:" Pss 8; 19; 29; 65; 104 as instances of natural theology. This is wrongheaded on two counts: (1) the Psalms as Scripture provide inspired interpretations of natural phenomena, and (2) they are composed and read within communities that have access to additional varied forms of special revelation (prophecy, law, other psalms, narrative accounts, dreams, visions); also see David S. Dockery, "Special Revelation," in *A Theology for the Church*, ed. Daniel L. Akin (Nashville: B&H, 2014), 103–53.
35. E.g., Gen 18:1–2; 12:7.
36. Isa 52:7–10; 56:1.

Gentiles along with the Jews as heirs of the bountiful blessings of Christ within the body of Christ, the church, discloses God's manifold wisdom to the angelic powers.[37] The Bible also records that certain individuals, such as Nebuchadnezzar, Daniel, and Peter, received revelations by dreams or visions in which God does not appear himself. Nebuchadnezzar's dream, in which God manifested to him future, successive historical kings and kingdoms, was interpreted only by another divine revelation received by Daniel through a vision.[38] Peter, too, received a vision that manifested that God shows no favoritism and welcomes both righteous Jews and the Gentiles who fear him by believing that Jesus is Lord, Judge, and Redeemer.[39]

Finally, within the category of forms of immediate revelation, is that of propositions where God manifests whatever he wills through spoken words. We have record, for example, of God speaking directly to Abraham when he sends him to Canaan, to Moses concerning the plagues that would befall Egypt, and to others, such as Jeremiah, when he commissions him to minister as a prophet.[40]

God the Father also speaks to us through the incarnate presence and ministry of his Son.[41] Christ, the Son and Word of God, reveals the Father to humanity along with grace, truth, and forgiveness.[42] As the image of the invisible God—who is in the bosom of the Father, radiates forth his glory, precisely represents his nature, and was sent forth in the fullness of all time—Christ is the pinnacle of revelation.[43] He is the Alpha and Omega, the first and the last.[44] All things in heaven and earth exist by and through him and are summed up in him.[45] Only in the Father's Word does creation have a future. As God created the heavens, the earth with its inhabitants, and light by his spoken Word, he also enlightens, re-creates, redeems, and provides rebirth to the same by means of his incarnate, victorious, personal Word, Jesus Christ.[46]

---

37. Eph 3:10.
38. Dan 2:1, 19–23, 28–30.
39. Acts 10:9–17, 34–43.
40. Gen 12:1–3; Exod 8:1–5, 16, 20–23; 9:1–5, 8–9, 13–17; Jer 1:9–10.
41. Heb 1:1–4.
42. Matt 11:27; John 1:1–4,14–18; Mark 2:10–12.
43. Col 1:15; John 1:18; Heb 1:3; Gal 4:4.
44. Rev 22:13.
45. 1 Cor 8:6; Eph 1:10.
46. Gen 1:1–31; John 1:1–5, 9–18; Isa 65:17–23; 2 Pet 3:1–13; Rev 19:11–16 (esp. 13); 21:1–8.

However, although Christ incarnate is the zenith of the Father's revelation, his being and his deeds must be explained by words. Propositions, at least prior to glorification, must complement all nonpropositional forms of revelation, even that of the incarnate Christ. Either he or others must interpret his acts through words. The prophets, evangelists, and apostles all proclaim the good news of Christ's person and work.[47] The only access we have to Christ as Revealer of the Father is in the Holy Bible. There we find testimony from those who anticipated his coming; those who witnessed his life, death, resurrection, and ascension; and those who await his return. Outside of Scripture's words, we know nothing of Christ. Even those who saw him in the first century were dependent on his and the prophets' words for any faith placed in him.[48] The personal Word of God (Christ) and the propositional Word of God are always linked, even when Christ provides his own interpretive propositions.

God or a mediator informed by God must speak or write in order to complement nonpropositional forms. Propositions bring necessary interpretive clarity and specificity to other forms of revelation, whether those are theophanies, acts of God among the nations, or dreams and visions. All require interpretive explanation. For instance, a voice explained to Peter the meaning of his vision; Daniel's words interpreted the mystery of Nebuchadnezzar's dream; and Isaiah's prophecy clarified, ahead of God's mighty activity, the divine blessings announced by Zion's victory. Without interpretive words all other forms of revelation remain ambiguous.

This, then, leads us into our second category of special revelation: revelation by human mediators. These intermediaries appear in the Bible as Old Testament prophets (including authors such as a lawgiver, psalmist, or king), New Testament apostles, and New Testament prophets (including authors who were disciples of the apostles, such as Mark and Luke).[49] God placed his words into the mouths of the authentic prophets of the Old Testament so that what they spoke and wrote were truly God's words.[50] In the same vein the Holy Spirit of truth revealed to the New Testament apostles the teachings, the words of the Lord Jesus, that originally were the

---

47. E.g., Acts 2:22–36; John 20:30; Eph 1:18–22.
48. E.g., Luke 4:16–21; John 10:1–30.
49. Deut 18:34; Acts 2:30.
50. Deut 18:15–22.

words of God the Father.[51] The apostles, having received the Spirit of God, received knowledge of the depths of God's wisdom and benevolence, which they speak forth in words taught not by human wisdom but by the Spirit of God.[52] Like the prophets of old, they proclaimed not a human word but the word of God—the gospel of God—as they exhorted, encouraged, and implored their communities.[53] The ascended Lord, by the Spirit, gifted some as New Testament prophets so that they acquired and revealed divine knowledge and insight into divine mysteries. By speaking forth the words given to them by God, in continuity with their prophetic predecessors, they edified, equipped, exhorted, and consoled the church by means of the words of God.[54]

Some of the words uttered by prophets of both Testaments and by the apostles were written down. The spoken became the written. Revelation, then, does not take place only as divine appearances, divine activity, or immediate or mediated divine speech. It does not only occur as dreams or visions. And although he is the summit of all appearances of God, the incarnate Christ does not eclipse all other forms of revelation. To all these nonliterary forms of revelation, we must add the literary, the written, the scriptural. Revelation occurs also as script when the God-given words of prophets and apostles are written down. The sequence in this process of verbal revelation, then, is (1) God speaks forth his words in an immediate or mediated fashion, and (2) human mediators write down these words of divine origin.

We can use the infinitive *to inspire* to speak of the divine act whereby the Lord "put his words into the mouths" of prophets, filled them with knowledge of divine mysteries by the Spirit's gifting, and governed their speech so that they prophesied—that is, spoke forth—his words.[55] We can apply it also to the ministry of the Spirit as he reminded the apostles of Jesus's words and gave them wisdom that they spoke in words taught

---

51. John 8:26, 28, 38; 14:10, 24, 26; 16:4, 12–15.
52. 1 Cor 2:1–16.
53. 1 Thess 2:1–13.
54. Eph 4:11; 1 Cor 12:9, 27–29; 13:1–2; 14:3, 30. We must assume that when Paul adopted the terms *prophet*, *prophecy*, and *prophesy* in order to refer to the gifts, ministry, and identity of certain Christians, he brought them into the Christian-ecclesial context with all the force and meaning they had acquired in the Old Testament and in the ministry of Christ. The same is true of Luke (Acts 21:8–10).
55. Deut 18:18; 1 Cor 13:2; 14:3.

by him.[56] Inspiration is the merciful act of God whereby he informs and governs the speaking and writing activity of prophets, apostles, and their scribes so that the words they speak and write are the words of God.

The Foundation of the Bible's Authority

Inspiration of Scripture

Paul, in 2 Tim 3:16 provides us with the term we normally translate as "inspired." We can also translate it "God breathed," and this helps us appreciate the force of the word. Paul teaches that all Scripture originates from God; it is God given. Although we would not be in error to think Paul believes God breathes out all written revelation, in this particular text, he probably means the Old Testament, the Law, and the Prophets.[57] Peter also speaks to the issue of the inspiration of the Old Testament Scripture, in particular, the prophets. His aim was to provide confidence in the divine origin of the inscripturated words of the prophets. He clarifies that the words spoken by the prophets originated from God as the Holy Spirit moved them.[58] In the same way, "no prophecy of Scripture" was a matter of human "interpretation."[59] In other words, what was written was not a human invention; it was not a departure from what the prophets had originally received from God and had orally prophesied. Those who read Scripture can rest assured that the same Spirit who moved the prophets to speak "from God" moved them to write God's words "from God."[60] Both the apostle to the Jews and the one to the Gentiles address the inspiration of the Old Testament.

When it comes to the inspiration of the New Testament, the God-breathed writings of the apostles, their disciples, and scribes, both apostles are equally clear. Peter believes Paul's letters are Scripture, a term

---

56. 1 Cor 2:12–13.
57. Cf. 2 Tim 3:15; Rom 1:2; 4:3; 9:17; 10:11; 11:12; 16:26; Gal 3:8; 4:30; 1 Tim 5:18.
58. 2 Pet 1:21.
59. 2 Pet 1:20.
60. Richard Bauckham (*Jude, 2 Peter*, Word Biblical Commentary [Waco: Word, 1983], 232–33; cf. Peter H. Davids, *The Letters of 2 Peter and Jude* [Grand Rapids: Eerdmans, 2006], 213) prefers to understand that the suspicion being answered by Peter is one that supposes a contrast between the trustworthiness of prophetic phenomena, such as dreams and visions, and the prophet's interpretation of those phenomena. Peter's concern, instead, seems to be the divine origin and character of both the speech of the prophets and what they (or their scribes) recorded in writing.

we have just seen him use for the prophetic writings that are "from God."[61] Paul tells us that all such writings are inspired.[62] Furthermore, Paul, as we have seen above, uses language for the apostles' teaching that puts it on the same plane with the prophets: it is not made up of human words derived from human wisdom, but it is the Word of God the Father given to them by the Spirit of God and of truth.[63]

The Bible discusses its own inspiration in order to establish that its writings are God given because the human involvement with its text and its historical, cultural dimensions are so apparent.[64] Though humans were actively involved, they were moved by the Spirit so that the Scriptures were not corrupted by human fallibility.[65] Inspiration does not minimize the text's human or historical facets; it highlights them and their capacity for corruption. However, it goes on to explain that what was written, although human and historical, is God's given word.

So we can speak of biblical inspiration as (1) plenary (it applies to *all* Scripture, all of the Old and New Testaments); (2) verbal (it applies to the *words*); and (3) spiritual (the *Spirit* is the effectual *means*).[66] The Spirit's ministry of inspiration involves leading, by revelation, the apostles into "all the truth" for he is the "Spirit of truth" and Christ is "the truth."[67] This accords precisely with what the Lord says of the prophets. Their authenticity is proven by the truth of their prophecies.[68] The truthfulness of medi-

---

61. 2 Pet 3:15–16; 1:20.
62. 2 Tim 3:16.
63. 1 Cor 2:1–16; 1 Thess 2:1–13.
64. Some, due to concern over perceived views of inspiration that minimize or deny the impact of the participation of humans from ancient cultures in the composition of Scripture, have become almost frantic to emphasize this point. Sometimes they do so in a manner that all but erases divine authorship or dismantles plenary inspiration and introduces human fallibility into the text. This concern largely informs Paul Enns's discomfort with the International Council on Biblical Inerrancy's statement on inerrancy ("Inerrancy, However Defined, Does Not Describe What the Bible Does," in *Five Views on Biblical Inerrancy*, ed. J. Merrick and Stephen M. Garrett [Grand Rapids: Zondervan, 2013], 29–58. Similar concerns associated with divine accommodation to human contexts inform his arguments in his *Inspiration and Incarnation* [Grand Rapids: Baker, 2005]). For him the Bible as a historical phenomenon, a text composed and assembled within the cultures of antiquity, does not conform to the parameters or expectations of biblical inerrancy. For instance, it includes unreliable records of historical events, myths, contradictions, and in his quotation of the language of C. S. Lewis, error; see also D. A. Carson, editor, *The Enduring Authority of the Christian Scriptures* (Grand Rapids: Eerdmans, 2016).
65. 1 Cor 2:5,13; 2 Pet 1:20–21.
66. (1) 2 Tim 3:16; John 14:26; 16:13 (2) Deut 18:18–19; John 14:10; 2 Pet 1:19,21; (3) John 14:25; 16:13–15; 1 Cor 2:10–13; 2 Pet 1:21.
67. John 14:6,17; 16:13.
68. Deut 18:22.

ated revelation is a corollary of inspiration, so the inerrancy of Scripture is a corollary of inspiration.

Inerrancy of Scripture

When we speak of the inerrancy of Scripture, we mean that Scripture is completely true, "being free from all falsehood, fraud, or deceit."[69] Inerrancy is a corollary of plenary inspiration. Since inspiration is plenary, inerrancy is also plenary. All the Bible's teachings, its claims and affirmations, are true and reliable whether they address matters of religion, science, history, spirituality, or redemption.[70] Whatever the Bible actually reveals and affirms about these issues is true.[71]

Biblical inerrancy is inferred from both the New Testament passages that teach inspiration and those that record Jesus's words on Scripture's authority. In 2 Tim 3:1–4:5, Paul is concerned with false teachers who are ignorant of the truth and oppose it, who deceive and are deceived, and with audiences who prefer myths to sound doctrine, the truth.[72] Within this context he inserts his teaching on inspiration of Scripture. For the apostle, contrary to the error and fraud of his day, the plenary inspiration of Scripture provides his disciple Timothy with a platform of truth, a depository

---

69. "The Chicago Statement on Biblical Inerrancy, Article 12" in *Inerrancy*, ed. Norman L. Geisler (Grand Rapids: Zondervan, 1980), 496. Technically, inerrancy is reserved for the original documents of the apostles, their disciples, and scribes. However, we extend inerrancy, without hesitation, to copies of those originals in so far as they faithfully represent those originals (Cf. Greg L. Bahnsen, "The Inerrancy of the Autographa," in *Inerrancy*, 151–93).

70. "The Chicago Statement on Biblical Inerrancy," A Short Statement, Article 12, 494, 496. Contrast the classical and influential position of Daniel P. Fuller who discriminated between "revelational" and "non-revelational" matters in Scripture ("Benjamin B. Warfield's View of Faith and History: A Critique in the Light of the New Testament," *Bulletin of the Evangelical Theological Society* 11 [1968]: 75–83; "The Nature of Biblical Inerrancy," *Journal of the American Scientific Affiliation* 24 [1971]: 47–51). The concept of "limited inerrancy" or "errant inspiration" is common among critics of inerrancy. Dewey M. Beegle (*Scripture, Tradition and Infallibility* [Grand Rapids: Eerdmans, 1973], 265–66; 307–8) emphasized human fallibility and a view of divine condescension in the act of inspiration that did not prevent errors in the transmission or recording of all biblical teachings. Some biblical teachings are "primary revelation" while others are not, and in these instances God did not inspire the biblical writers in a manner that prevented their fallible natures from introducing defective material into the Scripture.

71. What the Bible means, how it is to be interpreted, and what particular information it is really presenting on these matters are other questions entirely related to hermeneutics, the method and process of interpretation. Questions of genre, figures of speech, phenomenological language, rhetoric, use of numbers, and the like are hermeneutical issues. Unfortunately many evangelicals have become obsessed with these issues of interpretation to the neglect of offering a resounding, unqualified affirmation of biblical inerrancy.

72. 2 Tim 3:7–8, 4:3–4.

of wisdom, that he can continue to trust for salvation and thorough equipping for the virtuous life.[73]

Peter makes a similar argument in 2 Pet 1:1–2:3. He assures his readers that God's power granted blessings to them through the true knowledge of the Lord Jesus in which they have been established.[74] Nevertheless, he exhorts them to continue to live virtuously in continuity with these blessings and his teaching and to recall his instruction after his death.[75] They should abide in his teaching, particularly about Christ's coming as judge, for it was not based on fictitious stories.[76] Rather, he was an eyewitness to both Christ's majesty and the veracity of the Spirit-inspired prophets.[77] Contrary to false prophets and teachers who will introduce heresies and blaspheme the truth, his readers have surety that the claims of the Old Testament prophets are true.[78] Both Peter and Paul introduce discussions of Scripture's inspiration in order to undergird confidence in Scripture's inerrancy.

The apostles merely followed the Lord Jesus on these issues. The Lord's words in Matt 5:17–19 teach that Scripture, in all its parts, corresponds to reality. R. T. France offers a helpful interpretive paraphrase: "The law, down to its smallest details, is as permanent as heaven and earth, and will never lose its significance; on the contrary, all that it points forward to will in fact become reality."[79] Jesus's words in John's Gospel echo those in Matthew: "Scripture cannot be broken," it cannot be annulled or set aside; it must be fulfilled.[80] "Scripture cannot be emptied of its force by being shown to be erroneous."[81] His denial that Scripture manifests error also comes forth in John 17:17, where Jesus states that God's "word is truth." Earlier, in

---

73. 2 Tim 3:16–17. Plenary inspiration ("all") is the basis for Scripture's ability to thoroughly ("every") equip.
74. 2 Pet 1:1–4.
75. 2 Pet 1:5–15.
76. 2 Pet 1:16.
77. The phrase recorded in 2 Pet 1:17 concerning the declaration of God on the mount is similar to Matt 17:5 (cf. Luke 9:35). Both are a confluence of the prophetic teaching of Ps 2:4 and Isa 42:1.
78. 2 Pet 1:19; 2:1–3.
79. R. T. France, *The Gospel of Matthew* (Grand Rapids/Cambridge: Eerdmans, 2007), 186.
80. John 10:35. Cf. Raymond E. Brown, *The Gospel According to John I–XII*, vol. 29, *Anchor Bible Series* (Garden City, NY: Doubleday, 1966), 403–4, 410; F. F. Bruce, *The Gospel of John* (Basingstoke: Pickering & Inglis, 1983), 234.
81. Leon Morris, *The Gospel According to John* (Grand Rapids: Eerdmans, 1971), 527.

John 10:35 he identified God's word as Scripture. Therefore, in the teaching of Jesus, Scripture is true in what it claims.

The Canonicity of the Bible

Knowing that all Scripture is inspired and inerrant raises a crucial question for the believer: which writings are inspired? This question takes us to the issue of the Christian canon, the standard, authoritative list of books believed by Christians to be inspired. Those books the Spirit inspired and the church recognizes as such define the parameters of the canon. The church has considered several factors in its reception of these writings.

The Old Testament

It is important for the church that both the Law and the Prophets were esteemed within ancient Israel as authoritative Scripture. The Old Testament refers to them repeatedly and testifies to the nation's commitment to collect and preserve these texts unaltered.[82] Between the Testaments (c. 190 BC) the twelve Minor Prophets already constitute a single sacred group alongside the Major Prophets, and the community knows a threefold canon by around 130 BC.[83] In the New Testament the Old Testament appears as an authoritative, fixed, closed collection of writings, "the Scriptures," containing two or three divisions, the Law and the Prophets (and Psalms).[84] Before Christ's day the collection is set and known, but later sources provide further clarity. Although the Mishnah indicates the authoritative status of writings within the third division, Josephus is most helpful.[85] Writing at the end of the first century (c. AD 98) he provides insight into several old, commonly held Jewish beliefs: (1) inspiration and prophetic writing were limited to the prophets in their own days; (2) consequently, for a long

---

82. E.g., Josh 1:7–8; Dan 9:11–14; Jer 25:11–12; and Dan 9:2; Deut 10:5; 31:24–26. Deuteronomy reflects a commitment to the fixed and immutable nature of the law as it is in Deuteronomy, if not in the whole Pentateuch (4:1–2; 12:32). In Dan 9:2 the prophet refers to "the books," a reference to a collection of prophetic writings including Jeremiah. Later prophets referred to earlier ones (Zech 1:4–6; Hos 6:5).

83. Sir 48:22–49:12 (esp. 49:10); Prologue.

84. E.g., John 1:45; Luke 24:4, 27, 32, 45. The twofold division, "Law and Prophets," was also in use for the whole canon in the intertestamental period, c. 124 BC (2 Macc 15:9).

85. Mishnah Yadaim 3.5. The debate over these texts (Song, Eccl) seems to be about their ritual status. They were already viewed as Scripture. Cf. John Barton, "The Old Testament Canons," in *The New Cambridge History of the Bible*, vol. 1, *From the Beginnings to 600*, ed. James Carleton Paget and Joachim Schaper (Cambridge: Cambridge University, 2013), 160–61.

time ("ages"), a fixed list of Scriptures had existed, probably comprised of the writings of the Hebrew Bible (or the LXX without apocryphal books), divided as the books of Moses, the prophets after Moses, and hymns and precepts; (3) the Jews had refused to add to, subtract from, or change these writings; and (4) their devotion and loyalty were limited to these listed writings.[86] Sometime after the last prophet, but at least 160 years before Josephus, the Old Testament canon seems to have existed among the Jews as a revered, fixed collection of authoritative books.

The New Testament

Again with the New Testament the issue was recognition of inspired texts. The process was already well underway in the apostolic period. Churches in one city, for example, were reading Pauline epistles addressed to another community. Also, Paul and John were having their writings read publicly, a practice that imitates the reading of Scripture within the synagogues and one Paul expected to continue in the churches.[87] Furthermore, Paul was citing written teachings of Jesus (perhaps from Luke's Gospel) as authoritative and comparing them with Scripture (Moses's Law) while Peter was referring to Paul's letters as Scripture, comparing them with the Old Testament writings.[88]

The Gospels and Paul's epistles were used by the apostolic fathers (c. AD 95–130) more frequently than the Old Testament, suggesting that these writings held an early, common, sacred status among geographically

---

86. Josephus, *Against Apion* 1.7–8. Josephus mentions that for ages the Jews have known this particular collection and treated it with utmost respect. Cf. Roger Beckwith, *The Old Testament Canon of the New Testament Church* (Grand Rapids: Eerdmans, 1985), 118–19, for an estimation of the books within the three divisions. Some provide earlier dates based on texts that inform us about a collection by Judas Maccabeus, c. 164 BC, and an acute awareness in Israel about the long-endured cessation of prophecy, c. 100 BC (2 Macc 2:14; 1 Macc 9:23–27). These have brought forth dates for the close of the canon associated with those dates. For the earlier date see Beckwith, *The Old Testament Canon of the New Testament Church*; for the later, David G. Dunbar, "The Biblical Canon," in *Hermeneutics, Authority and Canon*, ed. D. A. Carson and John Woodbridge (Grand Rapids: Zondervan, 1986), 301–15. Cf. Sid Z. Leiman, "Inspiration and Canonicity: Reflections on the Formation of the Biblical Canon," in *Jewish and Christian Self-Definition*, vol. 2, *Aspects of Judaism in the Graeco-Roman Period*, ed. E. P. Sanders, A. I. Baumgarten, and Alan Mendelson (Philadelphia: Fortress, 1982), 61; and Moshe Halbertal, *People of the Book: Canon, Meaning and Authority* (Cambridge: Harvard, 1997), 16, for the date, c. 150 BC. The early Jewish sources can count the same, familiar collection of thirty-nine books as numbering twenty-two (Josephus *Ag. Apion* 1.7–8; Jub. 2.23; cf. Jerome, *Prologus Galeatus*) or twenty-four books (2 Esd 14.44–48; B. Bat. 14b; cf. Jerome, *Prologus Galeatus*).

87. Col 4:16; 1 Thess 5:27; 2 Cor 10:9; Rev 1:3; Luke 4:14–20; Acts 13:15; 1 Tim 4:13.

88. Luke 10:7/1 Tim 5:18/Deut 25:4; 1 Cor 7:10–11; 2 Pet 3:15–16; 1:20. Cf. Michael J. Kruger, *Canon Revisited* (Wheaton: Crossway, 2012), 205–7.

dispersed churches.[89] At least by Justin Martyr's time (c. AD 156), churches were reading both the Gospels and Prophets publicly in worship.[90] Irenaeus (c. 180), whose ecclesiological background connects Asia Minor, Rome, and Gaul, unequivocally attests to a fourfold Gospel canon, rejects other competing gospels, and refers to all the New Testament writings except for three.[91] Although our earliest canonical list, contemporary with Irenaeus, names all New Testament books save four, fourth-century lists are complete.[92] Eusebius (c. AD 311–325), clear about the church's rejection of competing uninspired texts, lists all twenty-seven New Testament books as canonical but notes that five, while received by most, were disputed by some.[93] Athanasius (AD 367) lists all the canonical books without qualification.[94]

The church employed several criteria in rejecting illegitimate canonical theories and in separating inspired writings from competing and sometimes edifying, sometimes heretical, uninspired texts. It quickly dismissed Marcion's theory (c. AD 144) that rejected the Old Testament and all New Testament texts other than ten of Paul's letters and Luke's Gospel, carefully edited. The church stood firm on the belief that the Lord and his disciples had embraced the Law and the Prophets. This established a fundamental criterion. All books received into the New Testament must reflect unity with the Old Testament. Other criteria employed by the church included (1) apostolicity (the book had to be authored by an apostle [Matthew, John] or the disciple of an apostle [Mark, Luke]); (2) universality (the book had to be revered by communities throughout the Mediterranean world); and (3) theological continuity (e.g., monotheism, unity of the history of redemption, the true incarnation, crucifixion, and resurrection of the one Lord Jesus Christ). All four were essential to disavowing the legitimacy of

---

89. Kruger, *Canon Revisited*, 210–25.
90. Justin, *1 Apol.* 67.3.
91. Irenaeus, *Ag. Her.* 1.31.1; 3.11.7–9. Irenaeus does not refer to Phlm, 3 John, or Jude. This does not mean he rejected these texts. He does not refer to several Old Testament writings in his polemical/summative work. Cf. D. Jeffrey Bingham, "Irenaeus of Lyons," in *Encyclopedia of the Bible and Its Reception*, vol. 13 (Berlin: De Gruyter, 2016).
92. The Muratorian Fragment, without clarification, does not list Heb, Jas, 1 Pet, or 2 Pet.
93. Eusebius, *Eccl. Hist.* 3.25.1–7. The five disputed writings are Jas, Jude, 2 Pet, 2 John, and 3 John.
94. Athanasius, *Ep.* 39.5.

the numerous, alternative volumes set forth by the Valentinians and Gnostic groups in the second century.[95]

Already in the first quarter of the second century, the church was demonstrating recognition of the inspiration of the four Gospels and Paul's letters. By the middle and latter part of the same century, the church was making discriminating canonical decisions and employing the New Testament writings broadly in worship, apologetic, polemic, and theological construction. Some books were used more frequently than others; some found full acceptance earlier than others. However, this process only demonstrates the immensity of the task faced by early Christians as they insisted on the canonicity of the Old Testament, included new writings along with it, rejected countless other texts, and identified some as edifying but not inspired. This process also shows the care early Christians exercised in this sacred task.

The Meaning of the Bible's Authority

Generally

The authority of the Bible arises from the inspired and inerrant nature of its fixed collection and applies to the faith and conduct of all human beings, the church in particular. It speaks, as the word of God, to what all human beings are to believe about God and his relationship to his creatures. It faithfully and uniquely reveals to us Jesus Christ and his words. Apart from the Bible we have no knowledge of Jesus Christ. Whatever it affirms, whatever it claims, is to be believed and obeyed. Therefore, it serves as the primary source for theological and ethical reflection and the final judge over each and every other source, whether tradition, reason, culture, or experience. It judges kings, bishops, priests, councils, presidents, parliaments, congresses, the individual, and the human majority. As the Word of God, it determines and informs our perspectives and behaviors related to war, euthanasia, abortion, incarceration, capital punishment, sexuality, marriage and family, biomedical issues, ethnicity and race, gender, and ecology. As the Word of God it determines and informs our dogmatics,

---

95. See the texts discovered at Nag Hammadi in 1945 and other gnostic writings (*The Nag Hammadi Scriptures: The Revised and Updated Translation of Sacred Gnostic Texts*, ed. Marvin Meyer (New York: HarperCollins, 2007); *The Gnostic Scriptures: A New Translation with Annotations and Introductions*, ed. Bentley Layton (New York: Doubleday, 1987).

homiletics, and evangelism. Interpreted well, the creed it fills is the doctrine of God; preached well, the sermon it fills is the voice of God; heralded well, the news it fills is the gospel of God.

In Theological Education

All of the above are ways the Bible holds authority over humanity and the church. However, I would like to address, specifically, some ways the Bible's authority relates to theological education and administrations of theological schools. First, we must recognize that in evangelical perspective the Bible judges not only kings and bishops but also presidents, provosts, deans, faculties, trustees, committees, accrediting agencies, and institutional constituencies. Therefore, in the same way theologians employ the Bible as their first source in constructions of doctrines, administrations of theological schools must employ the Bible as their first source in determining and evaluating concerns such as (1) philosophies of leadership, (2) institutional strategic objectives, (3) curricula, (4) modes of delivery, (5) programs, (6) codes of conduct, (7) the role of faculty in institutional governance, and (8) recruitment and advancement methodologies.

Frequently, enrollment and, subsequently, finances drive initiatives related to such concerns. If not enrollment, other powerful competing sources include accrediting agency guidelines and models, competition from other institutions, culture wars, cultural expectations and cultural forms, government regulations, interests or disinterests among prospective student populations, and technological innovations. The anxiety of administrations can reach a fever pitch when confronted with pressures from one or more of these. Sometimes the last question to be asked under such circumstances is, What does the Bible affirm or claim about an issue? Particularly, perhaps, this is the case when the curriculum of those institutions is Bible centered and the administration considers itself biblically informed. Sometimes in those contexts assumptions are made, and renewed attention to Bible teaching is bypassed. And yet we have seen these qualities about the Word of God: (1) it inaugurates life, brings order out of chaos, and offers solace; (2) it illuminates the darkness; (3) it is eternally valid; (4) it is the ground for human flourishing; (5) it is God breathed in its written form; (6) it is entirely true in its written form; and (7) in the Old and New Testaments of the Bible, it is wholly authoritative.

May I address, as examples, two concerns? First, I wish to speak to a curricular matter. Evangelical administrations and faculties may be under the impression that the issue of biblical inerrancy within "evangelicalism" has been settled because of concentrated attention in the last two decades of the last century. Such an impression, compounded by the pressures for other courses in the curriculum, might motivate curricular changes or syllabi modifications away from emphases on inspiration and inerrancy. To any who imagine that inerrancy is settled and prominent within evangelicalism, I would recommend a quick read of Jim Hinch's 2016 essay "Evangelicals Are Losing the Battle for the Bible. And They're Just Fine with It."[96] Likewise, those who think canonicity is an issue of the distant past will be interested to read Robert W. Funk, "The Once and Future New Testament," and Bart D. Ehrman, *Lost Christianities: The Battle for Scripture and the Faiths We Never Knew*.[97] Administrators, from trustees to department chairs, need to make sure these topics have a steady and perhaps increasing role in the institution's theological curriculum. One seminary I know just increased their MDiv theology core from two three-hour courses to three three-hour courses, with the addition of a course devoted to bibliology and theological method.

Second, administrators of theological schools, especially in an age inundated with books on leadership, personal effectiveness and success, and management need to take inventory of their sources. Are their philosophies of leadership informed in first place by the primary evangelical source that judges all others? Philip Ryken, president of Wheaton College (Illinois), has taken this question seriously. Early in his presidency he developed a leadership model for the Christian College president informed by the three offices of Jesus Christ—prophet, priest, and king.[98] In this case a biblical and theological paradigm illuminates how a president goes about defining and carrying out his responsibilities.

So here are a few questions to consider. Does Scripture largely inform your philosophy of leadership? Is the doctrine of Scripture precisely stated

---

96. *Los Angeles Review of Books*, February 15, 2016. See, too, Gregory K. Beale, *The Erosion of Inerrancy in Evangelicalism: Responding to New Challenges to Biblical Authority* (Wheaton: Crossway, 2008).

97. In *The Canon Debate*, ed. Lee Martin McDonald and James A. Sanders (Peabody, MA: Hendrickson, 2002), 555; For responses see Kruger, *Canon Revisited* and Charles E. Hill, *Who Chose the Gospels? Probing the Great Gospel Conspiracy* (Oxford: Oxford University, 2010).

98. Philip Graham Ryken, "Christ-Centered Presidency: The Threefold Office of Christ as a Theological Paradigm for Leading a Christian College," *Christian Scholar's Review* (forthcoming).

in your statement of faith? Does it have a sufficient place in the curriculum? Does your administration, at all levels, nurture an environment that invites Scripture to judge its objectives and initiatives? Finally, are you confident in your own faith concerning the Scripture, and are you adequately prepared to help someone else with theirs?

Questions for Further Reflection

1. Robert Louis Stevenson says, "The cruelest lies are often told in silence." How would you interpret this statement?
2. How do you personally relate to the illumination of God's Word regarding it potency for life and external validity?
3. Considering human flourishing, how would you explain the ways God reveals himself and his revelation to his creation?

Sources for Further Study

Barton, John. "The Old Testament Canons." *The New Cambridge History of the Bible*, vol. 1, *From the Beginnings to 600*. Ed. James Carleton Paget and Joachim Schaper. Cambridge: Cambridge University Press, 2013. 145–64.

_____. *The Spirit and the Letter: Studies in the Biblical Canon*. London: SPCK, 1997.

Beckwith, Roger. "Formation of the Hebrew Bible." *Mikra: Text, Translation, Reading and Interpretation of the Hebrew Bible in Ancient Judaism and Early Christianity*. Ed. Martin Mulder and Harry Sysling. Philadelphia/Assen/Maastricht: Van Gorcum/Fortress, 1988. 39–86.

_____. *The Old Testament Canon of the New Testament Church*. Grand Rapids: Eerdmans, 1985.

Carson, D. A., ed. *The Enduring Authority of the Christian Scriptures*. Grand Rapids: Eerdmans, 2016.

_____, and John Woodbridge, ed. *Hermeneutics, Authority and Canon*. Grand Rapids: Zondervan, 1986.

Frame, John M. *The Doctrine of the Word of God*, vol. 4, *A Theology of Lordship*. Phillipsburg, NJ: P&R, 2010.

Geisler, Norman L., ed. *Inerrancy*. Grand Rapids: Zondervan, 1980.

Hill, Charles E. *Who Chose the Gospels? Probing the Great Gospel Conspiracy*. Oxford: Oxford University Press, 2010.

Kruger, Michael J. *Canon Revisited*. Wheaton: Crossway, 2012.
Merrick, J., and Stephen M. Garrett, ed. *Five Views on Biblical Inerrancy*. Grand Rapids: Zondervan, 2013.
Packer, J. I. *"Fundamentalism" and the Word of God*. Grand Rapids: Eerdmans, 1958.

Chapter Six

THE LANGUAGES OF THE OLD TESTAMENT[1]

KENNETH A. MATHEWS

The heart of all theological education for Christian ministry is the study and proclamation of the Bible. By definition, understanding the Bible requires a cross-cultural experience, bridging the *then* and the *now*. The cultural gaps that must be spanned include time, geography, systems and institutions, and language. In effect, the church in all its aspects is the "mediator of a foreign culture."[2] Language is especially the window on the heart of a people group, for it captures the conceptualization of reality and the general worldview of a group. Although scholars can reconstruct provisionally some aspects of an ancient people's history and culture on the basis of material artifacts alone, the recovery of written texts provides the flesh that gives life to the skeleton of cold archaeological remains. What enables modern readers to understand the original message of ancient texts, despite the cultural gaps, is the common humanity the past and present share. Since humans are all created in the image of God (Gen 1:26–27), all people share in the same fundamental human interests and needs. We are made up of the same essential constitution. Since God himself transcends time and culture, his Word is eternally valid.

In this chapter we will explore the character and value of the Hebrew Old Testament (OT) for the modern reader. We will first summarize the general features of the Hebrew and Aramaic languages that comprise the OT.

---

1. A special thank you goes to Sarah Morris, my TA and research assistant on this project.
2. Claire Kramsch, *Context and Culture in Language Teaching* (Oxford: Oxford University Press, 1993), vii.

We will next review the formal discipline of Hebrew study in the academic and professional training of God-called ministers for the mission of the church at large. We will conclude with an explanation of how competency in Hebrew/Aramaic is a powerful tool in the life and ministry of Christian leaders who are better able to aide their congregations and denominations in a deeper understanding of and walk with God.

But first I want to debunk two common mythologies about language study for interpreting the Bible.

1. A common misconception is intense language study has a negative impact on a person's spiritual life. If this were so, it is hardly due to the language or to the study of language but rather due to the person's spiritual walk with God. There is no necessary correlation between knowledge and spirituality, as in, the more you know the less spiritual you are or the less you know the more apt you are to be spiritually disciplined. Of course, human wisdom and knowledge can be misused (1 Cor 8:1–3). Yet we only need a cursory look at the great heroes of the faith to see that this is not the case. Jason DeRouchie gathers quotes from these luminaries in church history who advocated language training as necessary for Christian ministry—Augustine, Martin Luther, John Calvin, Ulrich Zwingli, John Owen, B. B. Warfield, and J. Gresham Machen.[3] William Carey, the father of modern missions, for example, taught himself Latin, Greek, and Hebrew. He is said to have translated the whole Bible into six languages and portions into many other native tongues. Early Christian missionaries of the nineteenth century translated and printed portions of or the whole of the Bible when on the field, including Chinese, other Asian dialects, and Indian languages.[4]
2. The pendulum might swing to the other equally false conclusion that people competent in languages must be more spiritually devoted to God than the ordinary Christian. No, the ultimate Teacher is the Holy Spirit, and we are accountable to him (1 Cor 2:13–14;

---

3. Jason S. DeRouchie, "The Profit of Employing the Biblical Languages: Scriptural and Historical Reflections," *Themelios* 37 (2012): 32–50.

4. John H. Yieh, "The Bible in China: Interpretations and Consequences," in *Handbook of Christianity in China*, vol. 2, *1800–Present*, R. G. Tiedemann, ed. (Leiden: Brill, 2010), 891–913.

1 John 2:27), although human teachers gifted by the Spirit (Eph 4:11) benefit us. The Bible's teaching is sufficiently clear to provide God-given wisdom for a successful Spirit-filled life to anyone who obediently listens to his voice (Ps 19:7; Prov 1:4; 2 Tim 3:15; Jas 3:17). Training in the languages, a student soon learns, does not resolve all the exegetical challenges in the Bible. Language is a tool, not an end in itself.

Language Overview: Semitic Linguistic Family

The predominant language of the OT is Hebrew, but two substantial sections are in Hebrew's sister language, Aramaic, about 2 percent of the Hebrew Bible (Ezra 4:8–6:18; 7:12–26; Dan 2:4b–7:28).[5] As to what Aramaic is and why it occurs in the Bible, we will address below. Hebrew and Aramaic have much in common because they belong to the same Semitic linguistic family. The term *Semitic* may be misleading to some because of the prevalent expression "anti-Semitic" that refers to bigotry against ethnic Jews. A. L. von Schlözer in 1781 derived the word *Semite* from the Bible's Table of Nations, referring to Noah's son, Shem (Gen 10:21–31). Although the similarities in the languages of the region had been noted prior to Schlözer, his use of "Semitic" specifically marked similar languages as its own category. Although anti-Semitism targets individuals of Jewish decent, *Semitic* does not equate to any one specific people group; rather it reflects a number of ethnic groups whose languages share linguistic relationship. Therefore, by *Semitic* we refer to the tightly related languages in and around the Fertile Crescent in antiquity. *Fertile Crescent* describes the fertile green belt shaped like a crescent, bending northwest from the Persian Gulf via the Tigris-Euphrates Valley around the north Arabian Desert and south to include Egypt's Nile Valley. A striking feature of the Semitic languages is the duration of the languages, from the third millennium BC (Akkadian) to the present (e.g., Hebrew, Arabic).

Semitic languages are subdivided into the regions Northeast, Northwest, and Southwest. The prominent languages include Hebrew, Aramaic, Akkadian, Old South Arabic, and Ethiopic. There are many subbranches within these broad categories that indicate regional differences as well as

---

5. Bruce K. Waltke and Michael Patrick O'Connor, *An Introduction to Hebrew Syntax* (Winona Lake: Eisenbraun's 1990), 5.

ancient and modern variants. This is not surprising since language varies often according to geography and relative distance to surrounding civilizations. An example of this can be found in American English dialects and accents. Some of these variants are distinct and could nearly qualify as their own language. This would be the result of interaction with immigrants whose native tongue is not English. An example of this would be the Cajun Creole dialect in comparison to English spoken in Maine. Hebrew and Aramaic belong to different subgroups within the Northwest linguistic branch of the Semitic family. Hebrew and closely related languages of Moabite, Phoenician, and Punic constitute the Canaanite subgroup, and biblical Aramaic belongs to the Aramaic subgroup. Since the languages of the ancient Near East have linguistic correspondences, they help scholars understand and translate ancient Hebrew, such as rare words, idioms, and difficult grammatical/syntactical features.

As stated previously, the Semitic family is tightly related, sharing important features. First, they share phonological features. Semitic languages have a consonantal system with many uvular, laryngeal, and pharyngeal articulations (throaty, back of the mouth). The second similarity is they have a triconsonantal (three-letter) "root" system. This means the language consists of lexical morphemes of three consonants that serve as the base for multiple words. Third, they have morphological determination. With a pattern of prefixes, suffixes, and infixes added to the root, the function of the word is determined (noun, verb, etc.). The triconsonantal root *m-l-k* is common: e.g., in Hebrew, *malak* ("he reigned"), *melek* ("king"), *malkah* ("queen"), and *mamlakah* ("kingdom"). Fourth, the languages share a common syntax pattern. The syntax follows a simple coordination configuration ("and"), unlike Greek and English with their logical subordination pattern.

Hebrew Language

Before we begin, I mention two common mistakes by nonspecialists regarding the language: (1) the equation of "Hebrew(s)" as an ethnic term for Abraham's descendants and "Hebrew" as a language; and (2) the equation of biblical Hebrew and modern Israeli.

First, the etymology of the term *Hebrew* (*ibri*) is uncertain. It may have derived from the Hebrew verbal root translated "to cross over" (*abar*) or from the personal name Eber (*eber*, Gen 10:24–25), an ancestor of

Abraham. If the etymology is "to cross over," it may be an appropriate echo of Israel's ancestors whom God led across the Euphrates River to Canaan (Josh 24:3). An earlier view that *Hebrew* was another rendering of the *Habiru*, a group of renegades or outlaws, has been largely rejected. Where "Hebrew" appears in the OT as an ethnic term (cf. "Abram the Hebrew," Gen 14:13), it usually is used by foreigners to refer to the Hebrews, or the Hebrews use it when addressing foreigners (e.g., Gen 39:14; 41:12; Exod 1:15–16; 10:3; Jer 34:9; Jonah 1:9). Often the term used was "Israel" or the "sons of Israel." But the word *Hebrew* as a language was not used by the Hebrew people when referring to their own language. During the biblical period "language of Canaan" (Isa 19:18) or "Judahite" (2 Kgs 18:26, 28; Isa 36:11, 13; 3:24; 2 Chr 32:18) are used. [For the word *Judahite*, CSB translates "Hebrew" and ESV has "Judean."] Later, for the language Hebrew (probably a form of Jewish Palestinian Aramaic, not the classic Hebrew of the OT), it appears in Greek (*Ebrais*) in *Sirach* (132 BC) and in the first-century New Testament (NT; e.g., John 5:2; Acts 21:40; 22:2; Rev 16:16).

Second, Israeli, that is, modern spoken Hebrew, is the official language of the state of Israel, not ancient Hebrew, although they hold many features in common. After a protracted period from the third century AD to the late eighteenth century, Hebrew was virtually restricted to a literary and religious language, not a spoken language. It was usurped by spoken Aramaic, but Hebrew underwent a revival in the late nineteenth century to the present as a spoken language that led to its official adoption by Israel in 1948.

Hebrew Texts

Classical (biblical) Hebrew dates from the monarchy period of Israel (c. 1000 BC). There are few extrabiblical texts of classical Hebrew that are contemporary with the biblical period (from tenth century BC to sixth century BC). These include such inscriptions as scribal practice texts, monuments, letters, and economic texts. The largest and most notable discovery, however, was scrolls and fragments from a postbiblical period—the Dead Sea Scrolls (DSS). They were recovered near the site Khirbet Qumran at the southeast corner of the Dead Sea. Jewish sectarians (Qumranites) established a community from c. 150 BC to AD 70. The corpus dates from about the third century BC to AD 70. It includes nonbiblical manuscripts (sectarian in nature), many biblical manuscripts on leather and papyri, and translations of the OT in Greek (Septuagint) and Aramaic (Targum).

Although our knowledge of classical Hebrew is virtually confined to the Hebrew Bible itself, its preservation has been remarkable. From about 300 BC to AD 135, clear manuscript evidence exists of how the Scripture was transmitted, especially evidence drawn from the DSS. Before the discovery of these scrolls, we were limited to the Masoretic Text tradition (about AD 500–1000). The Masoretic Text (MT) is named for the Masoretes, Jewish scholars in the medieval period who were the caretakers of earlier Hebrew copies. They devised a system of grammatical notes and guides to aid in pronunciation of the biblical text. The earliest codices we possess of the MT are the Aleppo Codex (about AD 930) and the Leningrad Codex (AD 1008). The Leningrad Codex is the oldest complete Hebrew Bible and therefore is typically the standard edition of the Hebrew Bible used by scholars and students today.[6]

Paleo-Hebrew script is shaped in archaizing script that mimics Phoenician cursive in shape, not a real archaic script. Old Hebrew script, evidenced in epigraphic texts during the biblical period, has its origins in Phoenician script. Hebrew script did not break from the Phoenician style until the ninth century BC, although the Hebrew language existed long before this time. During the exile period Hebrew adopted the script style and square-form characters of Aramaic script that the Hebrew Bible appears in due to Aramaic's prevalence in the Babylonian and Persian Empires. In other words, scribes deliberately copied Hebrew manuscripts in angular forms to *appear* old, although they were not actually ancient copies. It is evidenced especially in some Pentateuchal manuscripts in the DSS corpus.

Hebrew Alphabet and Grammar and Syntax

For the purposes of this chapter, our discussion of Hebrew/Aramaic features in biblical Hebrew (MT) is a simple overview and does not consider the complexity every language possesses.[7] Hebrew is written from right to left

---

6. Karl Elliger and Wilhelm Rudolph, ed., *Biblica Hebraica Stuttgartensia*, 5th ed. (Stuttgart: Deutsche Bibelgellschaft, 1997).

7. For a useful summary of the languages, see Jeremy Hutton and Aaron D. Rubin, "Hebrew Language," *New Interpreter's Dictionary of the Bible* (Nashville: Abingdon Press, 2007) 2:768–78; and Michael D. Guinan, "Aramaic, Aramaisms," *New Interpreter's Dictionary of the Bible* (Nashville: Abingdon Press, 2006) 1:228–31.

and contains twenty-two characters representing twenty-three consonant sounds (one letter *ś/š* used for two different sounds). As explained earlier, like all Semitic languages, Hebrew operates off a root of three consonants with vowels indicated by diacritics (known as vowel points). The vowel sounds are classified according to vowel quality (a/i/u) and length (short/long). The insertion of the vowel diacritics between root consonants and additional affixes produce patterns that determine the parts of speech (nouns, pronouns, adjectives, verbs, verbals).

Hebrew nouns are two genders (masculine, feminine) and three numbers (singular, dual, plural); there is a definite article ("the") but no indefinite article ("a/an"). Unlike Greek with its highly inflected morphology (case endings that indicate grammatical function), Hebrew has lost for the most part its inflected endings (like English); therefore, the grammatical function of nouns and modifiers is usually identified by other indicators (such as prepositions and word order). Related to the grammatical function of nouns is the bound relationship between two nouns that are interdependent, that is, form one sense unit, usually possessive and descriptive (e.g., literally, "the palace the king" = "the king's palace"), reducing the need for adjectives in Hebrew. Pronouns may be independent, standalone words (as in English: *I, you, they*) or inflectional suffixes added to words.

As for the verb, the primary morphological feature already mentioned is the triconsonantal root system; infixed vowel patterns plus prefixes and some suffixes determine person, gender, and number. Although tense (time location) and mood (relation to reality) are important, "aspect" of the action (as it was understood by the speaker), namely, complete or incomplete (durative/injunctive) action is most important. Verbs have three voices (active, passive, reflexive). Since English is a tense-based system, translators must render the verb in terms of English tense and action, resulting many times in different English translations of the same verb because translators interpret them differently. Psalm 119:47, for example, shows renderings of the same two Hebrew verbs "to delight" and "to love" in different tenses: "I *delight* in your commands, which I *love*" (CSB), present tense meaning habitually; "And I *will delight* myself in thy commandments, which I *have loved*" (KJV), future tense followed by the present perfect; "*How I delight* in your commands! *How I love* them!" (NLT), a different view of the verbal mood, expressing strong resolution.

As for basic syntax, Hebrew sentences are classically of three types: (1) verbless clauses/sentences, also known as nominal clauses/sentences, that have no expressed verb, and therefore in English the verbal idea must be supplied from the context; (2) a verbal sentence in which the verb is expressed and the word order normally is verb followed by the subject; and (3) three volitional mood constructions that are imperative, cohortative, and jussive. As already mentioned under the Semitic family's characteristics, for connecting clauses Hebrew has a simple coordination pattern ("and . . . and"), possessing few explicit markers of a logical subordination pattern. Subordination is typically determined by the context.

Hebrew Lexicography

One of the advantages of learning Hebrew vocabulary is its economy of words. The surviving classical Hebrew vocabulary only contains approximately 8,500 words, and the total word count of the Hebrew Bible is 419,687. Memorizing just the top fifty words enables a student to gain knowledge of 55 percent of the total words in the Hebrew Bible.[8] Because of the cosmopolitan environment of ancient Israel, Hebrew gained Egyptian, Akkadian, Persian, Aramaic, and Greek loanwords. Compared to other languages in the Semitic family, however, Hebrew has few. There are approximately 3.5 percent (about 285) loanwords of the total vocabulary stock.[9] This is why archeological digs and continued ancient Near East research are invaluable as they add to the existing knowledge base. Semitic cognates assist scholars in defining unique or rare words occurring in the OT.

As this section on the languages associated with the OT has shown, the study of language and its development is vital to understanding the rich history of the text itself. The language of the OT is rich with cultural nuance that requires interpretation and context; otherwise such beauty and meaning could easily be lost in translation, and precisely these qualities were used by the Holy Spirit originally. Though language develops and cultures change, the Word of the Lord remains forever.

---

8. Miles Van Pelt and Gary Pratico, *The Vocabulary Guide to Biblical Hebrew* (Grand Rapids: Zondervan, 2003), ix.

9. Stefan Weninger, *Semitic Languages: An International Handbook* (Berlin: Mouton de Gruyter, 2011), 183.

Aramaic Language

Aramaic occurs briefly in Gen 31:47 (one word), Jer 10:11 (a sentence), and sustained embedded passages in Dan 2:4b–7:28 and Ezra 4:8–6:18; 7:12–16.[10] It also appears in the NT (Matt 27:46; Mark 5:41; 7:34; 15:34; 1 Cor 16:22; Rev 22:20). The language was spoken by the Aramean people (called Syrians by the Greeks). In the early centuries of the first millennium AD, Aramaic consisted of West and East branches, each possessing a number of subgroups. The West includes Nabataean, Palmyrene, Samaritan, Palestinian-Christian, and Judeo-Aramaic. The East includes Syriac, Mandaic, and the Babylonian Talmud. Aramaic had significant influence in the Northwest region of the Semitic world. Because of its longevity, Aramaic went through many phases/periods spanning from the late eleventh century BC to modernity. These phases largely align with military campaigns and changes in political players. The earliest phase (Old Aramaic) occurred during the decline of the major ancient Near Eastern empires around 925–700 BC, freeing the smaller states such as Aram to achieve regional power. This time period aligns with the divided monarchy of Israel and Judah, and the artifacts of this period contain the earliest extrabiblical reference to the house of David. Around the time of the Persian Empire, Aramaic was the primary language of trade, and its influence accompanied the Jews when they returned to Israel after the exile in the sixth century BC.

From 700 to 200 BC, Official Aramaic reached new heights. The expansion of the Assyrian Empire in the late eighth century began using Aramaic in official documents and correspondence. The surrounding of Jerusalem by King Sennacherib's Assyrian troops reported in 2 Kings 18 shows the influence of Aramaic for official diplomatic language between the Jews and an Assyrian representative (v. 26; cf. Isa 36:11). The succeeding empire of the Babylonians expanded the use of Aramaic, and by the sixth century the Persians adopted it as the *lingua franca* (common language) of the empire, much as English is the language used for international diplomacy and business today. As a consequence there is a large corpus of Aramaic. Although Aramaic was widespread at this point, there is little variation despite geographical range. This is likely due to its official use in governmental matters, regulating a particular form.

---

10. Probably the word *bar* is Aramaic "son" instead of Hebrew *ben* in Ps 2:12.

This phase is significant for OT interpretation because it is the setting for Daniel (Babylonian-Persian periods) and the Aramaic letters in the book of Ezra concern the reconstruction of the temple after the exile. Therefore, Aramaic, even its earliest form, was part of the cultural fabric of the OT from the monarchy to the postexilic periods. Aramaic is close to Hebrew in its basic features and vocabulary. Usually seminary students learn Aramaic after a grasp of Hebrew because the two languages have much in common. The square-form Hebrew script in the Hebrew Bible is derived from Aramaic script, although the language is Hebrew. This would be a modern equivalent of the Romance languages sharing the basic letter style yet being distinct languages. As Hebrew developed, it adopted the square-form script of Aramaic due to its prevalence in the Mesopotamian world of Israel's exile.

Ezra and Daniel, both texts written during the period of the exile, coincide with the widest usage of Aramaic in the Semitic world. Ezra 4:8–6:18 and 7:12–26 contain excerpts of Aramaic documents regarding the restoration of Jerusalem. The inclusion of the original Aramaic letters reinforces the authenticity of the Jews' claim to authorization from Persian rulers to rebuild the temple. The shift to Aramaic in Dan 2:4–7:28 corresponds to the accounts of Daniel and his friends and an apocalyptic vision—all in the context of God's view of the nations whose official language was Aramaic. Daniel's return to Hebrew in the prophecies of chapters 8–12 fit their focus on the future for the Jews. The appearance of Aramaic in the Hebrew canon is not surprising considering the interaction of the language within the OT world, especially in the period of the exile.

The Late Aramaic phase (AD 200–1200) saw the rise of Judaica in Jewish circles including a vast literary corpus of commentaries on law and stories. The Aramaic Targums are especially important to OT interpreters because they give insight into Jewish interpretations during the Second Temple period and because they provide another witness to the original wording of the Hebrew Bible for text-critical purposes. The Targums are translations/paraphrases of the OT from Hebrew to Aramaic during the postexilic period. The term *targum* is the Aramaic word meaning "translation or interpretation" (cf. Ezra 4:7). During this period Aramaic, along with Hebrew, was widely spoken among Jews. After the third century AD, Hebrew as a spoken language was virtually abandoned, and Aramaic took its place. The Targum's translations ranged from literalistic to periphrastic and included interpretive expansions and additions. Initially the targumic commentaries were oral explanations that accompanied Hebrew readings. At becoming written texts they were common in synagogue liturgy as readings that followed the Torah recitations.

Hebrew and Aramaic in Theological Education

The study of language is of critical importance for academia and society at large. Without a comprehension of language, the study of literature would be impossible. Language is inextricably tied to culture and is integrated into the way humans communicate and relate to one another. This is why understanding how language functions is crucial.

Learning Hebrew and Aramaic gives students a cross-cultural experience in education. Unfortunately, education in general in America is failing to give its students strong reading and composition skills. In effect students largely do not know how language works because they are not aware of the complexities of their own native language. Through thirty-six years of teaching OT and Hebrew, I have had students remark to me that they learned more English grammar and syntax in Hebrew and Greek classes than in their undergraduate days. Studying the language of the OT invites student and teacher together to delve into the literary and cultural world of an ancient civilization. By studying the mechanics of the language, they discover firsthand the dynamic of the concursus of the divine and human authorship. The script is foreign to the eye, and the sounds remind Western Christians that the Christian faith did not originate with their culture only to be read through their own modern lens. The Bible is rooted in history and in a culture far removed from today. The divine message of the Bible is not a mystical product whose message is available only to the few who enjoy a superior *gnosis* (esoteric knowledge). On the contrary the divine voice "travels" across all boundaries and is received through the open inquiry of human speech. The most telling significance of study in the Bible in its ancient language and context is the theological implication—namely that God has condescended in his remarkable grace by revealing his person and purpose for humanity through common speech.

Academically, the study of Hebrew and Aramaic is vital for Christian higher education. This is most evident in the area of English translations.

In my first year of university (PhD), students who had seminary training in biblical languages were better exegetes of the text, possessing a firmer grasp on vocabulary and grammar and syntax than those who did not experience seminary instruction. Their knowledge came from American and Israeli universities. Exegesis involves a cautious detailed examination of the text, drawing out every implication of the language. The presupposition and motivation for such meticulous labor is the reality that a faithful minister of God's Word is a divine vehicle of grace.

Martin Luther said, "When the preacher speaks, God speaks." Although I would nuance his viewpoint, his point is valid when he acknowledges the authority of preaching. Without understanding the fine distinctions in the OT languages, faithful translations into any receptor language are deficient. Think of awkward translations in our culture today. For example, English subtitles of foreign films cannot convey the full extent of dialogue and the cultural colloquialisms. Another example would be the translation of different works of literature into English, such as Dostoyevsky's Russian literary works. Depending on the linguistic skills of the translator, *Crime and Punishment* in English can be easier to read, convoluted, or perhaps unreadable.

How true is this for ancient literature that is rendered in modern linguistic structure? With the many English versions available today, some could argue that study of biblical languages is unnecessary for understanding and communicating the message of the Bible. Additionally, English versions today are produced by highly qualified scholars whose products are thoroughly erudite and constantly under review by international and interdenominational translation teams. By advocating language preparation in higher education, we don't mean English Bibles today are especially suspect of misleading and therefore knowledge of Hebrew and Greek are required of all readers. I have contributed to English translations, and I am happy to see their continuing impact for good in the church. Yet the church must continue to produce Hebraists for the reason we have mentioned above. The stream of devoted scholarship to languages must not dry up because every generation faces the task of translating anew the Bible. New information, change in English idiom and vocabulary necessitate new versions. Moreover, because we have so many translations, there is chronic need for accountability, and only those who excel in the languages can evaluate the

The Languages of the Old Testament

accuracy of translations. Our educational institutions must invest in training an army of scholars and ministers who can meet the need for producing, evaluating, and evaluating English translations.

Additionally, and perhaps most importantly, specialists in the original languages and in translation theory are positioned to answer the growing cry for Bible translations in the native languages of the vast number of different people groups. This missionary impulse of providing the Scriptures for common people in their colloquial speech had its beginnings in the Jewish world when Alexandrian Jewry translated the Hebrew Bible into Greek (Septuagint) about 250 BC, and Jews in Palestine and Babylon produced Aramaic paraphrases (Targums) orally in the first century BC and written in the first centuries of the new era.[11] The Joshua Project data resource reports today that 2,643 people groups constituting 209,000,000 people do not possess written portions or audio recordings of the Scriptures in their primary language.[12] As we see from the NT, the church from its earliest days relied on the Greek translation of the OT when preaching the gospel. Christian missionaries benefitted from the broad use of the Greek language and were equipped with the Greek Scripture. Who will provide the training of such an army of translators to achieve this opportunity?

The importance of the academic study of language is well founded in the history of Christianity. Particularly during the Reformation, the study of the original language rose in importance for understanding the message of Scripture. If it were not the return to the study of the Bible—and deeper engagement with Hebrew and Greek—the established church would have continued to dominate the theology of the medieval church. Martin Luther was a staunch advocate for the study of the biblical languages instead of relying on native translations. In his letter *To the Councilmen of All Cities in Germany That They Establish and Maintain Christian Schools* (1245), Luther shows how such study would benefit the entire church body, not only ministers and theologians: "Although the gospel came and still comes to us through the Holy Spirit alone, we cannot deny that it came through the medium of languages, was spread abroad by that means, and must be preserved by the same means. For just when God wanted to spread the

---

11. Although debatable, some scholars believe the scribe Ezra translated and declared the Scriptures in the Aramaic vernacular of his audience (Neh 8:8 CSB; cf. Ezra 4:18).

12. Joshua Project, "Global Statistics," accessed January 14, 2017, https://joshuaproject.net/global_statistics.

gospel throughout the world by means of the apostles he gave the tongues for that purpose."[13]

The study of biblical language therefore is an integral part of the plan of God to further spread the gospel into all the world. By examining what was written, translators can make sense of the gospel for isolated cultures, thereby spreading the light of God in a world corrupted by sin and blinded by spiritual darkness. The preservation of the original language is key to defeating the peril of spiritual powers because Scripture is the one *offensive* weapon against the false gospels and false lights found within the world (Eph 6:17). How can these false, heretical words be combated except with the one true Word given in God's self-revelation in Scripture? For Luther the academic study of language, therefore, is one on the front lines of spiritual warfare, where Satan desperately tries to minimize the importance of language and its role in spreading the gospel. Study in the languages establishes a stronger safeguard against encroaching heresies within the church. Such heresies today normally appeal to the same Christian Scriptures (or alternate religious "scripture") for their authority. Who can better point out the error than a minister armed with a deeper knowledge of what the Bible teaches?

Denominational leaders and church leaders only help themselves by vigorously supporting and even requiring educators to provide language enabling ministers to effectively and accurately declare the faith.

Hebrew and Aramaic for Spiritual Formation

The value of the original languages is not limited to professional ministers. Rather, any Christian may reap spiritual benefits. You may think an individual must be a linguistic scholar to be blessed by the languages; however, even a minimal knowledge can be enlightening for spiritual formation.[14] If for no other reason, nonspecialists reap benefits from the progressively improved English versions, word study sources in English,[15] and more competent clergy.

---

13. Martin Luther, *Martin Luther's Basic Theological Writings*, ed. Timothy F. Lull and William R. Russell, 3rd ed. (Minneapolis: Fortress Press, 2012), 462.
14. Lee M. Fields, *Hebrew for the Rest of Us* (Grand Rapids: Zondervan, 2008); and William D. Mounce, *Greek for the Rest of Us* (Grand Rapids: Zondervan, 2013).
15. See, for example, William D. Mounce, *Mounce's Complete Expository Dictionary of Old and New Testament Words* (Grand Rapids: Zondervan, 2006); and Stephen D. Renn, ed., *Expository Dictionary of Bible Words: Word Studies for Key Bible Words Based on the Hebrew and Greek Texts* (Peabody, MA: Hendrickson Publishers, 2010).

First, as previously stated in this chapter, that the Bible occurs in Hebrew and Greek attests to the power of God to speak in a discernible, life-altering voice in human language (e.g., Deut 4:12, 33, 36; 5:22–33; Acts 2:6, 8, 11). The God who used the languages of ancient civilizations, far removed from today's context, is the same God bringing about his promises and kingdom today. These historical contexts show that Christianity finds its basis on firm, unchangeable power that is not of human origin, although given through real people and real historical circumstances. Biblical revelation is anchored in historical reality. There is a continuum between antiquity and the present by virtue of the eternal Word and the shared human condition. This gives the minister and the congregation more confidence in the authority of the preached Word.

Second, the meticulous nature of Hebrew causes modern readers to slow down when engaging Scripture. Ministers who consult the Scriptures in their original languages can better achieve a clear understanding of the text, its rich theological vocabulary, its vivid imagery and figures of speech, and difficult passages that are in dispute. Poetry is especially challenging for translators into a receptor language because much of the imagery and power of the text's intensity are marginalized in the process. Hebrew poetry is especially different from Western poetry because of Hebrew poetry's highly terse, balanced lines (parallel). As a consequence of reading Hebrew poetry, the minister is impacted more by the vibrancy and emotion of the poet and prophet. The emotions of David's confession of sin with Bathsheba in Psalm 51 can be felt by the reader with him as he confesses every dimension of his sinful state, virtually offering a lexicon for the sematic idea of sin. David uses four different Hebrew words, each with its shade of meaning: "transgressions" (v. 1), iniquity (v. 2), "sin" (v. 2), and "evil" (v. 6). Pastors and teachers are moved spiritually by the power of the living Word and only wish they could convey better the same reality of experience to their congregations. Many Hebrew wordplays and soundplays in a passage are not detected in English. Such literary devices are not for aesthetic purposes alone but often convey the message of the passage. Deuteronomy 30:1–10 has the word *shub* ("turn, return") seven times; it is rendered variously by the CSB as "come to your senses" (v. 1), "return" (vv. 2, 10), "restore" (v. 3), and "again" (vv. 3, 8–9). The translation is not at fault because it cannot give a verbatim translation without butchering the English language. The point of the passage is made clear by the wordplay of *shub*: when Israel "returns" to the Lord (v. 2), the Lord will "return" their fortunes and "return" Israel to the land (v. 3). There is a mutual "turning," a turning to God in repentance and God's "returning" the people after forgiveness of their sins.

Third, when a minister reads the text in Hebrew, the engagement with the passage moves the minister intellectually and spiritually. These private experiences in the minister's study, along with the life-transforming Word, provide an illumination the pastor is compelled to bring to the pulpit. The study of the text is enriching for the life of the pastor but also instills in the pastor a confidence in the Scriptures with an authority that is higher than his own. The student of the languages is humbled by the experience and emboldened by the confidence that the Spirit of God stirs up in his soul. The minister thus is relieved from attempting some gimmickry and relies instead on the exposition of the text—the Spirit's own voice—so that the congregation enters into the text with the pastor. And the congregation knows the pastor's firsthand embrace of the text at the deepest level because they see in the minister a person who has heard God's Word and now delivers it vigorously to lead them into a profounder understanding of the Scriptures. Every church member would be rewarded week by week if they would encourage and provide their pastor the time necessary for study and continuing education. The church would experience a foundation on Jesus Christ and not the personality of a leader who is here today but gone tomorrow. Truly the hungry soul finds satisfaction only in feasting on the divine Word.

Conclusion

From the early centuries of the church until the Renaissance and Reformation of the fifteenth and sixteenth centuries, Christian scholars depended largely on Jewish masters of Hebrew to learn from the Hebrew of the OT and gain the insights of Jewish commentators. The first Protestant to provide a brief Hebrew grammar (1504) was a Swiss Reformer, Conrad Pellican (1478–1556), but the German humanist Johannes Reuchlin (1455–1522) produced the first substantial grammar in 1506.[16] I end this

---

16. Sophie Kessler Mesguich, "Early Christian Hebraists," *Hebrew Bible/Old Testament: The History of Its Interpretation*, vol. 2, *From the Renaissance to the Enlightenment*, Magne Sæbo, ed. (Göttengen: Vanderhoeck and Ruprecht, 2008), 254–75.

chapter by reminding us of how deeply we are indebted to our forefathers who took up the challenge to learn and enrich the Christian world with the languages of the OT. For a thousand years Christian interpreters worked in the OT virtually blindfolded because of their incompetence in Hebrew. Although I cannot imagine a future in the church when Christian scholars and their students will be so woefully handicapped, I know we must not let the flame of theological and spiritual renewal grow dim. We hold the torch. As Christian educators, it is our turn to decide how strong the torch's flame we pass to our descendants will be.

Questions for Further Reflection

1. What is the nature of divine revelation in English Bible translations compared to the original Hebrew and Greek Scriptures?
2. What are the theological implications of the multicultural world of ancient Israel for us in our multicultural, global era?
3. Is "distance learning" in seminaries and colleges for training Christian ministers sufficient for effective language training in the Bible?
4. Should ministerial training for those not preaching (e.g., music, youth, college, and pastoral care leaders) require facility also in Hebrew and Greek?
5. Since German piety in the eighteenth century revived study in the original languages, should we make language training more available to lay leaders?
6. Are there negative consequences for the church if pastors learn Hebrew and Greek? If so, what are they?
7. What steps can church leaders take to instill an ethos of deeper learning in the Scriptures in advancing individual Christian discipleship?

Sources for Further Study

Brunn, Dave. *One Bible, Many Versions: Are All Translations Created Equal?* Downers Grove: InterVarsity, 2013.

Byram, Michael, and Peter Grundy, ed. *Context and Culture in Language Teaching and Learning.* Clevedon, England: Multilingual Matters, 2003.

Currid, John D. *Calvin and the Biblical Languages.* Fearn, Ross-Shire, Scotland: Mentor, 2006.

Köstenberger, Andreas and David Croteau. *Which Bible Translation Should I Use?* Nashville: B&H, 2012.

Miller, Glenn. *Piety and Profession: American Protestant Theological Education, 1870–1970.* Grand Rapids: Eerdmans, 2007.

Spitzer, Peter James, and Thomas J. Finley. *How Biblical Languages Work: A Student's Guide to Learning Hebrew and Greek*, 2nd ed. Grand Rapids: Kregel Academic, 2004.

Tov, Emmanuel. *Textual Criticism of the Hebrew Bible.* Third edition. Minneapolis: Fortress, 2012.

Van Wolde, Ellen. *Reframing Biblical Studies: When Language and Text Meet Culture, Cognition, and Context.* Winona Lake, IN: Eisenbrauns, 2009.

Chapter Seven

THE STUDY OF THE LANGUAGE OF THE NEW TESTAMENT

CONSTANTINE R. CAMPBELL

Nearly one hundred years ago, the great Greek grammarian A. T. Robertson wrote, "The real New Testament is the Greek New Testament. The English is simply a translation of the New Testament, not the actual New Testament."[1] In his classic little work, *The Minister and His Greek New Testament*, Robertson claimed that knowledge of English translations is good, but for the minister whose special duty it is to teach the Word of God, "there will remain a large and rich untranslatable element that the preacher ought to know."[2] Robertson expected that those who love the truth would not take shortcuts in their handling of it. The man who loves the light is not afraid of the light. No amount of toil is too great for the lover of the truth of God. The true preacher wishes to plant his feet on the solid rock of real learning. Grammatical exegesis precedes the historical and the spiritual.[3]

In Robertson's day, however, there was an unhealthy attitude toward learning the language in which the New Testament was written. "But the chief reason why preachers do not get and do not keep up a fair and needful knowledge of the Greek New Testament is nothing less than carelessness, and even laziness in many cases. They can get along somehow without it,

---

1. A. T. Robertson, *The Minister and His Greek New Testament* (1923; repr. Birmingham: Solid Ground Christian Books, 2008), 17; also see David S. Dockery, *The Best of A. T. Robertson* (Nashville: B&H, 1996).
2. Robertson, *The Minister and His Greek New Testament*, 19.
3. Ibid., 85.

and so let it pass or let it drop."[4] Unfortunately, the same thing can be said today. But, as Robertson rightly pointed out, such an attitude is not acceptable. We excuse other men for not having a technical knowledge of the Bible. We do not expect all men to know the details of medicine, law, banking, and railroading. But the preacher cannot be excused from an accurate apprehension of the New Testament. This is the book he undertakes to expound. It is his specialty, and this he must know whatever else he does or does not know.[5]

The preacher of the Word of God has a special duty to know its contents, understand its message, and have command of its details. This chapter will argue that it is not possible to achieve such knowledge and accuracy in handling the New Testament without a working knowledge of the Greek language. The study of the language of the New Testament is thus an essential ingredient in theological education and ministry preparation.

First, we will explore the relationship between Greek and preaching; second, we will explore the relationship between Greek and New Testament studies.

Greek and Preaching

Since we are ultimately interested in the role of Greek in theological education and ministry preparation, we begin with the end first: preaching. Though theological education and ministry preparation do not all boil down to preaching, the ability to teach the Scriptures is a significant outcome for such training. So we begin by asking what relationship the knowledge of Greek bears on the practice of preaching. Is knowledge of Greek important for preaching? Does it really make a difference? Is such a scholarly pursuit truly aligned with this primary pastoral responsibility? First, we will address some common objections to preachers' need of Greek. Then we will move on to the positive benefits of Greek acquisition for the preacher.

Only for Specialists?

A common attitude today is that knowledge of Greek is the domain of specialists. Of course New Testament scholars and professors need to know

---
4. Ibid., 16.
5. Ibid., 19.

Greek, but preachers are neither scholars nor professors. We all rely on such people, but we don't need to *be* such people. The body of Christ is large and diverse, consisting of different gifts and abilities. As the apostle Paul says, it does the body no good if the whole body is an eye (1 Cor 12:17).

There is a place for specialists and experts, and we all rely on their insights, knowledge, and contribution. But that does not mean that the skill set and knowledge of the preacher should have *no* overlap with the scholar. On the contrary, the preacher must be a scholar, even if he is a small-*s* scholar. Indeed, even reading the work produced by serious scholars is an activity of scholarship. So the preacher who reads a commentary is engaging in scholarship even if he is not the one doing the research and writing.

Indeed, a preacher will share this kind of relationship to a number of fields. He will be a New Testament scholar, though himself no expert, by learning from the experts. By the same token, a pastor will need to be a counselor, though he may not be a trained counselor. Some skills and knowledge will overlap with the professional. Furthermore, the preacher will have skills and knowledge that overlap with the communications expert, without being an expert in that area either.

The preacher will be a practitioner of New Testament scholarship if he is to teach the text to his congregation. There is simply no way around that if he is to be a workman approved, correctly handling the word of truth (2 Tim 2:15). As a practitioner of New Testament scholarship, he has no legitimate reason to defer knowledge of Greek to "real" scholars. The preacher is a scholar, and the scholar must know Greek.

A ready example may be found in any university that is serious about the study of classical history. In any undergraduate classical history course, it is standard for students to learn both Greek and Latin. It is standard to assume undergraduate students will read several of the primary texts in their original languages. The studies of Aristotle, Plato, Thucydides, Herodotus, Lysias, and so on are conducted in ancient Greek. This is because history takes the primary sources seriously. And taking the primary sources seriously means reading them in their original languages. And just to reiterate: this is the expectation of undergraduate students. These are not experts in the field. These are not renowned scholars and researchers. No, these are students just beginning their tertiary education. If the discipline of history holds such expectations for their undergraduate students, why is it unrealistic to expect that postgraduate students of theology will study Greek and Hebrew?

We must resist the consistent dumbing down of expectations for preachers and pastors. The seriousness of training ministers in times past led to the foundation of the oldest universities in the Western world. Oxford, Cambridge, Harvard, Yale—alongside several others—all began as institutions devoted to theological training. The impetus that began Oxford has now dwindled to the attitude that a pastor does not even need to learn Greek! What a sorry state of affairs.

If we believe the preaching pastor is a doctor of souls, why would we tolerate sloppy and incomplete training? We would not tolerate incomplete training of a medical doctor or surgeon. After all, we put our lives in the hands of such people; they need to know what they are doing. How much more a doctor of souls? We put our eternal lives in the care of pastors and preachers, and yet we value their training less than that of the surgeon. Something is wrong with our perception of reality if we are willing to make such a concession. Either we do not believe in the seriousness of what's at stake, or we do not believe training really makes much difference. Both are significant errors.

Robertson said it well:

> The doctor does not complain at the details of his science. He has to know the minutiae of nature's handiwork. Nothing is too small for his investigation. He must know the laws of life, the ways of the cell, the habits of the bacilli and microbes that help and endanger human life, the value of all kinds of medicine, the idiosyncrasies of the individual, the wonders of the ductless glands and their influence on personality. Nothing is too small in order that one may save life. Surely the life of the soul is as important as that of the body.[6]

What About the Use of Greek in Sermons?

Many preachers are wary of referring to Greek in their sermons. They generally want to avoid mentioning issues related to the Greek text, citing

---

6. Ibid., 22.

Greek words, and so forth. While I am not opposed to referencing Greek in special situations, I am sympathetic to the concern overall. Preachers must avoid becoming "priests" who mediate access to God. While Protestants will rightly acknowledge that Jesus Christ is the great high priest who has done away with the need for human mediators (Hebrews 7–8), we can nevertheless unwittingly foster a priestly dynamic in preaching.

An overuse of Greek in the pulpit can lead to this priestly dynamic in preaching. Greek becomes the special knowledge held by one person, who thereby is the expert the congregation needs to approach God in truth. Since this knowledge is not available to all, and clearly holds the secrets to the text, Greek becomes an amulet of priestly power. Furthermore, over-reference to Greek in the pulpit can lead believers to lose confidence in their English Bibles.

If we are agreed that Greek should not be referenced in most sermons, what then is the point of learning it? This is probably the most common question I am asked by seminary Greek students. "If I don't even mention Greek in my sermon, why do I really need it?"

The question reveals a serious misunderstanding. The usefulness of Greek is not so the preacher can tell his hearers what the Greek says. The usefulness of Greek is that it will give the *preacher* deeper understanding of the text. That, in turn, will shape what the preacher says in the sermon.[7] Greek is for the preacher's preparation; it serves his study of the text. While it might, on occasion, come out from behind the curtains, Greek generally remains behind the scenes. And in this preparatory role Greek makes a significant difference to preaching.

When a mechanic works on my car, I do not always understand what he is doing. I am not a car guy and really just care about getting from A to B. So I do not need him to explain the technical details of his work. As long as he fixes the brakes, I don't care to know particulars. By the same token, it is usually not necessary for the preacher to share the technical details of his work. What's important is that the text is faithfully preached. But the technical side is essential for that task, just as it is for my mechanic. He needs technical competence; he needs to understand the details; he needs to know how all the parts work and go together. He would hardly be a

---

7. Constantine R. Campbell, *Keep Your Greek: Strategies for Busy People* (Grand Rapids: Zondervan, 2010), 10.

useful mechanic otherwise. So the preacher who does not understand and harness the technical aspects of exegesis is hardly equipped for the task set before him.

Exegetical Fallacies

Speaking of the technical aspects of exegesis, D. A. Carson's book, *Exegetical Fallacies*, continues to shed light on common mistakes made in New Testament interpretation. The importance of such "painfully frequent" exegetical fallacies is due to the responsibility inherent in "the faithful proclamation of the Word of God."[8] As Carson reflects, "We are dealing with God's thoughts: we are obligated to take the greatest pains to understand them truly and to explain them clearly. It is all the more shocking, therefore, to find in the evangelical pulpit, where the Scriptures are officially revered, frequent and inexcusable sloppiness in handling them."[9]

"Sloppiness" in handling the Scriptures is inexcusable in today's environment, in which tools and instruction are more readily available than ever before. It is not for lack of opportunity that preachers continue to make age-old errors in handling God's Word, since such problems are well documented. And yet, as Carson demonstrates even with the simple word study, preachers continue to commit the crimes of root fallacy, semantic anachronism, semantic obsolescence, appeal to unknown or unlikely meanings, careless appeal to background material, verbal parallelomania, and so on.

At the end of the day, Carson suggests that undergirding many such problems is deficiency in knowledge of Greek.

> Perhaps the principal reason why word studies constitute a particularly rich source for exegetical fallacies is that many preachers and Bible teachers know Greek only well enough to use concordances, or perhaps little more. There is little feel for Greek as a language; and so there is the temptation to display what has been learned in study, which as often as not is a great deal of lexical information without the restraining influence of context. The solution, of course, is to learn more Greek,

---

8. D. A. Carson, *Exegetical Fallacies*, 2nd ed. (Grand Rapids: Baker, 1996), 15.
9. Ibid., 15–16.

not less, and to gain at least a rudimentary knowledge of linguistics.[10]

Alongside word studies are Greek tense/aspect fallacies, errors relating to Greek conditional sentences, and other Greek-specific problems. Further exegetical problems are highlighted in my book, *Advances in the Study of Greek*.[11]

Exegetical Insights

In addition to avoiding errors, studying the Greek New Testament can lead to all sorts of observations that might be hidden to the reader of English translations. Such observations may not correct what we see in translation, but they may add depth of insight otherwise unavailable. Ephesians 2 offers some such insights. It is a well-known text, to be sure. Perhaps the preacher assumes there is nothing new to see here. But I would suggest such an assumption is misplaced. First, there is the connection between "walking" (περιπατέω) in 2:2 and 2:10. This may be seen readily in translations that render the word as "walking," such as ESV, but not all popular translations render the word this way (e.g, CSB and NIV). Without spotting the same word in 2:2 and 2:10, the preacher may miss the deliberate symmetry of 2:1–10, and, more importantly, the meaning conveyed by it. The symmetry of "walking" in verses 2 and 10 is that, in the first instance, it describes people walking in trespasses and sins, according to the ways of the world. In the second instance, it describes believers who now—thanks to the grace of God—walk in the good works that God has prepared in advance for us. In other words, 2:1–10 is bookended by "walking." Unbelievers are the "walking dead" while believers are those who walk alive in Christ. Dead people walk in sin; living people walk in good works.

Second, in Ephesians 2, we see that our union with Christ brings about our union with one another, and a small Greek preposition helps us appreciate that wonderful reality.[12]

---

10. Ibid., 64.
11. Constantine R. Campbell, *Advances in the Study of Greek: New Insights for Reading the New Testament* (Grand Rapids: Zondervan, 2015).
12. The following example is taken from my brief essay, "The σύν-Mirror of Christian Salvation and Christian Unity" in *Devotions on the Greek New Testament: 52 Reflections to Inspire and Instruct*, ed. J. Scott Duvall and Verlyn D. Verbrugge (Grand Rapids: Zondervan, 2012), 83–84.

Ephesians 2 provides a profound statement of salvation by grace (2:1–10) and the unity that Jews and Gentiles enjoy in Christ (2:11–22), and it is a carefully structured unit. The two halves of the chapter display a mirrored structure. In 2:1–10, there are the three main movements of the passage: (1) *problem*: sin to the core of our beings (2:1–3); (2) *solution*: made alive in Christ (2:4–7); (3) *consequence*: new creations (2:8–10). The same movements, but with different content, are seen in 2:11–22: (1) *problem*: disjunction between Jew and Gentile (2:11–12); (2) *solution*: Christ is our peace (2:13–18); (3) *consequence*: God's new household (2:19–22). The parallels between these two halves of Ephesians 2 demonstrate that Christ is the solution to sin and death, and he is therefore the solution to the disjunction between Jew and Gentile.

What is less easily seen in English translations is that the parallels between the two halves of the chapter do not end there. At the heart of the first half of Ephesians 2 are three Greek words prefixed by the preposition σύν: συνεζωοποίησεν, συνήγειρεν, and συνεκάθισεν. Believers have been *made alive with* Christ (2:5), have been *raised with* him, and are now *seated with* him in the heavenly realms (2:6). Clearly these σύν-prefixed words are significant for understanding a key theme of Ephesians—that of believers' union with Christ. But these σύν–prefixed words are also mirrored in the second half of the chapter. In 2:19–22, we read that Jews and Gentiles in Christ are now *fellow citizens*—συμπολῖται (2:19); are *joined together* in Christ—συναρμολογουμένη (2:21); and are *built together* for God's dwelling in the Spirit—συνοικοδομεῖσθε (2:22).

Is it merely coincidence that both halves of the chapter each have three closely spaced σύν-prefixed words, apparently in parallel? I think not. I believe these two sets of σύν-prefixed words are deliberately mirrored and reflect a profound theological reality. Part of the logic between the two halves of the chapter is that because we are saved by grace and not by works, law, or ethnic heritage, Jew and Gentile alike are now on the same footing before God in Christ. All people that dwell on earth may belong to the citizenship of God's household through Christ. And a central part of unity derives from a salvation by grace in which believers are made alive, raised, and seated *with* Christ. In other words, a consequence of being *with* Christ is that Jews and Gentiles are now *with* each other. They are fellow citizens of God's household; they are joined together in Christ; and they are built together for God's dwelling in the Spirit.

Truly our union with Christ brings about our unions with each other. And as we see in Ephesians 2, a small Greek preposition helps us appreciate that wonderful reality. As mentioned above, Ephesians 2 is a well-known text. And yet there are meaningful exegetical observations to be had through reading the Greek text. These offer depth of insight to the preacher that may otherwise be missed.

Syntax Diagrams

One of the most useful disciplines for the preparation of exegetical sermons is the construction of a syntax diagram of the Greek text. This is the first step I take when preparing a sermon, and I strongly commend it to my students who want to preach well. Syntax diagramming is one of those skills that is hard to appreciate until one has learned to do it properly. It is a little like trying to explain to someone who has never played music what you love about playing an instrument. I can only speak in general terms about the experience of playing music—it's fun, creative, expressive, communal, challenging, and so forth—but I cannot accurately convey the experience itself. You have to know it from the inside. You have to have done it too. I believe the same thing can be said about surfing—I'm told it's amazing, but I don't really know since I have never been able to do it properly. If you do not know it from the inside, you will never really understand it. I can affirm the value of syntax diagramming in general terms, but the reader will not understand its benefits until he or she has mastered it. To some extent you simply must trust me on this one until you have pursued the goal yourself.

Nevertheless, here are some general comments. First, syntax diagramming forces the preacher to analyze how Greek clauses relate to one another. The relationship between clauses is essential to understanding Greek text, and it is therefore essential for understanding any segment of the New Testament. Greek is a highly complex language when it comes to clauses. Unlike Hebrew, which generally employs a simple structure for the arrangement of clauses, Greek uses several levels of dependency. Subordinate clauses have subordinate clauses, which have their own subordinate clauses, which also have subordinate clauses—and so it goes. In order to follow the sequence of ideas in a Greek text, it is necessary to trace these levels of subordination, dependency, and correlation between clauses. The matrix of clauses, and how they relate to one another, is how Greek communicates complex ideas. When we construct a syntax diagram, the primary task is to identify the clauses and how they relate to one another. Below are some examples in English that demonstrate the importance of clausal syntax.

The **simple** sentence consists of:

Subject	*Verb*	*Object*	*(indirect object)*
The man	washed	the car	(for his friend)

The **compound** sentence consists of two or more simple sentences joined with a coordinating conjunction, such as *and*:

> The man washed the car, and he drove it to his friend.

The **complex** sentence consists of the simple sentence as the main clause, as well as one or more subordinate or dependent clauses:

> The man washed the car because he owed his friend a favor.

Greek demonstrates its clausal sophistication through the sheer complexity of its compound sentences. In Greek it is common to find very complex sentences, which, in English, might sound like this:

> The man, who lives next door, washed the car, using water and soap, because he owed his friend, who lives down the street, a favor since the friend bought him Cubs tickets, knowing that the man has been a Cubs fan since childhood—even though before 2016 they had not won the pennant in over a 108 years—but has never been able to attend a game.

Yes, Greek sentences are commonly that complex. Take Eph 1:3–6 as an example. In Greek that is one sentence. If that statement does not strike you, go read Eph 1:3–6 again. With such complexity surrounding Greek clauses, the syntax diagram is an essential tool for unraveling how everything fits together. The point is not to say to your congregation, "Did you know that Eph 1:3–6 is one sentence in the original Greek?" The point is for the preacher to understand that text as originally written. Since English translations will break long Greek sentences up into shorter ones, often the relationships between clauses becomes obscured. For instance, the NIV breaks this text into three sentences:

> Praise be to the God and Father of our Lord Jesus Christ, who has blessed us in the heavenly realms with every spiritual blessing in Christ. For he chose us in him before the creation of the world to be holy and blameless in his sight. In love he predestined us for adoption to sonship through Jesus Christ, in accordance with his pleasure and will—to the praise of his glorious grace, which he has freely given us in the One he loves.

In contrast, this wooden translation of the Greek text demonstrates what is really happening with the clauses:

> Praise be to the God and Father of our Lord Jesus Christ, who has blessed us in the heavenly realms with every spiritual blessing in Christ, just as he chose us in him before the creation of the world to be holy and blameless before him in love, having predestined us for adoption to sonship through Jesus Christ, in accordance with the pleasure of his will for the praise of his glorious grace, which he has freely given us in the One he loves.

The difference between the two translations ought to be clear. While the first makes for better English, the second more clearly demonstrates how the logic is unfolding. It is clearer that the main idea is found in 1:3—that God has blessed us with every spiritual blessing. What follows is the unpacking of these blessings. Now the preacher may come to the same conclusion by studying an English translation, but he will arrive there more surely by studying the Greek. English translations will provide hit-and-miss results when it comes to understanding how the original clauses were intended to be understood. Moreover, these shorter sentences will appear to be of equal status as independent sentences. But in Greek it is clear that these clauses are not of equal value, with some clauses driving the discourse while other clauses supplement such clauses. In other words, studying the

Greek text enables us to understand which clauses are most significant and which carry less weight. The bottom line is that Greek relies heavily on the structure of clauses to communicate ideas. But such information is often hidden in English translations because English does not structure its sentences in the same way as does Greek. Thus, the preacher who wants to see and understand how a New Testament author has structured his ideas simply must read them in Greek.

Conversing with Commentaries

One of the most common reasons preachers, or preachers-in-training, think they have no need to know Greek is that so many good commentaries are available. This has not always been the case, at least not to the same extent, so the preacher reasons that others—experts, no less—have done the hard work of analyzing the text—experts, no less. Why not trust these excellent resources? Will a minister's feeble knowledge of Greek add anything to the conversation?

I have already addressed the idea that knowledge of Greek is only for specialists (see above). Yes, specialists write commentaries. But with knowledge of Greek, the relationship between the preacher and the commentary undergoes a dramatic shift. The preacher who knows no Greek is beholden to the commentator whenever his or her insights relate to language. Commentators often decide exegetical complexities based on the language, or at least on their understanding of the language. And the preacher without Greek is completely unable to evaluate, much less challenge, such understandings. However, the preacher who knows Greek well is able to evaluate the claims made by commentators. He can observe the strength of argument. He can weigh whether too much is claimed given the evidence. He can dig into his own research tools to judge the exegetical issue for himself. This is a major shift in relationship between preacher and commentator. Yes, the commentator is still the expert, while most preachers are not. But rather than an impenetrable authority, the commentator becomes a conversation partner. The preacher can "dialogue" with the commentator rather than blindly trust his or her opinions relating to the Greek text.

Don't misunderstand me. I am not claiming that learning Greek will turn every preacher into a New Testament expert or that commentators will become obsolete. Not at all. Commentaries remain essential tools for faithful preaching. But there is a big difference between accepting every opinion of an authority and being able to weigh such opinions according to knowledge.

Evaluation of commentaries works best when the preacher has already done his own work in the Greek text. Study of the text—before consultation of a commentary—enables the preacher to form his own opinions, ideas, and questions. Then, when he consults a commentary, the preacher will engage it as a conversation partner, noticing when it differs in its reading of the text. Noticing such differences offers an opportunity for the preacher to test his understanding of the text. It may require supplementation. It may need some correcting. Or maybe it is a better reading than that of the commentary. Regardless, a "conversation" over the text is much better than just downloading the commentary. When the preacher does not study the Greek text before consulting a commentary, whatever the commentary says will tend to sound plausible. After all, the preacher has not formed his own opinions about the text, so he is easily swayed. It's called the power of suggestion.

This is not a good situation for the preacher who wants to be responsible for faithfully handling the word of God. For starters, commentaries are sometimes wrong; commentators are only human after all. And with so many commentaries available today, it is patently obvious that they often disagree—sometimes about significant matters—and so cannot all be right all the time. Discernment is required.

Furthermore, the preacher of God's Word needs to take responsibility for his handling of the text. He must own his reading of the text for himself rather than just adopting someone else's. This is a fundamental feature found among the best exegetical preachers: they have their own opinions about the text because they have studied the text carefully for themselves and formed their own conclusions. Commentators may have helped them, but their readings of the text nevertheless remain theirs. And they will thus preach with conviction and depth of knowledge.

Conversing with commentaries is necessary for good preaching, but sometimes it is not enough. Virtually any text will raise issues and questions that commentaries do not deal with. Sometimes this is due to the nature of the commentary—few are meant to be exhaustive. Other times commentaries simply don't address the issues we may be interested in. We cannot expect commentaries to have all the answers to the questions raised by the text.

Preachers ought to be equipped to chase down such questions for themselves. Lexicons, dictionaries, and other reference works may provide the information we need. But other times even these fine resources do not give us all we require. Preachers may need to do their own research with the use of Greek. With sophisticated Bible software tools at our disposal, we can perform all kinds of searches with relative ease. The results of a concordance can be produced in less than a second. Syntactical searches are a little more difficult to perform but are certainly not beyond savvy users. Indeed, there has not been a time when it has been easier to do one's own research on the Greek New Testament. But, again, many of the advantages of software are only available with some capacity with Greek.

Greek and New Testament Studies

The academic study of the New Testament is the study of the Greek New Testament. There is, therefore, simply no academic study of the New Testament that does not involve Greek—at least to some extent. And this is especially the case when it comes to exegesis of the Greek New Testament. There is no such thing as Greek exegesis that does not involve Greek.

While preachers do not need to be Greek scholars, good preachers will have some capacity in, and understanding of, New Testament scholarship. It is a necessary part of being faithful teachers of the Scriptures. And within New Testament studies, several important issues are directly connected to the Greek in which the New Testament is written. The following is a brief survey of some such topics.

Union with Christ

The theme of union with Christ has been a central concept in theological formation for millennia. Within modern New Testament studies, it has been a significant theme for over a century. There have been a variety of approaches to the subject, including antecedents research—comparing Paul's concepts to Greek and Jewish writings[13]—and theological

---

13. E.g., Albert Schweitzer, *The Mysticism of Paul the Apostle*, trans. William Montgomery (Baltimore: John Hopkins, 1998); E. P. Sanders, *Paul and Palestinian Judaism: A Comparison of Patterns of Religion* (Minneapolis: Fortress, 1977).

approaches—relating the theme to other biblical areas of thought.[14] In my own research on union with Christ in Paul's thirteen New Testament epistles, an analysis of his use of Greek prepositional phrases occupied much of the study.[15]

Careful examination of every relevant prepositional phrase, such as "in Christ," "with Christ," "into Christ," and "through Christ" yielded significant insights into Paul's theology of union with Christ. Naturally, the Greek versions of these prepositional phrases require elucidation. The Greek preposition ἐν ("in") is capable of widely different meanings in different contexts. Though the phrase ἐν Χριστῷ ("in Christ") may remain fairly well fixed in Paul's writings, it means different things according to the setting, and such meanings are largely dependent on the flexibility of the Greek preposition. Appreciation of the nuances of this preposition, and appropriate use of tools such as the Bauer-Danker-Arndt-Gingrich Greek-English Lexicon (BDAG) and the Louw-Nida Greek-English Lexicon, require knowledge of Greek. Indeed, it is not simply knowledge that is required but sensitive attention to the feel of the language.

While study of the wider theological theme of union with Christ cannot be limited to Greek prepositional phrases, nor can it succeed without them. In this sense I suggest that it is not possible to engage the study of union with Christ in modern New Testament studies without knowledge of Greek. Union with Christ is such a significant theme for Paul that, without the capacity to study it properly, students of the New Testament simply are not able to penetrate Paul's theology to sufficient depth.

The Deity of Christ

There is hardly a more important topic in New Testament studies than the deity of Christ. Does the New Testament clearly affirm that Jesus is God? Many skeptics answer negatively, claiming that Christ's status was elevated to that of God through subsequent centuries of church dogma. Several strands of evidence are found within the New Testament that support the full deity of Christ, and knowledge of Greek is key to much such evidence.

---

14. E.g., Richard B. Gaffin, *The Centrality of the Resurrection: A Study in Paul's Soteriology* (Grand Rapids: Baker, 1978); Michael S. Horton, *Covenant and Salvation: Union with Christ* (Louisville: Westminster John Knox, 2007).

15. Constantine R. Campbell, *Paul and Union with Christ: An Exegetical and Theological Study* (Grand Rapids: Zondervan, 2012).

Murray Harris's superb work, *Jesus as God: The New Testament Use of Theos in Reference to Jesus*, examines sixteen New Testament passages where the word θεός ("God") may be applied to Jesus.[16] He concludes that two of these texts certainly do refer to Jesus as God, four texts probably do so, and a seventh text probably does too. A key element in Harris's work is the use of the Greek article ("the"), which plays a decisive role in texts that evince Granville Sharp's rule and Colwell's rule. These syntactical rules for the use and nonuse of the Greek article are essential in determining whether Jesus is described as God. Daniel Wallace treats Granville Sharp's rule and Colwell's rule in depth in his intermediate grammar,[17] while the former is given special attention in Wallace's volume directly focused on that issue.[18] He likewise demonstrates the importance of these syntactical rules for affirming the deity of Christ. The rules surrounding the Greek article are complex and somewhat controversial, but they directly affect the New Testament teaching about the deity of Christ. Is any further warrant necessary to defend the essential contribution of Greek to New Testament studies? A proper understanding of the Greek article is enough to seal the fact that the New Testament affirms the full deity of Christ.

The Faith of Jesus Christ

Another significant issue that has occupied New Testament scholars in recent decades involves the meaning of the Greek genitive phrase, πίστεως [Ἰησοῦ] Χριστοῦ ("faith of [Jesus] Christ"), found in Rom 3:22; Gal 2:16; 3:22; and Phil 3:9. Since the Reformation this phrase has been understood as "faith *in* Jesus Christ," as reflected in standard English translations (e.g., CSB, ESV, NIV). But there is a long history of discussion in New Testament studies exploring whether this phrase would be better understood as "faith *of* Jesus Christ." The question revolves around the meaning of the Greek genitive case, [Ἰησοῦ] Χριστοῦ. The genitive case can be understood in several different ways according to context; indeed, Wallace lists

---

16. Murray J. Harris, *Jesus as God: The New Testament Use of Theos in Reference to Jesus* (Grand Rapids: Baker, 1992). See also the more recent work that draws on Harris's exegetical insights: Christopher W. Morgan and Robert A. Peterson, ed. *The Deity of Christ* (Wheaton: Crossway, 2011).

17. Daniel B. Wallace, *Greek Grammar Beyond the Basics: An Exegetical Syntax of the New Testament* (Grand Rapids: Zondervan, 1996).

18. Daniel B. Wallace, *Granville Sharp's Canon and Its Kin: Semantics and Significance*, vol. 14, *Studies in Biblical Greek* (New York: Peter Lang, 2009).

thirty-three distinct uses of the case.[19] In this instance, debate circles around whether the genitive should be understood as *subjective* ("faith *of* [Jesus] Christ") or *objective* ("faith *in* [Jesus] Christ").[20] While broader exegetical and theological matters impinge on the issue, it is primarily a question about how to understand a Greek phrase.

Once again it is clear that access to this major issue within New Testament studies is dependent on facility with Greek. The student without Greek is simply barred from the discussion.

Verbal Aspect

A third issue that has occupied certain spheres within New Testament studies is directly focused on Greek, namely its verbal system. The study of Greek verbal aspect has involved a paradigm shift in our understanding of how Greek verbs work, resulting in fresh approaches to exegesis and translation. Rather than a tense-based approach to Greek verbs, as though the language were like English or Latin, Greek is an aspect-dominant language. Aspect refers to *viewpoint*. The viewpoint is the way a verb is used to view an action, either from *outside* the action or from *inside* it.[21] Buist Fanning describes it thus:

> The action can be viewed from a reference-point *within* the action, without reference to the beginning or end-point of the action, but with a focus instead on its internal structure or make-up. Or the action can be viewed from a vantage point *outside* the action, with focus on the whole action from beginning to end, but without reference to its internal structure.[22]

As I further explain,

---

19. Wallace, *Greek Grammar Beyond the Basics*, 72–136.
20. The modern discussion can be traced back to Hays's argument for the subjective genitive reading; Richard B. Hays, *The Faith of Jesus Christ: The Narrative Substructure of Galatians 3:1–4:11* (1983; Grand Rapids: Eerdmans, 2002). Hays's primary opponent, arguing for an objective genitive reading, is Dunn; see, e.g., James D. G. Dunn, "Once More, ΠΙΣΤΙΣ ΧΡΙΣΤΟΥ," in idem, 249–71. For a relatively recent collection of essays on the subject, see Michael F. Bird and Preston M. Sprinkle, *The Faith of Jesus Christ: Exegetical, Biblical, and Theological Studies* (Milton Keynes: Paternoster, 2009).
21. Campbell, *Advances in the Study of Greek*, 106.
22. Buist M. Fanning, *Verbal Aspect in New Testament Greek* (Oxford: Clarendon, 1990), 27.

The external viewpoint (outside the action) is known as *perfective* aspect; the internal viewpoint (inside the action) is known as *imperfective* aspect. Perfective aspect views an action "from a distance," as a whole, and is often used to present an action in summary form—*this happened, that happened*—without reference to how it happened and without viewing it as though happen*ing*. Imperfective aspect views an action "up close," from within it, and is often used to present an action as unfolding or in progress—*this was happening, that happens*—without reference to the whole action.[23]

Rather than primary concern with indicating the *time* at which an action took place, Greek verbs portray actions in this *spatial* way: from inside or outside the activity. Understanding Greek verbs in light of aspect will enable interpreters to avoid some common exegetical errors, such as claiming that all aorists are "punctiliar" in nature.[24] It will also enable interpreters to make better-informed decisions about what verbs are doing in context, by considering the combination of aspect, lexeme, and context.[25]

This is not the place to explore the issue further. It is enough to say that verbal aspect represents a major advance in our understanding of the language of the New Testament, with far-reaching implications for exegesis and translation. And as such, the modern study of the New Testament must incorporate insights based on aspect. Consequently, this is yet another area of serious New Testament study that is inaccessible to the student without facility in Greek.

Discourse Analysis

A similar advance in the modern study of the New Testament is known as discourse analysis. It is a burgeoning field and is one of the most exciting new areas related to Greek exegesis. Discourse analysis is an interdisciplinary approach to understanding how units of text relate to one another in order to create the theme, message, and structure of a text.[26] Discourse analysts

---

23. Campbell, *Advances in the Study of Greek*, 106–7.
24. Ibid., 120.
25. Ibid., 120–24.
26. Ibid., 148–49.

are interested in identifying *discourse markers*—elements of language that mark out units of text.

I summarize discourse analysis as follows:

> The simplest way to think of discourse analysis is that it deals with text beyond the level of the sentence—the pericope, paragraph, wider units, and the text as a whole. In this way, it has obvious overlap with the interests of literary analysis (such as theme and structure) and also with the interests of rhetorical analysis (such as the way in which ideas are communicated). Discourse analysis does not attempt to replace these more traditional modes of exegesis, but is complementary to them. The most distinctive contribution that discourse analysis brings alongside literary and rhetorical analysis is its robustly linguistic nature. It generally moves from the grammar and syntax of a text out to these larger textual concerns, rather than starting with the big picture.[27]

A prominent exponent of discourse analysis is Steven Runge. In his book *Discourse Grammar of the New Testament*, Runge explores Greek issues such as connectives (conjunctions and other conjunction-like words and phrases), forward-pointing devices, information structuring devices, and thematic highlighting devices.[28] Runge has presented the building blocks of Greek discourse and has taken a significant step forward for New Testament studies. The work complements conventional grammatical insights but is also well grounded in contemporary linguistic principles. Discourse analysis is another area of New Testament research that requires knowledge of Greek. An exciting and quickly influential method for research, its impact on New Testament studies will only increase in the coming decades.

Conclusion

In some ways nothing has changed since the situation from which A. T. Robertson wrote one hundred years ago. Knowledge of the Greek New

---

27. Ibid., 149.
28. Steven E. Runge, *Discourse Grammar of the Greek New Testament: A Practical Introduction for Teaching and Exegesis* (Bellingham: Lexham, 2010).

Testament is as essential as it ever was. And yet some preachers continue to resist the need to grasp its significance. The same objections are raised today as then: "Greek is for specialists." "If I can't use Greek in my sermons, why bother?" "Surely I am not going to do better than the fine commentaries in my library," and so forth. But such are the complaints of those who don't know what they are missing. They are the least qualified to judge the matter. No one with a working facility with the Greek of the New Testament would question its value for preaching and teaching. As we move further into the twenty-first century, it is my hope that the prevailing anti-intellectual, or just plain lazy, neglect of serious study of the Greek New Testament will take a backseat. It is time for all of us to be involved in the work of theological education and to regain a vision of the scholar-pastor, who is well equipped to be a faithful teacher of the Scriptures.

Questions for Further Reflection

1. Other than those raised in this chapter, what are some objections to the study of Greek in preparation for preaching and ministry?
2. Do you think the average congregation would more likely be encouraged or threatened by a pastor with good knowledge of Greek?
3. With various demands on the time of a pastor, what can be said of the priority of retaining (and perhaps improving) his Greek knowledge?

Sources for Further Study

Carson, D. A. *Exegetical Fallacies*, 2nd ed. Grand Rapids: Baker, 1996.
Campbell, Constantine R. *Advances in the Study of Greek: New Insights for Reading the New Testament*. Grand Rapids: Zondervan, 2015.
Robertson, A. T. *The Minister and His Greek New Testament*. 1923; repr. Birmingham: Solid Ground Christian Books, 2008.

Chapter Eight

Introduction to the Old Testament

ERIC J. TULLY

As a teenager I attended a church whose motto was, "The Bible, the whole Bible, and nothing but the Bible." It was printed on leaflets and recited, from time to time, in sermons and congregational meetings. Some days the motto seemed a bit hackneyed, adapted as it was from the oath that witnesses take in a courtroom. I also found it comforting because it was an explicit reminder that we knew *all* Scripture to be authoritative. The whole Bible, Old and New Testaments, was the final arbiter of truth and our guide for faith and practice. Yet, if my memories are correct, the Sunday morning, evening, and Wednesday prayer meeting sermons were always taken from one of the New Testament epistles. In Sunday school and youth group we studied the New Testament. There were exceptions: Isaiah 6 was mentioned on Missionary Sunday and Micah 5 at Christmas, but these were rare; there was no sustained proclamation of the Old Testament. How strange that a church that articulated a ministry based on "the whole Bible" should, in practice, neglect more than 75 percent of it.

The Need to Study the Old Testament

In fact, my experience as a teenager is common. Personal convictions and doctrinal statements on the inspiration and authority of the Old Testament are not always reflected in ministry priorities. While children are taught some of the Old Testament stories, adults encounter the Old Testament

(OT) only in piecemeal: sermon illustrations, decontextualized references in regard to social ethics or messianic prophecies, wisdom from a proverb, and perhaps a psalm here or there. This relative neglect of the OT is understandable when we think about the difficulties it presents to the modern reader.

First, the OT takes place in a foreign world. The authors and original readers of the OT lived long ago in a different culture and society. Imagine life in a small village where the most important political authority is one's grandfather. During the day the children do not go to school; they stay home to work in the fields and to help make the daily food. At night, goats and sheep sleep in the house, on the ground floor, while the family takes advantage of their body heat by sleeping in the loft above. If they want to eat meat, they have to kill it themselves—there are no grocery stores. The new technology everyone is talking about is iron or a new mixture of clay for pots.

Second, modern readers struggle with the geographic and historical references that fill the text. How many of us can find Hebron or Edom on a map? How many modern readers understand the political implications of the Syro-Ephraimite coalition, which threatens Judah in Isaiah 7? We have enough difficulty remembering the major players in World War I.

In some cases the values in the OT seem primitive and barbaric. The OT regulates slaves, commands the annihilation of the inhabitants of the Promised Land, and requires a sacrifice following a woman's menstrual period. In our own family devotions one evening, I was faced with explaining to my two young daughters why David (good king David!) killed an Amalekite man on the spot after he admitted to killing King Saul, who would have died anyway (2 Sam 1).

Worship in the OT can seem foreign to us as well. In contrast to our own church services, which often include doughnuts, padded seating, and PowerPoint slides, worship in the OT is raw and earthy. In Exodus 24, Moses slaughters oxen and then throws some of the blood on the people. In Deuteronomy 21, the people are told to take a cow into the valley, break its neck, and then wash their hands over it. In the psalms we find laments and curses in which the authors cry bitterly and call on God to destroy their enemies. The prophets illustrate their messages with bizarre sign acts. Isaiah is told to walk around naked (Isa 20:2). Ezekiel is told to cook his food over human excrement (Ezek 4:12) and to refrain from weeping for his deceased wife (Ezek 24:16).

These few examples illustrate why many Christians struggle to understand the OT and why many pastors are wary of teaching and preaching it. It is challenging to understand the text, to create interest in the congregation, to integrate the text with Christian theology, and to make it relevant in a modern context. Nevertheless, if we are to preach and teach the whole counsel of God, we must not neglect the OT.

The Old Testament Is Scripture

Whenever the New Testament (NT) refers to "Scripture," it is referring to the OT. Paul says in 2 Tim 3:16–17, "All Scripture [i.e., Genesis–Malachi] is inspired by God and is profitable for teaching, for rebuking, for correcting, for training in righteousness, so that the man of God may be complete, equipped for every good work." Here Paul is speaking of the OT, which he considers to be not only inspired and the words of God but also useful and relevant in church ministry. He goes on to charge Timothy to persist in proclaiming the message whether convenient or not (2 Tim 4:1–2). The OT can lead people to faith in Christ, as when Philip led the Ethiopian eunuch to faith and baptism after they read together the book of Isaiah (Acts 8:27–39).

The OT was Jesus's Bible. He states in John 10:35 that "Scripture [i.e. the OT] cannot be broken." In the book of Luke, he does not pick and choose only portions of the OT that he deems relevant. Rather, he refers to the entire OT canon when he says, "Everything written about me in the Law of Moses, the Prophets, and the Psalms must be fulfilled" (Luke 24:44–45).[1] We see Jesus's knowledge of, and reliance on, the OT when he is tempted by Satan in the wilderness in Matthew 4. Jesus responds to Satan with Deut 8:3 ("Man does not live on bread alone"); 6:16 ("Do not test the Lord your God") and 6:13 ("Fear the Lord your God, worship him"). The OT was authoritative for Jesus and was the foundational guide for his life. He uses it to establish his identity as the Christ, quoting from Ps 110:1

---

1. In the Hebrew OT (the Masoretic text), the OT is divided into three parts: the Law (Genesis–Deuteronomy), the Prophets (Joshua–Malachi), and the Writings (Psalms–2 Chronicles). Jesus's reference to "the Law of Moses, the Prophets, and the Psalms" is a reference to each of these three parts and is thus a reference to the whole OT canon, from beginning to end.

(Matt 22:41–46). On the cross he speaks Ps 22:1 as a lament over his own death (Matt 27:46).

The Old Testament Has a Distinctive Message

Living on this side of the cross, we may be tempted to question the enduring theological significance of the OT. We may ask, even explicitly, Is the OT about Christ? To what extent? We know the NT teaches that Jesus Christ is the climax of God's redemptive program. The assumption is that unless we can demonstrate that the OT is directly about Christ, it may be theologically outdated and has lost its legitimacy in a Christian context. But Jesus and the writers of the NT had the opposite perspective. Their concern was to use the OT to legitimize the NT. The genealogies in Matthew and Luke, the OT allusions in the Gospels, the statements that Jesus had fulfilled OT prophecy, and references to major points in the grand narrative of redemption are there not to maintain the OT's relevance but to demonstrate that Christ's ministry and the church were in keeping with what the OT had promised.

We may be tempted to say that we cannot understand the OT without the NT. If the NT reveals Jesus Christ, then how can we hope to understand the OT without direct and explicit reference to him? But this is backward. The OT allows us to properly understand the NT. Beginning with the NT (or focusing exclusively on it) is like joining a conversation already in progress at a party. You don't know what everyone has been saying, but they are presupposing all that has been said already and are basing arguments on points already agreed upon.[2] Similarly, when we start with the NT, it is like coming in at the climax of a complex dramatic novel or film—too late to comprehend the significance of what is happening. We have no sense of who God is, who we are, how we relate to God in our sinful state, what God's holiness requires, the inability of people (even God's chosen people) to solve their rebellion, and the lengths to which God will go to show mercy.

In reality, the chronological and cultural foreignness of the OT is one of the reasons it has so much to say to us today. People are always inclined to think their own values, in their own historical and social contexts, are the

---

2. Christopher Wright, *How to Preach and Teach the Old Testament for All Its Worth* (Grand Rapids: Zondervan, 2016), 20.

right ones. They are also inclined to think their values and the values taught in the Bible must be the same, and they look for ways to conform the two.³ The writers of the OT, separated from us geographically, chronologically, and socially, have the opportunity to reveal our blind spots and to critique conventional wisdom, which we take for granted but is sometimes deeply problematic. For example, the OT has a particular interest in care for the poor and justice for the oppressed. The psalms provide models of prayer, and it may be worth considering that our reflex against lament and cursing is actually an indicator that our own spirituality is anemic and out of balance. In the OT we read about the people of God who have gone before us. We have been grafted into the people of Israel (Rom 11:17), and these are our spiritual ancestors. One writer states, "What we really need is to be brought out of ourselves by seeing our lives set in the context of a bigger picture, a bigger story, the gospel story. . . . Yet we are so overwhelmed by our emptiness, isolation and insignificance that we don't pay attention."⁴

The testaments have continuity between them but not total overlap. The OT is preparatory for the NT in some ways, but it teaches us things about God, the world, and ourselves that the NT does not repeat. We cannot teach and preach only the NT (only 25 percent of the Bible) and expect our hearers to be well fed spiritually.

We Must Study, Teach, and Preach the OT Because It Is Difficult

The difficulty and foreignness of the OT is more reason to study it, not less. If there are historical and cultural gaps to be overcome, if the OT presents theological challenges, if we and the people to whom we minister find it problematic, then that is all the more reason we must study it seriously in order to understand it well. If a theologically trained pastor avoids the OT, how much more will the laypeople in the congregation avoid it? The pastor must commit to the time required to bridge the gaps, showing that the claims in the text are accessible, relevant, and authoritative.

In the academy as well, we must avoid decontextualized readings that ignore the gaps between ancient writers and modern readers and assume

---

3. John Goldingay, *Do We Really Need the New Testament? Letting the Old Testament Speak for Itself* (Downers Grove: IVP Academic, 2015), 148.
4. Ibid., 106.

that their respective questions, concerns, and values are exactly the same. We must let the OT text have its own voice, challenging preconceptions and critiquing imbalances. Theological education requires integration of the OT with other fields of study such as NT, church history, systematic theology, and practical theology; but it also requires a sustained and disciplined investigation in the OT itself, ensuring that we are not imposing our ideas on the text but rather learning from it and submitting to its authority as God's inspired and inerrant Word.

Five Major Aspects of the Study of the Old Testament

Formal, academic study of the OT addresses the gaps and foreignness of the text mentioned above through a wide variety of methods. In reality, it is difficult even to talk about the discipline of OT study. Rather, the field consists of a number of subdisciplines, each of which looks at a different aspect of the biblical text (though with significant overlap). The five major aspects of the study of the OT are (1) textual criticism; (2) history, archaeology, and ancient Near Eastern backgrounds; (3) the study of the composition of the text; (4) literary and linguistic exegesis; and (5) biblical theology. The order in this list is logical, not an indication of importance. It does not necessarily represent the order or proportion in which these subjects are taught in a theological curriculum.

The Establishment of the Text: Textual Criticism

Before we can interpret the OT text, we must know which text we are interpreting. The OT comes to us in the form of many ancient manuscripts, in the original Hebrew and in other languages. These were copied by hand, and therefore differ from one another in both insignificant and sometimes significant ways. The most important manuscripts are the Hebrew Masoretic text (early eleventh century AD), the Hebrew Dead Sea Scrolls (second century BC), the Hebrew Samaritan Pentateuch (second century BC), the Greek Septuagint (third–first centuries BC), the Syriac Peshitta (second–third century AD), the Aramaic Targums (second century BC to first century AD), and the Latin Vulgate (fourth century AD).[5]

---

5. For an overview of these witnesses to the OT text, see Ellis R. Brotzman and Eric J. Tully, *Old Testament Textual Criticism: A Practical Introduction* (Grand Rapids: Baker, 2016), chapters 3–4.

For example, there is a variant reading in Hos 14:2. The ESV translates, "We will pay with bulls the vows of our lips." In the Hebrew Masoretic text, the word "bulls" is *pr^{y}m*. The NIV, however, translates "that we may offer the fruit of our lips," based on the reading of the Greek Septuagint which apparently represents the Hebrew word *pr^y* ("fruit"). The difference between the two words "bulls" and "fruit" is only one letter: m. Complicating matters is the fact that the letter "m" at the end of a word in Hebrew can be an extra letter that is not translated. Therefore, it is possible that the Hebrew also intends to say "fruit" (i.e., the "m" is an extra letter) or that the Greek translator read the word *pr^{y}m* ("bulls") and interpreted the "m" as extra when it was not intended to be so!

This brief example shows the complexity of textual criticism. In one sense it is a science because it requires knowledge of languages (Hebrew, Greek, Aramaic, Syriac, and Latin), an understanding of scribal practice and manuscript production, and awareness of translation theory and interpretive skills. But textual criticism is also an art because the scholar must weigh evidence and evaluate variant readings, reconstruct historical processes, and choose the best text. But the challenges of textual criticism are not grounds for ignoring it. I heard Dennis Magary, one of my department colleagues, say, "If you decide not to do textual criticism, you've just done it." That is to say, if we privilege one manuscript (such as the Hebrew text) by default, then we have just accepted all of the distinctive readings in that text even though they may not always be the best and most accurate.

The World Around the Text: Archaeology, History, and Ancient Near Eastern Comparative Literature

As mentioned above, the OT was written in and refers to a particular geographical, historical, and cultural context different from our own. This ancient context is not simply the literary setting for the text as we would find in historical fiction. The authors of the OT anchor God's revelation in historical events. God brought his people out of slavery in Egypt; met with them in the theophany on Mount Sinai; provided manna, water, and quail in the wilderness; and defeated their enemies in the Promised Land. In these acts he not only revealed his character and power, but he also initiated relationships and furthered his redemptive purposes in actual people, in history, as he worked to bring an actual, historical Christ to die on the cross and rise again.

The historical context also matters because, though superintended by the Holy Spirit, human authors who lived and worked in that ancient world wrote the OT. As with any communication, the authors depend on a shared network of knowledge, experiences, and concerns with their implied readers.[6] Consider how in this chapter I have referred to modern realities such as "Wednesday evening prayer meeting" and my "department colleague" as well as to "doughnuts" and a "map," none of which an ancient Israelite reader would understand. In the same way, ancient biblical authors encode the text in distinctive literary genres and refer to politics, economic values, social statuses, and many other features of everyday life that were automatically understood by the original readers but require some additional study from us. It has been said that the OT was not written *to* us, but it was written *for* us.

The first window into this world around the OT text is archaeology. Excavations in Israel, Palestine, Egypt, Jordan, Lebanon, and Syria have uncovered dramatic material remains that teach us about daily life and assist with dating historical events. Foundations of houses and city walls provide insight into construction techniques, fortification systems, city planning, and population size. We learn about ancient agriculture from extant olive presses, wine vats, and clay jars used for storage. Seals and seal impressions as well as receipts for services rendered are remnants of ancient administration. The many wars referenced in the Bible are vividly illuminated by the discovery of weapons such as arrowheads, spear tips, and sling stones. The authors of the OT frequently condemn unorthodox worship and commitment to pagan idols. Evidence of these is everywhere in the form of temple complexes, altars, incense stands, and small figurines of calves and women with enlarged breasts and genitalia, possibly connected to fertility religion. Students in the theological curriculum can study archaeology in the classroom, but there are also often opportunities to participate in excavations in

---

6. *Implied reader* is a literary term that refers to the reader the author had in mind when he was writing. This is distinguished from the actual reader. For example, my implied reader in this chapter is someone who is not an expert in the field of OT but is seeking to gain a basic understanding of the discipline. Others, such as my department colleagues, may read the chapter, but they are not the ones to whom I am writing.

the Middle East. There in the hot sun they dig, carry dirt, clean pottery, and learn the scientific methods of survey and conduct excavations firsthand.

A second window into the world around the OT text is geography. The Bible is set not only in a particular time; it is set in particular places. Climate and available natural resources determine settlement patterns, crop selection, and wealth. Settlement leads to trade, administrative bureaucracies, and warfare. Geography affects troop movements and strategic military objectives. Sometimes the biblical authors use characteristics of the setting as a major element in the narrative. One fascinating example is found in Judg 16:3 when Samson rips up the city gates of Gaza and carries them to Hebron during the night. Readers unfamiliar with those two locations may not realize that this is a distance of some forty miles! If Samson walked three miles per hour, this would have meant he carried massive gates, uphill, for thirteen hours. His miraculous strength is even more impressive with knowledge of the geography.

A third window into the world around the text comes in the form of extrabiblical texts from the period of the OT. Some of these have been discovered in the land of Israel. For example, the inscription from the Siloam Tunnel tells of the celebration when King Hezekiah's workers finally completed the underground channel designed to provide water to Jerusalem during the coming siege by the Assyrian army (cf. 2 Kgs 20:20). In the Lachish Letters, a short note written in ink on a broken piece of pottery reveals communication between Judahite soldiers during the Babylonian siege of the city of Lachish, the second most important city in Judah after Jerusalem (cf. Jer 34:7). In addition to inscriptions from ancient Israel, there are thousands of texts from the ancient Near East (ANE) written in Ugaritic, Aramaic, Sumerian, Egyptian, and Akkadian as well as other languages and dialects.

It is difficult to overstate the significance of these extrabiblical texts for our study of the OT. They provide valuable linguistic data for research in the Semitic language family that in turn improves our understanding of biblical Hebrew. Just as importantly, they assist us in identifying the genres used by biblical authors. For example, we have examples of treaties and covenants between kings and their subservient lords that contain the same elements and follow the same pattern as the covenant between God and Israel in Exodus 20–25. Actually, it might be more accurate to say that God followed the pattern of *those* covenants. By using conventional social and political patterns from the time period, God formalized the relationship with his people in a way they would understand with all of its implications and entailments. We could give many more examples, including comparison of Genesis 1–3 with ancient accounts of the beginning of the world, comparisons of the book of Joshua with ancient conquest accounts,[7] and comparisons of Egyptian poetry with the Song of Songs.[8] Finally, extrabiblical texts provide us with historical information and convey the values and beliefs of the peoples that lived around Israel and interacted with them.

Some in theological education get nervous about comparative literature as a hermeneutical key to the Bible, believing it could skew interpretation or impoverish its canonical and theological meaning. There is a spectrum of views, even among OT scholars, on how much knowledge of the ancient context and background of the OT is necessary in order to interpret it correctly.[9] In my view the text itself is sufficient to apprehend the author's essential meaning, but the interpreter who understands the historical and social background will gain a great deal of insight in important nuances, distinctions, and implications.[10] Studying the ancient Near East context of the OT is part of doing all we can to join the authors and their original readers in that network of shared knowledge on which they depend in order to communicate accurately and effectively.

---

7. See K. Lawson Younger, *Ancient Conquest Accounts: A Study in Ancient Near Eastern and Biblical History Writing* (Sheffield: JSOT Press, 1990).

8. Michael V. Fox, *The Song of Songs and the Ancient Egyptian Love Songs* (Madison: University of Wisconsin, 1985).

9. On one end of the spectrum, we might place John Walton who writes, "Israel, while being the recipient of divine revelation that gave her a unique theological distinctiveness, reflected in many ways the culture of the ancient Near East. Such a reflection implies that Israelite thinking *cannot be understood in isolation from its ancient Near Eastern cultural context,*" Ancient Israelite Literature in Its Cultural Context (Grand Rapids: Regency, 1989), 13 (emphasis added). On the other end of the spectrum, we might find John Sailhammer who argues that the biblical authors tell us everything we need to know. For Sailhammer, when we bring extrabiblical knowledge to the text, we are potentially undermining the specific focus of the author. This is because, "as far as the reader is concerned, the world of historical events (*res gestae*) in the Bible comes mediated through the 'textual world' (*verba*) . . . [N]o matter how true or accurate the text is, the accuracy of the Scriptures should not be allowed to obscure the fact that the text is, in fact a representation of those actual events," *Introduction to Old Testament Theology: A Canonical Approach* (Grand Rapids: Zondervan, 1999), 45.

10. Meir Sternberg argues that the Bible is a "foolproof composition." He writes, "I mean that the Bible is difficult to read, easy to underread and overread and even misread, but virtually impossible to, so to speak, counterread," *The Poetics of Biblical Narrative* (Bloomington: Indiana University Press, 1985), 50.

The History of the Text: Higher Criticism

The formal study of the OT involves not only the history *in* the text (i.e., the history to which the text refers) but the history *of* the text (i.e., how it came to be in the form we have in our Bibles). As long as there have been texts, there has been an interest in authorship and the interpretive significance of how and when a text was written. (See Jesus's argument about Davidic authorship of Psalm 110 in the example above from Matt 22:41–46.) In the Middle Ages a heightened interest in Jewish *peshat* ("straight" or "literal") interpretation of the OT (as opposed to interpretation which explored theological implications) led to more interest in certain details that might be clues to the authorship and formation of a book. Then, in the Enlightenment period, especially in nineteenth-century Europe, scholars who sought to interpret the text within a naturalistic worldview and the scientific method developed methods of higher criticism. (These methods are referred to as "higher" criticism because they build upon the establishment of the text in textual ("lower") criticism. "Criticism" does not necessarily mean scholars critique the text, only that they think critically, analyzing it with rigorous methodology rather than being guided by tradition.)[11]

One example of a higher critical method is *source criticism*, which seeks to identify and recover the written sources that lie behind the biblical text. Some biblical authors claim explicitly that they have drawn on sources (e.g. 1 Kgs 14:19; 1 Chr 9:1). In other cases two biblical passages are identical, indicating either dependence or a mutual source (e.g. Isa 36–39/2 Kgs 18:13–20:19). However, source criticism is usually concerned with uncovering hypothetical sources in biblical texts that do not claim to be made up of sources—as in the case of the Pentateuch. Sources are identified using a list of criteria: (1) variations in style and vocabulary; (2) contradictions and inconsistencies; (3) duplications and repetitions; and (4) ideological patterns. For example, if two paragraphs seem to repeat the story, perhaps they originally came from two different sources. Or, if two paragraphs seem to have different views about the nature of God, that would also indicate they were originally from two different sources—from two different authors—and were combined into the text we have now.

---

11. Of course, the guild of critical biblical scholarship, like any field, has established its own tradition which functions to determine what is "orthodox" and what is not.

If valid, there are several reasons this could be important for interpretation. First, how should we talk about the historical context of a passage? Did Moses write it in the wilderness? Or was it written by two different authors, separated by three hundred years, in completely different times in Israel's history, with different theological views? Second, what is the literary context of the passage? One of the key rules of interpretation is that we must also consider what has been said before and after a given passage. But if the text is made up of different sources, what constitutes the context?

A	*B*	*A*	*B*	*A*
(vv. 1–4)	(v. 5)	(vv. 6–8)	(vv. 9–14)	(vv. 15–16)

In this hypothetical example, the context of verses 6–8 would originally have been verses 1–4 and verses 15–16. Theoretically, all of the passages from source A could be pulled out of the biblical text and linked together to form a continuous whole. According to mainstream critical biblical scholars, interpretation that does not take into account these hypothetical sources is simplistic and naïve. We must account not only for the synchronic dimension of the text (i.e., the form we have in our Bibles) but its diachronic (i.e., "through time") development.

Source criticism not only has implications for interpretation, but it also potentially enables scholars to reconstruct the history of Israel behind the text. Practitioners of this methodology often conclude that in its final form (again, the form we have in our Bibles), the OT text is a melting pot of theological views and ideologies that lost their distinctive character when they were combined. However, if we can identify distinct sources in the text that come from different individuals and time periods, then we have "strata" that can show the development of ideas and perspectives over the course of Israelite history. The most famous and influential of these attempts was that of Julius Wellhausen (1844–1918), a German scholar who identified, on the basis of the work of previous scholars, four earlier sources which comprise the Pentateuch: J (c. 950 BC), E (c. 750 BC), D (c. 650 BC), and P (c. 550 BC). Wellhausen argued that by reading each of the four sources independently, one could see theological and religious trajectories in ancient Israel.[12] For example, in J and E the authors believed Israelites

---

12. Julius Wellhausen, *Prolegomena to the History of Israel* (1885; Eugene, OR: Wipf and Stock, 2003).

could worship at many different altars and locations throughout the land. One hundred years later the author of D believed worship was only legitimate if it took place in Jerusalem. Finally, one hundred years later, after the Babylonian exile, the author(s) of P *assume* centralized worship and believe it must be accompanied by a technical, complex priestly apparatus.[13] These views have come under increasing criticism in the past fifty years, although they are still the basic view of many scholars.

These higher critical methods, and especially the presuppositions that go along with them, have had profound ramifications on the study of the OT. For one thing, there is a consensus that much of the OT is the result of internal wrangling between groups and authors of opposing views. Although later editors have attempted to smooth over these inconsistencies and contradictions, they can still be perceived in the biblical text. John J. Collins writes, "The internal pluralism of the Bible, both theological and ethical, has been established beyond dispute."[14] The consensus therefore runs counter, in many cases, to the Bible's own claims about its authorship and provenance. Mainstream critical scholars usually deny the possibility (or necessity) of predictive prophecy and view statements about the religious faith of Israel as fragmentary and descriptive rather than authoritative, unified, and prescriptive.

It may be helpful to illustrate the ramifications of mainstream higher criticism by contrasting two different views of the OT text. The first diagram below represents an evangelical high view of Scripture that holds to the authority, inspiration, and inerrancy of the biblical text. This view takes seriously the internal claims of Scripture and has confidence in the trustworthiness of the biblical authors.

---

13. Ibid., 17–51.
14. John J. Collins, *The Bible After Babel* (Grand Rapids: Eerdmans, 2005), 160–61.

THEOLOGY, CHURCH, AND MINISTRY

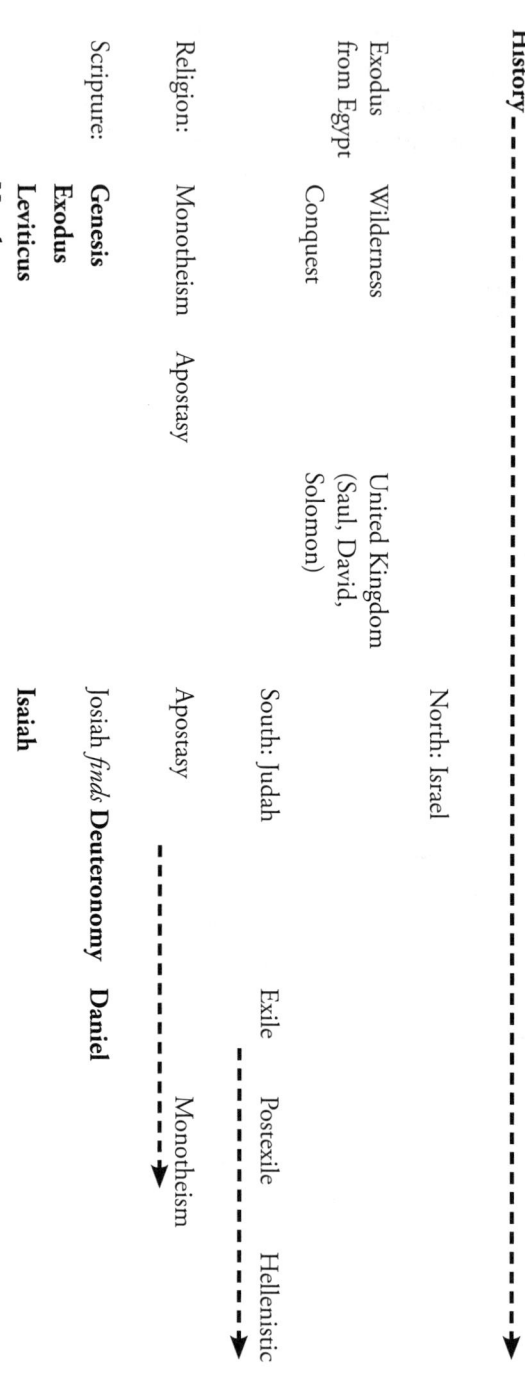

History						
		North: Israel				
Exodus from Egypt	Wilderness	United Kingdom (Saul, David, Solomon)	South: Judah		Exile	Postexile Hellenistic
	Conquest					
Religion:	Monotheism	Apostasy	Apostasy			Monotheism
Scripture:			Josiah *finds* **Deuteronomy**	**Daniel**		
			Isaiah			
	Genesis					
	Exodus					
	Leviticus					
	Numbers					

The evangelical view holds that the vast majority of the Pentateuch (Genesis–Deuteronomy) was written by Moses in the wilderness period after God brought Israel out of slavery in Egypt.[15] God revealed himself to Moses and Israel on Mount Sinai at that time, explaining that he was the only true God and that Israel would be tempted to polytheism once they entered the Promised Land. He also anticipated the establishment of a holy city (Jerusalem) where he would dwell with his people. Much later the prophet Isaiah ministered in the seventh century in Jerusalem and foresaw, in great detail, the Babylonian exile. Isaiah's predictive prophecy was a major proof that God could and would save. First, he would return Israel from exile. Later, in the undefined future, he would transform Israel spiritually along with the entire world. In 2 Kings 22, Josiah initiates repairs to the Jerusalem temple and finds "the book of the law" which had been long discarded. This was probably the book of Deuteronomy, because its discovery led to nationwide reforms that relate to the distinctive concerns therein. During the exile the prophet Daniel ministered and foresaw not only things in the immediate future but also the distant future of God's redemptive program in detail. Thus, the evangelical view has a high view of the Bible's historical accuracy. Monotheism was the creed of Israel from the beginning, but the nation fell into polytheism and apostasy, which led to the exile. Predictive prophecy is an essential part of the prophetic office both in the short term and in the eschatological future.

A second view is that of mainstream critical scholars. In reality, there are many different critical views, but the following diagram is an oversimplified illustration of one version of the classical view.

---

15. There is some evidence that later scribes or editors made updates to the text here and there. In addition, most evangelical scholars believe someone else wrote the narrative of Moses's own death in Deut 34.

"Memory" - - - - - -> History ->

Exodus   Wilderness   United Kingdom   North: Israel———
from Egypt   (Saul, David,
          Conquest   Solomon)
                                        South: Judah———| Exile   Postexile   Hellenistic

Religion: Polytheism   Monolatry   Monotheism

Scripture: J(ahwist) E(lohist) D(eut)   P(riestly)
                                              1st Isaiah   2nd Isaiah
                                                           ↑
                                                           - - - - - - - Daniel

In this view we have no reliable documentary evidence of Israel's history prior to the time of King David (c. 1000 BC).[16] Prior to that, the biblical narrative is "historical memory" which may contain nuggets of reliable history but otherwise consists of legends and tales. Parts of Genesis through Deuteronomy (the sources: J, E, D, and P) were written during the course of the Israelite monarchies, but the shape and final completion of the Pentateuch comes from the period after the exile. Although 2 Kings 22 states that the supporters of King Josiah *found* the book of the law / Deuteronomy, in reality they *wrote* Deuteronomy at that time in order to reinforce the religious reforms they had already planned in an effort to solidify their power. As mentioned above, the sources of the Pentateuch reflect an evolution of Israelite faith. Israel did not enter the Promised Land by conquest (as told in the book of Joshua). Rather, the nation of Israel was formed when Canaanites already in the Promised Land formed a new group around the worship of a god named Yahweh. Thus, Israel's faith evolved over time from an initial polytheism to monolatry,[17] and eventually to monotheism. Only parts of the book of Isaiah (i.e., some of chapters 1–39) come from the prophet Isaiah, whom critical scholars call *First Isaiah*. Later, anonymous authors who lived in the times they discuss wrote other parts of the book. Therefore, what looks like predictive prophecy is actually commentary on the prophets' contemporary circumstances. Likewise, the book of Daniel comes from an anonymous author in the Hellenistic period who reviews the past and constructs it to look like predictive prophecy for effect.

Critical biblical scholars are asking important questions, and there is much to be learned from their detailed and sophisticated analysis. There are also perils, for the consensus view is often incompatible with a high view of Scripture. Future pastors must be trained to evaluate scholarly claims, to read commentaries judiciously, and to serve as a resource for their congregations. There is also a need for evangelical students with deep convictions, who love Scripture and submit to its claims on their lives, to study the OT at a high academic level and to contribute to the work on these kinds of pressing questions that concern the history of the biblical text.

---

16. Note that some scholars would argue that we have no reliable history in the Bible until later in the divided kingdom period or even after the exile.

17. *Monolatry* is the belief that many gods exist, but it is appropriate to worship only one of them. *Monotheism* is the belief that only one god exists.

The Message in the Text: Exegesis

The fourth aspect of OT study—exegesis—refers to reading and analyzing the text for the purpose of uncovering the author's intended meaning. We do not want to foist our own values and ideas on the text; rather, we want to let it speak fully and freely to us as God's authoritative Word. In exegesis (from Greek, "to lead out of") we seek to derive meaning *out of* the text.

Exegesis that allows the biblical text to speak on its own terms is "historical-grammatical exegesis." It is historical in the sense that we are seeking to uncover the author's intended meaning in his original literary and historical context. Once this is established, we can apply that meaning to our own varied situations. It is grammatical because we seek to understand the biblical text according to the natural, linguistic sense of the words. We do not, for example, mine the text for secret theological meanings below the surface. Therefore, exegesis involves dialogue with the three aspects of the study of the OT surveyed above: (1) the establishment of the best text; (2) the historical, social, and literary context; and (3) a consideration of the identity, time period, and audience of the author.

The ability to read the text in the original languages of Hebrew and Aramaic is an important skill for exegesis (see chapter 7). This allows the interpreter to observe the particular choices the author has made: one word instead of another, this preposition instead of that one, this certain verbal tense, and so forth. Biblical authors write with precision and intentionality in order to emphasize certain elements or to avoid ambiguity. The ability to detect these choices in the original language is a significant advantage in interpretation.

Another key tool in exegesis is literary analysis. In many cases the literary texts of the Bible are not reducible to propositional statements. The authors want to make us feel something; they want to engage us.[18] Like linguistic analysis, literary analysis is another way of observing the particular choices of the author. How the author tells a story or shapes a

---

18. Note, for example, the difference between the propositional statement, "Do not murder" (Exod 20:13), and the narrative of the Cain and Abel episode (Gen 4). After Cain kills his brother, God says to him, "What have you done? Your brother's blood cries out to me from the ground!" Longmand and Ryken point out that the narrative does not even use the word "murder," but it affects us. In watching these events unfold, we have not merely been given new information. We have undergone an experience. Tremper Longman III and Leland Ryken, "Introduction," in *A Complete Literary Guide to the Bible* (Grand Rapids: Zondervan, 1993), 17.

prophetic oracle is often the key to his purpose. In the literary analysis of narrative, we examine the author's use of characterization, plot, and the shaping of time. In the analysis of poetry, we examine the poetic structure and use of figurative language. This overlaps with our discussion above about the importance of genre. Biblical authors use the genres of history, law, wisdom, lament, praise, oracles of judgment, oracles of salvation, and prophecy, among others, to set up reader expectations.[19]

The Entailments of the Text: Old Testament Theology

The final aspect of the study of the OT is moving from exegesis (what the text says) to theology (what it teaches). Here we seek to answer questions such as, What is God like? What is his redemptive plan? Who are we? What is the nature of sin? How can we be in relationship with God? How should we worship him? What is ethical behavior for the people of God? What is the meaning of our lives and our deaths? What does the future hold for us?

There is great diversity in the field of OT theology. Phyllis Trible writes, "Biblical theologians, though coming from a circumscribed community, have never agreed on the definition, method, organization, subject matter, point of view, or purpose of their enterprise."[20] There are several inherent challenges in the discipline of OT theology. First, the OT is large and complex. Second, scholars have often struggled to find the theological center of the OT: is it the idea of covenant? Communion with God? Promise? The choice of one center may make it difficult to include all parts of the OT canon (e.g. Wisdom literature). Third, how should we relate the OT to the NT? There is a tension here. On the one hand, the OT needs to have its own voice, to speak for itself with all of its distinctives intact. On the other hand, it needs to relate to the NT as part of one biblical canon—one story—that tells of God's one redemptive plan.

Conclusion

The OT is not a long introduction to the important part of the Bible (the NT); it is not just a prologue. It is the Word of God, just as relevant for

---

19. See D. Brent Sandy and Ronald L. Giese, *Cracking Old Testament Codes: A Guide to Interpreting Literary Genres of the Old Testament* (Nashville: B&H, 1995).

20. Phyllis Trible, "Five Loaves and Two Fishes: Feminist Hermeneutics and Biblical Theology," *Theological Studies* 50, no. 2 (1989), 282.

us today as it was three thousand years ago in the time of David and two thousand years ago when it was studied and quoted by Jesus. As individuals, we need to read and study the OT. To study it is to study the majority of Scripture as the whole counsel of God. In the pages of the OT, we get to know God through story, law, poetry, and prophetic oracle. If the OT seems foreign and problematic, this may be an indication that we are too much a product of our own time and culture and that we have constructed a god in our own image. We need the OT to speak to us with authority about its own distinctive concerns including God's holiness, the destructive nature of sin, the source and character of true wisdom, the need for social justice, the dangers of idolatry, and the ultimate victory of God. In the OT we join those who have gone before us in a historical faith, and we see our place in the long development of God's plan of redemption.

The church needs the OT as well. It needs to hear not only offhand references and to read children's Bible stories but to encounter sustained, serious proclamation. The people in our churches need theologically trained teachers and preachers who have confidence, conviction, and competence to lead them in the study of the OT.

The academy needs the OT. Those who have expertise in the OT can speak into other disciplines in an integrative and cooperative environment. The study of the OT can make significant contributions in disciplines such as apologetics (e.g., the defense of Scripture), practical theology (e.g., worship and preaching), New Testament (e.g., the use of the OT in the NT), and systematic theology (e.g., worldview and ethics).

> *"His delight is in the LORD's instruction,*
> *and he meditates on it day and night."*
>
> (PS 1:1–2)

Questions for Further Reflection

1. What do you think is the most significant reason Christians avoid the OT? Has that been your experience? Are there other reasons, apart from those described in this chapter? How might we address those concerns?

2. In what ways does the OT prepare us, theologically, for the advent of Christ in the NT?

3. What is your perspective on the place of contextual studies (such as archeology and ancient Near Eastern texts) in the study of the OT? How necessary are they?
4. Consider the contrast in presuppositions and methods between an evangelical view of Scripture and that of the mainstream consensus. What are the theological ramifications of the mainstream approach? If you studied the OT in that environment, what would be nonnegotiable?
5. How is the study of the OT different from the study of the NT? How is it the same?

Sources for Further Study

Bar-Efrat, Shimeon. *Narrative Art in the Bible.* Bible and Literature Series, vol. 17. Sheffield: Almond, 1989.

Barton, John. *Reading the Old Testament.* Louisville: Westminster John Knox, 1996.

Brotzman, Ellis R., and Eric J. Tully. *Old Testament Textual Criticism: A Practical Introduction.* 2nd ed. Grand Rapids: Baker Academic, 2016.

Chisholm, Robert B. *Interpreting the Historical Books: An Exegetical Handbook.* Grand Rapids: Kregel Publications, 2006.

Futato, Mark David. *Interpreting the Psalms: An Exegetical Handbook.* Grand Rapids: Kregel Publications, 2007.

Goldingay, John. *Do We Need the New Testament? Letting the Old Testament Speak for Itself.* Downers Grove: IVP Academic, 2015.

King, Philip J., and Lawrence E. Stager. *Life in Biblical Israel.* 1st ed. Library of Ancient Israel. Louisville, KY: Westminster John Knox Press, 2001.

Provan, Iain, V. Philips Long, and Tremper Longman III. *A Biblical History of Israel.* 2nd ed. Louisville: Westminster John Knox, 2015.

Smith, Gary, and David M. Howard Jr. *Interpreting the Prophetic Books: An Exegetical Handbook.* Grand Rapids: Kregel Academic, 2014.

Vogt, Peter T. *Interpreting the Pentateuch: An Exegetical Handbook.* Handbooks for Old Testament Exegesis. Grand Rapids: Kregel, 2009.

Chapter Nine

INTRODUCTION TO THE NEW TESTAMENT

RAY VAN NESTE

The goal of theological education is to know God, the true God of the world, whom we must worship and serve. Indeed, this is the ultimate aim of all of life (John 17:3; Jer 9:23–24). Constant attention to this goal by both educators and learners can prevent the deadening of theological education. We've all seen the student, once passionate about Jesus and evangelism, engaging in a type of theological study that dampens his zeal to an extent that he is only interested in the finer points of theology. However, there is a course of study that, if properly imbibed, will lead to a flowering of the student's love for God. The centerpiece of this curriculum must be the fullest revelation of God, God's disclosure of himself that comes in the New Testament (NT).

Systematic theology contemplates the character and perfection of the God we love, and *ethics* explores the way he calls us to live. *Church history* tells us the story of our brothers and sisters as they have sought to follow God and God's gracious interaction with them. The *Old Testament* shows God creating for himself a people through whom he will reveal his majesty and glory as well as his gracious covenant-keeping love. Finally, in the NT, we see the ultimate unveiling of God in the person of Jesus Christ, the incarnate Son of God. This is the crescendo of revelation, the climax of God's gracious manifestation. The love of God, wondrously displayed in the OT, reaches its zenith at the crucifixion of Jesus, such that the apostle John can say, "God's love was revealed among us in this way: God sent his one and only Son into the world so that we might live through him" (1 John 4:9).

The NT displays this Jesus whom we love, the One for whom we first decided to pursue theological education. The NT is not merely the record of human experiences of God or the best of humanity's ideas about how to relate to God. It is the culmination of the self-revelation of God, eyewitness testimony to the life and work of Christ, and the deposit of the apostles' teaching. Through the NT, we see how the OT pointed to Christ and how we must now live in light of Christ. As such, it deserves our devotion and careful study. The NT is central to theological education, and no effort would be too great, no cost too high, to gain understanding of such a book. As A. T. Robertson flatly stated, NT study is of the highest importance because "the NT is the fountainhead, the sourcebook of Christianity."[1]

This is not to say that the NT is all that is important or necessary. As will be discussed below, we cannot separate the NT from the OT. They are integrally related, and each is needed to understand the other as together they form one coherent message as Christian Scripture. However, there is an element of discontinuity as well. As the Epistle to the Hebrews tells us, in the past God spoke to us by the prophets, but "in these last days, he has spoken to us by his Son" (1:2). While the OT law possessed only a shadow of the good things that were to come, the NT reveals their true form (10:1).

In the study of the NT, we investigate ancient history, ancient literature, and Christian theology. We devote attention to ancient Near Eastern culture. Political history and geography provide the context for two-thousand-year-old Gospels and Letters. Meanwhile, the documents themselves are some of the most important sources for understanding the NT period. The NT has been justifiably reckoned the most significant literary corpus in the history of Western civilization, if not the world. Though this may sound like hyperbole, it is not. The Bible, the OT and the NT, is the founding document of Christianity and the most decisive shaper of Western civilization and the world. Even from a merely historical perspective, we are studying some of the most significant literature ever produced.

---

1. *New Testament Interpretation, Notes on Lectures of Dr. A. T. Robertson*, taken and neostyled by W. E. Davidson, 2nd ed. (New York: Revell, 1916), 19.

What Is the NT?

The Continuation of the OT

The NT presents itself as the continuation and fulfillment of the OT. It is impossible to understand the NT properly without reading it in conjunction with the OT. The NT writings quote the OT and allude to it extensively. In the four Gospels, Jesus expounds the OT, showing he is the One to whom the OT pointed. The apostles followed this example. The NT assumes a number of key concepts from the OT such as the identity of God, the Messiah, sin, and atonement. As Donald Hagner has stated, "Of all that could be mentioned as important for the understanding of the NT . . . nothing supersedes the Scriptures of the OT."[2] Thus, the theological and interpretive exercise fails from the outset if we ignore or isolate the OT. Theological education must always be rooted in a biblical exposition, which keeps both testaments together. Any methodology that claims to produce understanding of the NT but does not focus on knowing the OT intimately is false and misguided from its beginning. As Dennis Kinlaw says, "One of the reasons the New Testament does not live for us is because we do not really know the Old Testament the way we should."[3]

In theological education we have separate classes for OT and NT simply to allow us to focus on details, but this curricular separation must not translate into a partition in our thinking, theologizing, or preaching. Teachers of each testament should be integrating their subject matter with the entire enterprise of theological and spiritual formation (since theological education is a means to spiritual formation).

The Word of God

The NT, like the OT, presents itself as the Word of God. We pursue theological education because we believe this claim to be true. We must keep this truth clearly in focus as we pursue our studies. It is possible to get lost in the details. The copious amount of available (and still compiling) information can be dizzying, such that NT studies can become drudgery. Or we can become intoxicated with our new knowledge and thus become puffed

---

2. Donald Hagner, *The New Testament: A Historical and Theological Introduction* (Grand Rapids: Baker Academic, 2012), 26.
3. Dennis Kinlaw and John Oswalt, *Lectures in Old Testament Theology* (Anderson, IN: Francis Asbury Press, 2010), 17.

up. Either response shows that we have lost sight of what we are dealing with in the NT. We can maintain a proper vision in two ways. First, if we continually remind ourselves that we are digging deeply into God's self-revelation of his gracious purposes in redeeming sinful people like us, then it will not be drudgery. Second, if we truly comprehend and meditate on the message of the NT (God's holiness, our sin, and his gracious work to rescue us despite ourselves), we will find that pride can hardly thrive in that context. As a dear, aged professor once said to me, "Now, sir, you show me a man who is proud, and I will show you a man who has yet to understand the cross!"

As we approach the NT, whether as a student or a professor, we must come eagerly anticipating an encounter with God. We must think hard about all the data—attend to the Greek syntax, historical background, genre, and literary context—to the end of hearing more clearly the voice of the God who has loved us with an everlasting love. Biblical interpretation can only be done well as a lover's pursuit. In this way the rigor and toil of theological education will seem light, as did the seven years to Jacob as he worked for Rachel (Gen 29:20). Only those who seek God in faith study the NT aright. Those who hunger and thirst for God in this pursuit will be filled.

A Word for the Church

Any serious historical and literary interpretation of a text must take into account its intended audience. Even a casual examination of the NT reveals that it was written to and for the church. This is not to deny its evangelistic purpose, but by and large the NT is addressed to the church. This should shape our study in various ways. First, if we are not deeply involved in the life of a local church, we will not be able to grasp fully the burden and concern of the NT. This is true for everyone, but it is particularly true for one involved in theological education and preparation for ministry. I tell my students that if they are not involved in the community life and gospel work of a local congregation, they are wasting their time in theological study and fooling themselves as to what they are about. The famous dictum of Hillary of Poitiers, the fourth century bishop, rings true: "Those who are situated outside the church are not able to acquire any understanding of the divine discourse."[4]

---

4. Cited in Mark Gignilliat, *A Brief History of Old Testament Criticism: From Benedict Spinoza to Brevard Childs* (Grand Rapids: Zondervan, 2012), 26.

Second, if we interpret the NT correctly, we must always be asking what the text means not just for an individual but also for the church. Of course we will pursue many technical details which will not themselves be suitable for a prominent point in a sermon or lesson, but all of these details should help us understand what God is saying to the church.[5] Howard Marshall, who was described as the "dean of New Testament evangelical interpretation," provides us an example. While initiating and editing a leading series of commentaries on the Greek text and producing a bevy of standard technical works, he was rooted in the life of his small, local Methodist congregation where many of the members did not know he was a world-renowned scholar. They simply knew him as "Howard," who taught the young boys' class, played the church organ, and helped train lay preachers. His advice to theological students is pertinent: "I think it is important to be in a good Christian fellowship to have support from it and to be occupied in Christian work of one kind or another, and if possible to try and relate your studies to your practical Christian work."[6]

Lastly, Paul makes clear that we need the help of the Holy Spirit to understand spiritual things, including the message of the Scriptures (1 Cor 2:14). Therefore, we must be converted and indwelt by the Holy Spirit before we can fully understand the NT. As Alistair Wilson has stated, "The fundamental character of the NT as the breathed-out (2 Tim 3:16) utterance of the only God and Father of the Lord Jesus Christ demands that true interpretation of the NT can be achieved only by those who have been brought into a restored relationship with the Father and are equipped by the Holy Spirit of God (1 Cor 2:6–16; Rom 8:5–9)."[7] This is crucial as we seek to read sympathetically, entering the situation of the writers. J. I. Packer affirms this, writing, "The supreme requirement for understanding a biblical book—or indeed any other human document—is sympathy with its subject matter, and a mind and heart that can spontaneously enter into the author's outlook. But the capacity to put oneself in the shoes of Isaiah,

---

5. In my own experience, the best biblical scholars I have known have been devoted churchmen.
6. Carl Trueman, "Interview with Professor Howard Marshall," *Them* 26, no. 1 (Autumn 2000): 49.
7. A. Wilson, "Beginning to Study the New Testament," in *Encountering God's Word* (Downers Grove: IVP, 2003), 71. Note also Donald Hagner's comment: "Believers are the implied readers of the NT texts, and therefore believers are in the best place to make sense of the NT texts" (Hagner, *The New Testament: A Historical and Theological Introduction*, 10).

or Paul or John and see with his eyes and feel with his heart is the gift, not of academic training, but of the Holy Ghost though the new birth."[8]

Therefore, in all our efforts to understand Scripture, we ought to start with prayer to the Author of those Scriptures, asking for his illumination and guidance. And, since God will not answer requests to exalt ourselves (Jas 4:3,6–7), we must not pray and study to lift ourselves up but rather that God might be glorified as we grow in our knowledge of him, serving him and his church.

Unified Reading

In light of what we have just said about the nature of the NT, we should expect to interpret the NT, and the entire Bible, as a unified, coherent whole. However, modern studies have tended toward reading biblical texts in isolation from one another with an increasing assumption of discrepancy between texts. Such divergence seems to be a presupposition for many today. Thus we have Paul's ideas, which may be significantly different from John's, which may contradict Peter's or James's. This was not the way the church read the Bible through the first seventeen or so centuries of its history. The Bible was seen as a unified whole, so its interpretation required the coordination and theological integration of its various books.[9] The difference is rooted in what one thinks of the character of Scripture. If it is merely a human book written across centuries, then one would likely assume there will be large differences. If it is a divinely inspired book for God's people, one is likely to assume a high level of consistency and coherence as did most of the patristic, medieval, and Reformation era interpreters.

Evangelical convictions should lead us to studying the Bible, including the NT, in a unified way, expecting the Bible to help us interpret the Bible as we read each individual text in light of the whole of Scripture. This does not mean we flatten out the distinctive characteristics of each book. Gospel writers have distinct emphases, and Paul uses different language than John. It is valuable for us to notice this. In the end, however, they are testifying to the same truth of God in Christ reconciling the world to himself. We have the benefit of a variegated witness to a central reality.

---

8. J. I. Packer, *God Has Spoken*, 2nd ed. (Grand Rapids: Baker, 1994), 73–74.
9. Borrowing language from Christopher Seitz, *Colossians* (Grand Rapids: Brazos, 2014), 24.

Major Aspects of the Study of the New Testament

The various aspects of NT study can be grouped into five main categories: (1) textual criticism; (2) archaeological, historical, and cultural background; (3) study of the composition of the text; (4) exegesis; and (5) NT theology.[10] These are listed in terms of their logical progression in the actual practice of NT study, but one typically moves back and forth among these realms.

The Establishment of the Text: Textual Criticism

Before we can study the NT, we must establish the text itself. The NT was not handed down to us in a complete, single volume containing the original documents written by the apostles. Indeed, we do not have the originals of any of the NT documents (referred to as *autographs*). What we have is a multitude of manuscript copies from a wide range of locations and times. Some manuscripts are fragments, some have entire letters or books, and some have more than one letter. We also have early translations and quotations in the writings of early church fathers. Bruce Metzger has stated that the NT quotations in the writings of the church fathers are so extensive that we could reconstruct "practically the entire New Testament" from them![11]

We have an amazing wealth of manuscript copies of the NT. These include papyri (the earliest and rarest because they are more fragile), majuscules (so-called because they are written in all capital letters), minuscules (written in lower case), and lectionaries (collections of passages for assigned readings for certain days). From these categories we have well over 5,700 manuscripts.[12] No other ancient writing comes close to this level of textual evidence.

Among all these manuscripts, however, there are discrepancies in certain readings—some more and some less significant. In order to discern what the original document said, these differences need to be analyzed.

---

10. A later chapter treats NT theology, so that will not be discussed in this chapter.
11. Bruce Metzger, *The Text of the New Testament: Its Transmission, Corruption, and Restoration* (Oxford: Oxford University Press, 1968), 86.
12. Daniel Wallace, "Laying a Foundation: New Testament Textual Criticism," in *Interpreting the New Testament Text: Introduction to the Art and Science of Exegesis*, ed. Darrell Bock and Buist Fanning (Wheaton: Crossway, 2006), 39, mentions 5,745 manuscripts. More have been discovered since.

This analysis is called *textual criticism* because scholars critically examine these manuscripts in order to discern which readings are original.[13]

There are a large number of discrepancies among the thousands of manuscripts we have. Most, however, are insignificant for the meaning of the text. One example of this sort is variations in spelling. One manuscript might have the name John spelled *Iōannēs* and another with the spelling *Iōanēs*. This is a discrepancy, a variant reading, but it in no way affects the meaning of the text. There are also instances where the order of words is slightly different. While the word order may provide some nuance of meaning, the basic meaning is still clear. In a smaller percentage of cases, the variant reading does have an impact on the meaning of the text. Here the importance of textual criticism is seen (e.g., "we have" or "let us have" in Romans 1). The difference is between an omicron and an omega, which were probably pronounced the same in the first century as they are in later Greek.[14]

The work of textual criticism is, therefore, important, and any serious interpreter of the NT must be aware of this work. However, we must also note that the reality of variant readings in the manuscripts need not undermine our confidence in the Scripture. The large number of manuscripts provides a large sample for comparison, allowing us to make good decisions between the variants. Furthermore, we have old copies as well, dating back close to the time of the writing. As noted previously, no other ancient writing compares with the NT in terms of the number of manuscript copies available and their early date. For example, we have only 643 copies of Homer's *Illiad*, ten copies of Julius Caesar's *Gallic War*, seven copies of Plato's writings, and one copy of *Beowulf*.[15] For many of the other ancient works, the oldest copies we have date from thousands of years after the original. Scholars consider these other ancient works reliable, yet the NT has significantly more textual attestation. The stability of the NT text

---

13. There is an ongoing debate among scholars about terminology at this point, whether we should refer to "original" or "earliest" readings. While it is a significant topic, this is not the place to pursue it further. For a recent brief summary of the discussion, see Charles Hill and Michael Kruger, "Introduction: In Search of the Earliest Text of the New Testament," in *The Earliest Text of the New Testament*, ed. Charles Hill and Michael Kruger (Oxford: Oxford University Press, 2012), 3–5.

14. Examples drawn from Daniel Wallace, "Laying a Foundation: New Testament Textual Criticism," in *Interpreting the New Testament Text: Introduction to the Art and Science of Exegesis*, ed. Darrell Bock and Buist Fanning (Wheaton: Crossway, 2006), 37.

15. Andreas Köstenberger, Scott Kellum, and Charles Quarles, *The Cradle, the Cross, and the Crown: An Introduction to the New Testament* (Nashville: B&H Academic, 2009), 34.

can be seen in the fact that while numerous more manuscripts have been discovered over the last several decades, the decisions on variant readings have changed little.[16]

The World Around the Text: Historical and Cultural Background[17]

The NT was written in a specific historical and cultural setting, which is different from our own. This shapes the authors' styles and governs the sorts of things to which they allude or use for illustration. NT authors write in terms that were common and widely recognized by their readers but which at times are not so common today. They can assume their readers are well aware of the political, economic, and social realities they shared but which are alien to us. The better we understand the historical and cultural setting of the NT, the better we will understand its message; and we will be protected from numerous errors.

I often illustrate this to students by arguing from lesser to greater. Since I live and teach in the United States, I ask students what other culture is the most similar to ours. Certainly that is British culture with our shared language and significant shared history. Yet, as any American who has lived in Britain (and presumably the reverse) knows, the potential for misunderstanding between these two cultures is significant. Early in my family's time living in Scotland, we had to take one of our small children to the doctor. When we told family and friends we had taken him to the surgery, they were alarmed since to American ears that suggested the need for an operation. In Scotland it simply meant we went to the doctor's office. Humorous examples just from my family's experience abound. If there is this much potential for confusion between two cultures, which share so much in common, how much more potential for confusion is there between our setting and that of the NT, which is distant from us in time, language, and other cultural features?

This is not to say that we cannot understand the Bible at all unless we have advanced degrees in the history and culture of the first century.

---

16. Charles Hill and Michael Kruger, "Introduction: In Search of the Earliest Text of the New Testament," in *The Earliest Text of the New Testament*, ed. Charles Hill and Michael Kruger (Oxford: Oxford University Press, 2012), 5–6.

17. The most extensive recent coverage of this sort of material in one volume is Joel B. Green and Lee M. McDonald, *The World of the New Testament: Cultural, Social, and Historical Contexts* (Grand Rapids: Baker Academic, 2013).

Rather, our understanding will be enhanced and enriched, and we will be guarded against misunderstandings of various sorts.

The information we have on the historical and cultural background of the NT comes either from material that was intentionally preserved or from what has been discovered by archaeologists. Archaeology has been of great service to NT studies by uncovering all sorts of useful information ranging from biblical manuscripts (previously discussed), other texts, inscriptions, coins, and artifacts of daily life. Many of the items discussed below are available to us because of the work of archaeologists. The primary value of archaeology has been illuminating daily life in biblical times, helping us "see" the world of the NT and better understand what was going on in that time. Due to the work of archaeology, we have examples of homes, rich and poor, from Palestine and elsewhere around the Mediterranean and can reconstruct many activities of daily life.

In addition, archaeology has also given strong evidence of the historical reliability of the NT. "Finds [of archaeology] inevitably keep returning biblical studies to the realm of history and historical geography."[18] For example, John's Gospel has been shown to demonstrate an accurate awareness of the geography of Palestine, and discovered inscriptions have shown that Luke, in Acts, used the accurate terms for the various governmental leaders he mentioned.

Historical Events

Any specific time in history is shaped by the forces and events that preceded it, and the era of the NT is no different. Therefore, awareness of this historical background will be helpful in interpreting the NT. Much happened between the close of the OT and the opening of the NT, and these events and their effects are assumed by NT writers. For example, someone who has just completed reading the OT will find new concepts in the NT, which are introduced without explanation. Jesus and Paul visit synagogues, local Jewish assemblies, but these were not mentioned in the OT. Who are these groups called Pharisees and Sadducees? All of these can be explained by the history that preceded the NT era. During the exile from Judea, with the temple destroyed, the Jews had no place to gather for worship. They could not perform the prescribed sacrifices, but they gathered in their

---

18. John McRay, *Archaeology and the New Testament* (Grand Rapids: Baker Academic, 2008), 18.

communities to study the law. These gatherings became synagogues, and the practice of establishing synagogues continued after they returned from exile so that by the time of the NT there were synagogues throughout the Mediterranean world. The movements that became known as Pharisees and Sadducees began during the time in which the Jews were ruled by the remnants of Alexander the Great's empire. Antiochus IV forced Greek culture on the Jews with the threat of torture and death. Some groups were more willing to compromise (forerunners of the Sadducees) and some resisted compromise and called for purity (forerunners of the Pharisees). Furthermore, this persecution led to a revolt led by the Hasmonean family, who were referred to as the Maccabees, which eventually led to Jewish independence. The fact that the Jews had defeated a superior power to achieve independence in 164 BC and then lost that independence after defeat by the Romans in 63 BC no doubt helped fuel desires among many Jews to throw off the Romans during the NT era.

A basic awareness of the geography of the NT world is also quite helpful. The accounts of both Jesus and Paul are filled with travel, and it is helpful to know where they are going and the different terrains and political boundaries which are being crossed. Weather patterns also affect travel. In Acts Paul regularly stops traveling and spends the winter in a specific location. This is because sea travel largely shut down in the winter due to hazardous conditions. With this in mind, Paul's urging Timothy to "come before winter" (2 Tim 4:21) makes even more sense.

Texts

A wealth of texts have been preserved or discovered that illuminate various aspects of NT study. Large numbers of papyri letters have been discovered that illuminate daily life significantly. These are not texts intended for publication but everyday letters, notices, and inventories. As such they give us a glimpse into the lives of ordinary people. These documents also have furthered our knowledge of the Greek language as common people used it.

The wide range of Greco-Roman literature that has been preserved bears on NT study by giving us access to ideas and practices that were common in the era. Cicero died about four decades before the birth of Christ, but his discussions about letter writing help us understand Paul's letter writing. Ancient letters, treatises, speeches, and books give us insight into the life of slaves, popular religious ideas, and ideas about marriage for example. Sometimes specific cities or regions are described. For example, Polybius (second century BC) wrote that it was almost "impossible to find . . . personal conduct more treacherous or public policy more unjust than in Crete" (*Histories* 6.47 [Paton, LCL]). Cicero also stated, "Moral principles are so divergent that the Cretans . . . consider highway robbery honorable" (*De Republica* 3.9.15 [Keyes, LCL]). This reputation over a couple of centuries helps us understand the situation of the letter to Titus, who was ministering on Crete when Paul wrote him warning of the people's beastly behavior and urging him to teach the people the ethical implications of the gospel.

Even closer to the thought world of most of the NT writers is the Jewish literature that has survived.[19] Josephus, a Jewish historian, tells us much about the everyday life of first-century Jews and gives accounts of many key events including the destruction of Jerusalem in AD 70. Philo was a Jewish philosopher well acquainted with Greek thought. His expositions of the OT give us an example of how at least some Jews thought in the first century. We can see how Philo's handling of the OT compares with that of Paul, for example, or the author of Hebrews. The Dead Sea Scrolls and rabbinic literature (including Midrash, Targums, and Talmudim) give us examples of different religious expectations and approaches to the OT that come from at least close to the time of the writing of the NT.[20] All of this helps us understand some of the ideas that were in the air when Jesus came teaching or when the apostles preached Jesus as the promised Messiah. They help us situate the story of the NT.

The History of the Text: Higher Criticism

Formal study of the NT also addresses the question of how the texts we hold in our hands came to be in the form in which we have them. This is an issue students often do not consider before entering formal theological study, but it is an important topic. For example, how did we end up

---

19. Martin Hengel says it is certain "without qualification that Christianity grew *entirely* out of Jewish soil." ("Early Christianity as a Jewish-Messianic, Universalistic Movement," in *Conflicts and Challenges in Early Christianity*, ed. D. Hagner [Harrisburg, PA: Trinity Press International, 1999], 1).

20. For a helpful statement on the usefulness of rabbinic literature in NT interpretation and caution about dating of that literature, see J. Neusner, "Rabbinic Literature: Mishnah and Tosefta," in *Dictionary of New Testament Background: A Compendium of Contemporary Biblical Scholarship*, ed. Craig Evans and Stanley Porter (Downers Grove: IVP, 2000), 896–97.

with four Gospels, and how do we account for their striking similarities in certain places and dissimilarities in others? Who wrote the NT documents which do not have a stated author, and can we trust the claims of authorship that are present? Are certain books actually edited together from several different sources?

Some of these questions have been important from the early days of the church when its leaders examined writings to discern whether they were written by apostles and should thus be accepted as authoritative. The Enlightenment of the nineteenth century, however, elevated skepticism to a virtue and shaped the discussion of authorship in a new way. Until the nineteenth century the church basically accepted the stated authorship of NT books (the Epistle to the Hebrews, which does not claim an author, is a separate case). J. E. C. Schmidt and Friedrich Schleiermacher were the first to dispute the authorship of a NT letter, disputing Pauline authorship of 1 Timothy.[21] Early critics of Schleiermacher warned that this skepticism would spread to other NT books and thus erode the entire theological project concerning the Bible. The skeptics derided this as fear mongering, but this prophecy has been fulfilled. In modern NT studies the authorship of six of the thirteen letters attributed to Paul is widely disputed, and the apostolic authorship of the Gospels and several other epistles is called into question. This is significant for NT study since, as Donald Guthrie stated, "It is noticeable that challenges to traditional ascriptions of scholarship went hand in hand with rejection of authority."[22]

F. C. Baur furthered this skeptical viewpoint in the nineteenth century when he argued the NT itself was made up of books that were written against one another. Though Baur's basic thesis has largely been discredited, his acidic influence is still evident in the methodology of NT scholars who assume conflicts and contradictions between biblical books and even within books. This approach to scholarship brings to mind a scientist who

---

21. Apparently J. E. C. Schmidt was first in challenging 1 Tim in his *Historical-Critical Introduction to the New Testament* in 1804/5. But it was Schleiermacher's *Über den sogenannten ersten Brief des Paulos an den Timotheos. Ein kritisches Sendschreiben an J. C. Gass* (reprinted in Schleiermacher's Sämmtliche Werke, vol. 1–2, pp. 221–320) which really stirred up the conversation in 1807.

22. Donald Guthrie, "Questions of Introduction," in *New Testament Interpretation: Essays on Principles and Methods*, ed. I. H. Marshall (Grand Rapids: Eerdmans, 1977), 108. For further reflection on the tendency of such approaches to erode biblical authority, see Ray Van Neste, "Coherence and Authorship in 1 Timothy," *Global Journal of Classic Theology* 12, no. 3 (December 2015), accessed January 14, 2017, http://www.globaljournalct.com/wp-content/uploads/2015/12/Van-Neste-Vol-12-No-3-Coherence-and-Authorship-of-1-Timothy.pdf.

kills an animal, dissects its parts for a detailed study, and then declares he finds no life there. Or the scientist rebuilds the dissected animal in a way he sees fit, diverging from the condition in which he found it, and then declares that his completed reconstruction is the original condition of the animal. It is not putting too fine a point on it to say that this brand of scholarship remakes the NT in its own image. Too often biblical texts are criticized for not saying what we, as enlightened moderns, would have said.[23] Earle Ellis's assessment is worth quoting: "In Tübingen today there is properly a 'Ferdinand Christian Baur Street' to commemorate a great figure of the city's past. As is appropriate, it is a branch off 'Philosophers Way.' Equally appropriate, I believe, it is a *Sackgasse*, a blind alley. Baur produced a construct of early Christianity that was too artificial and exegetically too poorly grounded to serve as a viable historical representation."[24]

Other questions about the history of the text have been more useful. For example, redaction criticism focuses on differences between the Gospels, looking for evidence of the Gospel writers' interests and emphases. The value of such study varies, but it has usefully made the point that the Gospel writers were not mere recorders of events but were actually theologians. Canonical interpretation has pushed back against much of the concern with the history of the text, arguing instead that our focus should be on the text as we have it.

The Message in the Text: Exegesis

After the preparatory work we have just described, and in light of it, we must then interpret the text. We want to discern what the original intention of the text is so that we might believe it and obey it. Because we want to believe and obey what God has said, and not just whatever we can read into the text (eisegesis), exegesis must be done carefully.

---

23. Perhaps an anecdote would be helpful here. I once listened to a paper given by a systematic theologian who argued that Paul intended to say one thing in Ephesians 5 but that his theological reasoning got away from him, leading to a text which has left most of us over the ages thinking Paul was arguing something totally different. After the paper Howard Marshall spoke up declaring that he now had a new question for examinations: "Tell us how Paul should have written Ephesians in order to say what we know he meant to have said."

24. E. Earle Ellis, *The Making of the New Testament Documents* (Leiden: Brill, 2002), 445. For a fascinating critique of the skeptical approach from a literary perspective, see Anthony Esolen, "Pauline Scholar, Meet Homeric Scholar: How Textual Analysis Misses Authorial Genius and Literary Inspiration," *Touchstone* 26, no. 4 (July/August 2013): 22–26.

Historical-grammatical exegesis is the term often used for the approach that seeks to allow the biblical text to speak on its own terms. *Historical* refers to the effort to understand the author's meaning in his historical and literary context. We must understand what the text originally meant, and then we can ask how that meaning applies to various situations today. This approach is also *grammatical* in that we seek to understand the text according to the natural, linguistic sense of the words. We are not seeking to uncover secret or hidden meanings. Additionally, our approach can be described as *theological* since, as was argued above, we approach the text as the Word of God and anticipate a coherent message within the Bible.

The first step in any interpretation is to read the text carefully and closely. It is of immense help to the interpreter of the NT to be able to read the NT in the language in which it was originally written, Greek (see chapter 9). The author's specific word choices and broader structural elements that mark the flow of thought can be seen more readily in Greek. While we are blessed with many good English translations, the ability to read the NT in Greek is a serious advantage and is thus well worth pursuing in a theological education.

Also, to read a text properly, we must be aware of what sort of text it is. Different kinds of texts (genres) follow different patterns or rules. We know this intuitively in everyday life so that we don't puzzle over a train schedule or team roster looking for the plot or criticize it for lacking character development. We know to expect disparate topics and varying styles in science textbooks and mystery novels. When we turn to the NT, then, we need to be aware that there are several literary genres within it, and we must be mindful of them as we read. Basically in the NT we have three main genres: historical writing (Gospels and Acts), letters (Paul and the General Epistles), and apocalyptic (Revelation). The first two of these are generally familiar to us today. The Gospels and Acts narrate key events in a way broadly similar to historical writing we might encounter today, with some dissimilarities like the absence of a reference system for noting sources. We might note that the Gospels, as well as Acts, relate their stories in order to make a certain point, but this is usually true of any historical writing today as well.

Paul's letters begin with his name rather than the name of the recipient, but broadly speaking we understand that he is communicating his ideas to a person or group at a distance. He will typically use a health wish near the beginning of his letters that is common today as well ("I hope you're doing well!"). We know that letters (or even e-mails) can vary in length and can vary in style from casual to more instructive, and this was true of ancient letters as well. Paul's letters are more along the lines of instructing.

The NT genre least familiar to us is *apocalyptic*. This was a common genre in the ancient world, but it disappeared over time such that we do not expect to find an "apocalyptic" section in our local bookstores today. Since we have some other apocalyptic writings from the ancient world, we can discern some of the common features, such as an extensive use of symbolism and a focus on God's powerful intervention into the world. While the book of Revelation continues to present many challenges for the interpreter, an awareness of the apocalyptic genre helps clarify many things.

Within the genres are other aspects of study that can help us understand the structure and flow of thought in NT writings. For example, rhetorical and literary analysis help illuminate the ways ancient authors ordered their writings. Since these writings would be heard rather than read by most people, the use of certain words and the order or repetition of words could be helpful in comprehending the flow of thought and points of emphasis. For example, ancient writers would sometimes open and close a paragraph with the same ideas or words to mark the unit of thought.

A close reading of a text will necessitate placing that specific text within its broader literary context. A paragraph in a letter of Paul needs to be seen in light of what precedes and what follows it. Where does this specific paragraph fit in the overall argument of his letter? We must consider how a Gospel account is impacted by the stories around it. For example, if you are studying the text where Jesus is accused of breaking the Sabbath (Mark 2:23–28), it is helpful to note that this is the second of three narratives where Jesus disputed the way the Pharisees were interpreting the OT. An obvious theme in these texts is Jesus's demonstration of a proper understanding of OT law.

Thus, by close reading of the texts and their nuances within the literary, historical, and cultural context, we will be helped to accurately interpret the meaning of each text. Once understood, however, the text must be applied. No biblical study is completed with the acquisition of new information. Once again we must keep in mind the purpose of the Scriptures. God has not given them to us for mere historical inquiry but that we might know and obey him. Thus, we must apply the biblical truths and believe and obey what we have discovered.

Conclusion

NT studies done well is a rigorous, thrilling enterprise in pursuit of the knowledge of God and the service of his people. We cannot achieve theological education or hope for a healthy church without a deep awareness of the NT, so this task is vital. We must think clearly and diligently, making use of all the available tools and being aware of the current issues. We must approach the text with the right spirit as well if we want to encounter God since we know God resists the proud but gives grace to the humble (1 Pet 5:5). The prophet Isaiah also tells us that God will attend to the one who is humble, submissive in spirit, and trembles at his word (Isa 66:1–2). Let us be such people.

Questions for Further Reflection

1. How should the goal of knowing God shape your approach to biblical study? Is your approach to theological education currently shaped by this goal?
2. Are you involved significantly in the life of a specific local church? Do you believe this will have an impact on your study of the NT? How can you grow in your investment in the life of fellow believers and integrating this into your biblical studies?
3. How important is an awareness of the OT for the study of the NT?
4. How valuable are background studies for the interpretation of the NT? What can you do to increase your awareness of the history and culture of the Greco-Roman world?
5. Do you think it is important to approach the NT with the expectation that its various books agree with and help interpret one another?

Sources for Further Study

Arnold, Clinton E., ed. *Zondervan Illustrated Bible Backgrounds Commentary*. Grand Rapids: Zondervan, 2002.

Black, David A., and David S. Dockery, ed. *Interpreting the New Testament: Essays on Methods and Issues.* Nashville: B&H, 2001.

Bockmuehl, Markus. *Seeing the Word: Refocusing New Testament Study.* Grand Rapids: Baker, 2006.

Bird, Michael F. *Introducing Paul: The Man, His Mission and His Message.* Downers Grove: IVP, 2008.

Bruce, F. F. *The New Testament Documents: Are They Reliable?* 6th ed. Grand Rapids: Eerdmans, 1981.

Comfort, Philip W. *Encountering the Manuscripts: Introduction to New Testament Paleography and Textual Criticism.* Nashville: B&H Academic, 2005.

Evans, Craig, and Stanley Porter, ed. *Dictionary of New Testament Background: A Compendium of Contemporary Biblical Scholarship.* Downers Grove: IVP, 2000.

Fee, Gordon D. *New Testament Exegesis: A Handbook for Students and Pastors.* 3rd ed. Louisville: Westminster John Knox, 2002.

Green, Joel B., and Lee M. McDonald. *The World of the New Testament: Cultural, Social, and Historical Contexts.* Grand Rapids: Baker Academic, 2013.

Keener, Craig S. *The IVP Bible Background Commentary: New Testament.* 2nd ed. Downers Grove: IVP, 2014.

McRay, John. *Archaeology and the New Testament.* Grand Rapids: Baker Academic, 1991.

Seitz, Christopher. *The Character of Christian Scripture: The Significance of a Two-Testament Bible.* Grand Rapids: Baker, 2011.

Chapter Ten

THEOLOGY OF THE OLD TESTAMENT

DANIEL I. BLOCK

The task of introducing readers to the discipline of Old Testament theology in one short chapter is daunting for several reasons. First, the literature of the Hebrew Bible (our only resource for establishing an Old Testament theology) spans a wide range of genres (historiography, genealogies, hymnody and poetic lament, prophecy and apocalyptic, and wisdom texts). Second, since the composition of the books that make up the Hebrew Bible spanned more than a millennium, the theology that was taught evolved progressively with additional revelation, and the forms of communicating that theology changed as the people of Israel evolved from a migratory clan of patriarchs, to a full-fledged nation occupying the land of Canaan, to a remnant of exiles in Babylon, and finally to a small community huddled around Jerusalem in the Persian period.

Third, over time and space the institutions charged with the theological education of the citizenry changed. In earliest times this was largely in the hands of household and clan leaders, but the constitutional documents of the Pentateuch placed formal responsibility in the hands of the Levitical priesthood (Deut 33:9–10) and provided for Levitical towns throughout the land as bases of education for the people. These may have provided the bases for the synagogues that sprouted throughout the land in the periods of Persian and Greek domination.[1]

---

1. On this see, Daniel I. Block, "'The Meeting Places of God in the Land': Another Look at the Towns of the Levites," in *Current Issues in Priestly and Related Literature: The Legacy of Jacob Milgrom and Beyond*, ed. Roy Gane and Ada Taggar-Cohen, vol. 82, *Resources for Biblical Study* (Atlanta: Society of Biblical Literature, 2015), 93–121.

Fourth, the sheer bulk of the Hebrew Bible thrusts us into a library of literary resources and frustrates any who would try to condense First Testament theological teaching on the subject into one short essay. For these and other reasons, this chapter represents only a preliminary and summary foray into a much broader subject.

This chapter divides into two parts. In the first I shall review the history of Old Testament theology as a discipline and orient readers to the goals and nature of the discipline. In the second I shall turn to Deuteronomy as a focus text because it provides the bedrock for all Old Testament theology and presents Moses as a paradigmatic biblical theologian.

An Introduction to the Discipline of Old Testament Theology

Readers of the Old Testament are driven to study it for many different reasons: (1) its sheer literary value; (2) as window into the culture of a people on the eastern shores of the Mediterranean in the first millennium BC; (3) as the source of the three modern monotheistic religions (Judaism, Christianity, Islam); (4) as a devotional book for daily spiritual nurture; (5) as a resource for theological and ethical wisdom; and (6) as a textbook for biblical theology. In this chapter my concern is the last entry in this list.

The Roots of Old Testament Theology as a Discipline

While Christians have been engaged in biblical theology since the founding of the church, biblical theology as a recognized academic discipline is less than 350 years old. Many interpret J. P. Gabler's inaugural lecture at the University of Altdorf in 1787, "An Oration on the Proper Distinction Between Biblical and Dogmatic Theology and the Specific Objectives of Each," as the birthdate of what would in the twentieth century become a self-conscious movement within biblical scholarship.[2] Among other issues, Gabler highlighted the distinction between *biblical theology*, which originates in history and concerns what the writers of Scripture felt about divine matters, and *dogmatic theology*, which originates in didactics, being concerned to teach what theologians philosophize about divine matters. Whereas the latter depends on the theologians' abilities, their particular

---

2. The translation of Gabler's address from its original Latin by J. Sandys-Wunsch and L. Eldredge is conveniently reproduced in *Old Testament Theology: Flowering and Future*, ed. Ben C. Ollenburger, rev. ed., vol. 1, *Sources for Biblical and Theological Study* (Winona Lake, IN: Eisenbrauns, 2004), 497–506.

circumstances, age, locale, religious and intellectual tradition, and similar conditioning factors, the first task of biblical theology was to ascertain the biblical authors' thoughts and assertions on divine matters through grammatical and historical exegesis. Differences in perspective were not to be blurred but juxtaposed and compared. The second task of biblical theology was to evaluate biblical concepts and assertions in terms of their permanent and universal significance and deduce from these ideas that could serve as a basis for building a dogmatic theology.

In the rationalistic nineteenth and early twentieth centuries, critical Old Testament scholars focused on reconstructing the history of the religion of Israel and trying to fit the composition of the biblical books into the historical grid they had created. Commentaries such as the renowned International Critical Commentary series were preoccupied with lexical and grammatical matters and had little time or interest in theology; that was the responsibility of the church. However, we may identify a few notable exceptions, like Ernst Wilhelm Hengstenberg, whose particular theological interest is reflected in his classic four-volume *Christology of the Old Testament, and a Commentary on the Messianic Predictions*.[3]

With critical scholars' preoccupation with what is factually verifiable and its failure to account for the essentials of Israelite religion, specifically matters of faith, by 1930 many began to recognize its theological bankruptcy, and some called for the revival of Old Testament theology as a discipline. In fact, Steuernagel declared, "If it was necessary then [in Gabler's day] to free biblical theology from the shackles of dogmatics, so it is time now . . . to free Old Testament theology from the shackles of Old Testament history-of-religion."[4] The following decades would witness the appearance of several significant formal theological works, most notably, by Walther Eichrodt and Gerhard von Rad.

---

3. The set was published in German under the title *Christologie des Alten Testaments, 1828–1835*; the second edition was translated into English and published in 1871. A reprint of R. Keith's translation of the 1847 edition is available from Kregel Publishers (1970).

4. Carl Steuernagel, "Alttestamentliche Theologie und alttestamentliche Religionsgeschichte," in *Vom Alten Testament: Karl Martizum siebzigsten Geburtstage*, ed. K. Budde, BZAW 41 (Giessen: Alfred Töpelmann, 1925), 266. As translated in Ben C. Ollenburger, "Old Testament Theology Before 1933," in *Old Testament Theology: Flowering and Future*, 10.

The Nature of Old Testament Theologies

When we explore how the discipline of Old Testament theology has been pursued, we find the results to be extremely idiosyncratic; the theologies that have been proposed are as varied as the biblical scholars who have proposed them.[5] Although the studies of specific biblical theological topics are too numerous to mention, we may classify many who have produced synthetic Old Testament theologies according to their approach: (1) some identify a centralizing and unifying theme that could serve as an umbrella for the entire Old Testament,[6] (2) some identify a core theological text and seek to interpret the theology of the Old Testament under the rubrics suggested by that text,[7] (3) some identify the discreet theologies of sections of the Old Testament canon and/or books of the Old Testament,[8] (4) some highlight the competing and contrasting theologies represented in the Old Testament,[9] and (5) some offer eclectic discussion of key biblical theological themes.[10] From the bibliography cited, it is evident that as a discipline Old Testament theology has been a distinctly Protestant discipline. Jewish

---

5. The best survey of the history of the discipline (at least up to 1991) remains Gerhard Hasel, *Old Testament Theology: Basic Issues in the Current Debate*, 4th ed. (Grand Rapids: Eerdmans, 1991); see also John H. Hayes and Frederick Prussner, *Old Testament Theology: Its History and Development* (Atlanta: John Knox, 1984).

6. These include Walther Eichrodt, *Theology of the Old Testament*, trans. J. A. Baker; OTL, 2 vols. (Philadelphia: Westminster John Knox, 1991, 1967) (translation of the 5th edition; the first edition was published in 1933); Walter C. Kaiser, Jr., *Toward an Old Testament Theology* (Grand Rapids: Zondervan, 1991), further developed in *The Promise-Plan of God: A Biblical Theology of the Old and New Testaments* (Grand Rapids: Zondervan, 2008); Horst Dieter Preuss, *Old Testament Theology*, OTL, trans. Leo G. Perdue, 2 vols. (Louisville: Westminster John Knox,1995, 1996).

7. These include Gerhard von Rad, whose base text is "the little creed" (Deut 26:5–9), *Old Testament Theology*, trans. D. M. G. Stalker, *Old Testament Library*, vol. 1, *The Theology of Israel's Historical Traditions* (New York: Harper and Row, 1962); vol. 2, *The Theology of Israel's Prophetic Traditions* (New York: Harper and Row, 1965); see also Von Rad's *Wisdom in Israel*, trans. James D. Martin (Nashville: Abingdon, 1972); and Elmer A. Martens, *God's Design: A Focus on Old Testament Theology*, 4th ed. (Eugene, OR: Wipf and Stock, 2015).

8. For the former, see Brevard S. Childs, *Biblical Theology of the Old and New Testaments: Theological Reflection on the Christian Bible* (Minneapolis: Fortress, 1992); idem, *Old Testament Theology in a Canonical Context* (Philadelphia: Fortress, 1986). For the latter, see Paul J. House, *Old Testament Theology* (Downers Grove: InterVarsity, 1998).

9. Walter Brueggemann, *Theology of the Old Testament: Testimony, Dispute, Advocacy* (Minneapolis: Augsburg Fortress, 1997).

10. Robin Routledge, *Old Testament Theology: A Thematic Approach* (Downers Grove: InterVarsity, 2013). Here we should also include John Goldingay's massive three-volume opus, *Old Testament Theology*: vol. 1 *Israel's Gospel*; vol. 2 *Israel's Faith*; vol. 3 *Israel's Life* (Downers Grove: InterVarsity, 2003, 2006, 2009, respectively).

scholarship has been relatively disinterested in the subject,[11] and Roman Catholic scholarship has been so tied up with tradition it has been difficult to conceive of biblical theology as a separate discipline.[12]

The Nature of Old Testament Theology

While Old Testament *theologies* are the products of theologians, by definition Old Testament *theology* is fixed by the biblical text. Ideally, for the theology to be biblical, the task of interpreters is to get out of the way, to grasp the theology of the Old Testament, and to cast it in understandable forms for contemporary readers. Of course, this is not entirely possible. Readers come with their biases and predispositions to notice particular details. Nevertheless, the goal should always be to let biblical authors—and ultimately the divine Author—speak for themselves. Therein lies the Scriptures' authority for Christians. But what makes an Old Testament theology biblical? This question may be answered from several different directions.

The [Re]Sources of Old Testament Theology

By definition Old Testament theology will be based on the Old Testament. But what is the Old Testament? Jews, Roman Catholics, Eastern Orthodox Christians, and Protestants answer this question differently. Technically Jews do not have an Old Testament; they have only the Hebrew Bible (which includes small sections in Aramaic). By calling the Old Testament the "Old Testament," Christians identify this as the first part of a more complete Bible, which also contains the New Testament. In content and arrangement, the canons of what makes up the first part of the Christian

---

11. Several notable Jewish exceptions include Jon Levenson, whose theological ruminations are found in a series of books, including *The Hebrew Bible, the First Testament, and Historical Criticism: Jews and Christians in Biblical Studies* (Louisville: Westminster John Knox, 1993), and his more recent brilliant publication, *The Love of God: Divine Gift, Human Gratitude, and Mutual Faithfulness in Judaism*, Library of Jewish Ideas (Princeton, NJ: Princeton University Press, 2016). Although he does not mention John M. G. Barclay's *Paul and the Gift* (Grand Rapids: Eerdmans, 2015), this volume serves as a readily accessible Jewish counterweight. Levenson has interacted seriously with biblical theologians, though he insists that Jews and Christians do not read the same Bible. When Christians see in the New Testament the culmination of the message of the Old and the climax of revelation, they do something Jews could never do. For another recent constructive attempt, see Marvin Sweeney, *Tanak: A Theological and Critical Introduction to the Jewish Bible* (Minneapolis: Fortress, 2012). On the Jewish problem with biblical theology, see Ziony Zevit, "Jewish Biblical Theology: Whence? Why? And Whither?" *Hebrew Union College Annual* 76 (2005): 289–340.

12. For a notable exception, see John L. McKenzie, *A Theology of the Old Testament* (Garden City, NY: Doubleday, 1974).

Scriptures differ [see figure 1]. While the contents of the Protestant Old Testament are identical to the Hebrew Bible of the Jews, the books follow the order in the Roman Catholic and Eastern Orthodox Bibles (based on the Old Greek version).[13] However, the Hebrew Bible and the Protestant Old Testament are shorter than the Roman Catholic and Eastern Orthodox counterparts because the latter also contain a series of books identified as *deuterocanonical*, known more popularly as the Apocrypha.

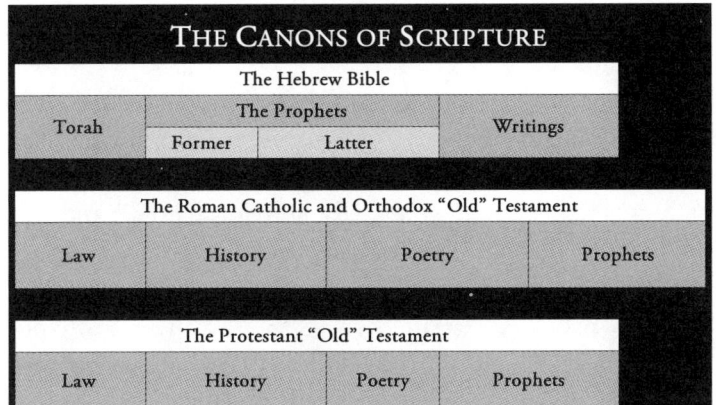

Figure 1

Inasmuch as most biblical theologians are Protestant, the primary source for Old Testament theologians is the Hebrew Bible. However, for Christians the pursuit of a comprehensive biblical theology is never complete until we have asked how the New Testament uses and develops Old Testament theological perspectives and how the appearance of Jesus the Messiah, who is at the same time Yahweh incarnate in human flesh, illuminates Old Testament texts.

---

13. Often referred to as the Septuagint (abbreviated as LXX, "the seventy"), though technically this expression applies only to the Pentateuch, which was supposedly translated independently but identically by seventy-two Greek-speaking Jewish scribes (six from each tribe) in Alexandria, Egypt, in precisely 72 days. Although the historical value of the document is often questioned, the origins of the translation of the Pentateuch are described in a letter written by Aristeas to Philocrates, dated from the mid-third century BC to the first century AD. For introductions to and translations of the text, see R. J. H. Shutt, "Letter of Aristeas," in *The Old Testament Pseudepigraph*, ed. James H. Charlesworth (Garden City, NY: Doubleday, 1985) 2:7–34; Erich S. Gruen, "The Letter of Aristeas," in *Outside the Bible: Ancient Jewish Writings Related to Scripture*, ed. Louis H. Feldman, James L. Kugel, and Lawrence H. Schiffman, 3 vols. (Philadelphia: Jewish Publication Society, 2013) 3:2711–68. Gruen also offers a helpful commentary on this text. Basing his report on Aristeas's letter, Josephus also provides a description of the event in *Jewish Antiquities* 12.11–118.

But this raises the question, how shall we identify the resource that Jewish readers prefer to call the Hebrew Bible? Since the designation for the New Testament is rooted in the New Testament (*diathēkē kainē*, "new covenant"),[14] on the surface the traditional rendering, "Old Testament," seems logical, and it has been helpful so long as antiquity and maturity were treasured values. However, the connotations of words change over time. In the current Western culture, "old" communicates "out of date, passé, irrelevant," and when applied to the Hebrew Bible, it reinforces neo-Marcionite tendencies to interpret the "Old Testament" as a negative foil against which to read the New Testament.

In the minds of many Christians, the "Old Testament" as a document and its theology are fundamentally flawed, and the function of the New Testament is to "fix" a broken system. But this view creates serious theological problems (Does God ever produce something that is flawed?) and casts doubts on Jesus's own statement: "Do not think that I came to destroy the Torah or the Prophets. I did not come to destroy but to fulfill" (Matt 5:17, author's translation). Because the expression, "Old Testament," connotes "out-of-dateness" and suggests to modern readers that God's earlier revelation has been supplanted and rendered obsolete by later revelation, it is best abandoned.

The Scriptures actually tell a single coherent story and communicate a single coherent theology.[15] The salvation offered in Jesus Christ in the New Testament is not an alternative *effective* plan replacing an *ineffective* Old Testament program, but the climax of the story by which God's saving grace is made available to all after we were driven from the garden because of our sin. In the present cultural context, "First Testament" communicates much better the relationship between ancient Israel's Scriptures and the New Testament, and in the remainder of this chapter this is the designation I shall use.

---

14. Hebrews 8:8,13; 9:15; 12:24. Obviously the expression does not refer to the New Testament. When Hebrews compares the previous covenant with the later one, he speaks of them as the "first covenant" (*prōto diathēkē*) and "new covenant" (*diathēkē kainē*) respectively (Heb 9:15).

15. Similarly John Goldingay, who observes, "[Old Testament] suggests something antiquated and inferior left behind by a dead person." *Old Testament Theology*, vol. 1, *Israel's Gospel* (Downers Grove: InterVarsity, 2003), 15.

Disciplinary Foils for First Testament Theology

To understand the nature of First Testament theology as a discipline, we must distinguish it from other kinds of theological investigation. The following categories summarize what First Testament theology is not.

First, First Testament theology is not a theology of the events of history. Although God's repeated intervention on Israel's behalf revealed profound theology (cf. Deut 4:32–40), First Testament theology does not try to recreate the events and then establish a theology based on that recreation. The only access we have to the events is through the divinely inspired interpretation of those events in the First Testament, and our theology must be grounded in that account.

Second, First Testament theology is not a theology of the sources behind the biblical texts. Critical scholars often begin by dissecting texts into their purported sources (e.g., JEDP in Pentateuchal studies). However, all such reconstructions are hypothetical, and whatever sources biblical authors might have used, their theological significance is determined by the canonical contexts in which they are embedded.

Third, First Testament theology is not a theology of the characters in biblical texts. It may be interesting to explore Samson's perspective on God and his views of human relations to Yahweh, but in the end it is the theology of the composers of biblical texts that is determinative and binding for Christians. Biblical characters often express heterodox and pagan perspectives.

Fourth, First Testament theology is not a theology of the New Testament. The New Testament does indeed reflect on First Testament texts in its reporting and interpretation of the coming of Christ, the climax of divine revelation. However, it is misguided to impose upon the First Testament the theology of the New. The texts that make up the First Testament were composed to make sense to their original readers/hearers, and while the full significance of many First Testament statements is not realized until much later, building a First Testament theology must begin with the rigorous search for the intended meaning of the texts within their own particular historical and cultural context.

First Testament texts do not all point to Jesus Christ. However, because they all represent and reflect a particular stage in the history of divine revelation and redemption, their ultimate significance may not be recognizable until we get to the New Testament (Figure 2). Hermeneutically we may—indeed must—read the First Testament Christo-telically, but it is theologically irresponsible to read it Christo-centrically, as if the Messiah is to be found in every text. Inasmuch as Jesus Christ is declared to be Yahweh incarnate, and every First Testament text teaches us something of Yahweh, the God of Israel, it will teach us something about Jesus—but not as the Messiah. Truly messianic texts are limited in number.

Figure 2: Christo-centric and Christo-telic Readings of the First Testament

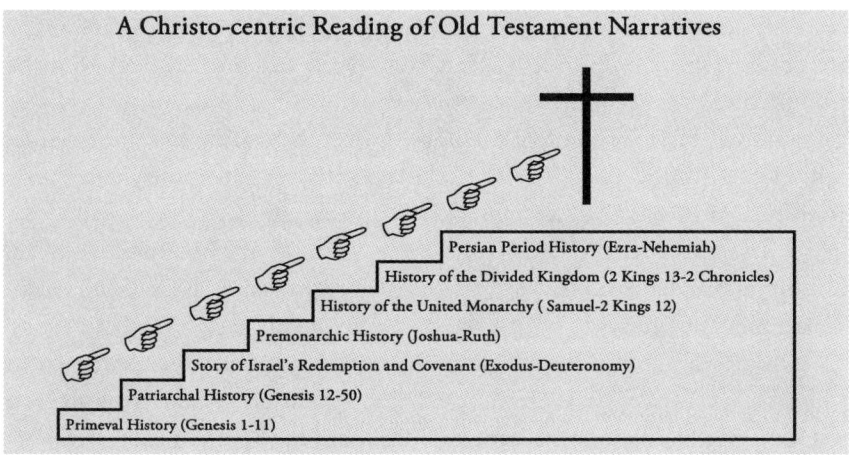

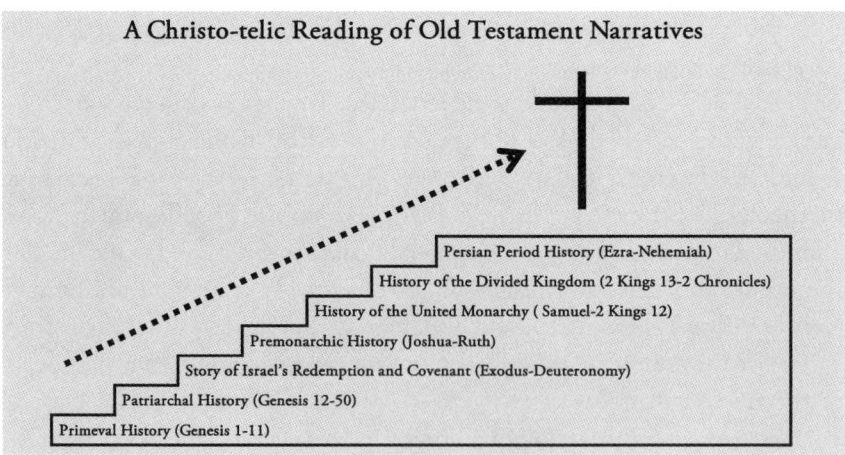

Fifth, First Testament theology is not a theology of the reader. All readers of Scripture come away with particular theologies and their own predispositions to notice particular details and to ignore others. However, within the context of the Protestant commitment to *sola Scriptura*, the more a theology is determined by the subjective prehensions of the reader, the less authoritative it is for the church. Ultimately reliable biblical theology is firmly rooted in the Bible itself and not in the persuasive power of the theologian. While Walter Brueggemann and Bruce Waltke and John Calvin may teach us many biblical truths, all interpreters render biased and jaundiced judgments. By definition First Testament theology is a "back to the Bible" movement.[16]

Sixth, First Testament theology is not systematic theology. Systematic theologians appeal to many sources of knowledge (Scripture, tradition, reason, natural revelation) and often arrive at theological conclusions through philosophical and rational deduction (see Table 1). First Testament theology is fundamentally exegetical and heavily dependent on inductive methods. Furthermore, while systematic theology seeks to organize the theology that arises from Scripture and elsewhere into categories that are appropriate to the culture of the theologian, biblical theology lets biblical texts determine the theological categories and seeks to explore both how these notions developed over time and how the nuances reflected in biblical texts differ. The goal of systematic theology is normative and prescriptive to define how the faith community should think and act. The goal of First Testament theology is first and foremost descriptive, exploring how theological notions were perceived by biblical writers, and then asking how believers should live out theology today.

Seventh, First Testament theology is not a history of Israelite religion (Table 1). In the heyday of rationalism, the First Testament was increasingly interpreted from the perspective of comparative religions. Miracles and mythological elements were dismissed as primitive superstitions, and a flood of archaeological discoveries in Egypt and Mesopotamia provided a cultural context within which to interpret the First Testament materials. Even when OT scholars used the word *theology*, they really meant "history of religion," a history that was interpreted along evolutionary lines, moving from primitive animism to ethical monotheism: (see Figure 3)

---

16. On reining in the subjective element in biblical theology, see Elmer A. Martens, "Accessing Theological Readings of Biblical Books," *Andrews University Seminary Studies* 34, no. 2 (1996): 236–37.

Table 1: A Comparison of the Disciplines Related to the Study of Scripture[17]

Rubric	History of Religion	Systematic Theology	First Testament Theology
Sources and Norms	Biblical and extra-biblical, literary and archaeological	Scripture, tradition, reason, human experience, and knowledge	First Testament canon
Method	Phenomenological and historical	Theological and philosophical	Exegetical and theological
Organization of Data	Chronological and genetic	Systematic and logical	Conceptual, topical, historical, and tradition-historical
Hermeneutics	Descriptive: What was it, and what did it mean to them?	Normative and constructive: What does it mean in the context of this faith community?	Descriptive and normative: What did it mean for them, and what is its significance for us today?

Figure 3: Categories of Religious Systems of Belief and Worship

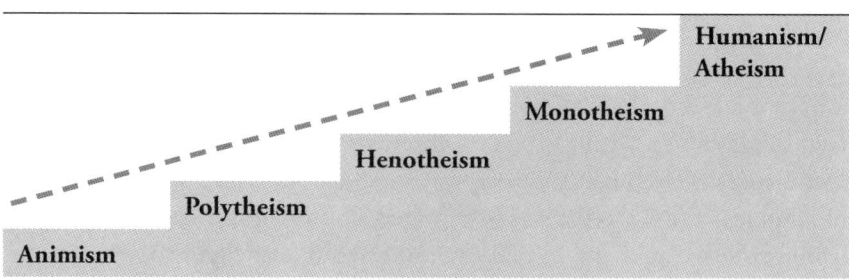

---

17. Adapted from Werner E. Lemke, "Theology: Old Testament," in *Anchor Bible Dictionary*, ed. D. N. Freedman (New York: Doubleday, 1992) 6:456.

Animism: Worshippers believe objects are inhabited by personalized supernatural beings, and these spirits govern human existence: object and supernatural beings are virtually equated.

Polytheism: Worshippers believe many gods exist simultaneously, and these gods govern human existence. These divinities may be closely associated with physical objects, but they exist apart from them. The gods are often being perceived as dwelling in a realm (heaven or otherwise) beyond the realm of human existence.

Henotheism: Worshippers believe many gods exist simultaneously, and many or all may govern human existence, but an individual or community is governed in particular by a single member of the pantheon. That god or goddess is perceived as the patron/matron of the community.

Monotheism: Worshippers believe there is only one God, and the existence of all other deities is categorically rejected.

Humanism/Atheism: Worshippers claim to believe in no deity at all, but in effect make self the measure of all things.

Julius Wellhausen's reconstruction of the history of Israel's religion was not a project in biblical theology but in comparative religion. Having reconstructed this image, he read his conclusions back into the biblical texts and made them fit his paradigm.

The Stress-Points of First Testament Theology

Having established what First Testament theology is not does not mean we have domesticated the discipline. On the contrary, this is an extremely complex enterprise, and biblical theologians are torn among a series of competing binary challenges (Figure 4).

First, should our enterprise merely describe the theology reflected in First Testament texts, or should it seek to establish normative perspectives? Is the concern of First Testament theology to describe the nature and structure of ancient Israelite belief or to determine and describe those theological realities that have abiding significance for any and every age? Lemke helpfully argues for the latter on four grounds:[18] (1) Even a self-consciously descriptive Old Testament theology assumes a normative structure in the way it selects, arranges, interprets, and presents data. Unbiased objectivity is impossible. (2) The biblical texts themselves require a response from the reader in every age and circumstance. Furthermore, the God who presents

---

18. Ibid., 455.

himself in Scripture demands a response to himself. (3) By definition *theology* concerns itself with "living faith," not just the history of religious ideas, and its conclusions suggest truths of abiding value. (4) The Bible has been preserved, read, and cherished through the centuries because it is God's Word to us. In it we find meaning and purpose for life.

Figure 4

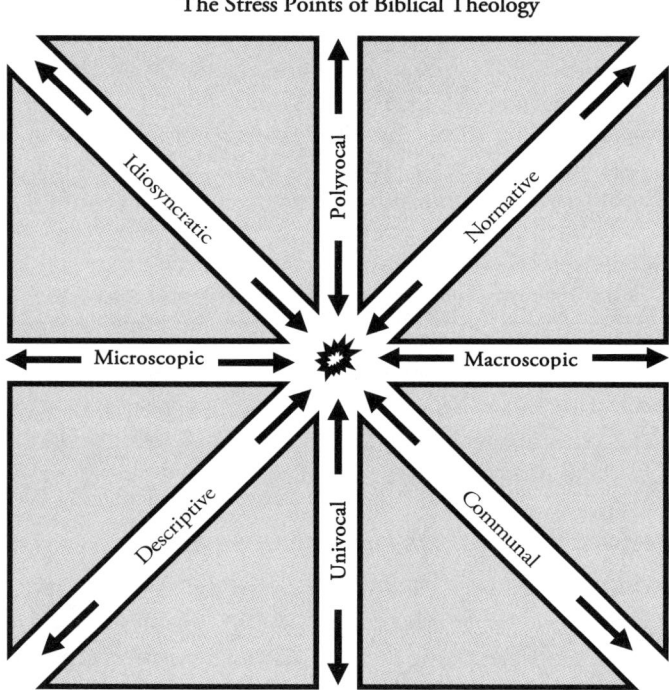

The Stress Points of Biblical Theology

Second, should biblical theology be a communal enterprise, or should scholars be free to go their own idiosyncratic ways? If we emphasize the latter, then the voice of mature reflection must surely take precedence over the enthusiasm and creativity of novices. Inasmuch as biblical theology is a synthetic enterprise, a responsible result will presuppose detailed analysis of large blocks of First Testament texts representing a wide array of genres found within the biblical material. Speaking from personal experience, I spent the first thirty years of my teaching career teaching biblical languages and exegetical and expositional courses on individual biblical books. I did not offer a course on First Testament theology until I was in my late fifties.

Even as we give priority to mature voices, the biblical-theological enterprise must be conducted in community. This is especially important if we find our conclusions to be departing from established paradigms. This does not preclude any new interpretations or theological perspectives; the deep ruts of tradition must be constantly subjected to the supreme authority of Scripture. But it means we communicate our findings in soft lead pencil and humbly seek responses from others.

Third, should First Testament theology be macroscopic, highlighting themes that tie all the Scriptures together, or should it be microscopic, focusing on distinctive perspectives of particular compositions within the First Testament? As intimated in the previous paragraph, the answer to this question may be determined by one's maturity or immaturity as a scholar. Ideally, a biblical theologian's growth will proceed in the following sequence: (1) mastery of the languages; (2) translation and exegesis of particular books, including reflection on the enduring theology of those books; (3) comparison and contrast of texts from the same period on the one hand and from different periods on the other; (4) synthetic explorations in the way theological themes are developed over time. In this last stage we begin to recognize that biblical theology is the epitome of the biblical sciences. Novices should probably begin by tackling small texts (such as the book of Ruth or one of the Minor Prophets), building up reserves of information and perspectives before they presume to pontificate on global theological matters. Having explored many texts at the microscopic level, we are prepared to move to macroscopic themes.

Fourth, should First Testament theology seek univocality, or should it celebrate the polyvocal witness of Scripture? The strength of the former is that it highlights the coherence of Scripture. In contrast to the New Testament, whose contents were all produced in a matter of decades after Jesus Christ's ascension to heaven, the texts that make up the First Testament were composed over a period lasting almost a millennium. However, inasmuch as all First Testament Scriptures were inspired by the same Spirit of God and share the goal of training the godly in righteousness and equipping them for every good work (2 Tim 3:16–17), we may expect them to speak with one voice on global matters: the character of God, the human predicament, the divine plan of redemption, etc.

However, the weakness of the univocal emphasis is that it may overlook the distinctions in approach and emphasis in the compositions that make up the First Testament. These texts were not produced in a vacuum but arose in response to particular historical and socioreligious circumstances and were recorded by humans with differing personalities and literary skills. Consequently, not only will the foci of divine revelation shift from book to book, but the ways in which divine revelation is recounted will vary. Mature First Testament theologians will resist homogenizing the messages of individual compositions and will celebrate the varieties of perspectives they represent, even as they seek to interpret each within the context of the Scriptures as a whole.

Deuteronomy as an Exercise in First Testament Theology

The Book of Deuteronomy: A Textbook for Biblical Theology 101

Deuteronomy is a good place to begin our pursuit of First Testament theology for several reasons. First, this book exercises greater influence on the rest of Scripture—including the New Testament—than any other book. Although it appears at the end of the Pentateuch, its retrospective influence is evident both in the extension of the generic designation for Moses's speeches in the book (*sēpher hattôrâ hazzeh*, "this document of the Torah")[19] to the Pentateuch as a whole (cf. Matt 5:17), and in its stylistic and conceptual influence on the preceding narratives.[20] The Torah of Moses represents the heart of the Hebrew Bible; this was the treasure priests were to teach and model,[21] that psalmists praised,[22] to which the prophets appealed,[23] by which faithful kings ruled[24] and righteous citizens lived (Psalm 1). And judging by the number of quotations and allusions to Deuteronomy, this was both Jesus's and Paul's favorite book. This impression is reinforced by

---

19. Deuteronomy 29:21; 30:10; 31:26; cf. 28:61, *sepher hattôrâ hazzō't*, "the document of this Torah."
20. For discussion of the latter issue, see Daniel I. Block, "In the Tradition of Moses: The Conceptual and Stylistic Imprint of Deuteronomy on the Patriarchal Narratives," a paper presented at Andrews University, April 3, 2016.
21. Deut 33:10; 2 Chr 15:3; 19:8; Mal 2:6, 9; cf. Jer 18:18; Ezek 7:26; Ezra 7:10.
22. Ps 19:7–14; 119
23. Isa 1:10; 5:24; 8:20; 30:9; 51:7.
24. 1 Kgs 2:2–4; 2 Kgs 14:6; 22:11; 23:25.

Jesus's distillation of the entire law into the simple command to love the Lord with one's whole being and to love one's neighbor as oneself (Matt 22:37; Mark 12:30; Luke 10:27). Although appeals for love for one's neighbor and the stranger occur earlier in the Pentateuch (Lev 19:18,34), the command to love God occurs only in Deuteronomy (6:5; 11:1,13; 13:3; 30:6). In short, the book of Deuteronomy provides the theological base for virtually the entire Old (and New) Testament and the paradigm for much of its literary style.

Second, with reference to form, genre, and intention, Deuteronomy offers the most didactic and systematic presentation of fundamental Yahwistic theology in the entire Hebrew Bible. In this respect, on the one hand we may compare it to Romans in the New Testament. On the other hand, since Deuteronomy reviews many of Israel's experiences of God's grace as recounted in Genesis–Numbers, a comparison with the Gospel of John may be more appropriate. Having had several decades to reflect on the significance of the death and resurrection of Jesus, John produced a profoundly theological Gospel; he was less interested in the chronology and facts of the life of Christ and more concerned with its revelatory significance. Similarly, according to Deuteronomy's internal witness, by the time Moses proclaimed the speeches in the book and committed them to writing, he had also had almost four decades to reflect on the significance of the exodus of his people from Egypt and Yahweh's establishment of a covenant relationship with Israel at Sinai.[25] Like the Gospel of John, the book of Deuteronomy functions as a theological manifesto, calling on Israel to respond to God's grace with unreserved loyalty and love. If we grasp the perspectives of this book, we will have grasped the foundations of biblical theology as a whole.

Third, contrary to popular opinion, which views Moses's role in the book as a legislator,[26] both the narrator and Moses himself viewed his role

---

25. The preamble to the first address and the book as a whole (1:1–5) suggests the speeches contain a distillation of Moses's teaching all along the journey from Horeb to the Plains of Moab.

26. Note the titles of books such as D. M. Murdock a.k.a. Acharya S, *Did Moses Exist? The Myth of the Israelite Lawgiver* (Seattle: Stellar, 2014); Thomas Keneally, *Moses the Lawgiver* (New York: Harper and Row, 1975); Julius Leibert, *The Lawgiver* (New York: Exposition, 1953); and William M. Taylor, *Moses: The Law-Giver*, Bible Biographies Series (Grand Rapids: Baker, 1961).

primarily as that of a pastor-teacher or pastor-theologian.[27] The opening line explicitly characterizes the contents of the book, not as statutes and ordinances (*huqqîm ûmišpāṭîm*) but as "the words Moses spoke to all Israel" (*haddĕbārîm 'ăšer dibber mōšeh 'el kol yiśrā'ēl*). The addresses that follow represent Moses's farewell speeches to his congregation before they crossed the Jordan and before he went to his own eternal reward (34:1–12). Deuteronomy casts these speeches as "instruction" rather than law (1:5; etc.). The Hebrew word *tôrâ* is a didactic expression, derived from the Hiphil form of *yrh*, meaning "to teach."

To be sure, the book contains statutes and ordinances, but they actually play subordinate roles, always being presented in support of the larger pedagogical and theological goals.

The Theological Agenda of Deuteronomy

The first generation of Israelites to come out of Egypt and the generation that stood before Moses on the Plains of Moab were dependent on the direct revelation of God as he acted in their own experience and history. Moses recalls the forms in which this happened repeatedly in Deuteronomy, but especially in 4:1–14 and 4:32–40. In the latter text he invites his hearers to research exhaustively all the historical and literary resources on earth to see if they could find any precedents or counterparts to Yahweh's rescue of Israel from Egypt and his encounter with them at Horeb. Assuming a negative answer, redundantly he added the theological goal of Yahweh's mighty revelatory acts: "You were shown *these things* so that you would know (*yāda'*) that the LORD is God; there is no other besides him" (4:35, emphasis added). "Today, recognize (*yāda'*) and keep in mind (*hēšîb 'el lĕbābekā*) that the LORD is God in heaven above and on earth below; there

---

27. The only role the book explicitly ascribes to Moses is that of "prophet" (*nābî'*, Deut 18:15; 34:10). The verbs used by the narrator to describe his speech actions include "to say" (*'āmar*, 1:5; 31:2; 32:6), "to speak" (*dibbēr*, 1:1; 4:45; 27:9; 31:1; 32:44–45); "to summon" (*qārā'*, 5:1; 29:1[Eng 2]; 31:7; "to teach" (*limmad*, 31:22); "to bless" (*bērēk*, 33:1); and "to set" [the Torah before the people] (*śîm*, 4:44). Only thrice (and not until after the bulk of the second address) does Moses "charge/command" the people (27:1; 31:10, 25). For full discussion, see Daniel I. Block, "Will the Real Moses Please Rise? An Exploration into the Role and Ministry of Moses in the Book of Deuteronomy," in Block, *The Gospel According to Moses: Theological and Ethical Reflections on the Book of Deuteronomy* (Eugene, OR: Cascade, 2012), 76–82. Moses characterizes his first address as teaching (*limmad*) as well (4:1, 5, 9, 14), and he casts the people as "learners" (4:10). Verbs used for the second address include "to say" (*'āmar*, 1:5; 31:2; 32:6), "to speak" (*dibbēr*, 5:1); and "to teach" (*limmad*, 6:1), while the people are "to learn" (*lāmad*) from him (5:2–5), though the tone of the second (5:1–11:32) and third addresses (12:1–26:19; 28:1–68) is entirely pastoral and sermonic. For full discussion, see ibid., 82–101.

is no other" (4:39). This revelation was to be permanently constitutive for the people of Yahweh. However, future generations—which are on Moses's mind throughout the book of Deuteronomy—will obviously not have participated in the dramatic events in Egypt, at Horeb, and in the desert on the way to the Promised Land. How then could their memories of those events be retained and their understandings of the theological significance of those events be maintained? The written copies of Moses's addresses, which were to be read every seven years at the Festival of Sukkot (31:9–13, 24–29), and the "national anthem," which Moses taught the people (32:1–43), provide answers to this question. The divine origin of both documents is clear: Moses delivered the addresses as Yahweh commanded him (1:3), and he transcribed and taught the song just as Yahweh had dictated it to him and Joshua (cf. 31:14–22,30; 32:44–47). The canonical status of the former is symbolized by Moses's handing the copies of the addresses to the Levitical priests, who ceremoniously place them beside the ark of the covenant (31:26), and of the latter by Yahweh's declaration that the song would function as a witness (*ʿēd*) against the Israelites in perpetuity (31:19–21). These documents represented the key to Israel's future well-being in the land and with Yahweh. As prescribed by Moses in 31:10–13, the pedagogical and theological function of the written Torah may be summarized this way:

Figure 5: The Deuteronomic Formula for Life

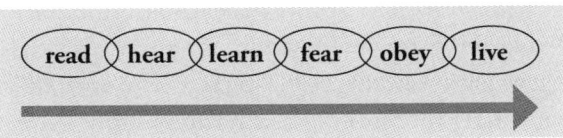

Read this Torah before all the people
    that they may hear,
        that they may learn,
            that they may fear,
                that they may obey,
                    that they may live.

We encounter this formula elsewhere in Deuteronomy (see Table 2). Although no single text contains all the elements, remarkably the most complete version occurs in 17:19–29, which presents the king as a model of covenant righteousness. This "charter for kingship" prohibits the king from using his office for personal advantage and calls on him to read the Torah for himself. Through this exercise he will learn to fear Yahweh, remain humble, stay on course in his obedience to Yahweh, and ultimately enjoy a long tenure on the throne. For ordinary citizens, the equivalent reward for obedience would simply be a long, full life in the land.

Table 2: The Importance of Hearing the Torah

Reference	Reading	Hearing	Learning	Fearing	Obeying	Living Well
1. 4:10		✓	✓	✓		
2. 5:23–29		✓		✓	✓	✓
3. 6:1–3			✓	✓	✓	✓
4. 17:13		✓		✓	✓	
5. 17:19–20	✓	[✓]	✓	✓	✓	✓
6. 19:20		✓		✓	✓	
7. 31:11–13	✓	✓	✓	✓	✓	[✓]

But how does hearing the Torah promote "fear" that yields obedient living and is rewarded with life? The answer is found in part in recognizing the variation in usage of the Hebrew word *yārēʾ*. The word is capable of a wide range of meanings. In Deuteronomy that range stretches from "sheer terror" to "trusting awe," and the term may actually function as a substitute for *heʾĕmîn*, "to believe, demonstrate confidence in" someone (Figure 6).[28] The word often occurs as a prelude to obedience and righteous living,[29] but

---

28. The roots of Deuteronomy's use of *yārēʾ* to mean "trusting awe," may be traced back to Abraham's proof of his faith in the sacrifice of Isaac (Gen 22:12; cf. v. 1). For full discussion, see Daniel I. Block, "Hearing Galatians with Moses: An Examination of Paul as a Second and Seconding Moses," in *Sēpher Tôrat Mōšeh: Studies in the Composition and Interpretation of Deuteronomy.*, ed. Daniel I. Block and Richard L. Schultz (Peabody, MA: Hendrickson, 2017); idem, "The Fear of Yahweh: The Theological Tie that Binds Deuteronomy and Proverbs," article forthcoming in the Festschrift for Willem VanGemeren, ed. Andrew Abernethy (Grand Rapids: Zondervan, 2017).

29. Deut 5:29; 6:2; 8:6; 10:12–13; 13:5[ET 4]; 17:19; 28:58; 31:12. Cf. Daniel I. Block, "'A Place for My Name': Horeb and Zion in the Mosaic Vision of Israelite Worship." *Journal of the Evangelical Theological Society* 58 (2015): 221–47.

its significance in the establishment and ethical demonstration of a biblical theology is evident particularly in the sequence of verbs in Figure 5 and illustrated in Table 2. For our purposes the fifth and seventh texts, which involve encounters with Yahweh through hearing the written Torah read, are especially significant.[30]

Whereas Israel's encounter with Yahweh at Horeb had terrified the people (4:9–14, 36; 5:5, 23–33; 18:16), Deuteronomy portrays worship at the place that Yahweh would establish his name as confident, intimate, and celebrative.[31] One of the functions of that worship was to promote *yārēʾ*, which obviously cannot mean "fright."

If we view the Torah (i.e., Moses's addresses in Deuteronomy) primarily as law, as many assume, hearing "the law" could evoke fear of negative consequences, analogous to the effect of hearing verdicts in criminal cases (13:12[ET 11]; 17:13; 19:20; 21:21). However, if we understand *hattôrâ* as "the instruction," whose goal was the promotion of *yārēʾ* in the sense of "trusting awe" (Paul's *pistis*), then its significance for this discussion is readily apparent.

Figure 6: The Semantic Range of ירא Words

| Terror | Fright | Anxiety | Awe | Reverence | Submission | Trust |

But how does hearing the Torah promote a true theology and a resultant firm faith in Yahweh? This chapter cannot offer a full discussion of the issue, but we may begin by asking, "When people hear the Torah read in community, what will they learn about God?" In short, how does Deuteronomy characterize Yahweh?

First, Deuteronomy portrays Yahweh in gloriously transcendent terms, pointing to a trustworthy deity. By itself this image could evoke fright/awe, but in context it is intended to promote confidence and trust (see

---

30. In the first three the sound of Yahweh's voice accompanied by awesome theophanic visual phenomena at Horeb evoked severe fright in the people. The fourth and sixth cases involve warnings against disregarding the divinely rendered decisions in criminal cases (17:13) or repeating the crime (19:20).

31. Signaled by the verb *śāmaḥ*, in 12:7, 12, 18; 14:26; 16:11, 14–15; 26:11 (cf. Lev 23:40). On the contrast between Israel's one-time encounter with Yahweh at Horeb and Israel's regular meetings with him at the central sanctuary, see Daniel I. Block, "A Place for My Name."

Isa 40:12–31). The concluding Song of Moses in Deuteronomy 32 opens by ascribing greatness (*gōdel*) to him (v. 3), a theme Moses declared elsewhere in doxological descriptions.

> 7:21 Yahweh your God is in your midst, a great and awesome God (*ʾēl gādôl wĕnôrāʾ*).
>
> 10:17 Yahweh your God is God of gods and Lord of lords, the great, mighty, and awe-inspiring God (*hāʾēl haggādōl haggibbōr wĕhannôrāʾ*).
>
> 28:5 That you may fear this glorious and awesome name, Yahweh your God (*haššēm hannikbād wĕhannôrāʾ hazzeh yhwh ʾĕlōhêkā*).

Yahweh's transcendent power and glory were demonstrated particularly through the "signs and wonders" performed against the Egyptians (4:34; 10:21; 26:8) and for Israel's benefit.[32]

Second, the Torah portrays Yahweh in graciously personal terms. Although the Hebrew word for grace (*ḥēn*) occurs only once in Deuteronomy,[33] Israel's confidence in future restoration after judgment was based on his compassionate character (4:31) and his change of heart toward his wayward people (32:36). But Moses laced his recollections of past events with stories of divine grace: Yahweh loved the ancestors and elected their descendants for his favor out of all the peoples on earth (4:37; cf. 7:6–7; 10:15; 14:2). He rescued his people from Egypt (4:32–40; cf. 5:6 *et passim*). He invited Israel to assembly in his presence at Horeb and established his covenant with them there (4:9–31; cf. 5:2–3); he revealed his will to Israel (4:1–8; cf. 5:1–22; 6:20–25; 30:11–20). He spared Israel and renewed the covenant at Horeb after the golden calf debacle (9:19, 25–10:5). He cared for Israel in the desert (1:31; 8:1–5). He gave them a fruitful homeland (1:7–8; 6:10–11, 23; 8:7–10; 11:9–12; 26:9, 15; 27:3; 32:14–14). He provided leadership in the forms of kings (17:14–20), prophets (such as Moses; 18:9–20), and Levitical priests (10:8–9; 18:1–8; 21:5; 33:8–11). He

---

32. Deuteronomy 11:2–7 includes Yahweh's care for the Israelites in the desert and his punishment of Dathan and Abiram among "all the great acts of Yahweh that he executed" (*kol maʿăśēh yhwh haggādôl ʾăšer ʿāśâ*). Cf. Exod 15:11.

33. The root *ḥēn* occurs only in 24:1, which notes its absence in the way a man treats a needy wife.

confirmed the covenant with the present generation in Moab (26:16–19; 27:9; 28:6–9[ET 29:1]; 29:11[ET 12]; etc.). He invited Israel to worship and celebrate in his presence (12:1–14; 14:1–21, 26; 16:11–14; 26:1–11), and he desired Israel's well-being (11:18–25; 12:7, 18; 15:10; 23:21[ET 20]; 28:1–14; 30:11–20). Even threats of punishment represent overtures of grace, reminding the people how passionately Yahweh treasured his relationship with them and warning in advance of the consequences of apostasy. Hearing the Torah would remind the people of all these graces, hopefully evoking in them not fear in the sense of terror, but as awed confidence in the One who had chosen them to be his treasured people.

Third, the Torah portrays Yahweh as faithful to his word. The exordium to the Song of Moses (Deut 32) begins by proclaiming Yahweh's greatness (v. 3), but the next strophe focuses on his faithfulness: "The Rock—his work is perfect; all his ways are just. A faithful God, without bias, he is righteous and true" (v. 4).

Earlier in 7:9 Moses had celebrated this faithfulness doxologically:[34] "The LORD your God is God, the faithful God who keep his gracious covenant loyalty for a thousand generations with those who love him and keep his commands." While this summary declaration is covenantal from beginning to end, the Torah of Deuteronomy proclaims the faithfulness of Yahweh with repeated reminders of how he has kept the promises associated with his covenant made with the ancestors, established with their descendants at Horeb,[35] and renewed with this generation:[36] (a) Yahweh has multiplied the population like the stars of the sky;[37] (b) as predicted in Gen 15:13, after centuries in a foreign land, the enslaved Israelites were rescued from their oppressors by Yahweh;[38] (c) now, after the failure of the Exodus generation (1:35; 4:25), Yahweh is about to deliver the Promised Land of Canaan into their hands.[39] But Yahweh's fidelity to his word is also reflected in his oath, with which he guarantees the negative consequences of infidelity built into the covenant (11:13–28; 28:1–69[ET 29:1]).

---

34. Cf. Exod 34:6; Ps 86:15.
35. Cf. Gen 17:6–8; Exod 6:2–8; 19:4–6; Deut 4:9–31.
36. On "the covenant with the fathers," see Jerry Hwang, *The Rhetoric of Remembrance: An Investigation of the "Fathers" in Deuteronomy*, Siphrut 8 (Winona Lake, IN: Eisenbrauns, 2012), 178–232.
37. Deut 1:10; 10:22; 26:5; cf. Gen 15:5; 22:17; 26:4.
38. Deut 4:37; 5:6; 6:12, 21–23; 7:8; 8:14; 13:6, 11[ET 5, 10]; 26:6–8.
39. References to the covenant oath involving the land occur a dozen times in the book: 1:8, 35; 4:21; etc.

Nevertheless, building on Lev 26:40–45, Moses declared that however horrendous the punishment for rebellion might be (4:26–28; 28:15–68; 29:19–27[ET 20–28]), the judgment would not be the last word. With compassionate heart and faithfulness to his commitments, Yahweh would bring his people back from exile and reestablish them in the land promised to the ancestors (4:30–31; 30:1–10; 32:43). The Israelites may soon forget their commitments by going after other gods (4:23; 6:12; 8:11, 14, 19; 31:16–18, 26–29), but Yahweh would never forget his covenant (4:31). God hereby guaranteed his people's future with his promise (32:36–43) and his oath.[40]

Why is hearing the Torah in community so important? In addition to its stimulating reverent awe (*yārē'*), hearing the reminders of Yahweh's compassion toward his people in the past and his declarations of his faithfulness to his words, his covenant, and his people in the future should evoke the same faith that Abraham exhibited in Gen 15:6 and 22:1–12. Since this confidence in Yahweh represents part of the fuller meaning of *yārē'* in Deuteronomy, hearing the Torah would be critical for inculcating in the people a sound theology and maintaining Israel's. At the festival of Shelters, the priests were to "read" the Torah that the people might "listen," that they might "learn" to "fear" (i.e., trust) Yahweh, that they might "follow," that they might "live" (Deut 31:9–13).[41] We now understand why the five markers of Israel's identity in Deut 10:12–13 begin with "fear/trusting awe" and then move successively through walking in the ways of Yahweh, demonstrating love for him, wholehearted and full-bodied service, and finally to obedience to the commands. We also learn that true biblical theology is demonstrated ethically in righteous living and has a teleological goal: well-being in the presence and under the blessing of God. Borrowing from Deuteronomy, the Wisdom writers had it right: "The fear of [trusting awe in] the LORD is the beginning of wisdom, and the knowledge of the Holy One is understanding" (Prov 9:10).[42]

---

40. Cf. the references to "a covenant . . . with an oath" in 29:11, 13, 20[ET 12, 14, 21].

41. This sequence reinforces Nahum Sarna's contention (in *Exodus*, JPS Torah Commentary [Philadelphia; Jewish Publication Society, 1991], 75) that "faith" in the Hebrew Bible "refers to trust and loyalty that find expression in obedience and commitment."

42. Cf. Prov 1:7; 15:33; Job 28:28; Ps 111:10. On "fear" and its relation to wisdom, see Moberly, *Theology of the Old Testament*, 265–77.

And now we also understand the conclusion to the book of Malachi, and indeed to the First Testament.[43] In a series of oracles from the Persian period responding to the absence of fear/trust in Yahweh in the restored community in Jerusalem, Malachi prescribed a remarkable solution: "Remember the instruction [Torah] of Moses my servant whom I charged at Horeb for all Israel" (Mal 4:4).[44] Let the theological reeducation program begin.

Conclusion

At the outset of the second part of this chapter, I suggested that Deuteronomy establishes the paradigm of biblical education that carries through the entire First Testament. This is true with respect to both its content and its pedagogical strategy. The importance of these two elements is reflected in Judg 2:7–12, a deuteronomistic text:

> The people [of Israel] worshiped the Lord throughout Joshua's lifetime and during the lifetimes of the elders who outlived Joshua. They had seen all the Lord's great works he had done for Israel. Joshua son of Nun, the servant of the Lord, died at the age of 110. They buried him in the territory of his inheritance, in Timnath-heres, in the hill country of Ephraim, north of Mount Gaash. That whole generation was also gathered to their ancestors. After them another generation rose up who did not know the Lord or the works he had done for Israel. The Israelites did what was evil in the Lord's sight. They worshiped the Baals and abandoned the Lord, the God of their fathers, who had brought them out of Egypt.

Obviously all the means for spiritual nurture of the people provided by the Torah of Moses had failed: parents stopped teaching Torah to their children; the Levitical priests failed in their pastoral duties; if the national festivals were remembered at all, they must have become perfunctory observances;

---

43. As arranged in the LXX and all Christian translations. The Hebrew Bible concludes with 2 Chronicles.
44. Malachi echoes Deut 4:1 and 4:14. Cf. also 6:1.

the national anthem was forgotten; the memorial objects and places were neglected.

No wonder Yahweh's ire was raised.

The Torah of Moses represents the heart of the Hebrew Bible and the heart of biblical theology. It also offers us guidance as we contemplate the place of biblical theology in our educational institutions. If biblical theology is the "queen of the biblical sciences," then at the heart of the curriculum should be instruction in the Scriptures. This will allow our students (Christian leaders of the future) to learn to fear [i.e., trust] the Lord who reveals himself in glory, grace, and trustworthiness, so that they might demonstrate covenant commitment to him in righteous living and faithful service. This will lead to flourishing spiritually in the presence and with the blessing of God—all to the praise of his glory!

Questions for Further Reflection

1. Explain how Deuteronomy provides the theological base for virtually the entire First (and New) Testament and the paradigm for much of its literary style.
2. Explain how Deuteronomy establishes the paradigm of biblical education that carries through the entire First Testament.
3. How does the Torah of Moses offer guidance as we contemplate the place of biblical theology in our educational institutions?

Sources for Further Study

Block, Daniel I. *For the Glory of God: Recovering a Biblical Theology of Worship.* Grand Rapids: Baker, 2014.

Goldingay, John. *Biblical Theology.* Downers Grove: InterVarsity, 2016.

Hasel, Gerhard. *Old Testament Theology.* Grand Rapids: Eerdmans, 1991.

House, Paul R. *Old Testament Theology.* Downers Grove: InterVarsity, 1998.

Kaiser, Walter C., Jr. *The Promise-Plan of God: A Biblical Theology of the Old and New Testaments.* Grand Rapids: Zondervan, 2008.

Routledge, Robin. *Old Testament Theology.* Downers Grove: InterVarsity, 2008.

Waltke, Bruce K., and Charles Yu. *An Old Testament Theology: An Exegetical, Canonical, and Thematic Approach.* Grand Rapids: Zondervan, 2007.

Chapter Eleven

THEOLOGY OF THE NEW TESTAMENT

CHRISTOPHER W. MORGAN

The Bible is a human book. It is deeply grounded in history and was written over a period of approximately 1,500 years, on three continents (Asia, Africa, and Europe). In one sense it is one book, but in another sense it is sixty-six books, written by forty or so authors from all walks of life (fishermen, doctor, tax collector, kings, prophets, tent maker, shepherd, governor, farmers, etc.). Each author is an individual with particular gifts, styles, and personality traits. The Bible is also written in human languages (the Old Testament in Hebrew and a few places in Aramaic, the New Testament in Greek), uses ordinary language of everyday speech, and includes loose quotations or approximations. The diverse authors also use a wide variety of literary genres, as D. A. Carson helpfully notes:

> Poetry and prose, narrative and discourse, oracle and lament, parable and fable, history and theology, genealogy and apocalyptic, proverb and psalm, gospel and letter, law and wisdom literature, missive and sermon, couplet and epic—the Bible is made up of all of these and more. Covenantal patterns emerge with some likeness to Hittite treaties. Tables of household duties are found with startling resemblances to codes of conduct in the Hellenistic world. And these realities, a by-product of the humanness of the Bible, necessarily affect how we must approach the Bible to interpret it aright.[1]

---

1. D. A. Carson, "Approaching the Bible," in his *Collected Writings on Scripture*, comp. Andrew David Naselli (Wheaton: Crossway, 2010), 26.

The Bible also addresses a wide range of human subjects: history, psychology, child-rearing, poetry, music, moral law, political law, military ideas, philosophy, science, and (fundamentally) salvation. It progressively tells the story of God and his relationship with people, especially his covenant people. The Bible bears human witness to God through stories of love and joy, pain and persecution, fear and hope. It was collected from its beginnings in the ancient Near East to its conclusion in the first century, and the church gradually recognized its individual books as authoritative (i.e., canonization). It is written for humans to know God, love God, love others, and live according to God's purpose in the world.

Yet, in the midst of all this human diversity among authors, cultures, contexts, periods, genres, and topics, there is amazing unity to the biblical message. This unity shines because Scripture is also a divinely inspired book. Scripture is routinely called (and is) the Word of God. This is evident from many passages, most famously 2 Tim 3–4. Paul reminds Timothy (and us) that Scripture is sacred (3:15), inspired by God (3:16); it is the Word of God (4:2) and the truth (4:4). Paul is not breaking new ground in saying this but reminding Timothy what he already knows through the Old Testament. Indeed, passages such as Ps 19:7–11 underline that Scripture is the Word *of God*, even using repetition for effect:

> The instruction of the LORD is perfect,
> renewing one's life;
> the testimony of the LORD is trustworthy,
> making the inexperienced wise.
> The precepts of the LORD are right,
> making the heart glad;
> the command of the LORD is radiant,
> making the eyes light up.
> The fear of the LORD is pure,
> enduring forever;
> the ordinances of the LORD are reliable
> and altogether righteous.
> They are more desirable than gold—
> than an abundance of pure gold;
> and sweeter than honey,
> dripping from a honeycomb.

> In addition, your servant is warned by them,
> and in keeping them there is an abundant reward.

Indeed, Scripture is the Word of God because God inspired it (3:16). The biblical *writers* were inspired by God, as Peter explains: "No prophecy of Scripture comes from the prophet's own interpretation, because no prophecy ever came by the will of man; instead, men spoke from God as they were carried along by the Holy Spirit" (2 Pet 1:20–21). And the biblical *writings* were inspired by God (2 Tim 3:16). God used the experiences, personalities, feelings, and thoughts of the prophets and apostles, yet he superintended what they spoke and wrote. This inspiration was dynamic, as God actively worked through the active human authors. This inspiration is also verbal, referring to the actual writings (2 Tim 3:16) and the words the prophets spoke (2 Pet 1:20–21).

The result is that Scripture is truthful in all it affirms. Carson summarizes the idea beautifully, stating that the inspiration of Scripture refers to the "supernatural work of God's Holy Spirit upon the human authors of Scripture such that what they wrote was precisely what God intended them to write in order to communicate his truth."[2] He adds, "The definition speaks both of God's action, by his Spirit, in the human author and of the nature of the resulting text."[3] Thus inspiration includes God's verbal revelation and historical human witness: "words of human beings and words of God, the truth that God chose to communicate and the particular forms of individual human authors."[4] Inspired by God and being the Word of God, Scripture is truthful, authoritative over our beliefs and lives, and a form of God's action in the world given to accomplish his mission (2 Tim 3:15–4:5)—so that people would glorify God through faith in Jesus, the Lord and Savior (see, e.g., John 20:28–31; 1 John 5:12–13).

Introduction to New Testament Theology

Like the other theological disciplines, biblical theology (including Old Testament theology, New Testament theology, and biblical theology in

---

2. Ibid., 31.
3. Ibid.
4. Ibid., 32.

general) is inherently shaped by these truths. And, as we will see, biblical theology struggles to find its identity and focus largely because of differing perspectives on these truths and the inherent tensions that emerge from Scripture's nature as both thoroughly human and the Word of God.

As a result, biblical theology is notoriously difficult to define, as attempted definitions are usually driven by the theological and ideological commitments of the scholars offering the definitions. As will be clearer later, evangelicals and more conservative scholars tend to define biblical theology in certain ways, whereas more liberal scholars tend to take it in other directions. In other words, biblical theology means different things to different people.

In general, though, biblical theology is the discipline that strives to set forth the message and theology of the Bible, of particular biblical books, and of their particular authors in their historical setting, terms, categories, and thought forms.[5] Unlike the interrelated discipline of systematic theology, biblical theology is not largely concerned with modern questions, terms, categories, and thought forms; instead, it focuses on the biblical material and its own historical concerns, themes, and theology. Adolf Schlatter classically framed the nature and goals of biblical theology:

> We turn away decisively from ourselves and our time to what was found in the men through whom the church came into being [i.e., the New Testament writers]. Our main interest should be the thought as it was conceived by them and the truth that was valid for them. We want to see and obtain a thorough grasp of what happened historically and existed in another time. This is the internal disposition upon which the

---

5. This definition is adapted from that of G. E. Ladd, *A Theology of the New Testament*, rev. ed. (Grand Rapids: Eerdmans, 1993), 20–28. For helpful introductions to biblical theology, see D. A. Carson, "Current Issues in Biblical Theology: A New Testament Perspective," *Bulletin of Biblical Research* 5 (1995): 17–41; Gerhard Hasel, "Biblical Theology: Then, Now, and Tomorrow," *Horizons of Biblical Theology* 4 (1982): 61–93; Edward W. Klink III and Darian R. Lockett, *Understanding Biblical Theology: A Comparison of Theory and Practice* (Grand Rapids: Zondervan, 2012); and Andreas J. Köstenberger, "The Present and Future of Biblical Theology," *Themelios* 37.3 (2012): 446–64. Charles H. H. Scobie offers another helpful definition: "Biblical Theology may be defined as the ordered study of the understanding of the revelation of God contained in the canonical scriptures of the Old and New Testaments"; see "The Challenge of Biblical Theology," *Tyndale Bulletin* 42 (1991): 36.

success of the work depends, the commitment which must consistently be renewed as the work proceeds.[6]

As a subdiscipline of biblical theology, New Testament theology strives to set forth the message and theology of the New Testament, its particular books, and its particular authors in their own historical setting, terms, categories, and thought forms.

One way to understand New Testament theology is to view it as a sort of bridge between New Testament exegesis and systematic theology.[7] While grounded in New Testament exegesis and studies of background, language, literary forms, and historical occasions, New Testament theology strives to describe further the message, themes, thought forms, and theology of the New Testament, its books, and its authors. Yet it does not seek to study how all of truth in all of life relates to it and coheres with it, as does systematic theology.

Most church leaders are acquainted with both biblical exegesis and systematic theology (whether or not they know the terms). They have been taught how to interpret the Bible and teach or preach it in an expository manner. They have also studied the major tenets of the Christian faith—God, humanity, sin, Christ, Holy Spirit, salvation, the church, and eschatology. Many, however, are not as familiar with biblical theology. They have studied the particulars and the major doctrines but are usually unacquainted with what lies between those vantage points. An analogy might help. If we wanted to survey a territory such as a city, we might do so from various points of view. We might walk around it, drive through it, or fly over it in a helicopter. In a way, walking around it would be like biblical exegesis. Every piece of the terrain in its specific location is observed. Flying over it is like systematic theology, which orients us to the major contours of the territory. Driving through it is comparable to biblical theology as it notices the bulk of the terrain and yet gives a fairly broad perspective. All three approaches

---

6. Adolf Schlatter, *The History of the Christ*, trans. Andreas J. Köstenberger (Grand Rapids: Baker, 1997), 18. I owe this quote to Köstenberger, "The Present and Future of Biblical Theology."

7. D. A. Carson, "Unity and Diversity in the New Testament: The Possibility of Systematic Theology," in *Scripture and Truth*, D. A. Carson and John D. Woodbridge, ed. (Grand Rapids: Baker, 1992), 94. Note that this is not a one-way bridge. These disciplines are not completely distinguishable, are interdependent, and inevitably flow back and forth into each other. Theology influences exegesis; exegesis shapes theology. Both shape biblical theology; biblical theology shapes both, etc.

have their place and offer particular insights the other perspectives cannot. Put together, these three perspectives yield more insight into the territory.

Inherent Tensions and Elements in New Testament Theology

As a discipline that is a bridge between New Testament studies and systematic theology, New Testament theology inherently strives to address both the historical and the theological aspects of the New Testament. New Testament theology also struggles in part to find its identity and focus because it strives to accept and manage the multifaceted inherent tensions that emerge from the thoroughly human and divinely inspired nature of Scripture. Three such tensions inherent in New Testament theology stand out.

Descriptive and Prescriptive

One tension facing New Testament theology is the question of whether the discipline is purely descriptive or is both descriptive and prescriptive. The goals and nature of New Testament theology often turn on this question. Because the Bible is not less than thoroughly human, written by humans with certain gifts, personalities, backgrounds, contexts, and goals to humans with certain needs and occasions, interpreting Scripture is properly seen as a historical and thus descriptive enterprise. Who wrote what to whom, in what setting, in what forms, and for what purposes? The investigative reporter's questions are valid for understanding any document, including the Bible: who, what, when, where, why, and how?

But is New Testament theology also prescriptive? Those who question the divine inspiration of Scripture naturally tend to undercut its prescriptive and normative character. Biblical studies in general, and New Testament theology in particular, are valuable to them only as a descriptive discipline.[8] This descriptive emphasis was voiced by William Wrede, who maintained that the role of New Testament theology was "to lay out the history of early Christian religion and theology . . . what was believed, thought, taught, hoped, required and striven for in the earliest period of Christianity; not what certain writings say about faith, doctrine, hope,

---

8. I. Howard Marshall in *Jesus the Savior: Studies in New Testament Theology* (Downers Grove, IL: InterVarsity Press, 1990), 15–34.

etc."⁹ In Wrede's approach New Testament theology is thereby reduced to a form of historical theology.

Yet other biblical scholars, such as Geerhardus Vos, aptly pointed out that the divinely inspired nature of Scripture means these historical documents are also God's Word.[10] God himself stands behind the intentions and words of Scripture (i.e., dynamic, verbal inspiration), has spoken through the documents to the original recipients, and speaks through these documents to his people today. Thus the historical message of the Bible is inherently authoritative over us, guiding our beliefs and lives. So, for evangelicals, New Testament theology is both descriptive and prescriptive. It was timely for its original setting and is yet timeless, applicable to everyone everywhere.

Unfortunately, some evangelicals who desire to receive authoritative teaching from God through his Word may inadvertently skip the hard work of descriptive analysis. But surely the theological message rests on the historical and descriptive work. For instance, how many sermons have we heard on Matt 28:18–20 as a rallying cry for missions? But how many times have we also heard that this Great Commission passage should first be read as the conclusion of the Gospel of Matthew? With these famous words Matthew concludes his book, a Gospel that is in a particular genre, organized by Matthew in a distinct way, written with particular goals to teach specific themes to particular recipients. Further, Matthew leaves his readers, who are in a historical context, with these words of Jesus, which are in a literary context. Matthew 28:18–20 follows the previous accounts of Jesus's genealogy, birth, baptism, temptation, formation of his messianic community, Sermon on the Mount, miracles, time with the disciples, betrayal, trial, crucifixion, burial, resurrection, and subsequent appearances.

The passage also reiterates and bolsters many themes Matthew has previously stressed: Jesus's messianic community, worship, doubt, faith, heaven and earth, Jesus's lordship and authority, discipleship, Jesus's teachings, obedience, God's covenant presence, the Abrahamic covenant, Jews and Gentiles in salvation history, and God's universal mission. Even more,

---

9. W. Wrede, "The Task and Methods of New Testament Theology," cited in Robert Morgan, *The Nature of New Testament Theology* (1897; London: SPCK, 1973), 84–85.

10. Geerhardus Vos, *Biblical Theology: Old and New Testaments* (Grand Rapids: Eerdmans, 1948). See also Peter Balla, *Challenges to New Testament Theology: An Attempt to Justify the Enterprise* (Grand Rapids: Baker, 1998); and Robert W. Yarbrough, *The Salvation-Historical Fallacy? Reassessing the History of New Testament Theology*, History of Biblical Interpretation (Leiden: Deo, 2004).

these final words in Matthew are both similar to and yet distinct from related commission statements in Luke, John, and Acts. Are these words from Jesus through Matthew prescriptive for us today? Yes, but we will understand how these words are prescriptive only after we have done the hard work of descriptive analysis.

Thus, for those holding to the Scripture as fully and simultaneously the words of humans and the Word of God, New Testament theology is both descriptive (historical) and prescriptive (authoritative/theological/revelatory). Even more, New Testament theology is first descriptive and then prescriptive.

Diversity and Unity

A related tension facing New Testament theology is the question of diversity and unity. The diversity in the New Testament is staggering: multiple authors, historical periods, cultural settings, authorial intentions, recipients, genres, and styles. Solid biblical interpretation and sound theological reflection should not flatten out the diversity but appreciate it. For example, there are four canonical Gospels and thus four portraits of Jesus. Yet there is one Jesus. Each of the Gospels truthfully presents him, each is necessary, and each contributes to a fuller portrait than any single one did or could produce.

Consider also the diversity of emphases surrounding the perennial question concerning the teaching of James and Paul on faith and works. James asserts, "You see that a person is justified by works and not by faith alone" (Jas 2:24). But Paul declares, "We conclude that a person is justified by faith apart from the works of the law" (Rom 3:28). Do these verses constitute a contradiction in Scripture? Does James refute Paul's teaching on justification, or vice versa? Those who highlight the human nature of Scripture but reject its divine inspiration readily embrace the diversity of James and Paul in such passages but often question the search for a unified message. Those who believe Scripture is both the words of humans and the Word of God fittingly prize the diversity and also anticipate unity. Unfortunately, some begin by asking the question of unity, but as Schlatter appropriately warned, "It does not make any sense to compare James to Paul before at least James has been understood."[11]

---

11. Richard Bauckham, *James: Wisdom of James, Disciple of Jesus the Sage* (London: Routledge, 1999), 119.

Better theological method starts with understanding the diversity and only then works toward unity. Sound methodology, for example, recognizes that the issues concerning James and Paul turn on three related but distinct questions. First is the historical (descriptive) question: what is the occasion (and teaching) for which the authors are writing? Second is the theological question: what are the authors actually teaching? Third is the canonical question: are the teachings of these authors compatible or inconsistent? Only after the historical and theological questions have been addressed are we even possibly capable of answering the canonical question. In the case of James and Paul, it appears they use the same terminology to speak to distinct theological and pastoral problems in diverse church contexts. James and Paul have different emphases and seem to use the faith of Abraham and the data somewhat differently, but both reflect theological and pastoral consistency. Using justification and works terminology, Paul cautions readers to remember that salvation is by God's grace and not because of anything they can contribute. Using similar language, James urges that true Christians do not merely verbalize faith but also live out Christ's teachings and love others.[12]

Thus, embracing the fact that Scripture is concurrently the words of humans and the Word of God results in an approach to New Testament theology that embraces both diversity and unity.[13] New Testament theology first examines the diversity in all its manifestations so as not to flatten out the distinctive theological and pastoral emphases and nuances of its books and writers. New Testament theology prizes this diversity (seeing no need for hyperharmonization) while finding an overall theological and pastoral consistency in the Bible.

Biblical Exegesis and Canonical Narrative

That the Bible is both the words of humans in and through multiple contexts as well as inspired by God results in another tension inherent in New Testament theology. Is New Testament theology focused only on the

---

12. For a more thorough treatment of this framework and historical, exegetical, and theological analysis of this issue, see Christopher W. Morgan, *A Theology of James: Wisdom for God's People*, Explorations in Biblical Theology, ed. Robert A. Peterson (Phillipsburg, NJ: 2010), 127–43; see also Bauckham, *James*, 119.

13. For good essays on unity and diversity in New Testament theology, see D. A. Carson, "Unity and Diversity in the New Testament: The Possibility of Systematic Theology," and David Wenham, "Appendix: Unity and Diversity in the New Testament," in Ladd, *A Theology of the New Testament*, 684–719.

messages of individual New Testament books, or does it also interact with the messages of other biblical books and authors?

The foundation of New Testament theology is to understand the meaning of New Testament passages, beginning with the biblical author's intention for each text. When studying a passage, interpreters must note the particular literary genre (narrative, parable, Gospel, epistle, apocalypse, etc.) and consider literary strategies unique to each. Literary context is also critical, as the placement of any given passage assists interpreters in understanding what a biblical author meant. The meaning of a word emerges through a careful study of the word in the phrases, clauses, and sentences in which it appears; the meaning of a sentence appears in its surrounding paragraphs or scenes; and the meaning of a scene surfaces in the episodes, sections, and overall book in which it is found. The historical setting is also formative, giving readers information about the occasion, recipients, author, and church context.

Yet every biblical passage has a larger context. The context is not only a particular book but also the entire canon, which places the biblical texts in God's unfolding plan moving from creation and the fall to redemption and new creation. This narrative frames, orders, and connects the doctrines. Further, it culminates in the person and work of Christ, which therefore gives Christological focus to what comes before and after the Gospels (Heb 1:1–4). Thus, New Testament theology locates passages within the biblical story line of redemptive history and relates them to other passages on the subject. It attends to how the Bible's story develops through the biblical covenants in the Old Testament—in the Law, Prophets, and Writings—as well as the New Testament in the dawning of the new covenant—in the Gospels, Acts, Epistles, and Revelation.

As a result and as a form of biblical theology, New Testament theology gives attention not only to specific biblical books but also to the central themes of each biblical author and the central themes throughout the Bible (covenant, kingdom, atonement, glory, love, holiness, etc.). In doing so, New Testament theology first enables readers to grasp the theological emphases within books and authors. Upon that exegetical foundation, New Testament theology then enables readers to see these theological emphases in connection with other major biblical books, authors, themes, and theology. This, in turn, helps readers understand and synthesize such themes and theology in their varied relationships, in proportion, and in Christological light.[14]

Methods in New Testament Theology

It should come as no surprise that a discipline interpreted so variously has varied approaches. Even among evangelicals there are several diverse methods of New Testament theology. We previously suggested that New Testament theology may be viewed as a bridge between New Testament exegesis and systematic theology. It may also be helpful to see that to some extent certain methods can be understood as closer to the land of New Testament studies, others to the land of systematic theology, and others closer to the middle of the bridge. While these distinct methods often show how scholars envision the nature and purpose of New Testament theology, they also show the inherent breadth of the discipline and its need for multiple methods to account for the inherent tensions and massively far-reaching goals. So multiple approaches are not only used but are, in a real sense, valid and even crucial.[15]

Among those closest to the land of New Testament studies is the single book-thematic-theology approach. This approach is reflected in *A Theology of James*.[16] This volume focuses on one biblical book, examines its historical, literary, and church contexts, examines the major themes in the book, and then demonstrates the book's overall theological teachings.

Similar to this method is the single author-single theme/theology approach. Books such as *The Glory of God and Paul* reflect this approach.[17] The volume focuses on the single theological theme of the glory of God in Paul, studies the major Pauline passages on glory, examines its usage in various contexts, clarifies its varied nuances, and relates it to other important Pauline theological themes.

---

14. See Matthew Y. Emerson and Christopher W. Morgan, "Toward a Holistic Hermeneutic: Exegesis, Narrative, Doctrine, the Church, and Application in Concert," *Journal of Mid-America Baptist Theological Seminary* 1 (2014), accessed January 15, 2017, www.mabts.edu/sites/all/themes/midamerica/uploads/pdf/emerson_morgan.pdf.

15. For other more technical classifications of approaches to biblical theology, see Carson, "Current Issues in Biblical Theology: A New Testament Perspective"; Klink and Lockett, *Understanding Biblical Theology*; and Köstenberger, "The Present and Future of Biblical Theology."

16. Morgan, *A Theology of James*.

17. Christopher W. Morgan, *The Glory of God and Paul*, New Studies in Biblical Theology, ed. D. A. Carson (Downers Grove: InterVarsity, forthcoming).

Another approach toward the New Testament studies side of the bridge is the author-thematic approach employed in Darrell Bock's *A Theology of Luke and Acts*.[18] The volume focuses on the author Luke's theology as found in his Gospel and Acts. It treats major theological themes in each chapter of those two books.

Also near the land of New Testament studies is the chronological-canonical-thematic-synthetic approach reflected in Frank Thielman's *Theology of the New Testament*.[19] Thielman follows a "roughly chronological approach, not so much to the texts themselves as to the history of Christianity they presuppose. Thus, I begin with Jesus as we know him from the four gospels, move to Paul, and then to the non-Pauline texts that treat the problems of heresy and persecution in the developing church."[20] So the approach is chronological, book by book, thematic, and then synthetic at certain key chapters along the way—most notably in his final chapter on the theological unity of the New Testament.

One approach closest to the middle of the bridge is the canonical-thematic approach demonstrated in G. E. Ladd's *A Theology of the New Testament*.[21] Ladd organizes according to the major sections of the Synoptic Gospels, the Fourth Gospel, the primitive church (Acts), Paul, Hebrews and the General Epistles, and the Apocalypse. He then treats the theological issues of each.

Another effort close to the middle of the bridge is the canonical-author-theology-theme approach of *A Biblical Theology of the New Testament*, edited by Roy Zuck and Darrell Bock.[22] This volume closely resembles New Testament studies in that it concentrates on each New Testament author,

---

18. Darrell L. Bock, *A Theology of Luke and Acts: God's Promised Program, Realized for All Nations*, Biblical Theology of the New Testament, ed. Andreas J. Köstenberger (Grand Rapids: Zondervan, 2012).

19. Frank Thielman, *Theology of the New Testament: A Canonical and Synthetic Approach* (Grand Rapids: Zondervan, 2005). For another example of this largely classic structure, see I. H. Marshall, *New Testament Theology: Many Witnesses, One Gospel* (Downers Grove: InterVarsity, 2004). See also Ben Witherington III, who also follows a classic approach, interacts with theology and ethics, and devotes a second volume on synthesis. See *The Individual Witnesses*, vol. 1, *The Indelible Image: The Theological and Ethical Thought World of the New Testament* (Downers Grove: InterVarsity, 2009); idem, *The Collective Witness*, vol. 2, *The Indelible Image: The Theological and Ethical Thought World of the New Testament* (Downers Grove, IL: InterVarsity, 2010).

20. Thielman, *Theology of the New Testament*, 10.

21. Ladd, *Theology of the New Testament*.

22. Roy B. Zuck and Darrell L. Bock, ed., *A Biblical Theology of the New Testament* (Chicago: Moody, 1994).

largely in canonical order. Yet it closely resembles systematic theology in that each book is organized in theological categories developed by individual themes.

Moving a bit toward the land of systematic theology is Thomas Schreiner's *New Testament Theology*.[23] His approach is narrative-theology-author-theme. He organizes the material around the biblical story line of God's saving plan and relates the story to the focus of God's glory in Christ. Schreiner then treats the New Testament's unfolding of this story and moves through it theologically chapter by chapter. In each chapter he addresses the material from the biblical authors and their subsequent themes. Along the way he points to his thesis of God's glory in Christ.

Structured similarly to Schreiner but more focused on developing a particular thesis is Gregory Beale's *A New Testament Biblical Theology*.[24] His approach is largely narrative-theology-author-theme but is distinctive in several ways. It relates the theological story line of the Old Testament, focuses on the plotline categories of thought, shows how important components of the story line are organically developed, employs much intertextuality, and is more focused on demonstrating his particular thesis than uncovering the numerous theological emphases in the New Testament.[25] Beale posits that the goal of the New Testament story line is God's glory and that "the main stepping stone to that goal is Christ's establishment of an eschatological new-creational kingdom and its expansion."[26]

Among those closest to the land of systematic theology is the theological-canonical-thematic approach exemplified in Donald Guthrie's *New Testament Theology*.[27] Guthrie traces the doctrines of God, humanity, Christ, the mission of Christ, the Holy Spirit, Christian life, the church,

---

23. Thomas R. Schreiner, *New Testament Theology: Magnifying God in Christ* (Grand Rapids: Baker Academic, 2008). For his broader biblical theology see Schreiner, *The King in His Beauty: A Biblical Theology of the Old and New Testaments* (Grand Rapids: Baker, 2013).

24. Gregory K. Beale, *A New Testament Biblical Theology: The Unfolding of the Old Testament in the New* (Grand Rapids: Baker Academic, 2011). An approach to biblical theology similar to that of Schreiner and Beale is the thematic-canonical approach found in *Central Themes in Biblical Theology*. Written and edited by evangelical biblical scholars committed to a "whole-Bible biblical theology," this volume seeks to trace unifying themes and overarching structural ideas through the Old and New Testaments, "in their entirety, in their final form, and in concert with one another." See Scott J. Hafemann and Paul R. House, ed., *Central Themes in Biblical Theology: Mapping Unity in Diversity* (Grand Rapids: Baker, 2007), 15–16.

25. Ibid., 1–15.

26. Ibid., 16.

27. Donald Guthrie, *New Testament Theology* (Downers Grove: InterVarsity, 1981).

the future, ethics, and Scripture. Under each, Guthrie normally treats the teachings and themes of the Synoptic Gospels, the Johannine literature, Acts, Paul, Hebrews, the General Epistles, and Revelation.

All of these methods are necessarily limited. Yet all of them also offer fresh vantage points into the theology of the New Testament. On their own they are helpful, but together they extensively broaden and deepen theological insight.

New Testament Theology, Theological Education, and Theological Formation

One might think that the importance of New Testament theology would be emphasized in seminary education. Unfortunately, according to my recent and brief look at the websites of the major evangelical seminaries in North America, courses in New Testament theology exist only as electives in most seminary curricula. Of the major seminaries I searched, only Beeson Divinity School requires a course in New Testament theology in its core master of divinity program (MDiv). It is also surprisingly rare to find biblical theology courses required in standard MDiv programs. Beeson Divinity School, Trinity Evangelical Divinity School, and Westminster Theological Seminary were notable exceptions. Beeson, in addition to requiring New Testament theology, also requires a course in Old Testament theology in its core MDiv curriculum. Trinity places biblical theology as an initial and foundational course in its MDiv program. Westminster mentions that biblical theology is in the curriculum because of the seminary's core values and requires two courses in Old Testament theology (listing them in the second year), though none in New Testament theology.[28] When I attended Mid-America Baptist Theological Seminary (1993–1996), both Old Testament theology and New Testament theology were required courses in its MDiv curriculum, but its MDiv program has undergone much revision since then. Now it often requires fewer units, incorporates more flexibility, and offers multiple concentrations from which students may choose. Few seminaries now require New Testament theology (or even biblical theology) as a part of an MDiv degree (let alone in the smaller and more specialized master of arts degrees).

---

28. Covenant Theological Seminary and Reformed Theological Seminary require their own particular versions of biblical theology with their covenant theology courses.

New Testament theology in particular, and biblical theology in general, can aptly serve as foundations in theological education, as Trinity and Beeson wisely understand. Such courses can ground students in the biblical story, develop a whole Bible analysis, and advance a framework by which the rest of the Bible can be interpreted. Such biblical theology courses can also build naturally on introductory courses in Old Testament and New Testament, as Westminster recognizes. Biblical theology can help students move forward and see the primary biblical themes of each book, author, and section. It can also help students trace such themes through the biblical story line; in time this ability enables students to develop their understanding and formation of systematic theology. As such, biblical theology is not merely one class in a curriculum but an opportunity to enhance the student's overall theological development as it strengthens the sustained and interconnected processes of exegesis, hermeneutics, biblical theology, and systematic theology. Further, it strengthens the student's pastoral ministry and preaching, as Schreiner aptly stresses:

> Our task as preachers is to proclaim the whole counsel of God. We will not fulfill our calling if as preachers we fail to do biblical theology. We may get many compliments from our people for our moral lessons and our illustrations, but we are not faithfully serving our congregations if they do not understand how the whole of Scripture points to Christ, and if they do not gain a better understanding from us of the story line of the Bible.[29]

Questions for Further Reflection

1. What is New Testament theology? How does it relate to biblical theology? New Testament exegesis? Systematic theology?
2. What tensions exist in New Testament theology that reflect the dual nature of Scripture as the words of humans and the Word of God?
3. What methods have been used in New Testament theology? In what ways is each helpful?

---

29. Thomas R. Schreiner, "Preaching and Biblical Theology," *Southern Baptist Journal of Theology* 10, no. 2 (Summer 2006): 28.

4. What seminaries currently require New Testament theology or biblical theology in their primary MDiv curriculum?
5. How does biblical theology help theological and pastoral formation?

Sources for Further Study

Balla, Peter. *Challenges to New Testament Theology: An Attempt to Justify the Enterprise.* Grand Rapids: Baker, 1998.

Beale, Gregory K. *A New Testament Biblical Theology: The Unfolding of the Old Testament in the New.* Grand Rapids: Baker Academic, 2011.

Carson, D. A. "Current Issues in Biblical Theology: A New Testament Perspective." *Bulletin of Biblical Research* 5 (1995): 17–41.

Hafemann, Scott J., and Paul R. House, ed. *Central Themes in Biblical Theology: Mapping Unity in Diversity.* Grand Rapids: Baker, 2007.

Klink III, Edward W., and Darian R. Lockett. *Understanding Biblical Theology: A Comparison of Theory and Practice.* Grand Rapids: Zondervan, 2012.

Köstenberger, Andreas J. "The Present and Future of Biblical Theology." *Themelios* 37:3 (2012): 446–64.

Ladd, G. E. *A Theology of the New Testament*, rev. ed. Grand Rapids: Eerdmans, 1993.

Schreiner, Thomas R. *New Testament Theology: Magnifying God in Christ.* Grand Rapids: Baker Academic, 2008.

Thielman, Frank. *Theology of the New Testament: A Canonical and Synthetic Approach.* Grand Rapids: Zondervan, 2005.

Yarbrough, Robert W. *The Salvation-Historical Fallacy? Reassessing the History of New Testament Theology.* History of Biblical Interpretation. Leiden: Deo, 2004.

Chapter Twelve

From Bible to Theology

KEVIN J. VANHOOZER

Seminary students and professors know that the "Department of From Bible to Theology" is a fictional conceit. Christian colleges and divinity schools typically have separate departments for Old Testament, New Testament, and Systematic Theology—as well as for other subjects such as church history and disciplines such as evangelism, preaching, counseling, education, and missions that fall under the broad rubric of practical theology. What is now the default fourfold curricular structure originated in the nineteenth-century at the University of Berlin, where the aim of theological education was preparing ministers for their profession.[1] The model draws and quarters the body of theology into different members—biblical, historical, systematic, and practical—distinct areas of specialization that, like the fallen Humpty Dumpty, cannot easily be put back together.

"From Bible to theology" names not a single department but an interdepartmental mandate to help students see the common task that unifies and governs theological education: to understand God and God's Word truly in order to live out our citizenship of the gospel under the lordship of Jesus Christ. This, ultimately, is theology: the display of understanding that is commensurate with the life of the disciple.

We begin by taking the measure of the problem: the fragmentation of theological education into various areas of specialized knowledge. I then suggest that understanding is the proper end of theology, that biblical

---

1. The unity of theological education according to this "clerical paradigm" is a function not of its subject matter but rather of its outcome (ministerial training). See further David K. Clark, *To Know and Love God: Method for Theology* (Wheaton: Crossway, 2003), 165–194.

interpretation is the means to that end, and that we must interpret Scripture in a way that accords with its nature, subject matter, and ultimate interest, which is the God of the gospel. The ultimate aim is to learn Christ, and this requires a properly theological approach to biblical interpretation, one whose aim is not simply to convey information but to form disciples who can follow the biblical words to the living Word. I then return to the fourfold curricular division and suggest that each academic department of the seminary plays a vital role in interpreting the Bible theologically, which is finally a matter of displaying our understanding of the Bible by making disciples and equipping the church for fitting participation in God's ongoing mission to the world.

Specialization, Professionalization, and Fragmentation: The Challenge of Theological Education

Specialization is today the operative term and the pressing challenge. In most institutions of higher education, specialists have greater academic status than generalists. In spite of the obvious benefits of specialized knowledge in science, medicine, history, and so forth, Edward Farley and others bewail its unintended effects in theological education, in particular, disciplinary fragmentation: "*Theologia* no longer forms part of a theological school's conception of its course of study, and the result is a loss of unifying subject matter."[2] Instead of providing a common subject matter, theological education tends to focus on helping students acquire the skill set and knowledge base deemed necessary for serving as a pastor—the "mastery" of "divinity," symbolized by an MDiv degree. There is a real danger of confusing knowledge of God with skills or information.

The well-known lines of T. S. Eliot's poem capture the plight of many seminary students, whose inability to connect theory and practice leads to curricular weeping and gnashing of teeth:

> Where is the wisdom we have lost in knowledge?
> Where is the knowledge we have lost in information?[3]

---

2. Edward Farley, *Theologia: The Fragmentation and Unity of Theological Education* (Minneapolis: Fortress, 1989), 151.
3. T. S. Eliot, "The Rock" (1934).

We are indeed awash in information. Of the storing of megabytes there is no end. But is education a matter of data transfer? Experts in information science and "knowledge management" regularly refer to the data/information/knowledge/wisdom hierarchy (also known as the DIKW pyramid).[4] On this model, "information" refers to useful facts gleaned from data and "knowledge" to descriptions of or theories about this information.

Theological Science: The Standard Model

Charles Hodge uses similar language in his description of how one moves "from the Bible to theology": "The Bible is to the theologian what nature is to the man of science. It is his store-house of facts."[5] For Hodge, we move from Bible to theology inductively. Scripture supplies the data/information, and theology provides the knowledge/theory (science) that explains the laws governing the facts: "The Bible contains the truths which the theologian has to collect, authenticate, arrange, and exhibit in their internal relation to each other."[6] Doctrines—the sum and substance of what the Bible says about God—may then be arranged, like butterflies pinned in so many display cabinets (theology textbooks). On this view, theology is a type of information processing, and education a delivery system that, like FedEx, guarantees the timely arrival of its packets of information (knowledge). This, at least, is the standard model of theological education as we commonly find it in modern seminaries.

The "from . . . to" construction of our chapter's title is a challenge to the model of education as information transfer and processing, inasmuch as it calls not for compartmentalization but, on the contrary, a bridge that connects the various theological disciplines organically (by orienting them to a distinct subject matter) rather than merely clerically (by orienting them toward preparation for a particular profession). The "from . . . to" progression also poses an implicit question: What kind of distance separates theology from the Bible? It arises from a dichotomy that runs from Lessing's famous "ugly ditch" between the accidental truths of history and

---

4. The notion is often attributed to Russell L. Ackoff's presidential address to the International Society for General Systems Research, comprised mainly of engineers, in which he distinguished what computer systems can do and what is distinct to humans ("From Data to Wisdom," *Journal of Applied Systems Analysis* 16 [1989]: 3–9).
5. Charles Hodge, *Systematic Theology* (Grand Rapids: Eerdmans, reprint 1977) 1:10.
6. Ibid.,1:1.

the necessary truths of reason through J. P. Gabler's 1787 lecture on "The Proper Distinction Between Biblical and Dogmatic Theology" to Krister Stendahl's influential distinction between "what it meant" and "what it means."[7] There are various ways to describe this dichotomy at the heart of the seminary curriculum (we shall examine three), but what is patently clear is that *a fissure runs through it.*

1. Past vs. present. One way of describing the meant/means dichotomy, signaled by the tense of the verbs, is the distance between past and present. Biblical scholarship describes the past (what the biblical authors thought about God); theology recasts past formulations in terms that people can understand today (what the church presently confesses about God).

2. Academy vs. church. Biblical scholars are particularly concerned not to read later theology back into the biblical texts. In principle even persons without faith can say "what it meant"—that is, what Israelites and Christians respectively thought about God. By way of contrast, church theologians read Scripture from within a confessional tradition, as the Word of God. This has led at least one scholar to contrast the "Academic Bible" with the "Christian Scripture."[8]

3. Religious studies vs. religio. Theology is more than religious studies. The latter is study of human belief and behavior oriented to the divine, but because humanity is the focus, it ultimately gets no further than anthropology. It is indeed possible to study the Old Testament under the rubric of "ancient Hebrew religion" or the New Testament under the rubric of "early Christianity." Nevertheless, examining what other people think and say about God is altogether different from speaking about God. The study of human religiosity is not yet *religio*, which for church theologians such as Calvin had more to do with the fear of the Lord and the Christian life, a point to which I shall return below.

---

7. Krister Stendahl, "Biblical Theology, Contemporary," *Interpreter's Dictionary of the Bible* 1 (1962): 418–32.

8. Michael C. Legaspi, *The Death of Scripture and the Rise of Biblical Studies* (Oxford: Oxford University Press, 2010), 9–10.

From Hermeneutics to Theological Hermeneutics: The Way Forward

Learning how to read the Bible, "correctly teaching the word of truth" (2 Tim 2:15), is arguably one of the most important things a seminary has to teach its students. This suggests an even simpler way of describing what we are calling the "from . . . to" movement that is the focus of the present chapter: *hermeneutics*. Its aim is not simply to teach students how to read—to recognize one word after another—but to read for understanding. But what is understanding, and can we understand the Bible the same way we understand any other book?

Hermeneutics, narrowly defined, is the art and science of textual interpretation. This narrow definition may encourage the idea that interpreters are "disengaged selves" who float above the messiness of history and culture, contemplating language and ideas as if their bodily location and context did not matter. This is the weakness of the inductive model. By way of contrast, twentieth-century hermeneutics has focused less on texts than on the conditions for understanding in general, in particular the significance of human finitude, temporality, and situatedness (e.g., "For now we see only a reflection as in a mirror," 1 Cor 13:12).[9] That interpreters are themselves historically conditioned problematizes the attempt to separate "what it meant" from "what it means," as if the interpreter's own situatedness and presuppositions were not a factor: "Hermeneutic philosophers contend . . . that our primary mode of perception is not theoretical but practical, and depends on our current desires or interests."[10] Hermeneutics is the disciplined search for understanding, but it involves far more than inductive information processing, for all textual understanding is also the search for self-understanding.

Hans-Georg Gadamer's important hermeneutic work *Truth and Method* challenges any attempt to insulate "what it meant" from "what it means."[11] By *method* Gadamer means technical procedures for studying things in ways that bracket out one's personal concerns, allegedly allowing a person to reason in a disinterested, objective manner. Induction is only one of the

---

9. See Clark, *To Know and Love God*, 50–51.
10. Jens Zimmerman, *Hermeneutics: A Very Short Introduction* (Oxford: Oxford University Press, 2015), 8.
11. Hans-Georg Gadamer, *Truth and Method*, 2nd rev ed. (London: Continuum, 2002).

methods for reading the Bible now on offer in the academic marketplace. Gadamer believes that method isolates us from the most important way of coming to understand classic texts, namely, by belonging to a tradition that has already decided to hold them in high regard. Christians study biblical texts because they are already deeply involved with them in personal, often practical, ways. *Truth* for Gadamer is a function of indwelling something greater than ourselves (e.g., language, culture, or tradition) that serves as the medium through which we read and engage texts.

Biblical interpreters need not abandon one dichotomy (meant vs. means) simply to fall captive to another (truth vs. method). The moral of this hermeneutical detour is simply that "from Bible to theology" is best viewed as an *interpretive* act, namely, the act of gaining understanding by (to paraphrase Johann Albrecht Bengel) applying oneself wholly to the biblical text and applying the biblical text wholly to oneself (and one's community).[12] In brief, theologians do not simply describe and summarize the informational content of the Bible; they interpret it. The goal is not simply gaining knowledge but understanding and, as we shall see, wisdom.

The Bible is both like and unlike every other text. It is *like* every other book because it has human authors who say something about something in some way. It is *unlike* every other book because (1) it has God for its ultimate Author; (2) it has God (Jesus Christ) as its ultimate content; (3) it has God (the Holy Spirit) for its ultimate interpreter; and (4) it has the church for its ultimate interpretive community. "From Bible to theology" ultimately calls for nothing less than a distinctly *theological* hermeneutic, an approach to biblical interpretation that accords with the nature, function, and purpose of God's written Word. The goal of theological hermeneutics is not simply to describe "what it meant" but to hear and obey God's living and active Word speaking in and through Scripture to the church today.[13] To anticipate the goal of theological hermeneutics is not merely to learn to read the Bible but to *learn Christ.*

---

12. See "J. A. Bengel (1687-1752)" *Dictionary of Major Biblical Interpreters*, ed. Donald K. McKim (Downers Grove: InterVarsity, 2007), 184–88.

13. See Scott Swain, *Trinity, Revelation, and Reading: A Theological Introduction to the Bible and Its Interpretation* (Edinburgh: T&T Clark, 2011).

"Learning Christ": Lessons from Calvin's *Institutes* on Reading Scripture Theologically

Theology is the search by people of faith for knowledge of God by means of understanding the Bible. Understanding is the goal, but what does it mean and how do we get it? Understanding involves more than knowing discrete bits of information. It has to do with grasping how things fit together. In particular: faith seeks understanding of how all things fit together or are summed up in Jesus Christ (Eph 1:10). This involves understanding how the story of Jesus is the revelation and fulfillment of the mystery of God's plan of salvation. The term translated "plan" is *oikonomia* and refers to the triune "economy" in which the Father carries out his redemptive purpose through the missions of the Son and Spirit. To learn Christ is to discover what God has done for us and our salvation. To understand how all things fit together in Jesus Christ is therefore to understand the God of the gospel and the gospel of God.

To understand is to know how to follow. We follow stories, arguments, and persons; and to attain faith's understanding of its unique subject matter, we must learn how to follow in all three ways. First, we must be able to follow the biblical story from creation through crucifixion to consummation, that is, to grasp how the various parts of the Bible fit into the canonical whole. Second, we must be able to follow the apostolic arguments about the significance of Jesus's person and works implied by that story. Third, we must follow the biblical words to the Word of life, and then we must follow that Word by walking in its way of truth and life (John 14:6).

Following the words of the Bible is ultimately a futile exercise if it does not contribute to the project of following Christ. It follows, then, that biblical interpretation is a form of discipleship. Discipleship, likewise, is a form of biblical interpretation. Why? Because to understand the Bible is ultimately a matter of being able to use it as its author intended. Whether a person understands the Bible will ultimately be demonstrated in practice by a person's ability rightly to use it for training in righteousness (2 Tim 3:16), godliness (1 Tim 4:7), and Christlikeness (1 Cor 11:1) as well as for formulating explicit doctrines or teachings: "One's understanding *is* one's abilities, and the measure of one's abilities is the exercise of them."[14]

---

14. Charles M. Wood, *The Formation of Christian Understanding: Theological Hermeneutics* (Eugene, OR: Wipf and Stock, 2000), 17.

"Faith seeking understanding" is about much more than processing and storing information, even if these activities seem to be what final exams reward. The vital tests of the Christian life are rarely multiple choice (choose the single best answer). More often, they are either true/false or fill in the blank—the "blank" being the span of one's life. Seminaries exist to foster biblical literacy and theological discernment, to teach disciples how to follow the way the biblical words go, from ancient page to contemporary practice, and how to help others do the same. While students pursuing ordination are called to teach others in an official capacity, the notion of the priesthood of all believers (cf. 1 Pet 2:9) reminds us that all Christians should be ministers of God's Word.

In seeking ways to reintegrate the shattered seminary curriculum, we do well to consult John Calvin, whose *Institutes* were intended to help students read Scripture rightly and whose work antedates the debilitating dichotomy between "what it meant" and "what it means." For Calvin, Christian doctrine was not simply the product of reading the Bible but an aid to Bible reading. Calvin was also an important precursor of what is sometimes referred to as theological interpretation of Scripture, which we can define as "interpretation of the Bible for the church."[15]

"Learning"

Christian theology begins not with a blank page but with a sacred page, with the address of the living God. In every other science the initiative begins with the human knower's interest in some area or aspect of the world. If we are to know God, the initiative must lie with him. In the words of the medieval scholastic adage, "Theology teaches of God, is taught by God, and leads to God." The Bible is the crucial ingredient in this teaching. It is testimony to God's stooping to speak, show, and share himself with human creatures. We speak of God only because God has first spoken to us. Theologians are not autonomous knowers but participants in an economy of revelation and redemption. It is a crucial point: we learn theology only by believing, and then understanding, what we have been told. Theological education has nothing to do with mastery and everything to do with learning.

---

15. Craig G. Bartholomew and Heath A. Thomas, *A Manifesto for Theological Interpretation* (Grand Rapids: Baker, 2016), ix.

Jesus taught that no one knows God the Father except the Son "and anyone to whom the Son desires to reveal him" (Matt 11:27). Immediately afterward he tells his disciples, "Take up my yoke and learn from me" (Matt 11:29). To take Jesus's yoke is to adopt his way; it is a figure of speech for becoming his disciple. Being a disciple means following his words in thought and deed. Education "from Bible to theology" is ultimately about learning how to live as citizens of the gospel (Phil 1:27)—members of "a royal priesthood, a holy nation" (1 Pet 2:9) that God calls into being to worship and bear witness to him. This is the skill set we need to move from Bible to theology: the ability to glorify in all we say and do the one true God who in Christ is "reconciling the world to himself" (2 Cor 5:19).

Learning Christ is an important Pauline theme. The modern academy privileges knowledge that can be quantified and observed theoretically, from a critical distance. But learning *about* Jesus is not the same thing as learning Christ.[16] When Paul says, "But that is not the way you learned Christ!" (Eph 4:20 ESV), he is referring to walking as those with darkened understanding do. To learn Christ means more than acquiring knowledge about him.[17] Learning Christ involves more than induction and rote memorization. The goal is not simply knowledge (the acquisition of information) but understanding (the ability to use information rightly, often by discerning what is to be done).

Some commentators suggest that "learning Christ" refers to the passing on of traditions about Christ. Calvin's commentary on this verse highlights the special kind of learning in view: "He whose life differs not from that of unbelievers, has learned nothing of Christ; for the knowledge of Christ cannot be separated from the mortification of the flesh."[18] Paul then specifies how the Ephesians did learn Christ: "You have heard about him and were taught in him" (Eph 4:21 ESV). F. F. Bruce thinks that to be "taught

---

16. Calvin is clear that theological understanding involves knowing the *benefits* of Christ, and this is a *knowledge of* as opposed to a mere *knowledge about*; see Matthew Boulton, *Life in God: John Calvin, Practical Formation, and the Future of Protestant Theology* (Grand Rapids: Eerdmans, 2011), 47.

17. Peter O'Brien notes that the phrase "to learn a person" is without precedent in Greek literature *The Letter to the Ephesians* (Grand Rapids: Eerdmans, 1999), 324. Equally intriguing is Markus Barth's observation that Paul's expressions in Eph 4:20–21 "evoke the image of a school" *Ephesians* (New York: Doubleday, 1974) 2: 504.

18. *Commentaries on the Epistles of Paul to the Galatians and Ephesians*, trans. William Pringle (Calvin Translation Society, 1854), 294.

in [Christ]" means being taught "in the context of the Christian fellowship."[19] This is a far cry from learning in the ivory tower, for to be "in Christ" is to be in the sphere of his personal influence. The contrast is with those who try to learn about Jesus outside the sphere of his influence: "The contrast is clear and decisive. Christ has transformed the Ephesians' pattern of perception and habits of thinking and feeling such that they now know the truth and can 'take every thought captive to Christ' (2 Cor 10:5)."[20] To learn Christ is to receive words about him and to make his own words the rule of faith, thought, and life.

We can now draw the various threads together: the purpose of theological education is to help students learn doctrine ("teaching") in order to become wise disciples, followers of Jesus who know how to follow his way and are able to teach others how to do so too through exposition (lessons) and example (life). It is no mere lexical coincidence that the Greek term Paul uses for "learning" Christ (*manthano*) is related to the term for disciple (*mathetes*), or that the Latin root of "disciple" (*discipulus*) resembles academic *discipline* and means "student," which explains why Jesus can say to his disciples both "Learn from me" (Matt 11:29) and "Follow me" (Matt 4:19). Being biblical and doing theology have this in common: both involve following the words that lead to Christ and to acting out Christ's life in us. Theological hermeneutics is the discipline of interpreting the Bible as an aspect of discipleship.

Paideia: *"A disciple . . . who is fully trained will be like his teacher" (Luke 6:40).*

Learning to read the Bible in order to follow Christ requires more than the transmission of information. The problem is less with the lecture format than with what is done in lecturing. The teacher is not simply a cog in a delivery system but a guide whose task is to develop a student's capacity to follow the words of Scripture to "learn Christ." As we shall see, this involves the ability not simply to recall information but, more importantly, to make

---

19. *The Epistles to the Colossians, to Philemon, and to the Ephesians*, New International Commentary of the New Testament (Grand Rapids: Eerdmans, 1984), 357.
20. Stephen Fowl, *Ephesians: A Commentary* (Louisville: WJK, 2012), 151.

judgments. The classroom is a place not simply to transfer information but to learn how to process and respond to it: to make right judgments.[21]

To understand the Bible is to know how the parts fit into a single redemptive history and where interpreters fit into its unified plot. Reading Scripture theologically involves learning not simply information (knowing propositions) but how to do things—in particular, how to participate rightly in the ongoing action. It is the difference between *Wissenschaft* and *paideia,* between Berlin and Athens.[22] *Paideia* has to do not with learning an academic specialization but with forming the whole person. *Formation* rather than information is the watchword in theological pedagogy.

This is not the place to enter into various debates about education. The basic point is the apostle Paul's: Scripture is profitable for teaching (*didaskalion*) and training (*paideia*) in righteousness (2 Tim 3:16). Christian doctrine is not an end in itself but a pedagogical tool for making disciples. Calvin's *Institutes* serves this practical purpose: "For Calvin, discipleship is *paideia,* 'formative education.'"[23] Calvin wrote his famous theology textbook to equip church leaders as readers—followers—of God's Word. Indeed, one scholar suggests that Calvin's title (*Institutio*) refers to the *paideia* mentioned in 2 Tim 3:16.[24] Learning to read Scripture theologically is itself an exercise in Christian discipleship.

Biblical interpretation involves both academic and spiritual disciplines. The aim of theological education is to teach interpreter-disciples how to use Scripture in order to discern what is fitting, or rather, how things fit together in Jesus Christ. This involves training our faculties "to distinguish between good and evil" (Heb 5:14). What is important is knowing not simply bits (or bytes) of information but, rather, how to make sound judgments about things—in particular, judgments about the form one's discipleship should take here and now.

How should disciples learn Christ and move from Bible to theology? Paul, in Gal 3:24 (NASB), refers to the law as "our tutor" (*paidagogos*) that

---

21. By *judgment* I refer to basic mental acts such as identifying ("this is an x"), making distinctions ("x is not y"), and making connections ("x is related to y because of z"). Judging is part and parcel of discernment inasmuch as disciples must constantly distinguish what is godly from what is ungodly.

22. See David H. Kelsey, *Between Athens and Berlin: The Theological Education Debate* (Grand Rapids: Eerdmans, 1993); and *To Understand God Truly: What's Theological About a Theological School?* (Louisville: Westminster John Knox, 1992).

23. Boulton, *Life in God,* 4.

24. Ibid., 57.

helps us learn Christ (probably by showing us our need for his righteousness). Yet there is an important sense in which not only the law but *all* the Scriptures serve a pedagogical purpose. The Reformers rightly acknowledged that Scripture is its own interpreter, which is another way of saying that Scripture itself teaches us how best to read it and how best to learn Christ.

Scripture is the disciples' royal pedagogical road to knowledge of God and themselves. To understand the Scriptures is to learn how all the biblical parts fit together in a canonical whole with Christ at the center.[25] To read the Bible rightly means achieving a kind of canonical competence. Students of theology must become apprentices of Scripture; this is the way to learn various canonical practices, such as seeing how all things lead to and fit together in Christ. David Starling argues in his *Hermeneutics as Apprenticeship: Allowing the Bible to Shape our Interpretive Habits and Practices* that biblical interpreters must learn from the biblical authors themselves the craft of reading the Bible.[26]

To move from Bible to theology requires canonical pedagogy. The canon leads readers *to* Christ and then forms the life of Christ *in* them so they can continue walking the way *of* Christ. Learning Christ is a matter of following, "putting on," or as we could say, *practicing* Christ. By reading God's Word, illuminated by the Spirit, disciples learn to think rightly, see rightly, judge rightly, and act rightly, that is, in a Christlike manner. Scripture offers precious remedial training to darkened hearts and clouded minds that enable them to see God, the world, and others as they truly are. Scripture is more than the "spectacles" of faith; it is the oculus that enables us to see and experience not virtual but eschatological reality, the real in Christ. Scripture restores us to our senses so we can see, hear, and taste the goodness of God and the gospel. This involves propositional and personal knowledge alike. By becoming apprentices to Scripture, a process of canonical pedagogy, we learn the mind of Christ (Phil 2:5 NIV), including his own way of reading Israel's Scriptures. As apprentices to Scripture,

---

25. I discuss the importance of becoming apprentices to the various canonical practices (such as typological interpretation) more fully in *The Drama of Doctrine* (Louisville: Westminster John Knox, 2005), where I set out a "canonical-linguistic" approach to theology. See also my response to I. Howard Marshall's proposal for going beyond the Bible biblically in Marshall, *Beyond the Bible: Moving from Scripture to Theology* (Grand Rapids: Baker, 2004), 92–95.

26. See David Starling, *Hermeneutics as Apprenticeship: Allowing the Bible to Shape our Interpretive Habits and Practices* (Grand Rapids: Baker Academic, 2016).

biblical interpreters receive not simply information about but formation in Christ.[27] In particular, they become canonically competent and eschatologically educated readers. In a word: they become faithful interpreters, wise unto salvation (2 Tim 3:15).

Wisdom

Knowing how to read the Bible to learn Christ requires biblical literacy, canonical competence, and interpretive excellence. It requires wisdom, which is more than theoretical knowledge. What counts in wisdom is not simply information and knowledge but understanding and discernment. Biblical wisdom pertains to a life that flourishes because it is in harmony with the created order and issues from the fear of the Lord. To understand a biblical text requires more than parsing its parts of speech; it requires knowing how to respond to what it says. Theological wisdom means knowing what to do in particular situations in order to glorify God and follow Jesus in ways that befit faithful disciples. Biblical wisdom means knowing how to embody the mind of Christ at all times, everywhere, and to everyone.

The kind of knowledge that comes to the fore here is not abstract theory (*theoria*) but practical reasoning (*phronesis*), which in a theological context pertains to knowing what to do in particular situations in order to promote peace, justice, and righteousness. Wisdom involves both cognition and character—dispositions, desires, and decision-making. As Daniel Treier defines it, wisdom is a kind of communicative praxis: the ability to say the right thing in the right way at the right time in order to speak the truth in love and glorify God.[28]

Understanding God is more than a theoretical exercise because God is not an abstract subject. On the contrary, theology's object is a sovereign speaking subject: God. Calvin begins his *Institutes* with the recognition that we can attain knowledge of God only by interpreting Scripture: "Nearly all the wisdom we possess . . . consists of two parts, the knowledge of God and of ourselves."[29] All of theology is for Calvin "an attempt to

---

27. Linda Cannell argues for a recovery of the church-based apprenticeship model for theological education in *Theological Education Matters: Leadership Education for the Church* (Newbergh, IN: EDCOT Press, 2006), 270–305.

28. See Daniel J. Treier, *Virtue and the Voice of God: Toward Theology as Wisdom* (Grand Rapids: Eerdmans, 2006) and his earlier programmatic essay, "Theology as the Acquisition of Wisdom: Reorienting Theological Education," *Christian Education Journal* 3 (1999): 127–39.

29. Calvin, *Institutes* I.1.1.

retrain disciples to believe, see, learn, and recall that they actually live in God by the grace of God."[30] The beginning of wisdom is knowing God as Creator and Lord and oneself as creature and servant. For Calvin, theology is always practical insofar as it guides disciples in a particular way of life: "being in Christ."

Calvin calls the Bible "spectacles": corrective lenses that retrain the eyes (of the mind, of faith, of the heart) to read the book of nature as the handiwork of God.[31] Scripture is a pedagogue that helps us see things—God, the world, and ourselves—as they really are and as they are gathered together in Jesus Christ. We need the Bible if we are to discern God's presence and activity in the world, which Calvin calls "this most beautiful theater."[32]

Elsewhere I have developed Calvin's theatrical model and argued that theological wisdom is essentially a matter of theodramatic discernment and disposition. If disciples have learned their script and know how to read the Scriptures, they will understand that Jesus Christ is the measure of truth, goodness, and beauty alike. Accordingly, they will be able to discern what discipleship means in their own particular situations, that is, what they should say and do in order to live out the life of Christ under new cultural conditions with new social scenery. Herein is wisdom: to see and do what is right in particular situations, something we can do only if we understand the whole drama of salvation history of which our own personal histories are a part.

We are now in a better position to understand theological hermeneutics as the ability to perform right interpretive acts, in particular, the ability to integrate particular things and situations into the meaningful whole that is redemptive history, or *theodrama*. For Calvin, "All theological knowledge comes down to *savoir faire*: know-how, knack, phronesis, practical wisdom,"[33] in particular, the "knack" of knowing how to act out the life of Christ in whatever scene we happen to be playing.[34]

---

30. Boulton, *Life in God*, 66.
31. Calvin, *Institutes*, I.6.1.
32. Ibid., I.24.20. Calvin employs theatrical imagery frequently both in the *Institutes* and elsewhere (see, *inter alia*, *Institutes* I.5.8, II.6.1; III.9.2).
33. Boulton, *Life in God*, 216.
34. Some writers on theological education now recognize the importance of *phronesis*: "The role of the teacher is being recast from that of an expert who distributes a store of knowledge to one who shapes tasks that compel a search for knowledge, develops capacities such as judgment and evaluation, and encourages skills of lifelong learning" (Cannell, *Theological Education Matters*, 281).

Carey Baptist Seminary in New Zealand conducts a seminar for its soon-to-be graduates on Integrative Theology, by which they mean the discipline that helps disciples participate fittingly in the mission of God by bringing everything they're learning to bear on contemporary issues. In the context of Carey, *from Bible to theology* means "through a biblical-theological grid to a pastoral outcome." Here, too, discerning what God has done, is doing, and will do in Christ is essential to right understanding (knowing) and right living (doing).[35] This is one way of teaching wisdom and learning Christ, and it has much in common with what I have called theodramatic understanding, which is a matter of knowing what God has done in Christ and what we as disciples are to do here and now in order to bear witness to the definitiveness of God's saving work. Scripture is the plumb line for understanding what God has done and hence the authoritative script disciples seek creatively yet faithfully to perform in their own times and places.

From "from . . . to" to "to and fro": Theologically Unified Organic Biblical Interpretation

There is no single department of "from Bible to theology." Nor should we think of "from Bible to theology" as a linear sequence from one department to the next. As we have seen, there is an intimate connection between following the way the biblical words go and following Jesus Christ. The purpose of the theological disciplines is to teach students to be disciples—followers of Scripture and of Jesus Christ—who can train others to be followers too. The present section aims to show how each of the four traditional seminary disciplines contributes to the aims and objectives of a theological education inasmuch as each contributes to the project of reading the Bible theologically to hear the voice of God addressing the people of God yesterday and today.

Here, then, is my thesis: theological interpretation of Scripture is not a specialization of its own; rather it is a joint enterprise of all the theological disciplines, working together to interpret and understand God's Word to the church yesterday and today. Again this follows from the goal of theological education, which is not simply to reap knowledge (information) from different fields but to help students become the kind of persons who

---

35. See Philip Halstead and Myk Habets, ed., *Doing Integrative Theology: Word, World, and Work in Conversation* (Santa Maria, CA: Archer Press, 2015).

perceive God, the world, and themselves through the spectacles of faith (Scripture) and are able to participate in what they see: God reconciling the world to himself in Christ (2 Cor 5:19). The goal is to produce not know-it-alls but disciples who know one big thing, namely, how to follow Jesus and live out with others their citizenship of the gospel with joy, integrity, and intelligence everywhere, with everyone, and at all times.

"From Bible to theology" is thus not another disciplinary specialization but a call to interdisciplinary cooperation. In this regard the disciplines must not imitate Jesus's disciples, who argued among themselves "who was the greatest" (Mark 9:34). No one seminary department has the upper academic hand or sits at the Lord's right hand. Rather, each discipline is a gift to the church, a particular perspective on the living and active Word of God that summons, addresses, and directs the people of God across centuries and cultures and transcends any one disciplinary domain.[36] The theological disciplines are organically connected: each is a necessary part of the whole that is theology. At its best this interdepartmental cooperation is the lifeblood of a seminarian's education—but only if the Holy Spirit staves off spiritual anemia—hence the importance of prayer, spiritual formation, chapel, and the local church.

Ultimately, it takes a whole seminary faculty working together in the partnership of the gospel to help students learn Christ. Other chapters in the present book treat in more detail the role of specific academic departments. The present section intends only to indicate ways each department contributes in its own way to the formation of biblical literacy, Christian understanding, theological discernment, and godly wisdom—in short, to the ability to read God's Word to edify God's people.

Biblical Theology

The integrity and unity of theological education ultimately depends on only one theological textbook: the Bible. God uses human words to communicate the meaning and significance of his incarnate Word, Jesus Christ. The Bible is supremely authoritative because it has God as its ultimate author; it conveys divine say-so. In an important sense, then, everything begins and ends with the way the biblical words go: Scripture's literal sense.

---

36. See Clark, *To Know and Love God*, 182.

Nevertheless, one must not too hastily infer that Hodge's inductive method of Bible study necessarily follows.

Exegesis asks the question, "What did the author mean in saying what he said?" Yet biblical interpretation involves more than determining the sense of words and sentences. D. A. Carson acknowledges the importance of the biblical languages, but he also knows that exegesis is never done in a vacuum, as if contemporary readers could ignore the various factors that influence their exegeses. We therefore do not move "from Bible to theology" along a straight line, as if biblical studies always precede historical, systematic, and practical theology. It turns out that "from . . . to" is more like "to and fro," where feedback loops from these other theological disciplines affect the way biblical scholars interpret the text.[37]

It is tempting to think of the Old and New Testament departments as more biblical than other areas in the curriculum. This is understandable but ultimately mistaken. The error lies in thinking that the meaning of the text is wholly a function of its grammar and original historical context. Learning about "the world behind the text" is frequently illuminating, and sometimes indispensable, for correctly discerning the sense of the biblical words. It is less helpful for discerning the bigger picture into which the words fit or for understanding their ultimate referent (i.e., what the biblical discourse is about).

Biblical interpretation is more than a subset of classics. The goal is not simply to recover the world behind the text, whether the ancient Near East or ancient Greece and Rome, but to hear God's Word. To follow rightly the way the biblical words go requires us to do justice not only to the sense they had in their immediate historical context but also to their redemptive-historical and canonical contexts. Sometimes only by taking these other contexts into account can we read the Bible *Christianly*, that is, in the creedal context of Trinitarian theology. Theological interpretation of the Bible means examining not only what the authors said (i.e., the sense of their discourse, what Augustine calls "signs") but also what they were talking about (i.e., the referent of their discourse, what Augustine calls "reality"). Christians know explicitly something the prophets saw only

---

37. See Carson's diagram of this to-and-fro interdepartmental interpretive process in his essay, "Unity and Diversity in the New Testament: The Possibility of Systematic Theology," in Carson, *Collected Writings on Scripture* (Wheaton: Crossway, 2010), 145–46.

vaguely, namely, that Jesus Christ is the fulfillment of God's promise (see 1 Pet 1:10–12).[38]

Biblical theology is that branch of biblical studies that sets forth the theology of the Bible on the Bible's own terms and in the Bible's own categories. The aim is to help readers understand their own world from the Bible's perspective rather than reading their own perspectives into the Bible.[39] It is essential to grasp the overarching story (the whole) in which the individual biblical authors are caught up, as well as the symbols the authors use to relate past and present (e.g., the temple motif which shows up not only in Israel's history but also in Eden, the story of Christ, and the church as a "living" temple). In particular, it is important to understand the theological judgments that lie behind the biblical authors' choices of terms and concepts. We may not have to use the same words, symbols, or concepts as the biblical authors, but if we are to be biblical in our understanding of God and the gospel and to adhere to biblical authority, we must make the same judgments they made. Indeed, "from Bible to theology" is largely the task of translating biblical judgments into a contemporary idiom.

The nature of the Bible itself requires more than biblical studies to understand it correctly. Everything depends on the unique nature of the Bible as God's address: "The Bible is not primarily an object of investigation from which emerges a set of impersonal propositions about its nature. It is a phenomenon to be entered into and engaged with."[40] Other texts do not focus on divine authorship, or demand to be read in redemptive-historical context with Christ at the center, or summon their readers to participate rightly in that ongoing history of redemption.

Historical Theology

It has been said that church history, particularly the development of doctrine, is the history of biblical interpretation. In this sense church history is an answer to prayer—Paul's prayer for the Ephesians, to be precise, and specifically that they would "comprehend with all the saints what is the length

---

38. See Gregory W. Lee, *Today When You Hear His Voice: Scripture, the Covenants, and the People of God* (Grand Rapids: Eerdmans, 2016).

39. James M. Hamilton Jr., *What Is Biblical Theology? A Guide to the Bible's Story, Symbolism, and Patterns* (Wheaton: Crossway, 2014), 23.

40. Timothy Meadowcroft, *The Message of the Word of God* (Downers Grove: InterVarsity, 2011), 27.

and width, height and depth of God's love" in Christ (Eph 3:18). Studying the history of Christianity may also be a means of learning Christ.

Much of what we know about Christ we have received from others. Paul says, "So then, just as you have received Christ Jesus as Lord, continue to live in him, being rooted and built up in him and established in the faith, just as you were taught" (Col 2:6–7). Tradition is both the process and the content of handing down to others what we have ourselves received. David Wenham's comment is apt: "You can't receive Christ without receiving the body of the tradition, which is His Word."[41]

Historical theology provides valuable lessons in how previous generations sought to preserve biblical judgments in terms of their own historical and cultural contexts. The Council of Nicaea provides an excellent case in point. Creeds and confessions represent attempts by earlier Christians to say for their own time and in their own terms what they must say on the basis of the Word of God. This was the case with the doctrine of the Trinity. Though the term *Trinity* is not in the Bible, the early church realized it had to confess the deity of the Son in order to make sense of the Gospel descriptions of his words and deeds and of the gospel of salvation in his name. The confession that the Son was *homoousios* ("of the same substance") as the Father is a doctrinal development that, far from deviating from the Bible, allows interpreters to dive in more deeply. The history of the church's interpretation of the Bible is thus a history of discipleship.

Not every development in church history served biblical understanding. Heresies and unsound doctrines, false ways of following the biblical words, cropped up too. Yet through the process of repeatedly trying to discern what faithful witness means in various times and places—from fourth-century Nicaea through sixteenth-century Wittenberg to twenty-first century North America—the whole church potentially gains a deeper grasp and appreciation of Jesus's person and work. The Holy Spirit leads the church into all truth largely through its struggles to be faithful in the case of new conceptual problems in new cultural contexts. It takes time to understand "the administration of the mystery hidden for ages in God" (Eph 3:9).[42]

---

41. David Wenham, *Paul: Follower of Jesus or Founder of Christianity* (Grand Rapids: Eerdmans, 1995), 392–410.

42. See further, Kevin Vanhoozer, "Improvising Theology According to the Scriptures: An Evangelical Account of the Development of Doctrine," in Gregg R. Allison and Stephen J. Wellum, ed., *Building on the Foundations of Evangelical Theology* (Wheaton: Crossway, 2015), 15–50.

Systematic Theology

Systematic theology is often misconstrued as abstract speculation that is further removed from the Bible than, say, exegesis. It is sometimes suggested that whereas biblical scholars follow the historical order of the Bible, other scholars, dictated either by logic or some ideological *–ism,* order their approaches in different ways. To be sure, there are pathologies of systematic theology, as there are in each of the theological disciplines. At its best, systematic theology is every bit as biblical as Old or New Testament exegesis to the extent that it renders the same underlying biblical (prophetic, apostolic) judgments in different conceptual terms.

Theology is systematic first and foremost because there is "one Lord, one faith, one baptism, one God and Father of all" (Eph 4:5–6) and one overarching story of God's gracious covenantal initiatives that climax in Christ. Systematic theology is the attempt to explicate the plan, and the planner, of salvation—the red thread that runs throughout the canonical Scriptures. The coherence and unity that characterize systems of theology ultimately stem from the unity and coherence of the triune God. John Webster only slightly exaggerates when he claims, "There is only one Christian doctrine, the doctrine of the Holy Trinity in its inward and outward movements. . . . All other doctrines are simply extensions of teaching about God and God's works."[43]

The task of systematic theology is to probe deeper into the conceptual grammar of the biblical text. For example, what must we say about God's being in order to account for his doing the things Scripture depicts him as doing? Or what should we say about the person and nature of Jesus Christ on the basis of Scripture's account of his words and deeds? Exegesis is relatively incomplete until one spells out the ontological implications of the Bible's referents. Only then do interpreters fully understand the judgments the biblical authors make as to the nature of the realities of which they speak. Systematic theology clarifies these judgments, and then it reformulates them in terms, concepts, and categories so that contemporary interpreters can understand what they have learned about divine things from following where the biblical words go.

---

43. Webster, "Principles of Systematic Theology," in *The Domain of the Word,* 145.

Systematic theologians therefore try to render the same biblical judgments in fresh ways, to say the same things the biblical authors said in an idiom that speaks to people in the present context. So it has always been. Today's systematic theology is tomorrow's historical theology. The ongoing mission of church leaders and theologians is to present the same biblical truths in forms that will be maximally intelligible to new generations. Both historical theology and systematic theology are actually forms of missional theology, and present-day missionaries (Christians who witness to the gospel in new cultural contexts) would do well to examine earlier attempts to communicate the truth of the gospel.

One fruitful way forward is to think of systematic theology as faith seeking theatrical rather than theoretical understanding. While biblical theology traces the plot of the unified drama of redemption that spans the Old and New Testaments, systematic theology offers detailed plot analysis: identifying the divine protagonist and the significance of the particular events in light of the whole action (e.g., why did Jesus have to die?). Doctrine on this view offers direction both for understanding what God said and did and for disciples who seek to bear true witness to God's speech and works in the present. On this model doctrine serves the project of cultivating a deeper understanding of the one drama of redemption to which the church has borne witness through the centuries and to which it continues to bear witness in its speech and life. Systematic theology thus aims at wisdom: helping disciples discern what to say and do then and now that faithfully attests and is in line with what God has done, is doing, and will do in Christ to reconcile humanity and renew creation.

Practical Theology

Practical theology, in the fourth position, may seem to be battling hermeneutical cleanup, applying to everyday life the wisdom won by and describing appropriating biblical judgments for real-life practices such as education, counseling, ethics, and missions. The idea that practical theologians apply the results of nonpractical interpretation, though common, is misleading. Practical theologians too are distancing themselves from the linear model according to which practice follows theory, preferring instead the to-and-fro between theory and practice. Practical theology is on this view "a dynamic process of reflective, critical inquiry into the praxis of the church in the world and God's purposes for humanity, carried out in the light of Christian Scripture and tradition, and in critical dialogue with other sources of knowledge."[44]

Whereas systematic theology is attuned to expressing biblical judgments in terms of contemporary thought forms, practical theology focuses on contemporary forms of social life and cultural contexts. These forms and contexts, important as they are, do not have more authority than the biblical texts: in order to minister the gospel to people living in the African Great Lakes region, one needs to know Swahili, but it doesn't follow that Swahili has authority over theology. Language and culture are simply the conditions under which the church has to pursue her mission and live out her citizenship of the gospel. Practical theology focuses on interpreting God's Word in forms of proclamation and practice that fit—speak to and are meaningful in—the contemporary context—that field, domestic or foreign, in which God's triune mission is now being realized.

Practical theology thus makes a vital contribution to the mission of "from Bible to theology" insofar as theology aims both at getting and then demonstrating understanding of God and the gospel, not least by encouraging certain practices that exhibit what it means to follow Jesus in real-life situations. Practical theology ministers understanding by indicating what discipleship means in practice here and now. Again the goal is not simply to understand what the biblical authors meant but to understand how to follow their words faithfully in and for every world situation the church happens to inhabit.

Conclusion: Lived Theological Commentary on the Living Christ

Paul's goal for the church at Colossae should be the goal of every theological educator: "That they may have the full riches of complete understanding, in order that they may know the mystery of God, namely, Christ, in whom are hidden all the treasures of wisdom and knowledge" (Col 2:2–3 NIV). Learning Christ is the beginning and end, the center and circumference,

---

44. Ray S. Anderson, *The Shape of Practical Theology: Empowering Ministry with Theological Praxis* (Downers Grove: InterVarsity, 2001), 22. See also Bonnie J. Miller-McLemore, "Introduction: The Contributions of Practical Theology," in Miller-McLemore, ed., *The Wiley Blackwell Companion to Practical Theology* (London: Blackwell, 2012), 1–20.

the matter and energy of theological education. It has as much to do with the spiritual disciplines associated with discipleship as it does the academic disciplines associated with being a seminary student. What disciples and seminary students have in common is the summons to follow Christ with all one's heart, soul, strength, and mind.

The theological disciplines form disciples. As we have seen, to be a disciple is to be an interpreter of the Bible, a follower of biblical words and the Word to which they bear witness. One important form of biblical interpretation is the biblical commentary. A good biblical commentary does justice to the historical, literary, and theological aspects of the text. In an important sense the life of the disciple, and of the local church, is the most appropriate form our biblical commentary takes: "What we do as the people of God is our interpretation of the Bible."[45] The ultimate aim of theological education is to help disciples be living commentaries, "Christ's letter" (2 Cor 3:3).

Seminaries exist to foster biblical literacy and theological understanding, in particular the ability to discern the voice of God speaking in the Scriptures and the ability to offer a fitting response. The goal is wisdom—lived knowledge of God—a matter of embodying the mind of Christ as the body of Christ everywhere, at all times, and to everyone. The purpose of theological education is to form faithful witnesses who know how to bear witness to the lordship of Christ by living out his life (Gal 2:20) in their own times, places, languages, and concepts—and who can train others to do the same. Learning how to move from the Bible to theology is a matter of learning Christ, of embodying the mind of Christ to the point where one can teach Christ to others.

Questions for Further Reflection

1. How has academic departmentalization both helped and hindered theological education?
2. What are the advantages and disadvantages of thinking of theology as a form of canonical wisdom (*sapientia*) rather than an inductive science of the Bible?

---

45. David Scott, "Speaking to Form: Trinitarian-Performative Scripture Reading," *Anglican Theological Review* 77 (1995), 145.

3. How is understanding more like a capacity or an ability than it is like a grasp of a body of knowledge?
4. What do you think of the author's proposal to make theological interpretation of the Bible the glue and goal of seminary education?
5. Do you agree that the ultimate aim of biblical interpretation is to "learn Christ"?
6. How might one use what Calvin says about the purpose of his *Institutes* (from Gk. *paideia* = "pedagogy") and the centrality of reading Scripture to form piety and reform theological education?

Sources for Further Study

Bartholomew, Craig G., and Heath A. Thomas, ed. *A Manifesto for Theological Interpretation.* Grand Rapids: Baker, 2016.

Boulton, Matthew Myer. *Life in God: John Calvin, Practical Formation, and the Future of Protestant Theology.* Grand Rapids: Eerdmans, 2011.

Charry, Ellen T. *By the Renewing of Your Minds: The Pastoral Function of Christian Doctrine.* Oxford: Oxford University Press, 1997.

Clark, David K. *To Know and Love God: Method for Theology.* Wheaton: Crossway, 2003.

Johnson, Keith L. *Theology as Discipleship.* Downers Grove: InterVarsity, 2015.

Meadors, Gary T. *Four Views on Moving Beyond the Bible to Theology.* Grand Rapids: Zondervan, 2009.

Osborne, Grant R. *The Hermeneutical Spiral: A Comprehensive Introduction to Biblical Interpretation*, 2nd ed. Downers Grove: InterVarsity, 2006.

Swain, Scott R. *Trinity, Revelation, and Reading: A Theological Introduction to the Bible and Its Interpretation.* Edinburgh: T&T Clark, 2011.

Vanhoozer, Kevin J. *Faith Speaking Understanding: Performing the Drama of Doctrine.* Louisville: Westminster John Knox, 2014.

_____, and Daniel J. Treier. *Theology and the Mirror of Scripture: A Mere Evangelical Account.* Grand Rapids: InterVarsity, 2015.

Webster, John. *The Domain of the Word: Scripture and Theological Reason.* Edinburgh: T&T Clark, 2012.

Wood, Charles M. *The Formation of Christian Understanding: Theological Hermeneutics.* Eugene, OR: Wipf and Stock, 2000.

Chapter Thirteen

SYSTEMATIC THEOLOGY

MALCOLM B. YARNELL III

During informal conversations, people often ask, "So, what is it that you do?" As soon as I respond, "I teach systematic theology," a cloud threatens to drench the conversation. The next question, usually asked with a timorous voice, is inevitable: "So, what does that mean?" Sometimes, even before I respond, there is a darting of the eyes, as if looking for an exit, an ominous withdrawal of breath. But at other times, as my acquaintance listens, a deep and enduring fascination develops. Knowing the conversation could go either way, I usually chuckle then offer two definitions: first, of *theology*, and second, of *systematic*. "Well, theology is talk about God. And systematic theology is where we talk about God in a comprehensive way."

A typically unstated third question arises. It appears in various forms, such as, "So what?" "Isn't that a rather esoteric subject?" "Why does that even matter?" (Some ask rather boldly, while most are careful not to injure my feelings.) But I continue the conversation to prevent it from drifting. My first apology for systematic theology is geared toward those captivated by Western pragmatism. "Systematic theology helps people get their minds around who God is and what God is doing. Christians with formal responsibilities for proclaiming God's Word find this useful. But systematic theology also assists every Christian who is concerned to learn what the Bible 'means' for them and for the people they know." I usually conclude with a challenge to my listener: "You know, God calls every human to be a systematic theologian."

Loving God with All Your Mind

Systematic theology is necessary for every human! On what basis would one make such a grand claim? Mark 12:29–30, where Jesus refers to the "most important" commandment, immediately comes to mind: "Love the Lord your God with all your heart, with all your soul, with all your mind, and with all your strength." As you probably know, Jesus is quoting another biblical text, one from the Old Testament, Deut 6:4–5, which is called the Shema. The Shema (the Hebrew statement beginning with עמש or *shema'*, meaning "Listen!") was the primary Jewish confession and was so important that it was repeated several times per day in prayer.

Do You Mind?

However, Jesus added something to the confession. Where Moses relayed the Lord's command as, "Love the LORD your God with all your heart, with all your soul, and with all your strength," Jesus added, "with all your mind." The original purpose of the Shema was to call every person to devote himself to God with everything that he is.[1] Thus Jesus did not materially change the Shema. He clarified it so that the command to worship God entirely now included, appropriately for the context, the Greek emphasis on the life of the "mind" (Gk. διανοία or *dianoia*). But the mind, according to Jesus, is not so much something you *have* as it is something that you *do*. The question is more appropriately stated, "Do you mind?" rather than, "What is the mind?"

Jesus's choice of wording here is important for discerning the scope of theology. Two important Greek words typically indicated the mind. Among the Greeks the first (Gk. νοῦς or *nous*) focused on the intellectual faculty of the mind. It meant that thing by which a human considers material facts and spiritual truths. But Jesus did not choose the philosophical and static term; he chose the second term, *dianoia*, which was often used with the more dynamic Hebrew view of humanity. He meant something holistic and process oriented. Jesus referred not merely to the intellectual activity of cognition but every activity within the human—feeling and choosing as well as thinking. If theology is to love God with the whole inner person,

---

1. For a detailed treatment of the devotional meaning of the *Shema*, see Malcolm B. Yarnell III, *God the Trinity: Biblical Portraits* (Nashville: B&H, 2016), chap. 3.

as Jesus commanded, then it must consider not just abstract items in the intellect but also the powerful affections in the imagination and the directive choices of the will.[2] All of this internal movement is intended to issue forth in outward action.

This command of Jesus, which he said was "most important" (Mark 12:29), must be delineated in order to see what systematic theologians are attempting to do. In addition to working with the whole of the inner human, the command offers basic answers to such necessary questions as: *Who? What? Why? Whence? Whither? How?* and *Where?*

Who?

Who should be engaged in this activity of directing the inner self toward God? The imperative is directed to everyone. Nobody is excluded. Back in the original context of the Shema, Moses made clear that entire devotion to God was to be taught to every succeeding generation at every possible moment in every place imaginable (Deut 6:4–9). If every human is to be taught to worship God, then that includes the reader of this chapter. So, yes, you must love God with all your mind, which means you must also be a theologian. But the universality in the call to love God with all the mind is not restricted merely to the subject of the action.

What?

What is the object of this inner human activity? To put it simply and singularly, the object of our inner movement is directed to one, God. Scripture reveals that God is the universal subject of creation (Gen 1:1), redemption (Col 1:20), and consummation (1 Cor 15:20–28). It is thus entirely appropriate that the subject of all things would also be the object of all devotion. In theology we have to do with God! This is not a delimiting but limitless claim. If God is the Creator of all that is (and he is) and if God is

---

2. The holistic, process orientation of Jesus was mirrored in the rest of the New Testament, where the entire word group affiliated with νοῦς and διανοία took on the holistic human meaning as well as a God-oriented direction in human thought. The primary distinction between νοῦς and διανοία seems to be that the first considered the faculty while the second considered the process. "Νοῦς, [etc.]," in *New International Dictionary of New Testament Theology and Exegesis*, 2nd ed., ed. Moisés Silva (Grand Rapids: Zondervan, 2014), 425–35. For a canonical example of the complex and holistic relation among the human internal faculties and their conduct, compare Paul's references to περιπατέω ("walk" or "way of life"), νοῦς ("thought" or "mind"), διάνοια ("mind"), καρδία ("heart"), ἐργασία ("practice"), μανθάνω ("learn"), διδάσκω ("taught"), ἀναστροφή ("life" or "behavior"), ἄνθρωπος ("self" or "man"), ἐπιθυμία ("desire"), and πνεῦμα ("spirit") in Eph 4:17–24.

the Redeemer of his creatures (and he is) and if God is the goal of everything that is (and he is), then God is the object of everything we do.

When we say that in theology we have to do with God, we include both God in himself and God in his acts. We include all that God is, which is bigger than everything else, and all that God does, which deals with everything else. Theology has as its object of consideration the immanent Trinity and the economic Trinity. This makes theology both simple and complex. It is simple in that there is one object, God, who is and who does. It is complex in that all other objects are by reason of creation, redemption, and consummation included in God's activity. Moreover, "in him we live and move and have our being" (Acts 17:28). To include God as the object of your study of love is to include all things that have their being in God, which is everything else besides God.

Why?

Why should we be engaged in this all-encompassing activity? Theology is not merely about thinking. Theology is about loving. "You shall love the Lord your God." The Hebrew word for "love" in Deuteronomy 6 (אהב or *'ahab*) indicated God's electing love, to which we ought to respond in love toward him. The Greek word for "love" in Mark 12 (ἀγαπάω or *agapao*) indicated a divine love free from selfishness and freely directed toward blessing the other. Divine love is love that originates with God and prompts human love toward God and others.

Humans are to be caught up in the divine love between the three persons of the Trinity (John 17:21, 23; Rom 5:5; 1 John 4:7–10). To be in love with the One who is the source and end of all things, including love, is to be devoted to him with the entirety of our being. This is why Jesus said we need to love him not only with our mind but also with our "heart," "soul," and "strength" (Mark 12:30; cf. Matt 22:37; Luke 10:27). These other aspects of human activity—heart, soul, strength—are not included alongside "mind" to indicate they are parts (or faculties) of the human being. They are included to show that loving God occurs with everything you are and do. Why do theology? For the love of God! For the purpose of loving God entirely, we must comprehend everything with our minds well.

Whence and Whither, Temporally?

Whence and whither is the activity of theology as loving God? The bookend questions of "whence" (origin) and "whither" (goal) are appropriate, and they have been partially answered with the questions of who and what. However, further dimensions of whence and whither should be considered in theology. We must answer this question from, among others, the perspectives of time and of space.

From the perspective of time, the Bible begins with God as preexistent reality. The first and foundational book in the biblical canon, Genesis, begins simply with the presupposition that God is: "In the beginning God." This is the highest reality, the being of God. The first activity the Bible emphasizes is that of original causation: "In the beginning God created." This is God's first external act, creation. However, after his blessing humanity with creation, Adam and Eve sinned and became subject to death. Nevertheless, God was not finished with humanity, and he began to promise through Abraham to provide a Savior. He would come to and through the people of Israel (Gen 12:1–3).

The second major activity of God in the Bible, after creation, became the divine act of redemption. All of creation is being restored through God's redemption of humanity (Rom 8:19–23). The redemption of humanity is effected in the cross of Jesus Christ and applied to the human heart by the Holy Spirit. But is redemption everything? Yes and no. Redemption is not merely restoring creation from the detriments of the fall. Redemption is God's activity of leading creation to its proper end in him. Redemption is occurring now in our transformation to Christ (Rom 12:2) and will be completed when we see him as he is (1 John 2:28–3:2).

The divine economy is thus centered in the redemption narrative of Jesus Christ, also known as the *gospel* (Eph 1:7–13; cf. 1 Cor 15:1–8). The plan of God, a former mystery now revealed, is to save our bodies through the incarnation, crucifixion, and resurrection of his eternally begotten Son. In Jesus, God became a human (called the incarnation). This Son of David atoned for our sins through his bodily death on the cross (the crucifixion). On the third day this Messiah (Gk. Χριστός or Christ) conquered death (the resurrection). Afterward, this same Son of Man ascended bodily (the ascension) to reign at the right hand of the Father on his throne (the heavenly session). From there Christ Jesus will one day return (the Second

Coming). He will give new bodies both to those who have died in faith and to those believers who remain alive (the first resurrection). The key factor in whether the ultimately universal resurrection of humanity results in eternal life or in eternal death (the second death) is the presence of faith in the subject human. This faith comes as a responsive calling to the proclamation of the Word of God, which must first be heard to be believed (Rom 10:14–17).

After redemption we may identify the third major activity of God, which has its goal in the future perfection of humanity and creation, as the consummation. The consummation includes the return of Christ, the final judgment, and the eternal city (Revelation 20–22). At the end of the consummation, Christ will have restored all things to their proper order before the sovereign God (1 Cor 15:28). The temporal perspective of theology includes everything from creation through the cross to the consummation. These works of God are also known as the divine economy, for it has to do with how God is managing his household. (Our English word *economy* comes from the Greek οἰκονομία or *oikonomia*, meaning "administration" or "dispensation"). God's economy includes all he created, which is all there is. Creation—redemption—consummation: this divine economy is the dramatic narrative of Scripture and provides the systematic theologian with a comprehensive and compelling view of God in relation to time.[3] From the problem of time, we turn to the problem of space.

Whence and Whither, Spatially?

Humans are living creatures who occupy not only time but space. We are not created as soulless bodies, nor are we created as bodiless souls.[4] Unfortunately, the scriptural words *soul* and *body* are often understood as if they were two separable pieces of the human being. This is a common but fundamental misunderstanding. When God created humanity, he formed the man out of dust and breathed life into him so that he became "a living being" (Gen 2:7). When the Spirit of God withdraws the gift of his breath (due to our sin), the human dies (Gen 6:3; 7:22). Because God loves humanity, he does not leave us to our deserved judgment, death.

---

3. Craig G. Bartholomew and Michael W. Goheen, *The Drama of Scripture: Finding Our Place in the Biblical Story*, 2nd ed. (Grand Rapids: Baker, 2014).

4. However, some of us for a time will exist in an "intermediate state" between death and resurrection at the second coming of Christ.

Rather, he promises life. It is necessary to affirm eternal life is located in resurrected bodies (1 Corinthians 15). Because we are composed of material (i.e., "dust"), human bodies occupy material dimensions. For the fallen human to gain life, he must be raised from death.

Since our entire existence and movement are in God, bodily life is necessarily brought under the purview of theology, too. Personal life is necessarily spatial because we are created as living, breathing beings. Personal salvation is necessarily spatial, too, because it requires the resurrection of human bodies. Personal salvation is necessarily spatial, moreover, because the gospel of Jesus must be heard in order to become the possession of a human.

A coordinate truth to the location of the person in body is the location of the person in community. Humans do not enter life alone; every human must be born of a woman. Nor can humans enter new life in Christ alone; every believer is "born again" when he or she hears and accepts the gospel from another person. Our embodied personhood requires embodied community.

From birth to rebirth and beyond, humans as embodied are simultaneously personal and communal creatures. We live in three basic human communities established by God, which we know as *family, society*, and *church*. While every human is born into a family, and while every human must exist in a rudimentary society in order to survive physically, only those who have been born again may truly be members of the third human community known as the church. The church is founded in Christ and fashioned by the Spirit. While being born again is a sovereign work of the Holy Spirit, he does not work apart from the preaching of the Word.

From both a personal and communal perspective, the fundamental spatial characters in the postascension and pre–Second Coming narrative of human salvation are four: the *hearer* of the Word, the *proclaimer* of the Word, the common *society* in which the hearer and the proclaimer share the capacity to communicate the Word, and the *church* that sends the proclaimer of the Word and receives through baptism the hearer of the Word. Note that each of the fundamental characters inhabits space. Proclaimer, church, hearer, and society all participate in the limits and capabilities of human bodies.

The movement of salvation thus occurs in a specific bodily direction. The proclamation of the Word of God moves from the church through the proclaimer to the hearer in the society.[5] The Word uses the means of spatial communication, and the Word is internally empowered with the Spirit. In this way God also freely chose to require preachers. And preachers must use human language to proclaim the divine Word. The human languages we use as the church's preachers are shaped in the context of the common society we share with our hearers. The Word is powerful and active to enable faith, but the Word chooses to be proclaimed in a language intelligible to the hearer and the society he or she inhabits.

While the church and the proclaimer bring to the conversation the divine and sufficiently powerful Word, the society and the hearer bring to the conversation the original divine gift of human *language*. Language is a gift of God (Gen 2:16–20; 11:1–9). But language has natural limits. Language, moreover, has been refashioned by human cultures with histories characterized by virtue and vice. Sin is not the only problem. Languages move in flux over time and are different among societies and subcultures within larger societies. Languages thus constantly need translation as the church proclaims. The Word must be translated or interpreted into numerous diverse and shifting human contexts so that people may understand its meaning (see Neh 8:1–12). The sociolinguistic problems could be seen as hopelessly insurmountable. This brings us to the question of how the church can accomplish its important role of theological communication.

How?

Providentially, the church is not without resources. The church has been given authority to accomplish the proclamation of the Word. This authority comes from the Lord who is always with the church and who possesses all power (Matt 28:18, 20). The Lord chose to use the church to proclaim his Word in order to make disciples (Matt 28:19). The Lord who gave the Word to his church also gives the Spirit to his church. In the earliest days of

---

5. This God-given structure to our physical reality and the conveyance of salvation must be emphasized. Note again the direction in the movement of these spatial truths. *Whence?* The proclamation of the Word derives in the church and proceeds through the proclaimer sent by the church. *Whither?* The Word moves toward the hearer who inhabits the same society as the proclaimer. Communally, the Word must move spatially from the church into the society. Personally, the Word must move spatially from the preacher into the ear of the hearer.

the church, the Spirit immediately connected the diverse speech and hearing of the various speakers and hearers (Acts 2). However, the long-term plan of God was for the church to learn and use language intelligible to its hearers. God gave Christians keen minds and "intelligible speech" so that they would proclaim the gospel with "meaning" in order to bring about the conversion of those speaking with "other languages" (1 Cor 14:1–25).[6]

The plan of God the Trinity for translation and interpretation may be seen in the teaching of Christ and the apostles about how the Holy Spirit works with the Word in the proclamation of the church. The Spirit of God inspired the original authors to write the Word they received from him (2 Tim 3:16). The church is the carrier of that Word, which is now located authoritatively in the canon prepared by the Holy Spirit (John 16:12–14). Moreover, the Spirit of God illumines the ears of the contemporary hearers of the Word to which the Lord has sent his preachers, ensuring they are able to understand it (2 Pet 1:20–21; 2 Cor 3:3–6). The God who gave the Word in the first place will lift up even the most difficult and compromised human languages to make them capable of conveying divine truth to the hearer. He does so through Spirit-guided lives and minds in the church.

At this point, we bring forward the witness of Karl Barth to see how theology is a necessary tool in the task of proclamation. Barth famously defined theology's task as critiquing the preaching of the church in the light of the gospel.[7] If the church stands in a society with a unique language requiring translation of the gospel from its original context, theology's role is to evaluate the preaching of the church in comparison to both the changing culture and the unchanging gospel. Systematic theology assists proclamation so the church can be faithful both to maintain the gospel and to interpret it for the world. The "true service" of theology, said Emil Brunner, is "to think through the message of God's work in Jesus Christ—think it through so long and so thoroughly that it can be spoken simply and intelligibly to every man in the language of his time."[8]

---

6. Malcolm B. Yarnell III, "Expository Notes," in *Studies in 1 Corinthians: Helping Your Church Stay on Course*, January Bible Study 2003 (Nashville: LifeWay, 2002), 64–66.

7. Karl Barth, *Church Dogmatics* I/1, *The Doctrine of the Word of God*, 2nd ed., ed. G. W. Bromiley and T. F. Torrance, trans. G. W. Bromiley (Edinburgh: T&T Clark, 1975), 6.

8. Emil Brunner, *Our Faith*, trans. John W. Rilling (New York: Scribner, 1962), iii.

Where?

Because of this comprehensive and critical role of the discipline Barth preferred to call "dogmatics,"[9] we now recognize where systematic theology fits among the various academic disciplines in a theological school. If we picture theological education as manufacturing arrows out of our students, who are intended to fly with the Word of God to accomplish the purposes of the Lord, systematic theology stands in the middle of the arrow.[10] On the one end of the shaft are the biblical disciplines, which like feathers guide the arrow in the proper direction. On the other end of the shaft, at the head, are the practical disciplines of proclamation, such as preaching, evangelism, missions, and counseling. The practical disciplines engage the church in direct ministry to the world.

Situated in the middle between the biblical and practical disciplines is the shaft of the arrow. The classical theological disciplines maintain the connection between the whence of Scripture and the whither of proclamation. Without a true shaft, an arrow will veer inevitably from its target. This shaft is occupied by systematic theology, which embraces the entire theological enterprise through critical evaluation. Joining with systematic theology in this work are other classical disciplines such as philosophy, church history, and theological ethics. The serene beauty of systematic theology is that it is privileged to engage all the disciplines. The complex difficulty for the systematic theologian is that he or she must know all the disciplines at a level of expertise conversant with their primary professors. Systematic theology is a middle discipline that demands its practitioners be more than middling.

Wisely Achieving Clarity of Mind

With the basis, participants, role, and locations of systematic theology established in the previous section, we now turn to consider the sources, norm, and method of systematic theology. I have written at length elsewhere on

---

9. Dogmatics is typically identified with the theological stance of a church, as drawn from its official doctrinal statements, while systematic theology is more of a personal enterprise.

10. In the Middle Ages, systematic theology was regarded as the "queen of the sciences." According to Aquinas, "sacred doctrine" is "nobler," because of its greater certitude and higher subject matter. Thomas Aquinas, *Summa Theologica*, trans. Fathers of the English Dominican Province (Westminster, MD: Christian Classics, 1948), Ia.1.5.

the issue of theological method,[11] so rather than repeating what has already been covered, we here note five necessary concepts that every systematic theologian would be wise to use. These sagacious notions include *condescension*, *correspondence*, *confidence*, *coherence*, and *comprehensiveness*. The purpose in using these tools is to achieve clarity of thought as we strive to love God with all of our minds.

Condescension

God himself is alone good (Mark 10:18; Luke 18:19). Any good existing in this world comes down to us from God, who transcends us far above (Jas 1:17). To the temporal and spatial perspectives of *whence* and *whither*, we must add a third dimension, condescending grace. By *condescension* we mean the overarching truth of divine grace whereby the transcendent God stoops to grant us every good and perfect gift: God condescends to create us; God condescends to redeem us; God condescends to complete us. All that we are, all that we have, all that we will be—everything is the result of divine grace, of divine *condescension*.

"Knowledge of God" (another way to define *theology*) is that particular good or grace that allows us to see God. Knowledge of God necessarily comes only from him as a gift and blessing. The highest goal of human existence is to see God (Matt 5:8). Such sight has been called "the beatific [blessed] vision." A famous statement ascribed to Thomas Aquinas encapsulates the movement of the grace of divine knowledge: "Theology is taught by God, teaches of God, and leads to God."[12]

Theology, however, does not begin with God's revelation of himself to humanity.[13] Rather, theology begins within the Trinity as God knows himself. First, note that God's knowledge of himself is a mystery to us, such that Brunner began his discussion of the divine attributes by saying, "He

---

11. Malcolm B. Yarnell III, *The Formation of Christian Doctrine* (Nashville: B&H, 2007); idem, "The Anabaptists and Theological Method: 'For What They Were Concerned with Was Not Luther's, but Rather God's Word,'" in *The Anabaptists and Contemporary Baptists: Restoring New Testament Christianity*, ed. idem (Nashville: B&H, 2013), 27–48.

12. "Theologia a Deo docetur, Deum docet, et ad Deum ducit." This is a summary of Aquinas's teaching in *Summa Theologia*, Ia.1.7; Kelly M. Kapic, *A Little Book for New Theologians: Why and How to Study Theology* (Downers Grove: IVP Academic, 2012), 36.

13. I am indebted to my former professor, the late John Webster, in these paragraphs. John Webster, "Principles of Systematic Theology," *International Journal of Systematic Theology* 11 (2009): 67–71.

is Mystery."[14] Second, God entirely and alone knows this singular divine mystery in his threeness: "No one knows the Father except the Son, and anyone to whom the Son desires to reveal him" (Matt 11:27). "No one comprehends the thoughts of God except the Spirit of God" (1 Cor 2:11 ESV).[15] God's knowledge of himself has been called *archetypal theology*,[16] but we describe it as the *first theology*.

Because God's knowledge of himself is an unfathomable mystery to his creatures, then God must freely reveal himself to us. God's revelation of himself is intended to bless us, to save us. Thus, theology is God's ultimate intention to save humans. God's revelation of his knowledge of himself as the God who not only creates but redeems is the greatest blessing. If God's knowledge of himself is first theology, then our knowledge of him, through revelation, is necessarily *second theology*.

Second theology, human knowledge of God, is not merely a cerebral exercise; it is a knowing inextricably bound with loving: "love is from God, and everyone who *loves* has been born of God and *knows* God. The one who does not *love* does not *know* God, because God is love. God's love was revealed among us" (1 John 4:7b–9a, emphasis added).[17]

And this love is revealed in the central eternal and historical event of the cross, when God's Son became "the propitiation for our sins" (1 John 4:10 ESV). Second theology traces the triune economy: it begins as an act of divine condescension motivated by God's love, was manifested supremely in the gracious work of Christ on the cross, and becomes our personal knowledge of God through the work of the Holy Spirit.

Correspondence

Human theology, second theology, comes from first theology, God's knowledge of himself as Trinity. God condescends knowledge of himself through revelation, which requires discussion of another matter of theological

---

14. Brunner, *Our Faith*, 12. Cf. Rom 11:33: "Oh, the depth of the riches both of the wisdom and of the knowledge of God! How unsearchable his judgments and untraceable his ways!"
15. The Greek word for "knowing" in Matt 11:27 is ἐπιγινώσκω or *epiginosko*, which indicates entire knowledge. The Greek word for comprehending in 1 Cor 2:11 is εἴδω or *eido*, which often indicates the faculty of sight.
16. Webster, "Principles of Systematic Theology," 62.
17. If in Matt 11:27, where God "knows" himself with ἐπιγινώσκω or *epiginosko*, indicating entire knowledge, then similarly here in 1 John 4, we may know God fully, though only by grace rather than by nature, and certainly in an ever increasing way into eternity.

wisdom, *correspondence*. Before the Enlightenment, people presumed that humans might receive divine truth. Disagreements arose over how that truth is accessed and interpreted, but most everyone believed humans could perceive the metaphysical, the realm of God. Alas, however, from Descartes to Hume to Kant, a wedge was driven between human ability to know the world and human ability to know God.[18] This thoroughgoing division in the modern mind handicaps believers' claims to know God truly from the Bible. This is most unfortunate.

In affirming that God has revealed himself truthfully, we are swimming against the modern philosophical tide. However, the Bible describes Jesus as the "Word of God" (e.g., John 1:1–14; Rev 19:13), the Bible itself as the "Word of God" (e.g. Acts 18:11; Heb 4:12), and our preaching of the Bible similarly (e.g. Heb 13:7; 1 Pet 1:21–23).[19] Thus, we believe God reveals himself supremely as the Word in Jesus, that his revelation is recorded in the writings of the prophets and apostles, and that his revelation can and should be proclaimed to humanity. Today our only certain external knowledge regarding Jesus comes from the writings of his apostles, which we call the New Testament. Under the guidance of the Holy Spirit, the thirty-nine books of the Old Testament and the twenty-seven books of the New were recognized by the church and collected into an official canon.

The Bible as the Word of God is a perfect gift that entirely corresponds to truth. God the Trinity brings this perfect Word to us in this way: God the Father began his revelation by speaking at various times and in various ways through the prophets. He climaxed his revelation by speaking most excellently in his only begotten Son (Heb 1:1–2). God the Father gave the words to his Son to teach, and God the Holy Spirit later brought the teachings of Jesus perfectly to the minds of the apostles, who subsequently wrote the New Testament (John 14:24–26; 15:26; 16:12–14). God the Holy Spirit inspired the writers of all the books of the Bible to write perfectly what they wrote, even as he allowed their personalities and contexts to shine through his Word (2 Tim 3:16–17). The divine Scriptures include the writings of both the prophets and the apostles (2 Pet 3:15–16). Like

---

18. The development of this problem is reviewed in Etienne Gilson, *The Unity of Philosophical Experience* (New York: Scribner, 1937), 198–239. Cf. Yarnell, *God the Trinity*, 89–98, 161–64, 230–34; and Roger Scruton, *The Soul of the World* (Princeton, NJ: Princeton University Press, 2014), 7–12.

19. "Word of God," in Anthony C. Thiselton, *The Thiselton Companion to Christian Theology* (Grand Rapids: Eerdmans, 2015), 850–51.

the original inspiration of the biblical books, so the interpretation of these same books is a work guided by the Spirit (2 Pet 1:19–21). As in other places, the final book of the Bible, Revelation, warns that the Word God as given to us should by no means be altered (Rev 22:18–19). God the Holy Spirit superintends the entire process by which the Word of God, the Bible, comes to us, so we can say with full confidence these "words are faithful and true" (Rev 22:6).

That is how perfect correspondence develops between Scripture and reality. The Word of God reveals God truly. Any attempt to derogate from the Word of God's truthfulness should be resisted as worthy of judgment. There are instances of such judgment in Scripture. Especially vivid are the narratives of Jeremiah. First, many prophets looked to cultural resources for divine authority, envisioned ideas in their own minds, and led the people astray. God judged these men for misrepresenting his Word (Jer 23:9–32). In another case Hananiah spoke under his own authority rather than being sent by God. Because Hananiah led people to trust in false hope, he was also judged (Jeremiah 28). Finally, one king of Judah, Jehoiakim, sliced up and burned Jeremiah's scroll. God promised to let Jehoiakim's corpse rot in the open for this and brought terrible judgment on the people who followed him (Jeremiah 36). God cares about the Bible, for it is his means for granting us eternal truth.

Theologians understand the truth revealed to us is eternal. They also understand the truth comes in human words. How is it that the eternal God uses temporal human language? Compensating for the limits of human language, God lifts up that language to make it capable of revealing him truly. The correspondence between God's perfect reality and our access to it through limited human language is made possible through God's "accommodation" of himself to our language and conceptual abilities. For instance, the Bible speaks of God's "arm" and "face," but we know God is spiritual rather than material (John 4:24). God used these human attributes to describe his power and his person. A divine act and the divine nature are revealed in human metaphors.[20] Correspondence is made possible through God's self-accommodation to human language.

---

20. S. N. Williams, "Accommodation," in *New Dictionary of Theology: Historical and Systematic*, ed. Martin Davie, et al. (Downers Grove: IVP Academic, 2016), 2–3.

Confidence

God has intentionally accommodated the expression of himself in our language such that an accessible correspondence between his knowledge of himself and our knowledge of him exists. From the perspective of his divine attributes, we can argue that because God is trustworthy, we know his revelation of himself is trustworthy. Similarly, because God is sufficient in himself, we know his self-revelation is sufficient for us. God's "sufficiency" (Gk. ἱκανότης or *hikanotes*, meaning "competency" or completeness") is the result of his all-encompassing knowledge, power, and presence. Our confidence in God results from knowing he is sufficient.

We can have great confidence in God because God himself is sufficient and has revealed himself accordingly in Christ: "Such is the confidence we have through Christ before God. It is not that we are competent in ourselves to claim anything as coming from ourselves, but our adequacy is from God" (2 Cor 3:4–5). Sufficiency is never a function of man but of God. Later in the same letter Paul says God shared his sufficiency with us through his Son, Jesus Christ. We are weak, but God powerfully works on our behalf through "grace" (2 Cor 12:8–9). So divine sufficiency is eternally in God and in his Son, Jesus Christ. How do we gain his sufficiency and confidence today?

In Christian history Scripture's sufficiency has not been widely discussed. Through separate exegeses of Psalm 19, John MacArthur and I recently concluded that Scripture must also be deemed sufficient. Psalm 19 "categorically affirms the authority, inerrancy, and sufficiency of the written Word of God."[21] Our understanding of Scripture as sufficient has five facets. First, Psalm 19 exalts "the truthfulness, goodness, and beauty of the Word of God."[22] Second, Isaiah 55; Hebrews 4; and Romans 10 present Scripture as operating dynamically. Through scriptural proclamation God works in our hearts. Third, Scripture is epistemologically sufficient to save us from sin. Fourth, Scripture is sufficient for the construction of doctrine. Fifth, Scripture defines what is truly relevant or applicable in human life. The Word of God gives confidence for our every need—our every "real need," it should be said, as opposed to ethereal "felt needs."[23]

---

21. John MacArthur, "The Sufficiency of the Word of God: Psalm 19," in *The Inerrant Word: Biblical, Historical, Theological, and Pastoral Perspectives* (Wheaton: Crossway, 2016), 25.
22. Yarnell, *The Formation of Christian Doctrine*, 25.
23. Ibid., 25–28.

The construction of the church's doctrines (in Latin *doctrina* means "teaching") from the Bible is, of course, more complex than merely affirming it is sufficient, inerrant, and authoritative. The Bible is the premiere source of Christian doctrine, but not the only influence on it. First, since the councils, the medieval papacy, and the Reformation, Christians have become painfully aware that countervailing traditions also impact our construal of biblical teaching. Second, in light of medieval scholasticism, scholastic Protestantism, and the Enlightenment, Christians learned that rational currents shape theologies. Third, after the rise of Pietism, Romanticism, and Wesleyan Evangelicalism, Christians also understood that experiences affect our doctrines.

Soon after the Reformation, Richard Hooker outlined the profound ways in which Scripture, tradition, and reason shape various churches.[24] And after the rise of the evangelical movement, Albert Outler coined the term, "Wesleyan Quadrilateral," to describe how experience joined the other three sources in constituting theology.[25] While evangelical theologians recognize that tradition, reason, and experience influence theology, most would agree Scripture is the normative source of Christian theology, using slogans such as *sola scriptura* or *suprema scriptura*.[26] The Evangelical Theological Society affirms the inerrancy of Scripture (and implicitly its authority),[27] while denominational statements often accommodate the other sources. The Bible, says one, is "the supreme standard by which all human conduct, creeds, and religious opinions should be tried."[28] As the "standard" or "norm" of truth, the Bible sufficiently and authoritatively conveys God's will. With it, we may confidently engage in theological construction.

---

24. Richard Hooker, *Of the Laws of Ecclesiastical Polity*, ed. Arthur Stephen McGrade (New York: Cambridge University Press, 1989).

25. Albert C. Outler, "The Wesleyan Quadrilateral—in John Wesley," *Wesleyan Theological Journal* 20 (1985): 7–18.

26. James Leo Garrett Jr., *Systematic Theology: Biblical, Historical, and Evangelical*, vol. 1 (Grand Rapids: Eerdmans, 2000), 206–9.

27. "The Bible alone, and the Bible in its entirety, is the Word of God written and is therefore inerrant in the autographs." Doctrinal Basis, Evangelical Theological Society.

28. "The Scriptures," *The Baptist Faith and Message*, accessed January 16, 2017, http://www.sbc.net/bfm2000/bfm2000.asp.

Coherence and Comprehensiveness

In order to teach the truths of God properly, one must thus know (1) that God *condescends* to reveal himself; (2) that his revelation *corresponds* to his reality; and (3) that we may have *confidence* in his Word as sufficient. However, two other matters of wisdom are necessary for theological interpretation of Scripture. The human mind must be able to perceive the connections between the many truths of divine revelation in a coherent and comprehensive way. One may understand a certain fact is true, but if that fact is not grounded in the universe of truth and properly located with regard to other facts in that universe, truth is compromised. As long as (4) *coherence* and (5) *comprehensiveness* are missing, systematic theology remains deficient.

An example may help the reader see this at work. According to early church theologians such as Justin Martyr, human thought (λόγος or *logos*) perceives truth through participation in the divine Λόγος ("the Word"). This Logos came into the world as the Lord Jesus Christ (John 1:1, 9, 14).[29] The beauty of Justin's "Logos theology" is that it draws on the central figure of the faith, Jesus Christ, granting him the dominant role in Christian theology. It also positively orients its system toward human salvation. The problem began when Justin went beyond the biblical text into the philosophy of the Stoics and Philo to construct his organizing motif. Moreover, "Logos theology" does not account properly for the personal relationships within the Godhead.[30]

This is not to say Logos theologians such as Justin Martyr and Tertullian transgressed the bounds of orthodox faith, nor is it to say they failed to make significant contributions. They most certainly did further orthodoxy, both with regard to the Word and the Trinity. (For instance, Tertullian coined the critical Latin theological term *Trinitas*). But they did not capture the comprehensiveness of the Christian faith, nor did they provide its most coherent description. There was still more truth, and fundamental truth about divine being at that, for Christians to observe as they peered

---

29. E. D. Cook, "Logos," in *New Dictionary of Theology*, 529–30.
30. This problem was perceived by the church's first systematic theologian. Origen, *Commentary on John*, fragment 2 in *Classical Christian Doctrine: Introducing the Essentials of the Ancient Faith*, trans. Ronald E. Heine (Grand Rapids: Baker, 2013), 61.

into the biblical text. Significant Christological and Trinitarian advances did not occur until after the time of the Logos theologians.

Then how do we arrive at a coherent and comprehensive theological construal of biblical revelation? We only note some general trends. The coherence of the Christian faith, presumed in the church through the early, medieval, and Reformation periods, was subsequently lost in the modern period.[31] By *coherence* I mean how the teachings of the canon hold together in a unified and compelling way. Kevin Vanhoozer argues the problem is that the human faculty of the imagination was compromised through either liberal misappropriation or conservative disdain.[32] The key to recovering the coherence of theology is through freeing the evangelical imagination from captivity. When the Trinity's work in the gospel to reconcile the world in Christ is emphasized, coherence should return.[33]

Vanhoozer says the theological recovery of the imagination begins in this way: First, the imagination identifies the "fittingness" of various theological "parts," showing how they "'belong' to a whole."[34] Second, the imaginative faculty engages the whole person, including mind, will, and emotions. Third, this requires both the visual and the verbal aspects of human knowing. Fourth, the imagination must strive to see what is invisible through "the eyes of [the] heart" (Eph 1:18). "Faith is the enduring ability to imagine God, the world, and ourselves in the light of the biblical story of salvation."[35] The imagination as described by Vanhoozer seems to be where the Holy Spirit's work of illumination is placed.

While Vanhoozer's "theodramatic" proposal is fascinating and helpful, we would emphasize two stipulations for properly constructing a coherent and comprehensive vision of theology. First, while there must be coherence in the proposal, this coherence may never contradict the elements of the biblical vision. Scripture retains visionary priority even when it may seem logically inconclusive. As Paige Patterson has explained privately, "Systematic theology is not a waffle iron into which one pours the batter of Scripture and demands conformity. No, theology must conform to Scripture."

---

31. E.g., C. S. Lewis, *The Discarded Image: An Introduction to Medieval and Renaissance Literature* (1964; reprint, New York: Cambridge University Press, 2012), 1–12.
32. Kevin Vanhoozer, *Pictures at a Theological Exposition: Scenes of the Churches Worship, Witness and Wisdom* (Downers Grove: IVP Academic, 2016), 18–19, 33–34.
33. Ibid., 36–39.
34. Ibid., 24.
35. Ibid., 27.

Our second emphatic stipulation is that the theme(s) used by a theologian to provide a coherent and comprehensive presentation must arise from the biblical text. With this in mind, I have detected a twofold approach from Scripture. From the divine perspective, we discern the movement of God as Father, Son, and Holy Spirit in his major activity of creation, redemption, and consummation.[36] From the human perspective, we discern the theme of personal and communal discipleship to Jesus as Lord.[37] The complementary movements of divine act and human response seem to offer the rudiments necessary for a coherent and comprehensive theological system.

Closing with an Open Mind

Because loving God "with all your mind" is commanded of everyone, the call to be a systematic theologian was deemed universal. And because the systematic theologian must discern God in his being and in his acts, each was called to embrace principles of theological wisdom. We conclude our chapter on the basics of systematic theology by showing how theological minds must be ordered theologically, oriented toward service, and open to further illumination.

Ordered Theologically

The life project of one of my former professors, the late John Webster, was to recall theology to its proper origin and goal, God. Theology in the modern period became a series of human self-reflections. Indoctrinated in this ethos, Webster eventually dissented and challenged contemporary academic theology to return to God as the source and end of all things. During his inaugural lecture at Oxford University, it was a privilege to be in the audience to hear him argue for a "theological theology," although many at the time were less than approving.[38] John Webster believed the order of theology must necessarily begin with God. "The first material object

---

36. Yarnell, *God the Trinity*, 234–36.
37. Yarnell, *The Formation of Christian Doctrine*, 11–16; idem, "The Anabaptists and Theological Method;" idem, "Anabaptist Spirituality," in *The Pure Flame of Devotion: The History of Christian Spirituality*, ed. G. Stephen Weaver and Ian Hugh Clary (Kitchener, ON: Joshua Press, 2013), 151–76; idem, *The Heart of a Baptist*, White Paper 2 (Fort Worth: Center for Theological Research, 2005).
38. John Webster, *Theological Theology: An Inaugural Lecture Delivered Before the University of Oxford on 28 October 1997* (Oxford: Clarendon Press, 1998).

of systematic theology is God considered in himself, the uncreated one eminent over all created being as its infinitely generous source and end."[39]

Only after beginning with God may one consider the second major part of theology, all the things that are within God or, to put it another way, all the things God does. But even as one proceeds from theological theology toward creaturely theology, God himself must remain in the foreground.[40] Since the economic "missions" are grounded in the eternal processions of God in the Son and the Holy Spirit, the missions may shape systematic theology.[41] We agree with John Webster's recovery of the traditional delineation but would orient the "loci" (or "commonplaces") of theology even more firmly within the frame of the Trinity.[42]

The scholastic ordering of the loci may be placed in a Trinitarian theological theology this way:

- Prolegomena;[43]
- God the Trinity; The Work of God in Revelation;[44]
- The Person of God the Father;[45] The Work of the Father;[46]
- The Work of God in Creation, Providence, Angels, and Humanity;[47]
- The Person of God the Son; The Work of the Son;[48]
- The Person of God the Holy Spirit; The Work of the Holy Spirit;[49]
- The Work of God in Salvation, the Church, and the End.

---

39. Webster, "Principles of Systematic Theology," 65.
40. Ibid., 65–68.
41. Ibid., 66.
42. John Webster, "Introduction: Systematic Theology," in *The Oxford Handbook of Systematic Theology*, ed. John Webster, Kathryn Tanner, and Iain Torrance (New York: Oxford University Press, 2007), 12.
43. In *prolegomena*, which means "the word that comes before," evangelicals locate issues of theological method. Roman Catholics typically call this "fundamental theology." The current chapter can be classified as such.
44. The choice of ordering between God and his revelation varies widely.
45. This is where the treatment of divine attributes would occur.
46. The focus here should be on election.
47. As part of anthropology or as a separate locus, human sin must also be treated in depth.
48. The work of the Son is centered on the cross, so this has often just been called, "The Atonement." However, the work of Christ extends from creation to consummation. The cross is central to salvation history and eternal in its impact, but Christ also does other work.
49. In some systems the Holy Spirit as person has been treated under theology proper, and his work has been subsumed under the locus of grace. The focus in the work of the Holy Spirit should be on perfection.

Oriented Toward Service

Above, systematic theology's service role is located within the church and among the disciplines. Hans Schwarz orients theology's service toward three audiences: the church, the world, and God. First, theology must be self-critical to preserve the integrity of the church's theological proclamation. This reflective service is necessary in order to learn how to address a shifting culture while remaining rooted in the eternal gospel. The church must "critically construe the content of our faith" to keep it from degenerating into either novelty or superstition.[50]

Second, theology serves the world. As we give an account of our faith to the world (1 Pet 3:15–16), theology reflects on the church's proclamation. We help the world see that God reveals himself in nature and conscience, but this general revelation is insufficient for salvation (Rom 1:18–2:16). This compels theology to be radically dependent on God's Word in proclamation. "Theology itself is a word, a human response; yet what makes it theology is not its own word or response, but the Word which it hears and to which it responds."[51] Finally, theology's service to the world depends on the Spirit, for the church must preach evangelistically, including repentance toward God and faith in Christ only alongside the conviction of the Spirit (John 16:5–12).

The third service of theology is directed toward God. In the act of praise, we reflect back toward God the knowledge of him received from him. This doxological service also shapes theology. Many traditions justify their dogma in the aspiration to worship God properly. This was true for Athanasius, the fourth-century hero of orthodoxy, who believed the proper worship of God in Christ compels a high Christology. Also important in this regard is the Church of England, whose theology was shaped by the liturgy of Thomas Cranmer's *Book of Common Prayer*. Finally, this is also true of the Baptists, who recovered believer-only baptism in order to worship God purely.[52] An old adage, *lex orandi lex credendi*, "the rule of prayer is the rule of faith," captures the correlation of worship and theology perfectly.[53]

---

50. Hans Schwarz, *The Christian Faith: A Creedal Account* (Grand Rapids: Baker, 2014), 20.
51. Karl Barth, *Evangelical Theology: An Introduction* (Grand Rapids: Eerdmans, 1963), 16–17.
52. Matthew Ward, *Pure Worship: The Early English Baptist Distinctive*, vol. 3, *Monographs in Baptist History* (Eugene, OR: Wipf and Stock, 2014).
53. Cf. Geoffrey Wainwright, *Doxology: The Praise of God in Worship, Life, and Doctrine: A Systematic Theology* (New York: Oxford University Press, 1980).

Open to Further Illumination

Even if one's systematic theology is ordered theologically, oriented toward service, follows the five aspects of theological wisdom, and embraces the call to comprehend God and his creation entirely, it will remain incomplete. Many people look at the difficult work required to engage in systematic theology and are tempted to make excuses. It takes effort to remain perennially attentive to the Word and the Spirit. And our created limitations and our sins inhibit the proper reception and construal of knowledge of God. But surrender is not the antidote for difficulty.

We will never reach a perfect system in this life. Paul wrote, "Now we see only a reflection," and "now I know in part" (1 Cor 13:12). In other words, no matter how hard we try, we see God incompletely in this age. If *first theology* is God's knowledge of himself, and *second theology* is our incomplete knowledge of him, then *third theology* will be the knowledge we receive in glory, when "I will know fully, as I am fully known" (1 Cor 13:12).[54] But this, too, is no reason for quitting. What is one to do? Forsaking the call to theologize is not an option, for Jesus commanded each of us to "love God with all [our] mind."

Finally, within church history and through contemporary encounters with other Christians, one discovers a wide variety of theological systems. Many were even fashioned in conflict with one another. The sheer choice of theologies indicates that surrendering your responsibility to theologize to another is also not an option. We are engaged in an intense spiritual conflict and must be careful to "take every thought captive to obey Christ" (2 Cor 10:5). Systematic theology is necessary, yet there are so many systems. But maybe that is part of God's plan. After all, Paul did not say, "I have the mind of Christ," but "*we* have the mind of Christ" (1 Cor 2:16b, emphasis added). Systematic theology is the work of the whole body of Christ, so it is necessarily a community effort.[55]

With experience one learns to appreciate architecture, especially church architecture. There is something beautiful in almost every theological system just as there is in almost every church building. Etienne Gilson

---

54. Alternatively, Webster distinguishes three phases of human theology: (1) *theologia ante lapsum*, "theology before the fall"; (2) *theologia viatorum*, "theology on the way"; and (3) *theologia beatorum*, "theology in paradise." Webster, "Principles of Systematic Theology," 62.

55. For a description of an ecclesial approach to theology, see Malcolm B. Yarnell III, "To the End of Glorifying Jesus: The Scholar's Calling to the Churches," *Faith and Mission* 19, no. 1 (2001): 25–32.

famously compared medieval Christian philosophy to magnificent cathedrals of thought.[56] The soaring elevation of stone upon stone in column after column of Paris's Notre Dame Cathedral reminds one of the similar comprehensiveness and coherence of the greatest Roman Catholic system, the *Summa Theologia* of the Paris theologian, Thomas Aquinas. Alternatively, one must appreciate the engaging nature of an Eastern Orthodox system such as that of Gregory of Nazianzus, whose theological architecture draws the inner mind to gaze upon and worship him who is three yet one. The iconic focus of Orthodoxy reflects their beautiful doctrine of God.

Again, as one enters a Reformed church, a relative simplicity is detected. The congregation has gathered in two ways, toward the pulpit and around the Communion Table. The Reformation ideal of worship as empowered by the Word and manifested simply in baptism and the Lord's Supper shapes both Protestant architecture and Protestant systematic theology. Finally, as one enters a Baptist church, the Reformation influence is clear, but the placement of the baptistery at the entrance, before the pulpit, or even above it tells you about the liturgical faith therein, a faith that also shapes Baptist theology.

If one counted the systematic theologies within the major Christian traditions, and many others besides, the number balloons. The immensity and diversity of systematic theologies, all claiming to represent God's truth, ought not concern us. What should concern us is whether this or that system, and this or that doctrine within a system, is true. Proper worship of God demands proper identification of who God is, and that means theology remains key to worship and salvation.

Many have distinguished essential from nonessential doctrines and called for charity among Christians regarding the latter. This is doubtless true, but identifying exactly what is essential also requires theological discernment, which is always performed in a systematic context. Thus, even the famous Moravian proverb—"In essentials unity; in nonessentials diversity; in all things charity"—ultimately requires further engagement in systematic theology.[57] The diversity of systems and the incompleteness of our knowledge of God in this age mandate an extraordinary virtue for every

---

56. Etienne Gilson, *Christianity and Philosophy* (New York; Sheed and Ward, 1939), 114.
57. This sentiment has been introduced into systematic theology most recently under the rubric of "theological triage." R. Albert Mohler Jr., "The Pastor as Theologian," in *A Theology for the Church*, rev. ed., ed. Daniel Akin (Nashville: B&H Academic, 2014), 723–28.

systematic theologian: humility. As you love God systematically according to his wisdom, and as you place confidence only in his Word, humbly pray the Holy Spirit will enlighten the "eyes of your heart." Such an understanding of systematic theology is illuminating and informative for the overarching work of theological education.

Questions for Further Reflection

1. Why is systematic theology important for every Christian?
2. What are first theology, second theology, and third theology?
3. With what subject should theology begin? Why?
4. What is the standard that allows us to engage in theology with confidence?
5. What do you believe is the coherent message of Scripture that comprehends everything?
6. Why is humility necessary in systematic theology?
7. How is theology an act of worship?

Sources for Further Study

Akin, Daniel L., ed. *A Theology for the Church*, rev. ed. Nashville: B&H Academic, 2014.

Augustine. *On Christian Teaching*. Trans. R. P. H. Green. New York: Oxford University Press, 1997.

Barth, Karl. *Evangelical Theology: An Introduction*. Grand Rapids: Eerdmans, 1963.

Gregory of Nazianzus. *On God and Christ: The Five Theological Orations and Two Letters to Cledonius*. Trans. Frederick Williams and Lionel Wickham. Crestwood, NY: St. Vladimir's Press, 2002.

Kapic, Kelly M. *A Little Book for New Theologians: Why and How to Study Theology*. Downers Grove: InterVarsity Press, 2012.

Thielicke, Helmut. *A Little Exercise for Young Theologians*. Trans. Charles L. Taylor. Grand Rapids: Eerdmans, 1962.

Webster, John, Kathryn Tanner, and Iain Torrance, ed. *The Oxford Handbook of Systematic Theology*. New York: Oxford University Press, 2007.

Yarnell, Malcolm B., III, *The Formation of Christian Doctrine*. Nashville: B&H Academic, 2007.

Chapter Fourteen

CHURCH HISTORY AND HISTORICAL THEOLOGY

GREGORY A. WILLS

The study of the history of the church is critical to theological education. We receive instruction from the greatest teachers in the history of Christianity. The leaders of long ago can become our teachers. Pastors and thinkers from past ages can transmit the insights gained from their successes and failures in their spiritual battles. We can gain instruction and insight from the most learned theologians. We can learn the keys to effectiveness from the most influential leaders of all church history.

The teachers of every age compete for our attention. Not all were equally gifted. As we look back over the generations, we find that some teachers help us see truth more effectively than others. We notice too that the teachers of some eras speak more powerfully to our situation than others. We gain different insights from different eras. Church history distills the hard-earned wisdom of former generations of Christians.

It hardly needs saying that church history trains us to recognize the variety of fundamental errors that have invaded churches throughout the generations. If we do not study the history of doctrine, we are liable to repeat the same errors and to relive the controversies and divisions of former generations. This fact alone justifies the fundamental place that church history has in theological education.

In short, those who have gone before us still teach us. From them we can learn truth from the divinely revealed Scriptures. Their grasp of truth was often the result of decades of Scripture study in the arena of intense controversy. Their characters derived from long practice of Christian virtue, often in the midst of worldliness and scorn. Their spirituality attained maturity as they relied on God's truth and mercy in Christ through great disappointments and griefs. Their wisdom was the result of long reflection on the nature of their duties, from careful analysis of their successes and failures. Their faithfulness was forged in periods of cruel opposition. They still have power to teach us.

The Persecuted Church Teaches Us

The history of the persecuted church teaches and equips us for faithfulness in our own day. Christianity spread rapidly in the first few centuries after Christ's ascension. In Rome, by AD 64, the number of Christians was sufficiently large so that Nero could plausibly blame them for the devastating fire that swept the city. In some areas the power and influence of Christian truth became evident as it transformed the social order. Pliny the Younger, governor of Bithynia, complained around AD 112 to the emperor Trajan that the Christian contagion had spread so widely there that the pagan temples were practically deserted.

As Christianity spread, it provoked the determined opposition of both the Jewish and the pagan communities. The Roman authorities held that proper veneration of the Roman gods was a civic duty and that worship of them was necessary to maintain the state. The gods who had supported the Roman people, it was believed, had caused Rome to prosper and had ensured Roman victories in war. Christians, however, refused to venerate the gods and make sacrifices to them and thus provoked the gods to displeasure, which jeopardized the peace and prosperity of Rome. Christians were therefore condemned as enemies of Rome.

Being a Christian was in itself a criminal act. Christians were therefore vulnerable to accusation and judgment at any time. By the time of Pliny, the practice of persecuting Christians was sufficiently common that it became customary. Roman judges promised Christians they could escape punishment by merely renouncing Christianity, generally demonstrated by cursing Christ, offering a sacrifice to Roman gods, and burning incense before a statue of the emperor. Some renounced Christ. Many others refused and confessed, "I am a Christian." The Roman authorities rewarded their steadfastness with torture, death, and the confiscation of property to ensure the complete destitution of any surviving family.

Roman emperors expected Roman authorities to punish Christians whenever someone was formally accused of being one. Christians were vulnerable to punishment anywhere and at any time, and multitudes suffered execution. Beginning in the middle of the third century, persecution increased in its intensity. In 250 the emperor Decius initiated a brutal persecution with the aim of abolishing Christianity. He required all persons in the empire to offer sacrifice to the gods and get notarized proof of compliance or face torture and death. The emperor Valerian ordered punishment of Christian clergy, Christian nobility, and Christians in state offices. In 303 the emperor Diocletian renewed the effort to abolish Christianity and led the most brutal and devastating assault on the early church. Many Christians refused to comply and suffered the confiscation of their property, torture, and execution. In many parts of the empire, systematic persecution continued until Constantine and Licinius published the Edict of Milan in 313, which granted legal status to Christians and ordered the restoration of confiscated property.

The persecution was a grievous evil. Christians nevertheless rejoiced even as they shed tears of grief. They gladly declared that Christ had shown them astonishing mercy through the suffering of Jesus Christ for their sake. And so they did not shrink from suffering for his sake. Their joyful testimony turned many to faith in Christ. Their public persecution gave many believers the opportunity to declare publicly that all were under God's wrath because of sin and that God offered mercy to all who repented and trusted in Christ. Their courage and joy in suffering the loss of all things credited the gospel they proclaimed. They prevailed "by the blood of the Lamb and by the word of their testimony; for they did not love their lives to the point of death" (Rev 12:11).

The faithful believers and teachers of the persecuted early church remind us powerfully that our faith in Christ is more precious than death, for by their faithful testimony in the face of torture and violence, they showed that they loved the Savior more than their own lives. They inspire renewed commitment to take up our crosses and follow Christ. And those, who on the contrary loved their lives more than faithfulness, admonish us and prepare us for ministry when some fall through weakness or faithlessness.

The Church in Controversy Teaches Us

The persecutions discouraged worldly persons and casual converts from identifying with Christ, but they did not prevent the spread of many serious errors among the churches. The church needed constant vigilance to remedy the many errors and infamies that frequently arose within.

Heresy confronted the church from its earliest days. The most successful heresies in the first few centuries included a set of ideas known generally as Gnosticism. It seems to have embraced central ideas borrowed from Neoplatonism and adapted them to the Christian faith. A number of gnostic teachers became popular and spread their teachings successfully among the churches.

It was, however, a poor adaptation. Gnosticism and Christianity differed in ways that made it necessary to alter the faith radically to be able to graft Gnosticism to it. It taught, for example, that humanity's fundamental problem was not a moral rebellion against their Creator but rather the imprisonment of the soul in the material world. Jesus saves humans, therefore, not by dying as a ransom for sin but by blazing a trail out of the material realm. In order to establish their claims persuasively, gnostic teachers established a set of authoritative texts as alternatives to the church's Scriptures. They rejected or altered the books that composed the Christian canon. Marcion, who was the most successful Christian gnostic, claimed that the Bible did not include the Old Testament, or indeed, much of the New Testament. The church's teachers labored extensively to oppose the various gnostic errors and impede its spread. They led the churches to reject these errors and to refuse recognition of those who taught them.

The teachers who opposed the gnostic heresies remind us that God gave the church an authoritative revelation by which to evaluate all truth claims. They show us that the authority the Scriptures have intrinsically did not need to wait upon a church council to attain recognition. The churches of the second and third centuries already accorded the books of the Old and New Testament Scripture status and opposed gnostic truth claims on that basis.

The Church Under Government Control Teaches Us

In the fourth century the church underwent profound alteration. Christianity became sufficiently popular that it became the favored religion of the Roman Empire and finally the officially established religion. This new relationship with the Roman government and the broader culture had vast consequences.

Constantine became sole emperor through a long and bloody civil war and reversed the Roman state's opposition to Christianity. He legitimized Christianity and gave it favored status among religious institutions. He professed his faith in Christ and was baptized on his deathbed in 337. Subsequent emperors strengthened state support of Christianity. In general, the state assumed oversight of the church. It deployed its vast power of grants and threats to superintend the church. The bishops of the most important Roman cities assumed vast influence in both church and society, and emperors generally controlled their appointment.

Many noble preachers defended truth and righteousness in the face of imperial opposition. In the fourth century a succession of emperors supported unscriptural teaching concerning the Trinity. Athanasius, bishop of Alexandria, and a small corps of faithful preachers defended biblical truth and by God's grace led the church and the emperors finally to recognize the orthodox doctrine. And bishops sometimes rebuked an emperor's sin, as when Ambrose required Theodosius to repent for having ordered the indiscriminate killing of thousands in Thessalonica. But the relationship between the church and the state did not alter fundamentally. The church was under the mighty sway of the state.

With or without the support of the imperial court, God led the churches to endorse scriptural views concerning the nature of God and the person of Christ. They affirmed the full and essential deity of Christ at the Council of Nicea in 325. They reaffirmed the point and defended the full and essential deity of the Holy Spirit at the Council of Constantinople in 381. At the Council of Chalcedon in 451, they defended the full union of Christ's humanity and deity in his person in order to maintain the full integrity of his human and divine natures and the integrity of his one person. With some significant exceptions, most Christians since have endorsed the correctness of the views endorsed in these councils.

The pastors and theologians who opposed the many errors concerning the person and work of Christ, and the character of God as Father, Son, and Holy Spirit, encourage us in our responsibilities to strive against error. Their victories for truth, gained by God's merciful providence, established foundations for faithful gospel ministry that still strengthen the churches today.

The pastors and theologians who struggled against emperors and heretics in the fourth and fifth centuries afford insight into the opportunities and dangers present when the gospel transforms an entire society. When civil government uses its power to advance the kingdom of God, the result is that the civil government entices and suborns the church to its own service. How can the church speak to political justice without being coopted by this world's politics and values?

The Churches in the Middle Ages Teach Us

The churches of the Middle Ages teach that the history of the church is a story of loss as much as a story of gain. As Muslim Arab armies conquered the Middle East, Anatolia, North Africa, and Spain, they constrained the Christian communities and sought to induce all citizens to become Muslims. The churches in many places withered and died and in others preserved a community of Christians as marginalized citizens. Other factors played important roles also. The churches of the East, once stretching from the Mediterranean Sea as far east as India, slowly diminished to a shadow of their former substantial strength.

In the tenth century, movement began in the Western church to free it from the state's control. Civil rulers had long controlled the appointment of bishops to important dioceses. As the wealth and power of the church grew, and as bishops assumed substantial roles in civil government, secular rulers felt strong interest in controlling the choice of the leaders of the church. The result was a church imposed upon by a set of worldly and ambitious bishops who used the church's power for political and personal ends.

Some teachers in the Western church, however, asserted that the civil ruler's authority in the church could be exercised only in subjection to the will of the bishop of Rome. They began a movement that opposed the corruptions resulting from the state's interference and its imposition of political appointees. Though only partially successful in restraining the power of kings and princes over the church, this reform movement produced many lasting results. The churches of this era remind us of susceptibility to worldliness in the church and of the need for reform in the churches.

In the twelfth century a movement arose to establish the right relationship of faith and science, of the Bible and reason. It sought also to combat errors relating to the incorrect application of reason to divine truth. Does reason function rightly only when it operates on the basis of the fundamental truths of the Christian faith? Or does reason operate rightly independent of our faith in God and the truths revealed in Scripture? And if reason operates independently, do reason and faith corroborate each other's conclusions? Or does reason operate rightly only in matters of the world of sight, and does faith operate rightly only in matters of the spiritual world?

Those who strove for certainty amid skepticism in the twelfth and thirteenth centuries guide us in understanding and evaluating arguments concerning the relationship between the world we see and the world that is unseen. In making their case for how reason and faith relate to each other, they show us the possibilities and limits of human reason.

The Churches of the Reformation and of the Modern Era Teach Us

In the fourteenth and fifteenth centuries, a number of teachers began to argue that the church should be returned to the people and that Scripture, not the church hierarchy, had ultimate authority. When Martin Luther tugged at the fraying edges of Roman Catholicism, the entire fabric began to come apart. His Ninety-Five Theses, published in 1517, protested certain abuses of the practice of penance, and they exposed certain fundamental errors. The Protestant Reformation that ensued insisted on the correction of those errors by insisting on the nonnegotiable character of the doctrines of justification through faith alone and the Scriptures alone as authoritative in matters of religious doctrine and practice. Many preachers of righteousness died at the hands of mobs, armies, or judges. The violent opposition experienced by Luther and his fellow Protestants evokes gratitude for God's grace to his churches and encourages us to value the fundamental truths of the Scriptures.

In the sixteenth century those who challenged the errors relating to indulgences, penance, and sacramentalism, and who defended the inspiration and authority of the Scriptures alone and justification by faith alone developed a critique of the doctrines and practices of the late medieval church that remains cogent today. Their teachings concerning justification, faith, and the authority and character of the Bible stand as fundamental truths of Scripture.

Those who advanced evangelical preaching and piety in the seventeenth and eighteenth centuries warn us of the church's liability to develop formal conformity to the Scriptures without the reality of hearts made new by personal repentance and faith—that correct doctrine does not guarantee the actual reality of believers born of the Holy Spirit and justified through faith in the crucified and resurrected Lord.

Those who defended the historical integrity of the Scriptures in the nineteenth and twentieth centuries warn us that when we seek to defend the Christian faith from the powerful criticisms of modern scholarship and modern science, we must not surrender our commitment to the historical integrity of the Bible in order to defend the truth of its religious teachings. Those who did so initiated a movement that ended up with few historical or religious claims to defend. It turned out that the historical predications of the Bible cannot be relinquished without relinquishing the religious truths the movement sought to defend. Christianity's fundamental religious claims are inextricably and irreducibly also historical claims. From the creation of the world to the incarnation and resurrection of Jesus Christ, to the sending of the Holy Spirit and the establishment of Christ's church, and to Christ's return, Christianity is irreducibly reliant on claims that God acted in history.

The Pull and Power of History

How can the history of the church teach us truth? God's activity in history differs from his speech. The history of the church is not equivalent to Scripture; it is not God's Word. How, then, can it be so critical to understanding Scripture?

People widely recognize history's power. In the public square it is common to advance moral values based on appeals to history with such phrases as "in this day and age," and "the day is long past when," and "history has proved." Such appeals generally lack intellectual cogency, but they are generally regarded as sufficient arguments. Such appeals to history generally count as valid arguments. Historical argumentation is thus often abused. Too often questionable reconstructions of historical events become the justification for our new programs. Incorrect interpretations of historical events undergird arguments. Indeed, the policy makers and reformers in almost every endeavor appeal to history as a fundamental support of their programs. The abuse of historical reason is so common that many historians have complained that the past is condemned to perform whatever tricks our present needs require of it. There are, however, valid historical arguments also. Whatever has power and value gets imitated and counterfeited. History is so often abused because the right use of historical reason has such great power.

Historical argumentation has credibility because it has the power to provide insight into our own experiences, identities, and natures. This insight is often so compelling that we predicate our arguments on historical insights. This is an appropriate and highly useful form of reasoning. Almost without exception, serious arguments appeal to history.

This is not to suggest that history is authoritative. It is not, in fact, a source of divine truth and morality. The Bible is. History, however, enables us to recognize, understand, and apply the truth revealed in the Bible. Carefully reconstructed, judiciously interpreted, and rightly applied, history plays a critical role in advancing insight and understanding of the biblical truths—enabling us to recognize the truth about ourselves, our world, the church, and the gospel. This is essential, of course, to a judicious analysis of our present circumstances and to grasping the biblically informed wisdom for making plans to meet them.

Just because church history is not prescriptive does not mean it is dispensable. Study of history is critical to forming a clear understanding of biblical doctrine and to its defense. To grasp the full meaning and implications of God's revealed truth is the ongoing duty of the church in all ages. Church history is a kind of laboratory for the proper assaying of the various claims of truth. By the variety of examples of doctrines, experiences, and controversies, we are able to examine truth with greater clarity.

History is critical to understanding Scripture in other ways. Throughout history, opponents of Christianity have attacked the Bible's historical claims, beginning with its history of creation. In the last two centuries especially, attacks on Scripture's historical statements have multiplied in number and force. Many Christians have responded by granting the validity of such criticism. They have sought to accommodate the Bible to the dismissal of historical validity in a way that preserves the Bible's authority for matters of religious faith and practice. The result, however, has always undermined the faith this accommodation sought to preserve. The reason is simple: Christianity is intrinsically and inextricably a historical religion. At its center is God's incarnation in the flesh in time and space. Its fundamental religious truth is a historical event: Christ crucified and resurrected on the third day. To reject the Bible's historical claims therefore necessarily undermines that Bible's central claim.

Getting the History Right

History has power, then, because it provides insight into scriptural truth. But we cannot learn the lessons history can teach us unless we get the history right. This requires careful hearing. The Christians of other eras speak to us with unfamiliar accents. They speak on the basis of different presuppositions and preunderstandings, and they can use familiar language with unfamiliar meanings. If we do not listen carefully, we can easily misunderstand what they are actually saying.

Christian thinkers of earlier eras have plausible arguments that many found persuasive. If we would judge their views justly, we must understand their arguments clearly. We must, therefore, attend carefully to their actual words. All too often we are content with secondhand reports. To understand the history accurately, we cannot rely merely on the works of modern historians. We must read what our predecessors actually wrote. We cannot read everything that they penned, but that is no excuse for reading little or nothing.

In order to read the teachers of the past, we must have access to their writings in a language we understand. The teachers of the churches over the ages have left their teachings in languages that are now known by relatively few scholars. The most extensive bodies of teaching survive in Latin, Greek, and Syriac, and large numbers of texts in these languages alone remain untranslated into English. Scholarship for the sake of the church must, therefore, encourage the study of the languages of our teachers from bygone eras.

Even when we have access to and read the teachings of earlier eras in our own language, we cannot gain much benefit unless we are prepared to subject our own views and assumptions to the critical inquiry of Christians from other periods. We do not learn well if we listen only to criticize. We must not assume that because Christians of earlier eras hold different ideas, they are wrong. We must give them a fair hearing. We must ask them to justify their views. Why do they say what they do? What evidence and arguments do they adduce to establish their views?

History cannot teach us anything if we study the past merely to condemn it and vindicate our own views. To learn from history, we must be willing to allow Christians of former eras to question us. They will give us fair hearings. What will we say when they ask us to justify our views? Why do we say what we do? What evidence and arguments can we bring forward to establish our views? We are no smarter than the Christians of other eras. Indeed, the Christians whose ideas we can still read have been preserved through the years because many persons have found their views helpful and insightful. In all likelihood the Christians whose writings we are reading are more capable and perhaps more intelligent than most of their modern readers. We still read their writings and sermons because they applied intelligence to their situation with wisdom and insight.

History is not self-interpreting. Thus, in order to get the history right, we must not only understand the words and context of our teachers from the past, but we must understand where we fit in the scheme of history and recognize our own predispositions, presuppositions, and worldviews. We must understand who we are.

History Helps Us Understand Who We Are

Church history is also our story. We learn something of our own identities by hearing the stories of the Christians who came before us. Our identities in Christ are both individual and corporate. Jesus has given us commands both as individuals and as corporate churches. He has saved and incorporated us into this body, the church. We are members of it.

Israel's identity was rooted in God's promise to Abraham and in the history of his fulfillment of the promise by bringing the people of Israel out of Egypt and into the land of Canaan. The memory of the exodus was foundational to the identity of Israel. When Israelites presented the first of their produce in thanksgiving to God, the gratitude included remembering that "the LORD brought [them] out of Egypt with a strong hand and an outstretched arm, with terrifying power, and with signs and wonders" (Deut 26:8). God included the history of his deliverance of his people from

Egypt as fundamental during his giving of the Ten Commandments: "I am the LORD your God, who brought you out of the land of Egypt, out of the place of slavery" (Exod 20:2). Our identities as Christians are rooted in the same promise and the same history; all who are in Christ are sons of Abraham and heirs of the same promise.

Our identities as individuals are often, in some important respects, something we choose. When we choose to become Christians, however, we do not construct our own Christian identities to suit ourselves. We choose an identity that already exists. It is an identity that is already well defined. When we accept our identity as Christians, we do not define what it means to be a Christian. Christ determines that. It is given to us. We are who we are because Christ has purchased us with his own precious blood, adopted us, and incorporated us into his body, the church, which is "God's household" and "the pillar and foundation of the truth" (1 Tim 3:15).

Church history, therefore, is our own history. The experience of the church throughout history helps us understand and assume our proper identities as Christians. Our Christian identities are strengthened by the history of God's mercy to his people in the long warfare against the evil one. Satan seeks to devour Christ's sheep, to destroy all who hold the testimony of Jesus. We, with all the saints throughout history, take up the spiritual armor to oppose the spiritual forces of evil who rule over this present darkness. And we, with all the saints, conquer "by the blood of the Lamb and by the word of [our] testimony, for [we do] not love [our] lives to the point of death" (Rev 12:11).

Satan wishes us to forget who we are, where we came from, and how we got here. He wants us to forget the history of God's saving works through the ages. He wants us to forget the history of God's faithful work in our own lives. Satan strives to make us forget. God wants us to remember. Indeed, he commands it, from remembering the redemption from Egypt to remembering Lot's wife to remembering our leaders.

Church history teaches us to remember. It reveals where we came from. It teaches us where our practices came from. Even when we seek deliberately to make a fresh start in order to escape the expectations and assumptions of our traditions, we transcend only the outer bands of our history. Often there is a sound, scriptural basis for our practices. Over time we sometimes lose the memory of why we do things the way we do them. Ecclesiology was once important to most Christians. Its substance guided many of the distinct practices and expectations of the churches. The ecclesiology was forgotten, and so was the basis for many practices. Church discipline, similarly, was once practiced from a carefully developed understanding of how to apply various scriptural truths and commands. Many churches still attempt something in the way of discipline, usually in desperate cases, but they are generally ill equipped for the task because churches have forgotten what they once knew. And so history often explains not only why we do the things we do but also why we don't do some things that perhaps we should do.

God created us to develop character as individuals and as communities. Character consists, in part, in the predetermination of what is right and true and in the commitment to act and respond in accordance with justice and truth. When a community develops its conclusions concerning justice and truth and commits itself to act and respond accordingly, those decisions become part of the community's tradition and culture. Such development is both good and inescapable. The question is not whether to adopt a culture. Culture is inescapable. The question is whether its components will be in accordance with truth and justice.

Consider What God Has Done

Remembering the past, then, is fundamental to our faithful service in the present. History, however, is not merely remembering. It is retelling. It is teaching what God has done so the next generation will know, will consider, and will order their lives in accordance with God's creation, rule, and redemptive purposes. Church history is the record of what God has done. It is the evidence of the accomplishment of God's purposes. Retelling it serves, therefore, to credit his power and his truth.

In Psalm 66, the psalmist's praise is founded on remembering and recounting the history of God's mercy to him: "I will tell what he has done for me" (Ps 66:16). In Psalm 64, David wrote that human respect for God rises when they learn of his acts of judgment in history: "Then everyone will fear and will tell about God's work, for they will understand what he has done" (v. 9). Samuel encourages unfaithful Israel to respond in obedience to the history of God's mercy toward them: "Above all, fear the Lord and worship him faithfully with all your heart; consider the great things he has done for you" (1 Sam 12:24).

The Scriptures frequently appeal to God's past actions as the basis of the saints' current praise. God calls his people to remember his activity as a basis of trusting in his mercy. They are to tell of his mighty works so that his people may know him rightly. And he calls his people to remember the sins of Israel, as well as his own mercy, that they may walk after him. Remembering and retelling play fundamental roles in our faithful service to God. History informs the substance of our gratitude.

Church History Trains Us for Right Interpretation

Studying church history also provides direct support for the study of the Bible. God gave us his Word in historical form. Men who lived in specific cultural and historical contexts wrote in the languages and forms of speech of those contexts. They addressed matters of their historical contexts. Biblical interpretation, therefore, is necessarily historical interpretation. The eternal God speaks unchanging truth that addresses people in all times and all places as he speaks to us in historical human language addressed to a specific time and place. To interpret eternal truth, therefore, requires sound historical sense.

To know the Word of God is to know it in its situated historical character, to discern its historically situated meaning accurately, and to show how its historical meaning reveals its meaning for all persons in all places. This is how the apostles interpreted the Old Testament. They made arguments concerning the historical situation of Old Testament texts and explained their meaning for the church, for the Scriptures "were written for our instruction" (1 Cor 10:11).

So it is not surprising that the study of Christian history is critical to understanding God's truth. When we see doctrines debated, refined, and instantiated in living Christians and actual churches, we are equipped to gain clearer and deeper insight into the substance and character of revealed truth.

History Trains Us for Discerning Error and Unrighteousness

Church history teaches us that error erupts suddenly and spreads rapidly. Error, immorality, confusion, and alienation beset churches in every generation. We cannot avoid these entirely until Christ consummates his kingdom. Error can take many years, and sometimes generations, to defeat. The occurrence of so much error throughout history serves notice to subsequent generations to be on their guard. We must not be surprised when error or immorality appears in our midst. Less common are times when peace and unity prevail for long periods without error and strife. Knowledge of church history teaches that such periods are by God's mercy and call us to offer praise to our Lord.

Studying the controversies that have afflicted the church, we also learn that we cannot escape controversy in the church any more than we can escape illnesses and injuries in our bodies. When God blesses the proclamation of the gospel of life and establishes churches of the redeemed through faith in Jesus Christ, Satan sends saboteurs to infiltrate the church and denature it. At the same time, sincere, good-hearted Christians often disagree concerning the precise interpretation of Scripture. They disagree concerning how to arrange and conduct gathered worship and its ordinances. They disagree about how to respond to church members who commit unchristian acts or who teach error. Even churches that are spiritually mature and grounded in the Scriptures must reckon constantly with susceptibility to creating alienation and division over such disagreements.

Church history also warns of the difficulty involved in recognizing error when it appears in the church. Every significant heresy advanced on the claim that it honored Christ and advanced his kingdom. Errors succeed in misleading vast numbers of sheep because they look so much like truth and holiness. False teachers do not begin their movements by announcing that their goals are to pervert the Scriptures and mislead the saints. False teachers generally have excellent reputations for purity, spirituality, soundness, and intelligence.

History Sharpens Our Judgment by Providing Context

Knowledge of history aids our ability to evaluate ideas and proposals by comparing them to similar ideas and proposals at various times in history. This is perhaps the most common way people use knowledge of history. Would-be reformers urge us to accept their ideas, or their proposals often press their agendas by claiming that the church is facing an unprecedented crisis. The uniqueness of the crisis, they argue, requires the adoption of their agenda. Knowledge of church history affords a sound basis for evaluating such claims.

Many church leaders in recent decades, for example, have argued that insistence on the literal truth of the Bible drives a wedge unnecessarily between Jesus and the people whom the church is seeking to draw to Jesus. Contemporary persons, educated in the scientific and moral values of our culture, cannot be expected to believe in Jesus if it requires them to believe that God suddenly created out of nothing the vast expanse of the universe and its millions of ancient stars, or that God created the earth and its creatures and made the first man and woman, or that God condemned humanity by a universal flood and by subsequent violent destruction of entire communities and nations, or that a baby was born of a virgin.

Knowledge of church history, however, demonstrates that this crisis is not a new one, for such objections have long been raised against Christianity. The Greek philosopher Celsus raised such objections in the second century. Christians teach as doctrine childish myths, Celsus wrote, for they claim the world is less than ten thousand years old, that God formed the first man and breathed life into him, that Noah built an ark and preserved a pair of every kind of animal in it from destruction by flood.

Many others made similar attacks on Christian doctrine. Indeed, such objections became rare only after Christianity became so popular and influential that emperors and kings effectively quashed all objections by favoring Christianity and burdening those who dissented from it. When religious tolerance emerged in the modern era, such objections were renewed. The intellectual culture of Europe and America drifted away from the distinctive truth claims of the Bible in favor of a philosophically established theism and morality.

In the eighteenth and nineteenth centuries, a vast number of scholars and philosophers attacked the historical assertions of the Bible as demonstrably false. They attacked many of the Bible's moral judgments as demonstrably immoral. They attacked many of the Bible's statements concerning the creation of the world and its creatures as scientifically disproved. The persuasive scholarship of biblical criticism thus rendered claims of biblical authority increasingly implausible to many.

Many Christians did not recognize that such objections, though taking new forms, were not new. They were therefore less prepared to oppose them, and many Christians erred in granting the validity of the main objections. In response, they developed a view of the Bible that could accommodate these criticisms. But the only view of the Bible that could accommodate such criticisms must include acknowledgment that many of the Bible's statements were erroneous. They concluded that the Bible had two meanings, a literal or historical meaning that was often false and a spiritual meaning that was true. This approach, known broadly as modernism or liberalism, proved ineffective in accomplishing its own goal of rescuing the Bible from criticism. The character of its accommodation eroded the Bible's authority broadly. Careful study of church history equips us to recognize the fundamental character of such plausible appeals, and it affords demonstration of its errors and ineffectiveness.

In the final analysis, seminaries teach church history and historical theology because the church is at war. Studying church history prepares us to engage the enemy with the spiritual weapons of prayer and faith and the Word of God. Church history equips us to apprehend more clearly God's revelation. It challenges our assumptions, broadens the range of our perceptions, demonstrates the power of the gospel, and warns of our liabilities to error. Through church history we gain wisdom as we open a window to the experience of Christians through the ages. And we are inspired by the examples of the faithful witnesses who have preceded us.

By studying church history, we learn theology, apologetics, leadership, and homiletics—enlarging powerfully our knowledge in these areas but more importantly, enlarging our souls, our hearts—for as we identify with faithful heroes of former generations, we remake ourselves, as we must do, if we would faithfully stand "against the rulers, against the authorities, against the cosmic powers of this darkness" (Eph 6:12). The seminary is a war college. Pastors and teachers are equipped to recognize the enemy's agents and stratagems. They must be trained in the weapons and tactics God has assigned his church for its warfare. Church history is a critical component of that preparation.

Questions for Further Reflection

1. What authority does church history have? How does it relate to the authority of Scripture?
2. How does church history teach us who we are?

3. How does church history train us to read the Bible more accurately?
4. How does church history prepare us for opposing error?
5. How does church history help us endure patiently?
6. How does church history train us for effective ministry?

Sources for Further Study

Arnold, John. *History: A Very Short Introduction.* New York: Oxford University Press, 2000.

Bebbington, David. *Patterns in History: A Christian Perspective on Historical Thought.* Vancouver, BC: Regent College Publishing, 1990.

Bendroth, Margaret. *The Spiritual Practice of Remembering.* Grand Rapids: Eerdmans, 2013.

Fea, John. *Why Study History? Reflecting on the Importance of the Past.* Grand Rapids: Baker Academic, 2013.

_____, Jay Green, and Eric Millers, eds. *Confessing History: Explorations in Christian Faith and the Historian's Vocation.* Notre Dame: University of Notre Dame Press, 2010.

Finn, Nathan. *History: A Student's Guide.* Reclaiming the Christian Intellectual Tradition Series. Wheaton: Crossway, 2016.

Green, Jay D. *Christian Historiography: Five Rival Versions.* Waco, TX: Baylor University Press, 2015.

Chapter Fifteen

APOLOGETICS

R. ALAN STREETT

The purpose of this chapter is to explore the historical progression of apologetics from being a practice of the local church to a theological discipline of higher education. We will look at key personalities who influenced the course of apologetics and how many of their ideas helped shape the apologetic curricula used in many present-day evangelical seminaries.

The First Apologists

Christian apologetics is a reasoned defense of one's beliefs and actions, often in response to the accusations of a hostile opponent. Its history reaches back to NT times. Apologetics in general, however, predates Christianity by several centuries. It was first associated with philosophical discourse. Plato's (c. 428–347 BC) *Apology* recounts how Socrates successfully defended himself in 399 BC before a jury of his peers in Athens when charged dually for corrupting the minds of his young followers and promoting atheism (i.e., a rejection of numerous Greeks gods).[1] One can readily see a parallel between Socrates's speech and Paul's encounter with the philosophers on Mars Hill (Acts 17:22–34).

Aristotle (384–322 BC), a brilliant student who attended Plato's Academy, devised a multistage process known as "The Five Canons of Rhetoric" that enabled orators to develop strong persuasive speeches. The five steps were (1) invention, the process of crafting and developing one's argument;

---

1. Plato, *The Apology of Socrates*, trans. George Theodoridis, 2015, cited May 31, 2001, accessed January 16, 2017, https://bacchicstage.wordpress.com/plato/platos-apology.

(2) style, the decision on how best to present the argument; (3) arrangement, the structuring or placing of materials in a certain sequence to get the best results; (4) delivery, the preplanning of how to use gestures, volume, pitch, speed, and enunciation most effectively to make a convincing case; and (5) memory, the rehearsal of the speech and key points in order to drive home the argument.

The world's greatest debaters and orators, non-Christian and Christian alike, have relied on the five canons of rhetoric in their apologetic efforts. The apostles used rhetorical devices in their speeches to persuade their pagan and Jewish audiences to abandon their misinformed traditions and to follow Christ. They used emotion, reason, ethical arguments, exhortation, appeal to evidence, and Scriptures (Acts 2:14–40; 13:43; 17:1–4; 18:4, 13; 19:8, 29; 26:27–29; 28:23–24).

The Birth of Christian Apologetics

Our English word *apologetics* is translated from the Greek *apologia* and appears in various grammatical forms throughout the NT (Luke 12:11; Acts 22:1; 25:16, 24; 1 Cor 9:3; 2 Cor 7:11; Phil 1:7, 16; 2 Tim 4:16; 1 Pet 3:15). Several other instances of Christians defending their faith can be found in the NT, where the term *apologia* does not appear.

The first believers were apologists out of necessity. Their theological assertions were being challenged and their lives threatened. Opposition came at the hands of Roman governmental officials, Jewish religious leaders, and Greek intellectuals. No seminaries or Bible colleges existed where one was taught how to defend the faith. Believers learned through trial and error and depended on the Holy Spirit, the divine teacher, to help them succeed. Christ's followers were hauled before both Roman and Jewish judges and tribunals to give a rationale for their beliefs (Acts 4:1–20; 5:22–32; 7:1–60; 13:45–50; 16:16–24; 17:22–32; 18:12–17; 22:1–22; 23:1–10; 24:10–21; 25:13–21; 26:2–32). Jesus forewarned his disciples, "Whenever they bring you before synagogues and rulers and authorities, don't worry about how you should defend (*apologeomai*) yourselves or what you should say. For the Holy Spirit will teach you at that very hour what must be said" (Luke 12:11–12).

Christians mainly defended their belief in Jesus as the Jewish Messiah. Many Jews were looking for a conquering messianic figure to overthrow

Rome and establish God's kingdom on earth. When the apostles offered an alternative view of the kingdom, based on Christ's death and resurrection, they immediately faced resistance from Greeks who thought the claim was ridiculous and from Jews who saw it as a stumbling block (1 Cor 1:23).

The apostles and other Christian leaders also wrote letters to local congregations, urging them to stand against false prophets and teachers who had infiltrated their house churches. Luke used the written word to persuade Theophilus, a Roman person of influence, about the validity of Christianity. In his two treatises he appeals to eyewitness testimony, historical inquiry, transformed lives, and oral tradition as evidences that the accounts about Christ are accurate. The One Rome executed as a false messiah and political subversive had risen from the grave and was now, as reigning Lord, empowering his people to do great works.

Peter admonished the churches throughout northern Asia Minor to be ready to defend the faith (1 Pet 3:15) and Jude called his audience to contend for the faith (Jude 3). Each Gospel and NT epistle contains a significant amount of apologetic material. In fact, one might conclude, apologetics was a key motivation for writing these texts. The authors, being cognizant of the attacks on Christianity, responded to their opponents by offering credible evidence and logical arguments to support their claims for Christ. While no book is specifically written as an apology, they all offer an apology.[2]

Apologetics and the Postapostolic Era

As the first century came to a close, second and third generations of Christians faced many challenges from opponents such as Gnostics, rabbinic Jews, and Roman pagans; all wanted Christianity snuffed out and its followers punished. With the apostles now dead and buried, new apologists stepped forward to defend the faith. They set the stage for how to do apologetics and became models for others.

Justin Martyr (c. 100–167), a convert from philosophical Platonism to Christ, was the best-known apologist of the second century. He wrote two books on apologetics aimed at Roman officials and argued against

---

2. Avery Dulles, *A History of Apologetics*, rev. ed. (San Francisco: Barnes and Noble, 2007), 19.

Christianity being condemned based on the unreliable rumors started by its enemies.[3] He claimed Christianity was a true religion, based on reason, moral rectitude, and the Hebrew Scriptures. He referred to the eternal *Logos* in John's Gospel in order to show that the seeds of Christianity actually predated Plato and Platonism. He contended that Christians were good citizens who supported the government and were not a threat to society. He dispelled rumors that Christians were cannibals who drank human blood. In his *Dialogue with Trypho,* Justin recounted his conversion in AD 130 through the witness of an old believer who spoke to him about true philosophy. Using the Hebrew Bible, Justin defended Jesus as Messiah and called on Trypho, a Jew, to become his follower. Justin's unwavering faith in Christ led to his beheading in Rome.

Irenaeus (c. 140–202), the bishop of Lyons, defended Christianity against the major heresies of his day, including the growing threat from Gnosticism. His main opponent was Marcion, who believed only in the God of love of the NT and rejected the God of justice in the OT. Irenaeus convincingly showed the relationship between the two testaments and how the former predicted the coming of Christ.

Origen (c. 185–254) of Alexandria, Egypt, was the most famous apologist during the third century. He responded to the writings of Celsus, a late second-century Greek Platonist philosopher and critic of Christianity. Celsus was familiar with Christian doctrines but interpreted them incorrectly in light of Gnosticism. He claimed Jesus was the offspring of Mary and a Roman soldier and that Christ's miracles were performed by sorcery.[4] Origen brilliantly answered each point, distinguishing Christianity from both Gnosticism and paganism. He also made a strong argument for the bodily resurrection of Jesus Christ. Origen's apology has been described as the "most convincing defense of the Christian faith" known in the ancient world until that time.[5]

---

3. Gerald L. Bray, "Justin Martyr" in *New Dictionary of Christian Apologetics*, ed. W. C. Campbell-Jack and Gavin McGrath (Downers Grove: InterVarsity, 2006), 382–83; see also Cullen I. K. Story, *Nature of Truth in "the Gospel" and in the Writings of Justin Martyr* (Leiden: Brill, 1970).

4. Origen, *Contra Celsum*, trans. Henry Chadwick (Cambridge: Cambridge University Press, 1980), 32.

5. Williston Walker, *A History of The Christian Church*, rev. ed. (New York: Scribner, 1984), 75.

Key Personalities Who
Laid the Theological Foundation for Apologetics

Just as the church for three centuries relied on key Christian thinkers to defend the faith intellectually, so it was during the ensuing centuries.

Aurelius Augustine (354–430), "the greatest theologian and apologist of the first Christian millennium,"[6] was converted to Christ from a life of debauchery and pagan philosophies. As he contemplated his sinful condition, he heard a youthful voice twice say, "Pick up and read." Perceiving this to be divine guidance, he read Rom 13:12, and instantly his heart was "infused . . . [with] something like the light of full certainty and all the gloom of doubt vanished away."[7] He argued convincingly for Christianity against Manichaean dualism and the Neoplatonist belief that all reality emanated from an impersonal god. He also challenged accusations that Christianity was responsible for the downfall of the Roman Empire.

Augustine presupposed the existence of God and defended Christianity from that starting point. He held that all humans possess knowledge of moral law and their inability to keep it results in guilty consciences that continually remain troubled and unsettled. Since God is the source of the moral law and the best explanation for humanity's awareness of it, the human heart is restless until it can find rest in him.

Anselm (1033–1109) was a scholar and classical apologist who mastered the ontological argument for the existence of God. His influence was widespread though his writings and his rise in the church to the office of Archbishop of Canterbury.

Thomas Aquinas (1225–1274) was the foremost philosopher, apologist, and theologian during the Middle Ages. He was a prolific writer, and his *Summa Contra Gentiles*, written to help missionaries evangelize Muslims, stands out as his most important apologetic work.[8] For Aquinas both faith and reason pointed back to God, who is the author of both.

---

6. Ted Cabal, "Notable Christian Apologist: Augustine," *The Apologetics Study Bible* (Nashville: Holman, 2007), 1797.

7. Augustine, *The Confessions*, trans. Albert C. Outler (New York: Barnes and Noble, 2007) 8.12.29, pp. 125–26.

8. David A. Horner, "Notable Christian Apologist: Thomas Aquinas," *The Apologetics Study Bible* (Nashville: Holman, 2007), 957.

Blaise Pascal (1623–1662) was a French intellectual, mathematician, and philosopher whose radical conversion led him to believe humans had a God-centered vacuum in their lives that could be filled only by Christ. He appealed to both experience and logic in defense of Christianity. Known for "Pascal's Wager," he challenged his doubting inquirers to consider the following proposal: "If Christianity is true, you have everything to gain. If it is false, you have nothing to lose."[9]

C. S. Lewis (1827–1963), a fellow of Magdalen College, Oxford (1925 to 1954) and chair of Medieval and Renaissance Literature and fellow at Magdalene College, Cambridge (1954 to 1963), was converted to Christ out of skepticism. He wrote many popular books, including *The Lion, the Witch and the Wardrobe*. Among his best-known apologetic works are *Miracles*, *The Problem of Pain*, and *Mere Christianity*. The latter, based on his live radio talks over the BBC network during WWII, was voted in 2000 as the best book of the twentieth century.[10] In it he challenges the view that Jesus was a great moral teacher but not God. He argued that since Jesus claimed divinity for himself on several occasions, he either was a liar, a lunatic, or indeed the Lord as he said. There were no other options.

Carl F. H. Henry (1913–2003) served as the first editor in chief of *Christianity Today* and did more to influence theology than any other person in the mid- to late-twentieth century. His book *The Uneasy Conscience of Modern Fundamentalism* served as a wakeup call to evangelicals. Henry critiqued the separatist tendencies of most Christians, even scholars, to disengage with the culture and called believers to give attention to social justice and public ethics. Gordon Clark, who served on the Wheaton College faculty and who served later as professor of philosophy at Butler University, greatly influenced Henry's thought. Henry embraced his mentor's rationalistic and presuppositional apologetics model. Henry believed that to be a good theologian one also must be an apologist. In his six-volume magnum opus *God, Revelation and Authority* (1976–1983), Henry identified all truth as propositional and defined Christian doctrines as "the theorems derived from the axioms of revelation."[11]

---

9. Blaise Pascal, *Pensées*, trans. W. F. Trotter (New York: Collier and Son, 1910), Part III, para 233.
10. "Books of the Century," *Christianity Today*, 44, no. 5 (April 24, 2000), accessed January 16, 2017, http://www.ctlibrary.com/ct/2000/april24/5.92.html.
11. Carl F. H. Henry, *God, Revelation, and Authority* (Waco, TX: Word, 1973), 1:234.

The Development of Apologetic Schools

As the church studied the writings of the above scholars and apologists, several schools of apologetic thought emerged. While not able to be neatly classified or separated from one another (since they overlap at many points), the following categories describe in broad strokes the different schools of apologetic thought.

Classical apologetics might be branded as preevangelism. Since many people have intellectual difficulties with Christian theism, they have difficulty believing in the veracity of miracles, particularly the resurrection of Christ. A classical apologist seeks to remove this obstacle by appealing first to natural theology (i.e., rational thinking) and second to historical evidences. This two-step approach is called classical because early Christian thinkers used it, including Anselm, Augustine, and Aquinas. More recent scholars such as William Lane Craig and J. P. Moreland are classical apologists. Taking these two steps in order is essential. If one does not believe in God's existence, it makes no sense to believe God raised Jesus from the dead.

The classicist makes four arguments based on (1) causality, (2) design of the cosmos, (3) moral consciousness, and (4) the existence of being. These are known as cosmological, teleological, axiological, and ontological arguments for God. If the case for an all-powerful God can be made, then the apologist asserts that miracles are possible. In such a case, Christ's resurrection can be viewed as credible.

Evidential or *historical* apologetics stresses the need for preponderance of evidence to support Christian truth claims. This evidence may come from reason, history, archeology, ancient nonbiblical documents, NT documents, transcendental experiences, and fulfillment of OT prophecy. John Warwick Montgomery and Gary Habermas are two proponents of this methodology. Like a forensic scientist, the apologist gathers evidence to find the most plausible explanation for an event—in this case, the resurrection of Jesus. The evidence demands a verdict.[12]

Experiential apologetics appeals to an existential encounter with God or conversion to verify and convince one that God exists. Mormons use this method to win converts. They request that their prospects pray and ask

---

12. Josh McDowell, *Evidence that Demands a Verdict* (San Bernadino: Campus Crusade for Christ, 1972).

God to give them a "burning in their bosom" to verify the truthfulness of Mormonism. Many converts to Christ from Islam testify of having a dream or visitation from Jesus. This apologetic method has been effective.

Existential apologetics claims that the Christian faith is real because it satisfies the deepest needs of the soul and gives meaning to life. Blaise Pascal and Søren Kierkegaard were proponents of this subjective apologetic method. The latter called for people to take a "leap of faith."

Presuppositional apologetics starts with God's self-revelation, apart from which no one can know God or truth. Based on the premise that there is a God who has intervened in history and spoken in the Bible through propositions, the apologist asks the opponent to accept this starting point. As the Word of God takes hold, the opponent begins to think God's thoughts after him. Thus, apologetics becomes a gospel-focused presentation. Gordon Clark, Cornelius Van Til, Carl F. H. Henry, and Ron Nash were presuppositionalists.

The Birth of Catholic Seminaries to Defend During the Counter-Reformation

In response to the Protestant Reformation, the Roman Catholic Church deemed it prudent to establish training centers where young men, beginning at the age of twelve, might be properly educated in church dogma to defend their faith against the Protestant heretics. A strong emphasis was placed on the study of both philosophy and theology. This was apologetics from a Roman Catholic perspective.

In the twenty-third session of the Council of Trent, the church called for a "method of establishing Seminaries for Clerics, and of educating the same therein."[13] The responsibility for training lay mainly with the local diocese. Bishops were charged with selecting candidates with high moral character who might have an inclination to one day serve as priests. Those sensing a clear call to the priesthood then entered college for further education, where they were taught the Scriptures, introduced to ancient Catholic writings, read sermons by famous priests of the past, learned to administer the sacraments and take confession. When the bishop was

---

13. The Council of Trent, XXII Session, chapter XVIII, 188.; also see John W. O'Malley, *Trent: What Happened at the Council?* (Cambridge: Harvard University Press, 2013), 279–83.

satisfied a candidate had met all priestly qualifications, he appointed him to a parish.[14]

Apologetics and Protestant Theological Education

There were no Protestant seminaries in existence in the mid-1500s. The European reformers looked to the Bible alone as the best tool for learning theology and defending the faith. *Sola scriptura* was their watchword. The printing press made the Scriptures readily available to all who could read. And the pulpit, not the Communion Table, became the focus of weekly worship in Protestant churches.

Harvard was the first college to open its doors in North America. It was founded in 1636 for the stated purpose of educating clergy and others in the traditions of Puritanism.[15] Nearly one-half of its alumni entered the ministry. Students received a classical education, including instruction in ancient languages, theology, rhetoric, logic, ethics, metaphysics, and the sciences. Harvard's motto was *Veritas Christo et Ecclesiae*, translated as "truth for Christ and the church." By the early 1700s, a strong emphasis was placed on mastering systematic theology, enabling its graduates to defend the Christian faith. Harvard was the center for theological education in New England until the mid-eighteenth century when it veered from its orthodox moorings as many of its professors embraced Unitarianism.

Formal seminary education in America began with the founding of Andover Seminary in 1808 and with Princeton Theological Seminary in 1812, marking a paradigm shift in theological education. The goal was to move away from the classical liberal arts model of Harvard or Yale and toward a more professional-theological model of education that was designed exclusively to train those specifically called to the ordained ministry, mainly in the General Assembly of Presbyterian Churches. Other denominations followed Princeton's cue and established seminaries of their own. But for nearly a century, Princeton set the standard for seminary education. The "Princeton theology" stood for bedrock Christianity from a Reformed perspective and against all challenges to orthodoxy. It was the

---

14. Ibid., 170–92.
15. George M. Marsden, *The Soul of the American University* (New York: Oxford University Press, 1996), 41.

academic hub for serious theological education. Princeton graduates were the best-trained ministers of their day.

Apologetics and the Birth of the Bible School Movement

The Bible School movement was the main educational response to creeping liberalism in denominational seminaries, especially in the northeastern region of the United States. In an effort to stem the tide, local pastors and lay leaders joined together to start independent Bible institutes. These new educational entities sought to educate laypeople, especially Sunday school teachers, in the fundamentals of the faith. They usually offered a three-year curriculum with classes held one or two evenings a week. Their purpose for existence was to help church members detect doctrinal heresy, defend the faith, and teach the truth to others.

Prominent among the Bible schools were Moody Bible Institute of Chicago, Detroit Bible Institute, Bible Institute of Los Angeles, and the Philadelphia School of the Bible. By the 1930s, some of the more established schools started a pastoral track for nonseminary-educated pastors.[16]

Nearly all Bible institutes required courses in systematic theology, dispensationalism, Old and New Testament books, and at least one course in apologetics—usually offered under the title of Christian Evidences. As the title suggests, an evidential methodology was taught to prove the existence of a personal God, creation by fiat, the inspiration and inerrancy of the Scriptures, Christ's deity, his substitutionary atonement, and his bodily resurrection. Particular emphasis was placed on fulfilled prophecy as a main support for many of the claims.

Although many Bible school students may never have heard the word *apologia*, they were being trained as apologists, nonetheless. They, in turn, served as doctrinal watchdogs for their denominations by standing up for "the faith that was delivered to the saints" (Jude 3). The Evangelical Teachers Training Association was formed in 1930 to provide curriculum and resource guidance for teachers and to offer certification for Bible school graduates.

---

16. Joel A. Carpenter, *Revive Us Again: The Reawakening of American Fundamentalism* (New York: Oxford University Press, 1997), 18.

Apologetics and the Birth of Conservative Seminaries

When German higher criticism jumped the Atlantic and found a home in many denominational seminaries, concerned evangelicals from across denominational lines joined forces to protect their orthodoxy. A crisis arose at Princeton in 1929 (and later at other denominational seminaries in the North), when the administration began hiring faculty either trained in Germany or those enamored with German liberalism. J. Gresham Machen, a prominent NT and Greek scholar, challenged the administration's wisdom and urged them to reconsider the direction they were taking the school. When he failed to prevail, he along with three other members of the faculty—Robert Dick Wilson, Oswald T. Allis, and Cornelius Van Til—resigned their posts and founded Westminster Theological Seminary (Philadelphia).

The new seminary was an instant success. All four men were competent scholars and apologists. As a result, Westminster became a hub for apologetics in theological education. For nearly a half century it remained the premiere seminary for those standing for the fundamentals of the faith and the infallibility of the Scriptures, particularly among those holding to Reformed theology. Machen was one of the most admired apologists of his day. His book *Christianity and Liberalism* (1923) made the point that Christianity and liberalism are two different religions altogether, and his classic *The Virgin Birth of Christ* (1930) is arguably the best defense of the doctrine ever written. Machen, however, is best known for the *New Testament Greek for Beginners* (1923). It is still used in seminaries throughout America.

Robert Dick Wilson was a linguist and scholar with a PhD from Princeton and postgraduate studies at Humboldt University (Berlin). He defended the book of Daniel and the Psalms from higher criticism. He famously claimed that no man was smart enough or knowledgeable enough to attack the veracity of the OT.

Oswald T. Allis was a strong advocate for the Mosaic authorship of the Pentateuch and the unity of Isaiah. His mammoth 509-page *The Old Testament: Its Claims and Its Critics* (1972) answered the many objections liberal scholars hurl at the Hebrew Bible.

Cornelius Van Til, a Dutch-born Reformed theologian and popular professor, did more to champion the presuppositional school of apologetics than any other person of the twentieth century. Through his classroom lectures and books, he influenced several generations of apologists including Francis Schaeffer, Ron Nash, and John Frame. As a result, many Reformed seminaries have adopted an apologetic curriculum based on this presuppositional model.

As more denominational seminaries drifted from their theological roots, new conservative seminaries began to spring up and offer an alternative ministerial education to those within their faith tradition. They often hired disenchanted conservative professors from the more liberal mainstream seminaries. Apologetic concerns usually were an impetus behind the founding of these schools.

Apologetics and Fuller Theological Seminary

In 1947, Charles E. Fuller, a well-known evangelist, radio preacher, and wealthy orange grower from Southern California joined forces with Harold John Ockenga, the Congregational pastor of Park Street Church in Boston, Massachusetts, to found Fuller Theological Seminary in Pasadena, California. The two envisioned a school that would be rigorously academic, thoroughly orthodox, and offer a strong dose of evangelism, missions, and apologetics. However, unlike many conservative seminaries that emphasized separation from the world, Fuller sought to prepare its graduates to engage in dialogue with liberal theology and secular thought.

The Fuller faculty included Carl F. H. Henry, Harold Lindsell, Wilbur Smith, George Eldon Ladd, Everett F. Harrison, and Edward John Carnell—an outstanding scholar and the top apologist of the 1950s—who became president of the seminary in 1954. The entire Fuller faculty, but especially Henry and Carnell, influenced a generation of students, pastors, and laypeople to do apologetics. Nearly all seminarians and Bible colleges of the mid to late twentieth century were impacted by their thoughts.

An Interdisciplinary Approach to Apologetics in Theological Education

Most theological schools do not offer a concentration or degree devoted specifically to apologetics, but most evangelical seminaries offer at least one course in the subject, either required or as an elective. Despite an overall lack of singular attention given to apologetics, nearly all theological courses interact directly or indirectly with the topic. This speaks to the interdisciplinary nature of apologetics.

In homiletics courses, for example, students learn how to prepare and preach persuasive sermons, including doctrinal messages, designed to keep their congregants from falling into theological errors. In world religions courses, divinity students are taught to recognize the differences between Christianity and its competitors. With the current advance of Islam in the West, students must be prepared to provide reasonable answers to members in their churches and community who ask questions about this and other groups. Courses on cults, sects, and alternative new age religions not only provide information on the history and theology of aberrant groups but seek to show how their truth claims differ with those of Christianity. This, in turn, prepares ministerial students to protect their flocks from the proliferation of alternative religions that search for converts.

Evangelism courses concentrate on helping students preach the gospel to all people, including those of other faiths or no faith at all. Graduates must be especially prepared to confront atheists who aggressively challenge the claims of Christ. In church history courses students learn about the many heretical movements and individuals over the centuries who distorted orthodoxy. They also study how the various church councils answered doctrinal error by formulating creeds that expressed the timeless truths of the Christian faith.

Old Testament theology courses grapple with the nature of God, creation, the age of the earth, God's self-revelation, redemption history, and God's faithfulness to his covenants—all of which have apologetic implications. Archaeology exposes students to the latest discoveries and data that support the legitimacy of key events, personalities, and sites in the Bible. Archaeology provides evidence for the veracity of the historical Jesus. New Testament theology deals with Christology, pneumatology, sin, the Trinity, atonement, Christ's bodily resurrection, and a host of other topics that are often attacked by opponents and that must be explained and defended. Because apologetics interacts with nearly all theological subjects, it is an eclectic discipline. Thus, the successful theological student who receives a well-rounded education will be equipped as an apologist.

Apologetics and the Challenge of Postmodernism

With the advent of postmodernism and the decline of Christendom in the Western world, it might be wise for evangelical seminaries to rethink their apologetics curriculum. Apologetic models that worked effectively in the twentieth century are fast becoming less relevant.

Many millennials and postmoderns think differently than their parents. They do not accept a single version of truth or believe that any one person or religious group has the right to speak on religious matters as if they possess the truth. Many do not trust authority figures or institutions. Science, medicine, government, corporate America, banks, Wall Street, police departments, the military, religion, and their representatives have often had their own interests at heart. Instead of serving their clientele, they have victimized them.

Postmoderns have lost confidence in institutions. They are leery of those claiming to possess truth or declaring a metanarrative that excludes, marginalizes, or condemns those outside the story. As a result, apologists may have to use alternative approaches in reaching this generation. Logic, axiomatic propositions, evidences, and philosophical arguments rarely change their points of view. Seminaries must consider how to train a new wave of apologists for the twenty-first century. Possibly the solution is to offer more courses in experiential and existential apologetics. Whatever the solution, many apologetics curricula will need to be retooled.

Apologetics and Theological Education in the Local Church

While traditional seminaries with campuses have been the main locus in the past for training men and women called into ministry, a shift is taking place. Besides the increase of online education, some larger evangelical churches have become training sites for those going into full-time ministry. Second Baptist Church in Houston, Texas, for example, has become a partner with Houston Baptist University (HBU) in training future pastors. HBU receives an annual grant from Second Baptist to train master of divinity students. In return, all MDiv students take their practical and pastoral theology courses at the church with the pastoral staff serving as the instructors. The remainder of coursework—including languages, theology, and church history—is taken on the HBU campus and is taught by the faculty.

Whether or not a local church decides to offer seminary-level courses, it has a responsibility to train its members to engage the culture and interact with the unchurched. Therefore, it is incumbent on these churches to teach apologetics and evangelism to their people. One of the most valuable resources a church can provide its members is *The Apologetics Study Bible*.

ATS and Regionally Accredited Programs in Apologetics

The following chart is a brief survey of a selection of accredited schools that offer a major or concentration in apologetics and have at least one full-time professor qualified to teach in the discipline.

School	Degree	Major	Accreditation
Asbury Theological	MA	Apologetics & Philosophy	ATS
Baptist Bible Seminary	MA	Biblical Apologetics	Regional
Biola University	MA	Christian Apologetics	Regional
Denver Seminary	MA	Apologetics and Ethics	ATS, Regional
Houston Baptist University	MA	Apologetics	Regional
Liberty Baptist Theological Seminary	PhD	Theology & Apologetics	Regional
New Orleans Baptist Theological Seminary	MDiv	Apologetics	ATS, Regional
Oklahoma Wesleyan	MA	Theology & Apologetics	Regional
Southern Baptist Theological Seminary	MDiv / PhD	Worldviews & Apologetics / Applied Apologetics	ATS, Regional
Southeastern Baptist Theological Seminary	MDiv	Christian Apologetics	ATS, Regional
Southwestern Theological Seminary	MA	Christian Apologetics	ATS
Wesley Biblical Seminary	MA	Apologetics	ATS

Questions for Further Reflection

1. How familiar should students of apologetics be with the writings of Plato and Aristotle?
2. Knowing that the Gospels and Epistles were written to exhort and help believers defend the faith, what resources need to be developed to help students study the Scriptures from an apologetic perspective?
3. What prominence should be given to the history of apologetics in an apologetics curriculum?
4. What action can an apologetic program take to ensure it does not skew its curriculum toward one model of apologetics over another?
5. How wise is it to devote an entire course to the life, writings, and apologetics of a single apologist such as C. S. Lewis, Frances Schaefer, or Cornelius Van Til?
6. Since we are living in a postmodern era, what adjustments must apologetic departments make in their curricula to train apologetic students to reach millennials?
7. Why is apologetics an important component of a theological education?
8. Should apologetics be interwoven into other courses, taught as a separate course, or offered as a concentration or major?

Sources for Further Study

The Apologetics Study Bible, gen. ed., Ted Cabal. Nashville: Holman, 2007.

Beilby, James K. *Thinking About Christian Apologetics: What It Is and Why We Do It*. Downers Grove: IVP, 2011.

Bush, L. Russell. *Classical Readings in Christian Apologetics*. Grand Rapids: Zondervan, 1983.

Craig, William Lane. *Reasonable Faith: Christian Truth and Apologetics*, 3rd ed. Wheaton: Crossway, 2008.

_____, et al. *Five Views on Apologetics*. Grand Rapids: Zondervan, 2000.

Dembski, William A., and Jay Wesley Richards. *Unapologetic Apologetics: Meeting the Challenges of Theological Studies*. Downers Grove: IVP, 2001.

Dulles, Avery R. *A History of Apologetics*, rev. ed. San Francisco: Ignatius, 2005.

Groothuis, Douglas. *Truth Decay: Defending Christianity Against the Challenges of Postmodernism*. Downers Grove: IVP, 2000.

———. *Christian Apologetics: A Comprehensive Case for Biblical Faith.* Downers Grove: IVP, 2011.

Kinnaman, David. *Unchristian: What a New Generation Really Thinks About Christianity and Why It Matters.* Downers Grove: IVP, 2011.

Kreft, Peter J. and Ronald K. Tacelli. *Handbook of Christian Apologetics* (reprinted). Downers Grove: IVP Academic, 1994.

Meister, Chad, and Khaldoun Sweis, ed. *Christian Apologetics: An Anthology of Primary Sources.* Grand Rapids: Zondervan, 2012.

Chapter Sixteen

THEOLOGICAL ETHICS

GRAHAM A. COLE

We live in morally confused times. Debates swirl around the propriety of abortion and euthanasia, sexuality issues, environmental concerns, religion, and politics to name just a few. These debates happen both inside and outside churches. As a consequence, pastors are facing increasingly complex cases of conscience. For example, a former student of mine was trying to start a Bible study as an outreach in a part of town where his church had no presence. At least he thought so until a new church member who had moved into that area volunteered to host a Bible study. The pastor was busy planning arrangements for the venture when in passing this new member said, "By the way, I used to be a man." What ought the pastor to say and do in response to a revelation like that?[1] The need to answer this last question especially brings questions of ethics and morality to the fore. Theological ethics deals with such questions among others.

For the purposes of this study, *theological ethics* refers to that discipline which addresses the moral questions and quandaries of the day within a theological framework that is informed by the theological interpretation of

---

1. Questions involving both ought-language and behaviors fall into the realm of *normative ethics*. *Normative ethics* is to be distinguished from *descriptive ethics*, which simply describes a person's actual moral standards. Both kinds of ethical inquiries are to be distinguished from *metaethics*, which is concerned with assumptions and concepts, used in any ethical theory. I am indebted to my ethics teacher Michael Hill for these distinctions. See Michael Hill, *The How and Why of Love: An Introduction to Evangelical Ethics* (Kingsford, NSW: Matthias Press, 2002), 17–19. On the question of transgender people, see Mark A. Yarhouse, *Understanding Gender Dysphoria: Navigating Issues in a Changing Culture* (Downers Grove: InterVarsity, 2015). For a brief history of Christian ethics, see Samuel Wells and Ben Quash, *Introducing Christian Ethics* (Chichester, West Sussex: Wiley-Blackwell, 2010), 84–111. The annotated bibliography is especially helpful.

Scripture and an evangelical understanding of theology.² In my view theological ethics as a normative and not merely historical discipline is a subset of systematic theology.

Two Helpful Distinctions

I find it helpful to follow Michael Hill in stipulating a distinction between morality and ethics.³ This distinction brings clarity to the discussion. Morality is what I actually do and say in a moral situation. A moral situation is one in which the language of right and wrong applies. For example, falling asleep does not constitute a moral situation. Falling asleep when on lookout duty in a war zone does. Contrastively, ethics is about the principles underlying my morality. For example, I worked in a factory one summer while going through university. At the end of a shift, the foreman handed me a pair of work gloves and invited me to take them home. He argued that the owners of the factory would never miss them. I refused the invitation. That was my morality showing itself in a moral situation. But why did I say no? Here my ethics came into play. I would not want someone to steal from me if I owned the factory. The ethical principle informing my behavior was the Golden Rule in this case: do to others as you would have them do to you (Matt 7:12).

Another helpful distinction comes from the eminent evangelical ethicist Oliver O'Donovan. He distinguishes between moral reflection and moral deliberation. He writes, "Christian moral reasoning involves the exercise of two kinds of thought together: 1. Reflection; and 2. Deliberation. Reflection is thought *about* something; when we reflect, we ask 'What is the truth?' Deliberation is thought *towards action*; when we deliberate, we ask 'What are we to do?'"⁴ O'Donovan elaborates: "The metaphors contained in the two words illustrate the difference: reflection is 'turning back' on something; deliberation is 'weighing up' alternative courses of action."⁵

---

2. For my take on what constitutes the theological interpretation of Scripture, see the appendix in *The God Who Became Human: A Biblical Theology of Incarnation* (Downer's Grove: InterVarsity, 2013), 171–74.
3. See Michael Hill, *The How and Why of Love*, 21.
4. Oliver O'Donovan, "Christian Moral Reasoning," in *New Dictionary of Christian Ethics and Pastoral Theology*, ed. David J. Atkinson and David H. Field (Downer's Grove, IL: InterVarsity, 1995), 122 (italics in the original).
5. Ibid.

For our purposes moral reflection has God's self-revelation as its object. God's Word written is truth. Moral reflection interacts with moral deliberation in bringing God's truth to bear on cases of conscience with a view to action. In terms of the example of my factory experience, moral reflection had distilled from Scripture the Golden Rule. Moral deliberation applied it to the invitation of the foreman. The result? I did not steal from my employer. The mention of Scripture as the object of moral deliberation highlights the importance of Scripture in evangelical theological ethics.

The Evangelical Theological Touchstone

The appeal to Scripture should not surprise. For an evangelical Scripture is the *norma normans* (the "norming norm"). Scripture is the touchstone of faith. A touchstone is a piece of quartz that was used in earlier days to test whether the ore that had been discovered was really gold and not iron pyrite. The touch of the quartz and subsequent reaction or lack of it showed the truth. It is a classic evangelical metaphor for Scripture.[6] We test our theological and ethical and moral proposals by appeals to Scripture. Is what is being proposed found in Scripture or consistent with what is to be found there? Failing the Scripture test is to fail to win assent among evangelicals. This high view of Scripture does not suggest that other authorities operate in the Christian's life such as tradition, reason, and experience. These are *norma normata* ("ruled norms"). *Sola scriptura* ("Scripture alone") means that in any contest between authorities, Scripture as the *norma normans* trumps the others. This view is not to be confused with *nuda scriptura*, which naively suggests that only Scripture operates authoritatively in our lives. Formally speaking, the *sola scriptura* principle that informs this chapter and the use of this principle make an evangelical theological ethic. Materially speaking, an evangelical theological ethic should in no way undermine the evangel (the gospel), which is the burden of Scripture.

The Divine Project

The rationale for studying theological ethics arises from reflection on what God is up to in his world. The divine project can be summed up in these

---

6. For example, J. C. Ryle, *Warnings to Churches* (London: The Banner of Truth Trust, 1967), 118: "Let us receive nothing, believe nothing, follow nothing, which is not in the Bible, nor can be proved by the Bible. Let our rule of faith, our touchstone of all teaching, be the written Word of God."

terms: to secure God's people living in God's place, under God's rule, in God's way, in God's loving and holy presence as God's worshippers. "God's people living in God's way" is the stuff of Christian ethics. Living in God's way needs to be informed by what God has made known about his character, will, and ways in Scripture. What theological reflection on the scriptural testimony reveals—or what the theological interpretation of Scripture reveals—is that the Bible presents a relational ethic; that is to say, relationship brings moral responsibility. This should occasion no surprise as the relational is the heart of reality since the triune God is relational on the inside (*ad intra*).

Basic to biblical ethical thought is the notion that relationship brings responsibility.[7] For example, the Ten Commandments do not locate moral obligation in an abstract set of rules. The obligations not to worship idols or take God's name in vain, observe the Sabbath, honor father and mother, not murder, not commit adultery, not steal, not bear false witness, and not covet flow from a relationship that God established with his people through rescuing them from Egyptian oppression (Exod 20:1–17). The opening verses of Exodus 20 make this clear: "Then God spoke all these words: I am the LORD your God, who brought you out of the land of Egypt, out of the place of slavery. Do not have other gods besides me'" (vv. 1–3).

New Testament writers such as Paul repeat this relational structure. The structure is the classic Jewish one of *haggadah* ("telling" the story) and *halakah* ("walk"). The walk is predicated on the story told of God's deeds. You cannot walk in God's ways unless you know God's stories. The obligations of Romans 12–15 flow from the relationship established by God with his people though the mercies shown us in Christ, especially in Romans 1–11. Paul opens Romans 12 in a way that makes this patent: "Therefore [given what Paul has written before], brothers and sisters, in view of the mercies of God [the gospel], I urge you to present your bodies as a living sacrifice, holy and pleasing to God; this is your true worship. Do not be conformed to this age, but be transformed by the renewing of your mind, so that you may discern what is the good, pleasing, and perfect will of God" (vv. 1–2).

---

7. For the substance of this section, I am drawing on my "Christianity as a Relational Religion," in *Jubilee Manifesto*, ed. Michael Schluter and John Ashcroft (Leicester, UK: InterVarsity and Jubilee Centre, 2005), 37–49.

This same structure appears in Paul's earliest letter. In the first chapter of his first letter to the Thessalonians, he reminds them of the evangel (the gospel), which they had embraced and which had transformed their lives: "Therefore, we don't need to say anything, for they themselves report what kind of reception we had from you: how you turned to God from idols to serve the living and true God and to wait for his Son from heaven, whom he raised from the dead—Jesus, who rescues us from the coming wrath" (vv. 8–10). In chapter four he reminded them of the ethics he left them to follow: "Additionally then, brothers and sisters, we ask and encourage you in the Lord Jesus, that as you have received instruction from us on how you should live and please God—as you are doing—do this even more. For you know what commands we gave you through the Lord Jesus" (vv. 1–2). In other words Paul not only preached the evangel to the Thessalonians, but he also left an ethic. The evangelical and ethical are not to be decoupled.

In light of the above, a question may rise in the minds of some whether this relational seating of obligation pertains to God's redemptive relationship with only some of humankind. However, the New Testament leaves us in no doubt on this score. The relationship of the Creator to his creation brings moral obligation on the part of creatures with it. To reverence God and give him due glory is the appropriate behavior of the creature before his or her Maker. This is the eternal gospel according to Rev 14:6–7: "Then I saw another angel flying high overhead, with the eternal gospel to announce to the inhabitants of the earth—to every nation, tribe, language, and people. He spoke with a loud voice: 'Fear God and give him glory, because the hour of his judgment has come. Worship the one who made heaven and earth, the sea and the springs of water.'" Paul presents the polar opposite to this behavior in Rom 1:18–32, where the pagan idolater who fails to give God his due faces the outworking of this rebellion in his lifestyle. For example, in Rom 1:21–23, we read, "For though they knew God, they did not glorify him as God or show gratitude. Instead, their thinking became worthless, and their senseless hearts were darkened. Claiming to be wise, they became fools and exchanged the glory of the immortal God for images resembling mortal man, birds, four-footed animals, and reptiles." It is sobering to read how God may give rebels up to the folly of their choices as an expression of his righteous (relationally appropriate) judgment as in Rom 1:24–25: "Therefore God delivered them over in the desires of their hearts to sexual impurity, so that their bodies were degraded among themselves. They exchanged the truth of God for a lie, and worshiped and served what has been created instead of the Creator, who is praised forever. Amen."

Since relationship brings responsibility, it is no surprise that when a New Testament writer such as Paul speaks of moral obligation, he does not leave it in generalities. This is plain when the household codes found in some of Paul's letters are considered. He writes of the obligations of masters to slaves and vice versa, of husbands to wives and vice versa, and of children to parents and vice versa (e.g. Eph 5:22–6:9; Col 3:18–4:1). Christian obedience is worked out along relational lines. The Christian has a relationship to the governing authorities too that brings responsibilities. In Paul's minimalist vision, the governing authorities are God's appointees for justice's sake and for human good. So the proper respect, honor, revenue, and taxes are due to them (Rom 13:1–7). In his letters he does not consider the problem of when such authorities turn hostile and demand the allegiance that only God should have. However, in the wider New Testament witness, the book of Revelation envisages that scenario and the Christian's duty is to remain true to the living God even to the point of personal harm (Rev 13:10–12).

Importantly, Jesus summed up moral obligation along relational lines in Matt 22:34–40. The vertical axis is love for God with all one's heart, soul, and mind; and the horizontal axis is love for one's neighbor as oneself. In this passage we see Jesus creatively combining Deut 6:5 with its accent on the love for God as we saw earlier and Lev 19:18 with its emphasis on love for one's neighbor. The life of Christ instantiated such love. The apostle Paul echoes Jesus in his summing up of human moral obligation toward one's neighbor. Love fulfills the law. But what does love of neighbor look like? Such love does not commit adultery with the neighbor's spouse or murder him or her, or steal or covet (Rom 13:8–10). The commands of the law provide love with eyes to see what to avoid (e.g., idolatry) and what to embrace (e.g., honoring parents).

Significantly, the commandments of God for the Christian are to be obeyed in a new location. The Christian is in Christ, not in Adam, to use some more of Paul's language (e.g. Rom 5:12–19; 1 Cor 15:22). The Christian lives not under Old Testament law per se but under grace in Christ. The Christian still needs to keep the commandments reaffirmed in the New Testament witness as they give Christian love shape. But the commandments are not the basis of relationship with God; they provide directions for the outworking of that relationship in real life. The Christian ethic is a response-to-grace ethic, not a ladder ethic. A ladder ethic consists of rungs of obedience that need to be climbed in order to win grace. A response ethic is "work[ing] out [note, not 'for'] your own salvation with fear and trembling" (Phil 2:12).[8] Therefore, with regard to Old Testament commandments, the New Testament testimony needs to be carefully noted because the flow of redemptive history and its accompanying revelation have made obsolete some Old Testament practices in the light of Christ's coming and cross (e.g., temple worship).

How, then, is Scripture to be read responsibly with the need of moral guidance in mind?

Reading Strategies

Evangelical readers of Scripture, broadly speaking, adopt one of two frameworks in the reading of Scripture. The dispensationalist reader, whether classic (e.g., Lewis Sperry Chafer) or progressive (e.g., Darrell Bock), makes periods of time in God's dealings with humankind the chief organizing principle. Covenantal readers make God's covenants the *leitmotif* (e.g., Michael Horton).

Whether one is a dispensationalist reader or a covenantal one, a responsible theological interpretation of Scripture places a biblical text in its context within its literary unit (e.g., parable, proverb, song, genealogy) in its book in the canon of Scripture in the light of the flow of redemptive history before making normative claims. Many of these biblical texts contain ethical principles, moral commands, moral proscriptions, or moral permissions. Once the moral burden of a text of Scripture is ascertained, theological ethics helps sort out the moral implications of the text with a view to answering the question of how we are to live. The pastor who expounds Scripture to feed the flock of God needs guidance here in order to be faithful to the burden of the text. The theological study of ethics aids in providing such guidance.

---

8. Even here grace is at work, for the text goes on to read: "For it is God who is working in you both to will and to work according to his good purpose" (v. 13).

Using Scripture in Ethics

In my reading of Scripture, I find four kinds of material that are especially relevant to matters of ethics and morality. First, there is much behavior simply described in Scripture: murder, lying, incest, rape, and so on. Because a certain behavior is described in Scripture does not mean it is to be imitated. Examples abound. Solomon had numerous wives (1 Kgs 11). It does not follow that polygamy is God's design for life. I have read arguments that contend that because such descriptions are found in Scripture, the definition of marriage is not biblically fixed and so same-sex marriage is a legitimate development. However, the argument based on mere description or report proves too much. Child sacrifice is reported in Scripture (2 Chr 28:1–4). "Is" must not be turned into "ought."

Second, God prescribes moral behavior and attitudes. We are to be holy as he is holy (Lev 19:2). We are to love him and our neighbors as ourselves (Matt 22:34–40). We are to walk in his ways. Here the flow of redemptive history is so important. Walking in God's way in general as in the Old Testament becomes walking in Christ's way in the New Testament (cf. Deut 8:6; 1 Pet 2:21). The flow of redemptive history affects the prescriptive material in Scripture in major ways. For example, given the sacrifice of Christ on the cross for the sins of the world, there is no need to offer sacrifices in the Jerusalem temple, even if it still existed (Heb 10:1–18).

Third, God also proscribes certain attitudes and behaviors. Idolatry, for instance, is forbidden both in the Old Testament and the New (cf., Exod 20:3–4; 1 John 5:21). Fourth, in some areas of life there is more than one path of obedience. For example, it is morally appropriate for some to be married and for others not to be (1 Cor 7:8–9). In this instance, permissive or concessive moral material is found in the biblical text.

Jesus the Teacher of the Moral Way

Jesus exemplifies the kind of moral deliberation to embrace. Indeed, Jesus lived by every word that proceeded out of the mouth of God (Matt 4:1–11). If there was a question about his behavior and an Old Testament Scripture spoke to the issue, then Jesus appealed to it. Luke 6:1–5 offers a case in point.

> On a Sabbath, he passed through the grainfields. His disciples were picking heads of grain, rubbing them in their hands, and eating them. But some of the Pharisees said, "Why are you doing what is not lawful on the Sabbath? "
>
> Jesus answered them, "Haven't you read what David and those who were with him did when he was hungry—how he entered the house of God and took and ate the bread of the Presence, which is not lawful for any but the priests to eat? He even gave some to those who were with him." Then he told them, "The Son of Man is Lord of the Sabbath."

A question arises, however. What if there is no specific biblical text that speaks to the issue in view? Jesus is our model here too. Luke 6:6–11 is another Sabbath controversy story that instructs:

> On another Sabbath he entered the synagogue and was teaching. A man was there whose right hand was shriveled. The scribes and Pharisees were watching him closely, to see if he would heal on the Sabbath, so that they could find a charge against him. But he knew their thoughts and told the man with the shriveled hand, "Get up and stand here." So he got up and stood there. Then Jesus said to them, "I ask you: Is it lawful to do good on the Sabbath or to do evil, to save life or to destroy it? " After looking around at them all, he told him, "Stretch out your hand." He did, and his hand was restored. They, however, were filled with rage and started discussing with one another what they might do to Jesus.

This healing miracle, like other miraculous deeds of Jesus, is about restoration.[9] The man was restored to wholeness. In the case of the disabled man, Jesus had no Scripture to which to appeal. So, what was his way forward? He dug down to ethical principle, which he put into an either-or form: "I ask you: Is it lawful to do good on the Sabbath or to do evil, to save

---

9. The miracles of Jesus restore order: the wind and seas are returned to order, a demon possessed man is restored to his right mind and community, a young girl is restored to life and family, and a woman with a bleeding problem is restored to cleanness and community (Mark 4:35–5:43). These restorations are of eschatological significance as they anticipate the great restoration to come with the creation of new heavens and a new earth.

life or to destroy it?" The importance of the parallelism ought not to be lost on the reader. The good resides in saving life. The evil resides in destroying life. Of course, this principle is eminently consistent with biblical texts stretching all the way back to Gen 9:4–6 about the value of human life as image bearers of the living God.

The Jesus Approach and Two Contemporary Controversial Issues

Two moral issues that are roiling the times in which we live are same-sex marriage and abortion. Many Scriptures speak to the issues of marriage and same-sex sexual expression. In the United States the Supreme Court made same-sex marriage effectively the law of the land. For Bible-believing Christians, this is problematic in the extreme. Why? The reason is straightforward; no biblical texts can be cited in support of same-sex sexual behavior. The contrary is in fact the case. Whether the Old Testament or the New is in view, the biblical materials are uniformly negative (e.g., Gen 19; Lev 18:22; 20:13; Judg 19; Rom 1:26–27; 1 Cor 6:9–11; and 1 Tim 1:8–11). Moreover, a positive strand of biblical evidence stretches from the Old Testament to the New that the appropriate context for sexual expression is the one-flesh union between a married man and woman (e.g., Gen 2:24; Song of Songs; Matt 19:4–6; 1 Cor 6:12–20; and Eph 5:22–33).

Abortion is another matter entirely.[10] Abortion is the intentional termination of the life growing in the womb. No biblical text describes or proscribes abortion per se.[11] The Christian ethicist consequently has to dig down into biblical principle just as Jesus did in the case of the man with the shriveled right hand. In fact that story is of great relevance because in it Jesus sees the destruction of human life as an evil. On any view, abortion—the destruction of an embryo or fetus—is the destruction of human life. The contemporary world prizes personality, the larger the better. Scripture prizes something even more fundamental: namely, human life.[12]

---

10. Another example would be the morality of organ harvesting. Increasingly sophisticated technology is creating moral dilemmas about which no biblical text directly speaks (e.g., genetic engineering).

11. A text often adduced in the abortion discussion is Exod 21:22–25, which is about miscarriage, not abortion. The text is relevant, however, to the question of the value of the life in the womb.

12. This is not to say that, biblically speaking, human life can never be forfeited as in the cases of capital punishment and war.

Why Study Secular Ethical Theories?

I have been championing the theological interpretation of Scripture either at the level of specific texts or the principles informing them. However, some may raise the question as to whether an evangelical Christian should study secular ethical theory as well as Scripture. Such a question assumes a more basic one concerning the Christian's relation to the surrounding culture. To build on Tertullian's (AD 160–220) celebrated cry, "What is there in common between Athens and Jerusalem? What between the Academy [Plato's school] and the Church?"[13] The repudiationist would have no time for the study of secular ethical theory except by way of critique. In other words, Jerusalem always, Athens never! The accommodationist may let the surrounding culture and its best thinking about ethics set the agenda. Athens always, Jerusalem at times! My own approach is that of engagement. Jerusalem always, and Athens at times. In other words, I say yes or no, but only after carefully considering the case in point.

Augustine (AD 354–430) has wisdom to offer here. He argued that there is correct reason outside the church, but there are certain premises for thought that can only be found in the church's holy books.[14] The Bible category that is relevant is that of wisdom. Any wisdom found in the wider world is the product of the common grace of God, which allows people far from him to make right judgments about nature, history, culture, and life. John Calvin (AD 1509–1564) argues strikingly,

> Therefore, in reading profane authors, the admirable light of truth displayed in them should remind us, that the human mind, however much fallen and perverted from its original integrity, is still adorned and invested with admirable gifts from its Creator. If we reflect that the Spirit of God is the only fountain of truth, we will be careful, as we would avoid offering insult to him, not to reject or condemn truth wherever it appears. In despising the gifts, we insult the Giver.[15]

---

13. Tertullian, *De praescriptione haerticorum*, quoted in *Documents of the Christian Church*, new ed., ed. Henry Bettenson and Chris Maunder (Oxford: Oxford University Press, 1999), 5.
14. Augustine, *De Doctrina Christiana*, in *Augustine on Education*, trans. George Howie (Chicago: Henry Regner Company, 1969), 359.
15. John Calvin, *Institutes of the Christian Religion*, II.2.15, accessed March 4, 2016, http://www.reformed.org/master/index.html?mainframe=/books/institutes.

Calvin's robust doctrine of creation and common grace are clearly evident. However, godly discernment is essential when engaging extrabiblical ethical theories.

There are three important families of extrabiblical ethical theory. The ancient-virtue ethical theories and modern ones accent the virtuous moral agent (e.g., Aristotle, 384–322 BC). By reason of their moral character, they act rightly in context. The deontological families of ethical theory emphasize moral rules and conformity to them as the Enlightenment thinker, Immanuel Kant (1724–1804 AD) taught. In this approach moral acts are to the fore. Another Enlightenment thinker, Jeremy Bentham (1748–1832 AD) turned the attention to consequences as the key to deciding whether an action is right or wrong. The consequentialist family of ethical theory—the best known of which is utilitarianism—predominates in today's Western societies. "The greatest happiness for the greatest number" is the mantra of many in such societies. Here the emphasis falls on the aftermath of an action as deciding whether the action was right or wrong, good or bad.

Fascinatingly, all three approaches to deciding moral questions are instantiated in Scripture. The New Testament especially focuses on the character of the moral agent in passages which speak of the fruit of the Spirit indwelling the believer who lives by, is led by, and who keeps in step with the Spirit (Gal 5:16–26). Commands and prohibitions of both the Old and New Testaments (e.g., Exod 20:1–17, and John 15:9–17, respectively) show the importance of the deontological (Gk. *deōn*, "duty") with its emphasis on moral action. The Wisdom literature, especially the book of Proverbs, reveals the role of consequences or moral aftermath in moral decision-making. The wise person sees and learns from the happy consequences for the ants that store up food in advance of winter (Prov 6:6–8). If you are lazy, then you might find as a consequence that winter will put you in great personal jeopardy (Prov 6:9–11).

The Triple-*A* Analysis and Case Studies

The phrase *theological ethics* might give the impression that it is a discipline solely concerned with theoretical matters. This is not the case. Theological ethics, as with systematic theology (of which in my view it is a subset) needs to engage the real world of human brokenness, for the tasks (e.g., the theological interpretation of Scripture) that make up theological ethics are situated in the midst of the groaning creation (Rom 8:18–25) and in these last days (Heb 1:1–2). Thus, the study of theological ethics should not be left in the abstract. Case studies are vital whether hypothetical or real.

Consider, then, this hypothetical case in the light of a tool I call the *triple-A analysis*. This tool attempts to synthesize the Bible testimony with its accents on the moral agent, the moral action, and the moral aftermath. The setting is in the majority world. A young widow is left destitute by her husband's death. She has a young sickly child in desperate need of medicine that she cannot afford. Her husband's family shuns her because she is not of their tribe. In this particular country there are no social services of which to speak. The way she earns the money to keep herself, her child, and pay for the medicine is through prostitution.

An exclusively deontological approach would judge her action as contrary to the revealed mind of God and quote biblical texts to show her so. Her action would be to the fore. A virtue approach would ask what sort of person does this. Here the agent is on view, and her motivations are full of care for her desperately ill child. And doesn't the Bible, indeed Jesus himself, effectively affirm the compassionate person such as the good Samaritan of Luke 10? As for the aftermath, the consequences—the child still lives because of her selfless actions. Who can gainsay such an aftermath?

The triple-*A* analysis would say that her motivation is noble, but her action is contrary to God's design for life, and the aftermath may be good short-term but over time may prove to be not so. Suppose she gets AIDS from her actions and dies before her child recovers. The triple-*A* analysis enables a far more rounded and human response to complex moral situations. The fact is that living as we do outside of Eden we are often in a quandary as far as knowing what is right is concerned.

Of course, the phrase *triple-A analysis* is not found in Scripture, so the reader will need to ask if it is consistent with Scripture and whether it represents a wise way or a foolish one. Such a tool helps the pastor be compassionate (acknowledging right motive) while offering criticism (drawing attention to wrong action) and cautioning that the moral aftermath may prove mixed over time.

Later in the Curriculum Rather than Earlier

The study of ethics ought to be a core course in any theological school curriculum. However, it is not a course for the beginner. The reason lies in the nature of the discipline. The study of ethics draws on Old Testament, New Testament, systematic theology, church history, and pastoral theology.[16] I have taught in places where some students do it as their first course, whereas in my view it ought to be the capstone study in a theological curriculum. Such a capstone course is more than a survey of the moral issues of the day. A theological framework for dealing with any issue needs to be provided to the student as well as selected worked examples drawn from contemporary controversies.

The theological framework would be a Trinitarian one. The doctrine of the Trinity illuminates the fact that at the heart of eternal reality are relational values such as love and righteousness. Importantly, therefore, the triune God of the Bible did not need to create before there were others to love and rightly (righteously) to whom to relate. Creation is an act of divine freedom, not divine necessity. Every ethical theory presupposes anthropology (a doctrine of the human). The theological framework would therefore also be informed by the biblical teaching that humankind is made in the image of God and has great value in God's eyes (Gen 9:4–6). The Christian has reasons for believing in the sacredness of human life that the secular world does not.

The worked examples should include issues that fall into the realm of personal ethics (e.g., divorce), those that fall into that of social ethics (e.g., euthanasia and racism respectively), and those of environmental ethics (e.g., greenhouse gas emissions). The wise old adage says that to give a person a fish feeds him for a day. However, teach that person to fish, and he is fed for a lifetime. The fact is that new challenges arise in the course of history, and what one was taught in a Christian ethics class twenty years ago may not have anticipated the new challenge. How could it? For example, I recall working through issues of personal and social ethics as a theological student but not environmental ethics. Furthermore, in my view at least one homiletics course in a theological school ought to give help to the budding preacher in preaching the morally freighted texts of both the Old and New

---

16. Every ethical theory presupposes anthropology (a doctrine of the human). Systematic theology is, traditionally speaking, the discipline that explores this topic.

Testaments. If competence in the systematic exposition of Scripture is the goal, then such passages are unavoidable.

Conclusion

Theological ethics addresses the normative question of how one ought to live in the light of special revelation from God. That revelation now in Scripture form informs us of God's character, will, and ways. Without the theological study of ethics, how are pastors to address matters of conscience in such a morally complicated world? How are pastors to preach and teach the morality of Scripture in a society that so often is challenging the legitimacy of that morality and the ethics informing it? The theological study of ethics helps the pastor be a better Bible reader, preacher, and counselor. The pastor learns to discriminate between the descriptive, prescriptive, proscriptive, and permissive in Scripture. The pastor also learns about the continuities and discontinuities in Scripture when engaging the moral testimony of the whole canon. It is no easy study because it presupposes just about everything in the theological curriculum. Moreover, in a highly complex social setting where technology generates moral conundrums that earlier generations did not face, the pastor needs to learn to dig deeper. The pastor needs to learn to go below the surface of the biblical text in some instances to find the ethical principle that applies (e.g., matters of bioethics). In this there is no better model than Jesus, who is not only the Savior of the world but also the Teacher of the moral way.

Questions for Further Reflection

1. What makes an ethical theory theological?
2. What makes an ethical theory evangelical?
3. What role should the Bible play in addressing moral questions?
4. What carries over from the Old Testament into the New Testament in terms of ethical principle and morality?
5. To what extent is Jesus our moral example?

Sources for Further Study

Feinberg, Paul D., and John S. Feinberg. *Ethics for a Brave New World*, 2nd ed. Wheaton: Crossway Books, 2010.

Gill, Robin, ed. *The Cambridge Companion to Christian Ethics*, 2nd ed. Cambridge: Cambridge University Press, 2012.

Hill, Michael. *The How and Why of Love: An Introduction to Evangelical Ethics*. Kingsford, NSW: Matthias Press, 2002.

McQuilken, Robertson, and Paul Copan. *An Introduction to Biblical Ethics: Walking in the Way of Wisdom*, 3rd ed. Downers Grove: IVP Academic, 2014.

Stott, John R. W., Roy McCloughry, and John Wyatt. *Issues Facing Christians Today*, 4th ed., Grand Rapids: Zondervan, 2006.

Wells, Samuel, and Ben Quash. *Christian Ethics: An Introductory Reader*. Chichester, West Sussex: Wiley-Blackwell, 2010.

_____. *Introducing Christian Ethics*. Chichester, West Sussex: Wiley-Blackwell, 2010.

SECTION THREE

*Theological Education:
Church and Ministry*

Chapter Seventeen

THEOLOGY, PREACHING, AND PASTORAL MINISTRY

ROBERT R. SMITH

This chapter will explore the integral and inextricable relationship between preaching, theology, and pastoral ministry. Eccl 4:12 reads, "A cord of three strands is not easily broken." These three strands—theology, preaching, and pastoral ministry—run through the fabric of Acts 17:16–34. They are not secondary in their importance but are essential and primary in God's encountering the hearer through the proclamation of the Word of God, in the relationship to theology, and for a view toward the necessity of pastoral ministry when theologizing and preaching.

Helmut Thielicke, the great German theologian and preacher, made a revolutionary statement that informs my thinking regarding the significance of theology, preaching, and pastoral ministry in relationship to theological education and formation. He said, "Theology investigates the basis of this proclamation when it has already been *heard*. Thus the message always precedes theology as a text precedes its interpretation."[1] In Thielicke's thought, people hear the Word of God through preaching (Rom 10:17) and have a salvific experience. They then begin to think theologically through the salvific experience they have had as a result of preaching. Preaching is crucial to theological education because preaching fosters salvation, but it rests on theological education. Theological education is necessary in order to give an *apologia* for the hope that lies in the believer (1 Pet 3:15). Theology

---

1. Helmut Thielicke, *The Evangelical Faith*, trans. Geoffrey W. Bromiley (Macon: Smyth and Helwys, 1997), 3:xix.

exists in order to make preaching as difficult as it needs to be. Theology is not initially meant to teach us what to believe but rather to challenge us to express why we believe what we believe in order that we might fully realize the goal of the marriage between theological education and theological formation (Col 1:28; Gal 4:19).

In Acts 17:16–34 the apostle Paul does corrective surgery on Athenian proclamation and false theology. He has a view toward the necessity for pastoral ministry to those who will believe his message and become followers of Jesus Christ—Dionysius, Damaris, and others (Acts 17:34). Athenian theology and proclamation are false and need to be corrected. Paul proclaims the gospel to these Athenian philosophers who are polytheistic, worshipping many gods. The Epicureans and Stoics are divided in their philosophies and theologies that result in their worshipping gods made of materials. This polytheistic approach influences their ways of life. They are erroneous in their proclamations and are open to new ideas and novel thoughts about the gods. Paul's preaching brings about the conversion of Dionysius, Damaris, and a number of other Athenian residents.

Preaching

John Calvin was convinced preaching was the process of the internal witness of the Spirit in which the Spirit, who reveals the Word of God in the preacher's exegetical conveyance of Scripture, also reveals and witnesses the truth of that Word to the hearer of the gospel by the preacher in a context of public worship. This dynamic is caused by an encounter or experience with the divine through the Spirit of God. This is an example of a divine-human colloquy.

Paul asked, "How can they hear without a *preacher*?" (Rom 10:14, emphasis added). In the same vein one may ask, "How can they preach without a hearer?" In Acts 17:16–34 the Spirit is acting upon the Word in the preaching of Paul to the Athenian philosophers. The Holy Spirit is not explicitly mentioned in this passage. However, Word and Spirit are indivisible and inseparable. Word and Spirit were inseparable in creation—God spoke on creation morning, and the Spirit moved upon the waters. Word and Spirit were inextricably connected in the incarnation—God as Spirit became what he was not, human, and yet remained who he was, God. The Word, Christ, spoke words, "When you were under the fig tree, I saw you"

(John 1:48), which reveal his operation in the spiritual as well as the physical realm. The Word and Spirit will be interrelated in the consummation and will give the last invitation to humanity: "The Spirit and the bride say, 'Come!'" (Rev 22:17). Together, the Spirit and the Word impact expositional preaching.

Some of the twentieth century's premier preachers have defined preaching. E. K. Bailey, the late pastor of Concord Baptist Church in Dallas, Texas, defines *expository preaching* as, "A message[2] that focuses on a portion of scripture so as to clearly establish the precise meaning of the text and to poignantly motivate the hearers to actions or attitudes dictated by that text in the power of the Holy Spirit."[3] God gives the *message* to the preacher, and the preacher exegetes both the text and the congregational context. John Wesley and Karl Barth believed the preacher simultaneously holds in his or her hand the Bible and the newspaper so that the revelation of the Word and its current relevance engage the hearers. This *message* focuses on a *portion* of Scripture.

The preacher exegetes a pericope, a preaching and teaching paragraph, rather than a single verse or a fragment of a verse. The pericope provides sufficient context out of which emerges a central idea or proposition that will serve as the glue to hold the main components of the biblical message together. The preacher's responsibility is to establish clearly the *precise* meaning or the authorial intent of the text. The preacher attempts to answer the *what* question, which provides the facts or truths of the biblical text in addition to answering the *so what* question—what does the ancient text mean to the contemporary hearer? The preacher also attempts to answer the *now what* question of practicality—what are the contemporary hearers to do in relation to what the ancient text meant to the original hearers?

In addition to the substance of the message, the preacher must present the message *poignantly* in order to motivate the hearers. Poignancy is related to keenness and cannot be accomplished without passion. Aristotle, in his *Rhetoric*, furnishes three modes of proof or three ways of persuading hearers: *ethos* (character), *logos* (content), and *pathos* (passion). The preacher must be passionate about the text that is under consideration and is being presented to the hearers. A preacher without passion is a preacher without

---

2. Bailey uses the word "message" instead of "sermon" in relation to preaching.
3. E. K. Bailey, *Ten Reasons for Expository Preaching* (Dallas: E. K. Bailey Ministries, 2003), 2:1.

fire. The preacher must not only have a head full of information but also a heart full of inspiration.

The two disciples arriving in Emmaus and recognizing the resurrected Jesus (who disappears out of their sight upon the breaking of the bread) acknowledge that they learned from Jesus, the Master Teacher—"while he was talking with us on the road and explaining the Scriptures" (Luke 24:32). They experienced passion or burning—"Weren't our hearts burning within us?" (Luke 24:32). If the hearer is going to be poignantly motivated, then the preacher must first assume that posture.

The distinction between motivating and manipulating the hearer is whether the hearer is moved to adopt actions or attitudes dictated by the text. If the preacher forsakes and abandons the text, then the hearer is being persuaded to actions or attitudes dictated by the preacher's agenda whether philosophy or pop psychology. However, when the preacher stays true to the text, then the motivation to adopt attitudes and actions is based on the Scripture being presented. This kind of presentation is text honoring and God glorifying. The above dynamics are not possible unless they are done in the power of the Holy Spirit. The Holy Spirit not only aids the preacher in the interpretation of Scripture, but he also empowers the preacher in the presentation of Scripture. Zechariah puts it this way: "'Not by strength or by might, but by my Spirit,' says the LORD of Armies" (Zech 4:6).

Haddon Robinson, former homiletician at Gordon-Conwell Theological Seminary, defines *biblical preaching* in this manner: "Expository preaching is the communication of a biblical concept transmitted through a historical, grammatical and literary study of a passage in its context which the Holy Spirit first applies to the personality and experience of the preacher, then through him to his hearers."[4] Robinson contends that expository preaching is really biblical preaching—preaching that exposes the truths in the biblical text. He will later posit that expository preaching must be done in the contemporary narrative world in which we live.[5] He acknowledges expository preaching is the communication of a biblical concept—that is, a concept that emerges and arises from the biblical text.

---

4. Haddon W. Robinson, *Biblical Preaching* (Grand Rapids: Baker, 1980), 20.
5. Michael Duduit, "Expository Preaching in a Narrative World: An Interview with Haddon Robinson," *Preaching.com*, accessed March 28, 2016, http://www.preaching.com/resources/articles/expository-preaching-in-a-narrative-world-an-interview-with-haddon-robinson.

Robinson believes the Bible is relevant and has something to say to our contemporary world. First, the *history* of the biblical text must be explored in order to acquaint the hearer with the events occurring at the time the original hearer heard the text. Second, this biblical concept is transmitted through a *grammatical* study of the words within that expository unit of Scripture. The grammar of the English versions of the biblical text as well as the original biblical languages (Hebrew, Greek, and Aramaic) must be applied to the text in order to arrive at its fullest interpretive meaning. Third, the passage must be seen through the lens of the *literary genre* in order to ascertain how the passage should be distinctively read and preached in relation to other biblical genres. The preacher must look at the *context* of the text under consideration—this is the expository unit that will provide what Haddon Robinson calls "the big idea"[6] or the propositional sentence. The Holy Spirit first *applies* the interpretation of the text to the personality and experience of the preacher. This is crucial because the Spirit involves the authentic self of the preacher instead of the preacher's imitation of someone else. The message must first be applied to the preacher before it is applied to the hearers; it must come through the preacher before it comes to the hearers.

The late, celebrated, Anglican preacher-theologian, John R. W. Stott, offers this pregnant definition of *expository preaching*: It "is the opening up of the inspired text with such faithfulness and sensitivity that God's voice is heard and his people obey him."[7] Stott is convinced of this and contends preachers of expository sermons possess at least these two convictions: first, they are firm in their convictions that the Bible is not *a* word of God, but *the* Word of God, inspired and God breathed. They are also firm in their convictions that the Bible is a closed book that must be opened by the Holy Spirit and "cut straight," that is, rightly divided by the preacher (2 Tim 2:15). Expository preachers have at least two obligations. They must be faithful to the text of Scripture, and they must be sensitive to the hearers. In reality, they not only exegete the text, but they also exegete the hearers.

Finally, expository preachers have at least two expectations. First, they are accurate in delivering the expositional message and can expect God's

---

6. Haddon W. Robinson, *Biblical Preaching*, 15.
7. Given at a conference on expository preaching, accessed, March 6, 2017, Sermon Illustrations http://www.passionforpreaching.net/sermon-illustrations/.

Word to be heard. Like Isaiah who cried out, "Who has believed what we have heard?" they might wonder if it is believed (Isa 53:1). They can also expect the people to obey God because his Word will get a hearing whether it is heard immediately or futuristically, in compliance or disobedience; his Word will not return to him void but will accomplish the purpose for which it is sent (Isa 55:11). Preaching may be defined endlessly, but it must be demonstrated in the preaching moment.

Theology

Theology is the discipline of speaking words about God. Simply put, theology is God talk. We know God through his self-revelation; however, no one can define God—God defines God's self. Harry Emerson Fosdick, who pastored the historic Riverside Church in New York City, described his theology in this fashion: "Theology, like a telescope, is made simply to help people see, and like a telescope it is meant to be looked through and not looked at."[8] Only God knows and interprets God. Jesus said, "No one has ever seen God. The one and only Son, who is himself God and is at the Father's side—he has revealed him" (John 1:18). Preaching must be done in a theological framework with a view toward pastoral ministry.

Preaching must rest on a theological and apologetic foundation. Peter asserts, "[Be] ready at any time to give a defense to anyone who asks you for a reason for the hope that is in you" (1 Pet 3:15). Theology does not primarily exist to teach us *what* to believe but rather to equip and enable us to articulate *why* we believe *what* we believe.

"What God has joined together, let no one separate" (Matt 19:6). Theology must reconnect transcendence and immanence. God is not only transcendent, above us; he is also immanent, with us. His transcendence is reflected in his sovereignty, but his immanence is portrayed in his humanity—"the Word became flesh" (John 1:14). The distance between deity and dust and divinity and humanity was bridged in the incarnation. The incarnation bridged the gap between the *aboveness* of God and the *withness* of God. Open theism and process theology attempt to bring about a greater identification of God with humanity. However, they lean toward severing the transcendence and immanence of God.

---

8. Robert Moats Miller, *Harry Emerson Fosdick: Preacher, Pastor and Prophet* (New York: Oxford University Press, 1985), 396.

In the incarnation God is not either-or, but he is both-and. He is wholly other. He is *mysterium tremendum fascinosum*; he comes to us as a tremendous mystery and leaves us transfixed with tremors so that when we worship him we do it with a sense of trembling adoration. God is omnipotent and yet resigns himself to becoming impotent at Calvary. The One who holds the world in the palm of his hand is the One who is held by nails on the cross. He is not even able to carry his cross to the crucifixion site. Helmut Thielicke was known to say, "The crib and the cross"—that is, the feeding trough and crucifixion stake—"are hewn out of the same wood."[9] However, three days later the crucified God is the resurrected Savior raised from the dead by the Holy Spirit (Rom 8:11).

Theology must keep in an inextricable relationship the *omnipresence* ("everywhereness") of God and the *omniscience* ("all-knowingness") of God. God is everywhere spatially and yet chooses to be present with his people by residing within them through the Holy Spirit. God's omniscience signifies he knows the end before the beginning begins (Isa 46:10). There is no place where God is not, and there is nothing God does not know. Isaiah extols the omniscience of God: "Even before they call, I will answer; while they are still speaking, I will hear" (Isa 65:24). The psalmist embraces the omnipresence of God: "Where can I go to escape your Spirit? Where can I flee from your presence? If I go up to heaven, you are there; if I make my bed in Sheol, you are there. If I live at the eastern horizon or settle at the western limits, even there your hand will lead me; your right hand will hold on to me" (Ps 139:7–10).

Distilled from the breadth of Jonathan Edwards's massive theological work is this truth: God has forever known himself in a sweet and holy society as Father, Son, and Holy Spirit. This teaching militates against modalism that portrays God as wearing three masks—acting in the Old Testament as the Father, in the New Testament as the Son, and in our present world as the Holy Spirit. The triune God has never acted outside of his triune nature. The triune God acts in sacred unity to perform the mighty acts of God through Christ in the power of the Holy Spirit. This is intratrinitarian presence. In his classic hymn, Reginald Heber expresses the unity of the triune community:

---

9. Thielicke, *The Evangelical Faith*, 3: xvi.

> Holy, holy, holy! Lord God Almighty!
> All Thy works shall praise Thy name in earth and sky and sea;
> Holy, holy, holy; merciful and mighty!
> God in three Persons, blessed Trinity![10]

Pastoral Ministry

Preaching and theology are servants for pastoral ministry. In Acts 2, Peter preaches a theological sermon based on the Old Testament Scriptures and approximately three thousand persons are convicted in their hearts by what John Calvin calls the internal witness of the Spirit. They asked, "What should we do?" (Acts 2:37). Preaching and theology are wings that provide the spiritual energy for pastoral ministry to answer this question. Authentic and powerful pastoral ministry is an echo or response to preaching and profound theology.

After Peter preaches his powerful sermon drawn from Old Testament texts (Psalms, Joel, etc.), about three thousand persons respond to the message and are baptized. They heard preaching and saw the theology of the biblical text; now they are in need of pastoral ministry. The first thing the apostles involved in this pastoral ministry do is provide an atmosphere in which these believers can be discipled and grow in the Christian faith. Luke articulates the components of the pastoral ministry that are adopted in order to mature these believers: "They devoted themselves to the apostles' teaching, to the fellowship, to the breaking of bread, and to prayer" (Acts 2:42). The first component is *doctrine*. The pastoral leaders or apostles knew the new believers had an immediate need to be grounded in the teaching of the Scriptures. The text says they devoted themselves—the inference is they immersed themselves to deepen their understanding of the Scriptures.

Peter's Pentecostal sermon lifted up a few familiar Old Testament texts and more fully exposed the new believers to the spiritual meaning behind those texts in their historicity. No wonder the apostle Paul says to Timothy, "All Scripture is inspired by God and is profitable for teaching, for rebuking, for correcting, for training in righteousness, so that the man of God may be complete, equipped for every good work" (2 Tim 3:16–17).

---

10. Reginald Heber, "Holy, Holy, Holy."

The second component is *fellowship*. This fellowship is more than Christianly socializing. Rather, it is *koinonia*. None in the Christian community lacked anything because the Christian community provided for each of its members. There were no greater or lesser Christians. The believers rejoiced when others rejoiced and wept when others wept. This is authentic Christian fellowship.

The third component is the *breaking of bread*. Breaking of bread certainly has a spiritual meaning; perhaps it is related to the Eucharist or the Lord's Supper. Luke, in his first volume, informs the reader that Jesus was recognized in the breaking of bread (Luke 24:30–31). It can also have a physical meaning because the church provided for the physical needs of its members. Luke, in his second volume (Acts 6:1–6), captures how the church provided for the physical needs of the Grecian Jewish widows who felt they were being overlooked in the daily distribution of food.

The final component is *prayer*. Prayer is stressed as an indispensable individual and/or corporate discipline. Preparation for the day of Pentecost began with prayer as 120 believers gathered in an upper room, awaiting the descent of the Holy Spirit. After ten days the Spirit descended on those gathered there and convicted nearly three thousand persons of their sins, and they were converted to Christ and the Christian faith. Now they are admonished to continue in prayer.

Prayer is a two-way spiritual dynamic in which believers talk to God and wait for God to talk to them. The early church will gain tremendous momentum because it is saturated in prayer. In Acts 3:1, Peter and John go to the temple at the hour of prayer. In Acts 4:31 the church prayed, and those in the prayer meeting were filled with the Spirit and spoke the Word of God boldly. In Acts 6:4 the apostles prioritized their ministry by giving attention to prayer and the preaching of the Word. In Acts 7:59–60, while being stoned, Stephen prays that the Lord would receive his spirit and not hold the sin of his persecutors against them. In Acts 8:15, Peter and John prayed that the Samaritan believers might receive the Holy Spirit. In Acts 9:11, Saul, the new convert, is praying. In Acts 10:4, Cornelius the centurion has been praying. In Acts 10:9, Peter goes up on the roof to pray. And in Acts 12:5, the church is earnestly praying to God for Peter who is imprisoned. These components of pastoral ministry—teaching, fellowship, breaking of bread, and prayer—strengthen the cord of three strands by serving to deepen the understanding of theology and the thirst for more biblical preaching.

Sermon

At this point I want to illustrate how the work of theological education discussed in the previous chapters of this book will help shape, inform, and craft a sermon. This message will weave the three strands of preaching, theology, and pastoral ministry into the fabric of a sermonic tapestry.

Title: Do You Know Him? (Acts 17:16–34)

Church father, lawyer, and rhetorician, Tertullian (c. AD 155–240) asked this perennial question: "What has Athens to do with Jerusalem?" That is, what has the Athens of the academy to do with the Jerusalem of Christianity? What has the Athens of culture to do with the Jerusalem of the church? What has the Athens of philosophy to do with the Jerusalem of theology? What has the Athens of reason to do with the Jerusalem of faith? What has the Athens of Socrates to do with the Jerusalem of Paul?

This question has often been quoted and yet is often misunderstood and misapplied. Paul is not saying that Athens and Jerusalem have nothing to do with each other because, after all, the threads of Athens and Jerusalem are inextricably tied and woven together in the garment of our mission. Jesus says in Matt 5:13, "[Believers] are the salt of the earth." And therefore Jerusalem, home of the salt, penetrates the rock of Mars Hill in Athens. Jesus says to us in Matt 5:14, "You are the light of the world." The Jerusalem of light illumines the dense darkness of Athens. Athens and Jerusalem share together in a mission God has ordained.

As we look through the lens of church history, we hear Tertullian ask, "What has Athens to do with Jerusalem?" Is he critiquing the Athens-type preachers who pose as those who really are proclaiming the gospel message of Jerusalem? Perhaps he wants to contend that some of the preachers who say they preach the gospel are really Athens-type preachers—wolves dressed in sheep's clothing (Matt 7:15). Yet they say they represent the proclamation of Jerusalem.

Paul describes the preachers at Jerusalem as being those who rightly cut straight "the word of truth" (2 Tim 2:15). Tertullian is really saying that Athens-type preachers are those who are not cutting it straight. They are not exegeting the text. They are eisegeting the text. They are twisting and perverting the text. Apparently Tertullian would be glad to call for a redemptive reversal of this question, "What has Athens to do with Jerusalem?" to "What does Jerusalem have to do with Athens?" This sanctified sequence really makes a difference. In his *Proslogion*, his discourse for the arguments for the existence of God, Anselm provides this dictum: "faith seeking understanding"—I believe in order to understand. The dictum is not I understand in order to believe, but I believe in order to understand. We start with faith. It is what Paul says to Timothy in 2 Tim 1:12: "I know whom I have believed and am persuaded that he is able to guard what has been entrusted to me until that day." We have faith, and we are on the way toward understanding. There are things we may not ever understand, yet we believe and worship. Ira Stanphill lyrically expresses Anselm's theological dictum in his song, "I Know Who Holds Tomorrow": "I don't know about tomorrow, I just live from day to day. I don't borrow from its sunshine, For its skies may turn to gray."[11] We may not know what, why, where, when, or how. But we do know *who* holds tomorrow and we know *who* holds our hands.

Acts 17:16

The apostle Paul finds himself alone in Athens. Timothy and Silas are going to join him from Berea, but they have not yet arrived. Paul enters the city of Athens, now eclipsed by Corinth, the great city. The glory and golden days of Athens of the fifth century BC are over. Athens has been reduced to a population of about five thousand people, but it is still an important city. Paul comes to this city alone. He looks around. The NIV says that he "was greatly distressed" by the multitudinous idols. The Greek word for "distressed" is *paroxino*. The word has the same Greek root for the word for "disagreement" used in Acts 15:39, where Paul and Barnabas have a sharp dissension over whether John Mark will go with them on the second missionary journey.

There was a sharp dispute or *paroxino* between them. This word suggests that Paul is provoked. He is irritated. He is exasperated because he sees many idols. Everywhere he looks he sees idols. He is a monotheist. He believes in the Shema: "Listen, Israel: The Lord our God, the Lord is

---

11. Ira F. Stanphill, "I Know Who Holds Tomorrow," © Singspiration Music.

one" (Deut 6:4). He is not a polytheist. Everywhere he looks he sees idols. Yonder there is Hades, the god of the underworld. Yonder there is Hermes, the god of speed and commerce. Yonder there is Aphrodite, the goddess of beauty. Yonder there is Apollo, the god of the sun. Yonder there is Artemis, the goddess of the moon. Yonder there is Nike, the goddess of victory. Yonder there is Eros, the god of love. Yonder there is Poseidon, the god of the sea. Yonder there is Zeus, the chief of the Olympian gods. Paul is frustrated when he sees these idols.

Acts 17:17

Paul goes into the synagogue. There must have been a sizable population of Jews in Athens to warrant the establishment of a synagogue—ten households of Jewish families over which a male was the head. Paul goes in the synagogue and reasons with the Jews. Some God-fearing Greeks there are on the verge of converting from polytheism to monotheism—belief in one God. Paul goes into the marketplace and reasons with the people there also. He reasons with them on the subject of the resurrection (Acts 17:18, 31–32).

Acts 17:18

There in the marketplace Paul inevitably encountered and confronted Stoics and Epicureans, two of the philosophical schools in Athens. They challenge him because the Epicureans do not believe their existence is fated by the gods. There is distance between humanity and the gods. They do not believe in the afterlife. The essence of Epicureanism is pleasure. Epicureanism is on full display in its essence in the story of the rich man in Luke 12:16–21. Listen to his soliloquy: "You have many goods stored up for many years. Take it easy; eat, drink, and enjoy yourself" (v. 19).

Epicureans have a form of disciplined hedonism and restrained pleasure. Epicureans believe once a person dies, it is all over. Paul borrows from their philosophy and confronts them with it. He says to them the pleasure they really need is that of seeking God (Acts 17:27). Paul urges these Athenian philosophers to seek God in hopes of finding God. God has put within humans a God-sized hole that nothing or no one else can fill or provide full satisfaction. Augustine asserted, "Thou hast formed us for Thyself, and our hearts are restless until they find rest in Thee."[12]

The other philosophical school is Stoicism. Stoics believe in life after death. They believe there remains a demiurge, a divine spark after the decomposition of the body. They believe the gods govern their lives. The essence of their philosophy is wisdom. They hate ignorance. Paul uses their belief system and turns it against them. In verses 22 and 23 Paul sees an inscription as he enters their precinct. It was an inscription to the *agnos theos*—the "unknown God." Paul posits, "You worship and pay homage to what you do not know." Paul attributes their actions to what the Stoics looked upon with great disdain—"ignorance" (v. 30). Paul uses their culture as a boomerang and throws it to confront them.

The Stoics believe individuals exist in a disembodied spirit after death. They charged Paul with being a babbler, that is a seed picker. This expression is a strong suggestion that Paul is like a bird flitting around trying to pick up bits of food with its beak. They label Paul an amateur. To these Athenian philosophers, Paul was a plagiarist just mirroring and parroting back ideas he heard from others. They accused Paul of not having any original thoughts. To them Paul's doctrine of the resurrection was a strange idea and an unheard of concept about a foreign deity's dying and rising from the dead! Can deity die? No wonder these Athenian philosophers thought Paul was a babbler. Evidently they did not know Paul graduated from the University of Tarsus in Cilicia and had sat at the feet of Gamaliel, the celebrated and famous Jewish rabbi. They could not know that Paul would later write over half of the New Testament.

Acts 17:19–20

They escort Paul to the Areopagus. The Areopagus is a place and an organization like Wall Street. It is a system. Wall Street is a street—23 Wall Street, New York, New York—but it is also a stock exchange organization. The Areopagus is a place and a system. In Greek this place is the Hill of Aries; in Latin it is the Hill of Mars or Mars Hill. On that hill approximately thirty elite members would sit and talk and discuss court cases, criminal and civil matters, and perhaps even whether new gods would be inducted

---

12. Augustine of Hippo, *Confessions*, trans. William Watts (Cambridge, MA: Harvard University Press, 1912), 1.

into the directory of deities. They invited Paul to come and defend his strange doctrine of the resurrection.

Acts 17:21

The text says all the Athenians and the foreigners who lived there did every day was talk about something new, novel, and innovative. They invite Paul to come and talk about the resurrection. They are at least open to discussing this new doctrine. This is not a hospitable crowd on Mars Hill, but they are willing to hear. Are we willing to hear even though we have denominational differences? Are we willing to hear even though we have ethnic peculiarities? Are we willing to hear even though we have liturgical preferences? Are we willing to hear even though we have theological particularities? Are we willing to listen and talk to one another?

Paul is invited to stand before this august body of philosophers and defend the doctrine of resurrection from the dead. Paul tells them as he entered their precincts, he could see they were religious—superstitious. He saw the pantheon and the idolatrous memorabilia inside. But he also noticed something unusual. He saw an inscription to an unknown God—an *agnos theos*. Paul informs them he knows and worships the God they did not know. In his book *Bonhoeffer's Seminary Vision: A Case for Costly Discipleship and Life Together*, Dr. Paul House says, "How Christians think about God determines how they think about everything else."[13] Today people caricature God because they want him to be the kind of God they want him to be. God has made us in his own image and after his own likeness, and we have tried to bring God down to our level and make God in our own image after our own likeness.

In his book *Your God Is Too Small*, J. B. Phillips provides several caricatures of God.[14] God is portrayed as the resident policeman who walks the heavenly beat looking down at us. When we sin, he takes his divine billy club and beats us on the head. God is portrayed as the grand old man. This is the God who is sovereign but has senior moments and senioritis. He is Almighty and is yet affected by amnesia and Alzheimer's. This is the God who is divine yet suffers with dementia, thus permitting individuals to get

---

13. Paul R. House, *Bonhoeffer's Seminary Vision: A Case for Costly Discipleship and Life Together* (Wheaton: Crossway, 2015), 55.
14. J. B. Phillips, *Your God Is Too Small* (New York: Touchstone, 1997), cited in James Montgomery Boice, *Romans* (Grand Rapids: Baker Books, 1992), 2:749.

away with their sin. God is also portrayed as the God-in-a-box. This is the God individuals seldom pay attention to until an emergency or crisis occurs. Then they rub his stomach and expect him to come out of the box to deliver them. These caricatures do not accurately portray the God of the Bible. The late S. M. Lockridge, who pastored the Calvary Baptist Church of San Diego, California, answered the question, "Do you know him?" many years ago in his poetic rendition "That's My King." He said, "My King was born King. The Bible says He's a Seven Way King. He's the King of the Jews—that's a racial King. He's the King of Israel—that's a National King. He's the King of righteousness. . . ."[15]

Paul declares the Word and the Spirit move in the hearts of those who hear the Word. The Spirit convicts the world of sin, judgment, and righteousness (John 16:7–9), bringing the hearers to repentance. Therefore, the unknown God is made known through the resurrected Jesus who calls all people to seek him in repentance through the power of the Spirit.

Acts 17:24

Paul says, "I know him." Paul articulates the truth about this great God he knows. God is Creator. He created everything. He is the triune God—Father, Son, and Spirit. In creation the Father stood on nothing and said, "Let there be light." The Spirit hovered over the face of the water. According to Col 1:17, by the Son of God, "all things hold together." So the Father, Son, and Holy Spirit are active in creation. The triune God creates all things and yet does not live in temples like the temple where the Athenians housed their gods. The fact that God does not live in temples made with human hands has to be a reflection on the dedicatory prayer of Solomon. In his prayer Solomon acknowledged the temple did not house God even though the temple was beautiful.[16]

Acts 17:25

God is the giver of everything. He gives everything, yet he does not need anything from anyone. He is no one's debtor. In fact, he even gives breath.

---

15. S. M. Lockridge, "That's My King," accessed March 26, 2016, http://www.youtube.com/watch?v=1qrS8-PIjLI&feature=related.
16. 1 Kgs 8:27.

Acts 17:26

God is the One who made the whole human race out of one person. All humans come from Adam and are the recipients of God's grace. The *missio dei* is less effective when Christians have an incorrect *imago dei*. Everyone on planet Earth has been made in God's image. Therefore, our mission is to everyone. Slavery in America could never have existed if the American church had a correct *imago dei*. A proper *imago dei* leads to an effective *missio dei* for the purpose of *Soli Deo Gloria* in anticipation of *maranatha*—the day of the Lord when Jesus comes again. We all come from one blood—one person—Adam.

Acts 17:27

The truth of verse 27 is the triune God wants us to seek him in order that we might find him. As a young man Siddhartha Gautama, the founder of Buddhism, desired to find God. Word got around his village that he wanted to do so. He was referred to sages in the hill country. Gautama went up to the hill country and found one of the sages and started talking to him about finding God. The sage took him down to a pool of water. Gautama and the sage dabbled their feet in the water and talked about finding God. Without warning, the sage, with an ironclad grip, took the back of Gautama's neck and plunged his head in the water. To no avail Gautama tried to free himself from the ironclad grip. Just when Gautama surrendered himself to die, the sage pulled his head out of the water. Gautama cleared his throat and began to protest how the sage mistreated him. The sage responded, "When you want God as much as you wanted that next breath, then you'll find God." Jeremiah relays God's Word: "You will seek me and find me when you search for me with all your heart" (Jer 29:13).

Acts 17:28

We are reminded this is the true God in whom we live, move, and have our being. We exist because of him. Paul quotes some of their poets when he asserts that we have our existence in God and because of God. Paul is scripturally accurate and culturally engaging as he borrows from Athenian poets.

Acts 17:29

Paul contends this God cannot be made with silver and gold. He cannot be fashioned. He is the God who is not malleable; he cannot be formed. He is sovereign and resists fitting an ecclesiastical, denominational, ethnic box. This God is the sovereign God of the universe.

Acts 17:30

There was a time God overlooked ignorance, but now the full revelation of God has come in the person of Jesus Christ, the incarnate Son of God. Now God calls people everywhere to repent. Repentance cannot take place without the movement of the Spirit. John Calvin posited it is the Spirit who takes the words of Scripture uttered from the lips of the preacher and applies those words by the Spirit's power to convict hearts to the point they respond to the proclamation with, "What must we do [to be saved]?" (Acts 2:37). Peter would respond to this inquiry by saying, "Repent and be baptized, each of you, in the name of Jesus Christ for the forgiveness of your sins, and you will receive the gift of the Holy Spirit" (Acts 2:38). The Holy Spirit stimulates repentance. The thesis drawn from verse 30 is this: The unknown God is made known by the resurrected Jesus who calls all people to seek him in repentance through the power of the Holy Spirit.

Acts 17:31

Paul establishes the fundamental doctrine of the Christian faith on which the whole church stands and falls—the resurrection. He preaches the literal resurrection of Jesus. Paul believes God will judge the world by righteousness and justice. God confirmed this by raising Jesus from the dead. Paul spends the entirety of 1 Corinthians 15 showing why the resurrection is indispensable to the Christian faith. It was not enough for Jesus to die. He had to rise from the dead. If Jesus was not resurrected from the dead, then Christians perform their ministries in vain.

Acts 17:32

At this point this group of Athenian philosophers began to sneer and mock Paul. They rejected him. Still others wanted to schedule another occasion for Paul to speak on the resurrection. This request is the opposite of Felix's fearful decision: "As [Paul] spoke about righteousness, self-control, and the judgment to come, Felix became afraid and replied, 'Leave for now, but when I have an opportunity I'll call for you'" (Acts 24:25).

Acts 17:33

Paul responds to their sneering and mockery by walking away from the crowd. Some think Paul did not just walk out but was mistreated and forced out. But Paul did not depart from this assembly without the Word having a witness. The Word will accomplish the purpose for which it was sent (Isa 55:11).

Acts 17:34

Just as there were negative reactions to Paul's message, there were positive responses to Paul's proclamation of the resurrection of Jesus. Dionysius, a member of the Areopagus, believed. Damaris, probably one of the leading women of the city, believed. Additionally, a number of persons heard Paul's preaching and became followers of Christ. The Word will make his own witness. Paul did not fail at Mars Hill due to a lack of preaching Jesus. On the contrary, he successfully preached Jesus who was crucified and resurrected from the grave (Acts 17:18, 32).

Dietrich Bonhoeffer faithfully preached the Word. He was rejected by the German church and even misunderstood by some members of the Confessing Church. On April 9, 1945, Bonhoeffer walked out of the Flossenbürg jail, saying good-bye to his fellow inmates. To them that day was the end of his life, but for him it was the beginning. Thanks to his close friend Eberhard Bethge, we are left with Bonhoeffer's poignant poem, "Who Am I?," which locates Bonhoeffer's true identity not in the response of others to his ministry of the Word, but in his relationship to the God of the Word! "Who am I? They often tell me I step out from my . . ."[17]! Faithful ministers of the Word may take comfort in the reality that they know *who* they are because of *whose* they are. Do you know him?

Conclusion

As we have seen in this sermon, much goes into the process of moving from text to sermon, extending the work of moving from Bible to theology. Biblical exegesis, biblical theology, and historical and systematic theology help inform a well-developed sermon. These aspects of theological education help preachers and teachers prepare for a lifetime of ministry. Theological

---

17. Dietrich Bonhoeffer, *Letters and Papers from Prison*, updated ed. (New York: Touchstone, 1997), 459–60.

education will not necessarily produce great preachers, but teachers and preachers who take seriously the preparation provided through faithful theological education will be ready not just for the next sermon but for a lifetime of ministry.

Questions for Further Reflection

1. What would biblical preaching look like in your congregation? What difference would it make in the spiritual health of your church?
2. To what extent does the personality of the preacher impact the theology of the church and its pastoral ministry?
3. How does theology shape the preaching moment in the life of the church?
4. Does the preaching moment impact the effectiveness of pastoral ministry, or can parishioners' needs be met without sound theology and biblical preaching?
5. Is a thriving corporate prayer life paramount for effective pastoral ministry to a congregation? (How does your community define "thriving corporate prayer"?) What would a thriving corporate prayer life look like in your congregation? What difference would it make to the spiritual health of your church?
6. How important is it to remain true to biblical authorial intent in the preaching moment when ministering to a congregation?
7. How does the church convey its theology to the outside community who might not hear the sermons but receive pastoral ministry?
8. How is biblical preaching challenged by the antiauthoritarian mood of the contemporary mind-set?

Sources for Further Study

Alcántara, Jared E. *Crossover Preaching: Intercultural-Improvisational Homiletics in Conversation with Gardner C. Taylor*. Strategic Initiatives in Evangelical Theology. Downers Grove: InterVarsity Press, 2015.

Andrews, Dale P. *Practical Theology for Black Churches: Bridging Black Theology and African American Folk Religion*. Louisville: Westminster John Knox Press, 2002.

Bailey, Raymond. *Hermeneutics for Preaching: Approaches to Contemporary Interpretation of Scripture*. Nashville: Broadman, 1992.

Bond, L. Susan. *Contemporary African American Preaching: Diversity in Theory and Style*. St. Louis: Chalice Press, 2003.

Chapell, Bryan. *Christ-Centered Preaching: Redeeming the Expository Sermon*. 2nd ed. Grand Rapids: Baker Academic, 2005.

George, Timothy, James Earl Massey, and Robert Smith, ed. *Our Sufficiency Is of God: Essays On Preaching in Honor of Gardner C. Taylor*. Macon, GA: Mercer University Press, 2012.

Harris, James H. *Pastoral Theology: A Black-Church Perspective*. Minneapolis: Fortress Press, 1991.

Kuruvilla, Abraham. *Privilege the Text! A Theological Hermeneutic for Preaching*. Chicago: Moody Publishers, 2013.

LaRue, Cleophus James. *The Heart of Black Preaching*. Louisville: Westminster John Knox, 2000.

Lischer, Richard. *A Theology of Preaching: The Dynamics of the Gospel*. Rev. ed. Eugene, OR: Wipf and Stock, 2001.

Lloyd-Jones, David Martyn. *Preaching and Preachers*. 40th ed. Grand Rapids: Zondervan, 2011.

Massey, James Earl. *The Burdensome Joy of Preaching*. Nashville: Abingdon, 1998.

Mitchell, Henry H. *Celebration and Experience in Preaching*. Rev. ed. Nashville: Abingdon, 2008.

Oden, Thomas C. *Pastoral Theology: Essentials of Ministry*. San Francisco: Harper and Row, 1983.

Simmons, Martha J., and Frank A. Thomas, ed. *Preaching with Sacred Fire: An Anthology of African American Sermons, 1750 to the Present*. New York: W. W. Norton, 2010.

Taylor, Barbara Brown. *The Preaching Life*. Cambridge, MA: Cowley Publications, 1993.

Webster, Douglas D. *Living in Tension: A Theology of Ministry*. Eugene, OR: Cascade Books, 2012.

Chapter Eighteen

THEOLOGY, EVANGELISM, AND MISSIONS

CHARLES (CHUCK) E. LAWLESS

It is difficult, if not impossible, to read the Bible and not see God's heart for evangelism and missions. He is the God who came seeking Adam and Eve after they had sinned against him (Gen 3:9), seeking them not because he did not know where they were but because he wanted a renewed relationship with them. More importantly, he announced the coming of One from the seed of the woman who would strike the head of the serpent even as he would be wounded in the process (Gen 3:15). Through this One—Jesus, the incarnate Son of God—God would provide redemption for a fallen world. Hence, the words of Gen 3:15 were much more than an announcement of judgment; they were God's announcement of ultimate victory over the serpent. God would reclaim his world, and he would reach that world through a singular means: his people proclaiming his message to the ends of the earth (Rom 10:9–14). That proclamation is the task of evangelism and world missions.

Evangelism and *World Missions* Defined

Evangelism is "sharing the good news of Jesus Christ by word and life in the power of the Holy Spirit, so that unbelievers become followers of Jesus Christ in His church and in the culture."[1] Central to this task is the proclamation of the message of the gospel. The English word *evangelize* is itself transliterated from the Greek word meaning "to announce good

---

1. Alvin Reid, *Evangelism Handbook* (Nashville: B&H, 2009), 31.

news," and the word was used in the ancient world to pronounce good news such as victory in war or any other joyous event.[2] In the case of Christians, we announce the good news of Jesus, trusting God to draw to himself unbelievers who follow him in repentance and faith. They, then, become witnesses to Christ themselves as they proclaim that same message to their neighbors and the nations. Guiding this process is the Holy Spirit, who empowers believers (Acts 1:8) and convicts the world of sin, righteousness, and judgment (John 16:8–11).

Thus, we cannot do evangelism without understanding the *evangel*—that is, the "good news" of Jesus Christ. Apart from understanding the spiritual lostness of humanity and the gracious intervention of God in redeeming that lostness, we will not likely evangelize others; a faith meant to be shared would then become only a faith kept to oneself. Hence, one role of theological training is to teach believers to know, love, and proclaim the story of the gospel through evangelism.

World missions, then, is carrying out this evangelistic task across cultural boundaries. It is the task of the believer who "intentionally crosses boundaries for the purpose of communicating the gospel to win people to Christ, discipling new believers, planting churches, training biblically qualified leaders, and ministering to the whole body of Christ in holistic ways."[3] Sometimes wrongly limited to those believers who indicate a calling to missionary service, this work is more clearly the task of all believers. All may not go full-time to the nations, but all are commanded to make disciples "of all nations" (Matt 28:19).

The work of world missions is not, however, limited to work that assumes an international setting. Especially as the world becomes both global and smaller through travel and technology, missions occurs whenever believers cross cultural boundaries in order to share the good news of Jesus. That task takes place whether a Caucasian American speaks the gospel to his Muslim immigrant neighbor or that same believer moves to Southeast Asia to do the same. In either case a follower of Jesus speaks the story of Jesus to a person who does not follow Christ; that is, the believer evangelizes the nonbeliever, who in this case is from a different culture.

---

2. *Theological Dictionary of the New Testament: Abridged* (Grand Rapids: Eerdmans, 1985), s.v. *euangelizomai*.

3. Zane Pratt, Jeff Walters, and David M. Sills, *Introduction to Global Missions* (Nashville: B&H, 2014), 3.

The Place of Evangelism and World Missions in a Theological Curriculum

It is not uncommon for scholars to debate whether the disciplines of evangelism and world missions belong in a theological curriculum. "The local church should be teaching those things," they say. "The theological institutions should cover the classical disciplines like biblical studies, church history, and theology, but the practical disciplines belong in the local church." The debate is a fair one, as other disciplines do indeed seem to fit more clearly into a theological curriculum; however, reasons for including practical disciplines such as evangelism and world missions in such a curriculum are numerous.

The Foundation of Evangelism and World Missions Is the Bible

Evangelism and world missions are, at their foundation, theological callings built on the foundation of the Bible. Christ followers do the work of evangelism and world missions because the Bible—that is, the writings we accept as the inspired Word of God, "profitable for teaching, for rebuking, for correcting, for training in righteousness" (2 Tim 3:16)—command that we do so. That Word is perfect, trustworthy, right, radiant, pure, and reliable (Ps 19:11–13); it's the infallible standard for Christian living that includes speaking the gospel around the world. Apart from the authority of this Word, we would have little reason to carry this message to the nations. Strong theological training prepares church leaders both to defend and to proclaim that Word that compels us to announce the good news.

The Gospel Is Itself a Theological Message

Christians do what we do in evangelism and missions because of what we believe about the nature of God, the lostness of humanity, and the salvation Christ provides. The God of the Bible is a perfect God, omniscient (1 John 3:20), omnipotent (Rev 19:6), and omnipresent (Prov 15:3). He created all things, holds all things together, and is the culmination of all things (John 1:1–3; Col 1:15–17; Rev 22:13). He made the first humans, Adam and Eve, in his image (Gen 1:27), provided all they would ever need, and lovingly commanded them to follow his every word—including not eating from the tree of knowledge of good and evil in the garden of Eden (Gen 2:16–17). Should they eat from that tree, the result would be death.

The first humans, though, rebelled against their Creator and ate from the forbidden tree. The consequences were catastrophic (Gen 3:7–24). The relationship of the humans was distorted as the husband blamed the wife (and ultimately, God) for his own wrong choices. Childbirth and physical labor changed. Creation itself began to groan for God's intervention and renewal (Rom 8:19–22). More specifically, God carried out his judgment, and death entered creation. Adam and Eve were cast from the garden and separated from their Creator.

Every human since then has been a sinner, and all have fallen short of God's glory (Rom 3:23). As the apostle Paul concluded, "There is no one righteous, not even one. There is no one who understands; there is no one who seeks God. All have turned away; all alike have become worthless. There is no one who does what is good, not even one" (Rom 3:10–12). Thus, the lostness of humanity pervades the world. Dead in sins, no one around the globe has hope apart from the grace of God.

The story does not end there, however. God so loved the world that he sent his Son Jesus—who was himself fully God and fully human—as the Savior (Luke 2:11), the sacrifice (Eph 5:2), the ransom (1 Tim 2:6), and the propitiation for sins (1 John 2:2). Jesus was the fulfillment of Gen 3:15—the One born of a woman, the One who crushed the serpent's head through his death (Col 2:15). Jesus then conquered death through the miracle of resurrection (1 Cor 15:54–57). He ascended to the Father after blessing his followers (Luke 24:50–51; Acts 1:11), and he will someday return in power and glory (Matt 24:30).

To those who turn to him in repentance and trust, Jesus promises eternal life (Mark 1:15; John 3:16). God gives that life as he forgives sin (Rom 4:7), remembering it no more (Jer 31:34), dropping it to the bottom of the sea (Mic 7:19), blotting it out (Isa 43:25), and separating sinners from that sin as far as the east is from the west (Ps 103:12). That salvation cost him his life, but Jesus graciously died for us "while we were still sinners" (Rom 5:8).

He not only redeems sinners, but he also folds them into a local church where he is both the cornerstone (1 Pet 2:7) and the head (Eph 5:23).

Within the local body, believers experience teaching, fellowship, equipping, and accountability. There we also receive our marching orders and our support to proclaim the gospel around the world. We go, and we commission others to go, because of the theology we believe.

God Is a Global God

The gospel message revolves around the theological truth that God is a global God. All humans in the world are lost without a personal relationship with Jesus, yet God loves the entire world; thus, world missions is a reflection of the heart of God. He called out a people in Abraham, through whom he would bless the nations of the world (Gen 12:1–3). He redeemed his people from slavery in Egypt, illustrating his power to the Egyptians in the process (Exod 14:25). He blessed his people so the nations would "rejoice and shout for joy" (Ps 67:4) as he was exalted (Ps 46:10). He sent the reluctant prophet Jonah to speak forgiveness to the Ninevites (Jonah 1–4), and the day will come when "the earth will be filled with the knowledge of the Lord's glory, as the water covers the sea" (Hab 2:14).

Lostness permeates the earth today, but Jesus will reign one day as the King of kings and Lord of lords (Rev 17:14) among those described as "a vast multitude from every nation, tribe, people, and language, which no one could number, standing before the throne and before the Lamb" (Rev 7:9). So important was this missions task to Jesus, in fact, that he spoke what is known as the Great Commission at least four times in the New Testament (Matt 28:18–20; Luke 24:45–47; John 20:21; Acts 1:8; see also Mark 15:7).

Each of the four Gospels includes a similar sending and proclaiming statement at the end of the gospel, suggesting a final and climactic emphasis on the Great Commission task.[4] Acts 1:8 then roughly outlines the approach the disciples would take to fulfill that calling. They would evangelize those nearest them in Jerusalem and then spread their witness in expanding circles to Judea, Samaria, and the ends of the earth. By the end of the book of Acts, Paul would proclaim the gospel in Rome "with all boldness and without hindrance" (Acts 28:31). Among the Gospel accounts of

---

4. Portions of the remainder of this subsection were first published in Chuck Lawless, "To All the Nations: The Great Commission Passages in the Gospels and Acts," *Southern Baptist Journal of Theology* 15, no. 2 (Summer 2011): 18–19.

the Great Commission, Matthew's account is most helpful for this chapter. Jesus's mandate to his disciples, and ultimately to all believers, was clear: "Go . . . and make disciples of all nations." Better understood as "as you are going," the verb "go" suggests that the disciples were to make disciples in any place among any people. They were to be on the offensive, proclaiming the good news to all the people groups who make up the nations of the world. Evangelism was thus a proactive response to the transforming power of the gospel in their own lives; in no sense were they to wait for others to come to them.

Their task was not complete with evangelizing, however. The disciples were to "make disciples," leading nonbelievers to follow Christ in faith and then to obey all that he commanded his followers to do. New Testament scholar Robert Plummer describes this responsibility of the church: The apostles must bring persons to the point where they knowingly and publicly align themselves with Jesus Christ by declaring their faith through baptism (Matt 28:19). This baptism is in "the name of the Father and of the Son and of the Holy Spirit"—implying that the one being baptized has come to know God as Father, Son, and Holy Spirit. That is, the convert is not one unwillingly immersed but one who has entered into conscious relationship with the triune God. The apostles are to teach the converts everything Jesus has commanded (Matt 28:20). If the new converts are to become mature disciples, they must continue to be schooled in the apostles' teaching, enabled by Christ's indwelling Spirit to love God and love neighbor (Matt 22:37–40).[5]

The goal is that those who follow Christ will live like Christ and lead others to do the same. Hence, a process of making disciples that ends with only the conversion of the evangelized is incomplete at best, disobedient at worst. In fact, the results of this omission can be disastrous. Untaught believers are ill equipped to face trials, untrained to recognize false teachings, and unprepared to teach others. They quickly become easy prey for an enemy who seeks to devour them (1 Pet 5:8). Disciple-makers must, therefore, be trained to equip others to be fully devoted disciples of Jesus. Theological trainers can play a significant role in this task.

---

5. Robert L. Plummer, "The Great Commission in the New Testament," *Southern Baptist Journal of Theology* (Winter 2005), v.9: 4.

Great Commission Believers Face Spiritual Warfare

Those who do the Great Commission face the reality of spiritual warfare and therefore must understand the theological underpinnings of this battle. The Scriptures variously describe nonbelievers as following the "ruler of the power of the air, the spirit now working in the disobedient" (Eph 2:2), their having been blinded by "the god of this age" (2 Cor 4:4), held in the "domain of darkness" (Col 1:13), under the power of Satan (Acts 26:18), and in the "trap of the devil" (2 Tim 2:26). The enemy aims his arrows at believers, seeking to remove us from the battle as God's proclaimers of life and freedom. We, though, have the full armor of God (Eph 6:10–17) at our disposal, giving us authority and power to conquer the enemy that Jesus has already disarmed through his cross (Col 2:15). The believer who does not understand these biblical truths will likely not persevere long under attack when he seeks to evangelize his neighbors and reach the nations.

Believers Do Evangelism and World Missions in the Power of the Spirit

God's choice for his followers to do the Great Commission surely reflects the theological truth of the believer's empowerment through the Holy Spirit.[6] In Matthew's account of the Great Commission, some gathered there on the mountainside still doubted the resurrection (Matt 28:17). Mark's account shows that some followers did not believe Mary's resurrection report; others did not believe two disciples who had been walking with the resurrected Jesus (Mark 16:11–13). Those same two disciples had struggled in their own postcrucifixion faith in Luke's account (Luke 24:13–27), and others battled doubts when Jesus was physically in their midst (Luke 24:36–39). In John, some of the disciples hid for fear of the Jews (John 20:19), and Thomas is still remembered as the "doubting one" because of his disbelief without proof (John 20:24–25). Even the disciples in the book of Acts were seemingly focused more on the kingdom of Israel than on God's kingdom (Acts 1:6), yet all of these men were the ones to whom Jesus gave the Great Commission. He knew they could never accomplish these tasks without the empowerment of the Spirit and promised them his presence even "to the end of the age" (Matt 28:20). Doing the Great

---

6. See Lawless, "To All the Nations," 22–23.

Commission cannot be disconnected from the power and presence of the One who gave the command.

Theology, of course, resounds throughout this entire section: theology proper, revelation, Christology, pneumatology, anthropology, soteriology, demonology, ecclesiology, and eschatology. Further, to accept and follow the command of Jesus to do the Great Commission, we must recognize the meaning and extent of his authority (Matt 28:18). He was not just another religious teacher; he is the Son of God. To baptize in the name of the Father, the Son, and the Holy Spirit (Matt 28:19), believers must have some grasp of the Trinity of God. If we are to teach others to do all that Jesus commanded, we must know and understand Jesus's teachings. Ultimately, we must cling to a biblical theology of suffering, knowing that doing the Great Commission in some places of the world may cost our lives. Theology especially matters when one faces persecution that comes as a result of Great Commission obedience. This summary reminds us that evangelism and missions are so connected to major areas of Christian theology that not to include these practical disciplines in a theological curriculum is a serious omission. Indeed, evangelism and world missions separated from theology risk losing their gospel message and becoming only man-centered pragmatism.

The Value of Evangelism and World Missions in a Theological Curriculum

The best theological training is not only about content but also about application. It is more than learning how to interpret the Word of God; it is also learning how to live out the Word and lead others to do the same. It is studying and appreciating the gospel so deeply that one cannot help but speak its transforming truths. Good theological training leads to scholar practitioners who do not separate the knowledge in their heads from the work of their hands.

That truth is perhaps more evident in the work of evangelism and missions than in any other practical discipline. While John Piper is correct that "missions is not the ultimate goal of the church. Worship is. . . . The goal of missions is the gladness of the peoples in the greatness of God,"[7]

---

7. John Piper, *Let the Nations Be Glad! The Supremacy of God in Missions* (Grand Rapids: Baker Academic, 2010), 63, 35.

the work of the Great Commission remains fundamental to the church. For that reason it must also be central in theological training that equips leaders for the church. Teaching potential leaders how to do evangelism and how to cross cultures with the gospel is a nonnegotiable task of ministry training, and theological training in particular provides means to approach these tasks.

Offering Practical Training

Many accrediting agencies require theological institutions to build supervised ministry training experiences into their curriculum. Those experiences must include not only the praxis of ministry but also reflection on that ministry. Consider, for example, the learning opportunities in the following real-life evangelism and missions scenarios of seminary students:

1. A seminary student was attempting to share the gospel with a neighbor, who halted the conversation as soon as the student said, "The Bible says . . ." To the student's naïve surprise, he was facing a man who denied the authority of the Bible, the foundation on which the student was building his position. He was forced by this experience to learn more about explaining and apologetically defending biblical authority in preparation for his next evangelistic encounter.

2. A student was excited about her opportunity to teach a small group overseas, and she spent many hours getting ready for the assignment. What she did not think about—and frankly, what her trip leaders did not help her to consider—was that her group consisted of several illiterate ladies who were oral learners. The young student realized quickly that her three-point outline based on their reading Scripture texts was not going to work.

3. "How can you be so sure you've got the right way?" a man visiting from Europe asked a group of students. "That's nothing but arrogance to think Christianity is the only way." The students had read about people who believed as he did, but they had never in their somewhat sheltered world met somebody who did. They were, by their own admission, unprepared to answer and quickly contacted a professor to learn more.

4. The student intern was certain his restaurant coworker was ready to follow Christ. He seemed so open, so willing to listen. To his surprise, though, the fellow rejected the gospel. Unbeknown to the student, the man and his wife had unexpectedly lost a baby in childbirth, and they were not willing to follow a God who allows such evil things to happen. When the student learned of the situation, the doctrine of theodicy stared him in the face.
5. The young student on a short-term mission trip was thoroughly ill equipped for the question, how would you reach out to and evangelize a transgendered person? The issue was a significant one in his culture, and the student suddenly had some homework to do.

The point is that actually doing ministry under the watchful eye of a mentor and professor is one of the best means to connect theology with practice. In these five ministry scenarios are such theological issues as revelation, exclusivity, theology, and ethics. Practical issues such as worldview analysis, orality, and apologetics are evident as well. The supervised ministry component brings ministry to life for the theological student, and the guiding care of a mentor and professor allows the student to learn, and perhaps to fail, without threat or fear—all within the context of doing evangelism and world missions.

Connecting Theological Training to the Local Church

Moreover, evangelism and world missions connect institutional theological training to its proper root: the local church. The work of the Great Commission is the work of the church—primarily, the local body of believers, though often in partnership with other believers around the world. Even independent or denominationally affiliated missions-sending agencies must find their candidates in the local church, and most require a local congregation to approve those candidates before sending them. Mission agencies often look specifically for candidates who regularly evangelize others, that is, who give evidence of an evangelistic heart long before going to the mission field. Even as the theological institution provides complementary training to the work of the church, God calls out and sends out believers through his church, modeled in the first-century Antioch church's sending out missionaries Paul and Barnabas (Acts 13:1–3). The church is both a partner and a goal in the missionary-sending task: a local congregation affirms, commissions, and prayerfully supports missionaries who seek to plant new churches to the ends of the earth. Those new congregations then become sending units themselves as they in turn raise up and deploy missionaries. Hence, for both the missionary and the locals, the body of Christ is essential to the task of the Great Commission.[8]

The wise theological institution makes sure students understand just how much ecclesiology matters in the Great Commission task.

In that light, theological institutions must prepare students not only to do the tasks of evangelism and missions personally but also to lead congregations to do them corporately. That expectation requires multiple tasks: introducing students to potential resources and methods, teaching them to critique resources and methods from a theological viewpoint, guiding them to know how to introduce new resources to different congregations, showing them how to train individuals to use the resources and then equip others to do the same, and teaching them how to adjust when resources and methods seem to be ineffective in a given congregation. In this sense the best "grade" a student receives cannot be adequately assessed until he or she attempts to implement such training in a local congregation, again rightly connecting the local church to the theological training institution.

Promoting Attention to Discipleship

Further, including evangelism and world missions in a theological curriculum necessitates attention to one of the weaker areas of many churches: discipleship. As noted earlier, the Great Commission demands that believers teach others to obey everything Jesus commanded (Matt 28:20). Churches that fail to do this task fail in doing the Great Commission, as New Testament scholar Craig Blomberg notes: "Teaching obedience to all of Jesus's

---

8. Chuck Lawless, "A Theology of Missions," in *Whom Shall We Send? Understanding the Essentials of Sending Missionaries*, ed. Joel Sutton (Charleston: CreateSpace Independent, 2016), 18–19.

commands forms the heart of disciple making. Evangelism must be holistic. If non-Christians are not hearing the gospel and not being challenged to make a decision for Christ, then the church has disobeyed one part of Jesus's commission. If new converts are not faithfully and lovingly nurtured in the whole counsel of God's revelation, then the church has disobeyed the other part."[9]

This task of discipleship is primarily reserved for the church, but the theological institution has an opportunity to model it as well. Many pastors and missionaries today give credit to university and seminary professors who took them under their care, demonstrated Christianity for them, and then challenged them to fulfill God's calling wherever he would take them. They disciple others today because professors who understood the discipling component of the Great Commission—and often taught it in their classrooms—modeled it for them.

A prime example of this kind of professor is Robert Coleman, longtime professor of discipleship and evangelism at several institutions, including Asbury Theological Seminary, Trinity Evangelical Divinity School, and Gordon-Conwell Theological Seminary. Coleman is the author of *The Master Plan of Evangelism*, the best-selling book that describes Jesus's method for selecting, training, and sending out his disciples.[10] In his decades of teaching, Coleman has followed Jesus's model by intentionally investing in young leaders—many who are now pastors, professors, and denominational leaders themselves. The professor has been the pastor/mentor/encourager who understands that "a few people so dedicated . . . will shake the world for God."[11]

Challenges and Opportunities Facing Evangelism and World Missions in Theological Education

All of theological education is changing rapidly. The world we Christians are striving to reach is changing even faster, and these changes offer multiple challenges to connecting theological education, evangelism, and world missions.

---

9. Craig Blomberg, *Matthew*, New American Commentary (Nashville: B&H, 1992), 432.
10. Robert Coleman, *The Master Plan of Evangelism* (Grand Rapids: Revell, 1993).
11. Ibid., 30.

Orality and Noninstitutional Instruction

When many of us think of theological education, we think about a classroom, a professor, textbooks, lectures, and written exams. We fail to realize that perhaps 80 percent of the world's population are primarily oral learners who cannot read or write, or who simply prefer to learn by oral rather than written or textual means.[12] They tend not to learn by our written texts and structured lectures but by stories, dramas, songs, and proverbs.

This reality is especially challenging as we train the next generation of pastors and missionaries. We train them through our customary methods, and they tend to emulate our approaches wherever they go until they learn that literate means of teaching do not always work among oral learners. Missiologist David Sills reminds us that oral learners often retain more information for longer periods of time than literates do, but most training materials are not designed for oral learners.[13] We must consequently prepare future missionaries and theologians to teach in oral-learning seminaries that have "no computer labs or libraries . . . or even pen, pencil, or paper."[14] Often that preparation includes learning to teach via biblical stories rather than through our outlined lectures.

Even doctoral studies are affected by this reality. For example, the recent PhD graduate who is ready to move overseas to train nationals in a theological institution must realize (1) language study will likely require years before that graduate is proficient to teach in the native tongue; (2) many "institutions" are only meeting places; and (3) teaching in a different context is much different from teaching in North America. The graduate trained at the highest level must also learn to teach in an oral culture.

Distance Learning

Online education is here to stay, and theological institutions must learn to maximize the opportunities this delivery system offers. While some professors and trainers see little value in the online approach to theological education, others see strengths in it. For example, the advent of online options now allows students to remain in a local ministry under the direction of

---

12. "Who Are Oral Learners?" International Orality Network, accessed January 17, 2017, https://orality.net/about/who-are-oral-learners.
13. M. David Sills, *Reaching and Teaching: A Call to Great Commission Obedience* (Chicago: Moody Publishers, 2010), 176.
14. Ibid., 187.

a caring pastor while still earning their degrees. Internships in a known local church then become possible, and students often have opportunity to do evangelism in a culture and location they recognize and understand, as opposed to moving to a campus where they are too often cocooned in a theological bubble.

Additionally, online classes sometimes include international students whose presence invites other students to broaden their worldviews. For example, imagine the learning/teaching opportunity in a missions class when Western students deny the possibility of demon possession, but African and Asian students take the opposite stance. Their online discussions push the class to consider worldview options, biblical teachings, and practical ministry applications. The resulting exposure to the globe may well encourage more students to consider international service.

The challenge for theological educators is to provide the best education possible via various delivery systems, and meeting that challenge cannot be separated from the local churches where distance-learning students live. We must not ignore distance learning options; we must instead learn to use them well in partnership with local congregations, as will be evident in the next section.

Local Church-Based Training

As noted above, distance-learning options now allow students to remain in local church settings while earning their degrees from accredited institutions. A corollary result is that local churches are now designing their own training programs and asking theological institutions to help their students earn credit for their training. Churches are now coming to the institution to ask for accreditation and affirmation of their local programs.

This trend is not entirely negative, however. First, it requires needed communication between the local church and the theological institution in order to coordinate teachers and curriculum to meet accreditation standards. Second, it provides another set of eyes in evaluating curriculum; local church leaders who are in the trenches of ministry have opportunity to influence the curriculum. Third, it forces theological institutions to evaluate their curricula in terms of effectiveness in preparing graduates for the local church. Fourth, it gives students an opportunity to do evangelism and missions alongside pastors and congregations they already know well.

Fifth, it allows students to learn from teachers who are themselves in the trenches—trenches that are changing so rapidly that educational institutions can hardly keep up with them.

In a similar vein, Perry Shaw, curriculum and faculty development consultant to regional schools throughout the Middle East, argues from a global perspective that local churches must be involved in assessing curriculum, particularly if "the ultimate goal of our work is to see missional impact in the community."[15] In fact, he contends that gifted lay leaders may be the best ones to help evaluate curriculum because they are often most open to change. Pastors and denominational leaders, on the other hand, often find it difficult "to consider creative alternatives for effective curricula" and "push for more traditional education rather than creative innovation."[16] While church leaders pushing for local church-based theological training would not typically fit this category, such an indictment ought to challenge church and denominational leaders as they consider twenty-first-century training for evangelism and world missions.

Lay Missionaries

More and more, missions-sending agencies are facing increased difficulties in securing on-the-ground access for missionaries. One of the responses to this difficulty has been the rise of various forms of "business as mission" (BAM), with businessmen and women carrying the gospel around the world.[17] Local churches and missions agencies alike are challenging believers to move overseas to work or to use their short-term overseas business trips more wisely for the gospel.

That call has given rise to a new need for theological education: training adults who may not want to earn a degree but do want basic theological and missiological training so they may be better equipped for the task when they arrive on international soil. Imagine, for example, the engineer who must somehow move a conversation to Jesus even as he hears the wail from the minaret in the background . . . or the teacher ministering among animists who have lost several loved ones to a natural disaster . . . or the

---

15. Perry Shaw, *Transforming Theological Education: A Practical Handbook for Integrative Learning* (Carlisle, UK: Langham Global, 2014), 57.
16. Ibid.
17. Mark L. Russell, *The Missional Entrepreneur: Principles and Practices for Business as Mission* (Birmingham, AL: New Hope, 2010), 22–23, lists several nuanced understandings of BAM.

CEO who has one week of opportunity to help atheists understand why she believes there is a God . . . or the college student who seeks to explain the Trinity to her international colleagues. The challenges are many, and the local church and theological institutions must help prepare laypersons for this work.

For the theological institution, this need means offering more educational options, including free online courses, certificate-level studies, practical ministry conferences, local church-based courses, and international classes. To reach the world, institutions must think beyond their local classroom and traditional delivery systems.

World Religions

The images are striking: the African offering animal sacrifices to pagan gods, the Muslim striving to do enough good works to enter heaven, the Buddhist spinning a prayer wheel, the Hindu offering chants, the people praying to false gods around the world, the families following elaborate burial rituals in hopes of ushering their loved one into a positive afterlife. These are people God loves, numbered among those for whom Jesus died, ones we are called to reach with the gospel. They are part of the approximately 53 percent of the world's population that self-identify as followers of a faith other than Christianity.[18]

Globalization now requires that theological institutions offer training in world religions. When believers are to make disciples of all peoples (Matt 28:19–20), and followers of world faiths are also now our neighbors, such study is imperative. This study is much more than the simple study of religion, however; it is study to teach believers how to share the gospel with adherents of other faiths. It is theologizing in two directions: understanding the theology of other world religions, and knowing how to counter that thinking with Christian theology. Only with this kind of understanding are we best prepared to do evangelism and missions in a world of other faiths. With this kind of theological preparation, however, we can tackle both the opportunity and the challenges that world faiths present.

---

18. "Religions of the World," Religious Tolerance, accessed January 17, 2017, http://www.religioustolerance.org/worldrel.htm.

Conclusion

John MacArthur has argued that evangelism "is the most urgent duty we as Christians have been given to do."[19] The cry of three billion people around the world who have little or no access to the gospel only magnifies MacArthur's words. The New Testament church has the privilege and responsibility of taking the good news to our neighbors and the nations, and theological training institutions have the opportunity to prepare leaders for this task.

That training may look different around the world. Some of it will occur in large lecture halls, but some will take place under a tree in Africa. Some teachers will use textbooks, while others will teach with only stories and poems. Some students will earn degrees, but others will train only to be better prepared to share the gospel. Regardless of the format, though, the foundational goal remains the same: raising up leaders to proclaim to the world the message, "The Son of Man has come to seek and to save the lost" (Luke 19:10). In his power, we can accomplish this task.

Questions for Further Reflection

1. What motivates you to do evangelism and world missions? What keeps you from doing these tasks?
2. What theological issues would you want to study more to be better equipped to do evangelism and world missions?
3. How much is your church involved in evangelism and world missions? In theological training?
4. How might you better support theological institutions that are seeking to produce pastors, missionaries, and evangelists who do the Great Commission? Pray? Give? Attend?
5. What world faiths are most evident where you live? How might you be better equipped to reach followers of those faiths?

Sources for Further Study

Coleman, Robert. *The Master Plan of Evangelism*. Grand Rapids: Revell, 1993.

---

19. John F. MacArthur, *Evangelism: How to Share the Gospel Faithfully* (Nashville: Thomas Nelson, 2011), viii.

Moreau, A. Scott, Gary Corwin, and Gary McGee. *Introducing World Missions*. Grand Rapids: Baker Academic, 2015.
Packer, J. I. *Evangelism and the Sovereignty of God*. Downers Grove: IVP Books, 2012.
Pratt, Zane, Jeff Walters, and David M. Sills. *Introduction to Global Missions*. Nashville: B&H, 2014.
Reid, Alvin. *Evangelism Handbook*. Nashville: B&H, 2009.
Shaw, Perry. *Transforming Theological Education: A Practical Handbook for Integrative Learning*. Carlisle, UK: Langham Global, 2014.
Terry, John Mark. *Missiology*. Nashville: B&H Academic, 2015.

Chapter Nineteen

THEOLOGY, WORLDVIEW FORMATION, AND CULTURAL ENGAGEMENT

OWEN STRACHAN

I heard a voice that cried,
Balder the beautiful
Is dead, is dead—

This is how Henry Wadsworth Longfellow translated lines of a poem by Esaias Tegner.[1] Many years after Longfellow's translation, a young C. S. Lewis read these lines. In the midst of a childhood speckled by tragedy and trial, Lewis experienced an epiphany. "I knew nothing of Balder, but instantly I was uplifted into huge regions of northern sky, [and] I desired with almost sickening intensity something never to be described (except that it is cold, spacious, severe, pale, and remote)."[2]

Lewis elsewhere articulated this brush with the transcendent as a sensation of "pure Northern-ness." In the twenty-first century we might feel uncomfortable with such statements. Awe, particularly metaphysical awe, does not play well in a postmodern world where scientism and postmodernism train us to be rigid advocates of reason in certain spheres even as

---

1. See "Tegner's Drapa" in Alphonso Gerald Newcomer and Alice Ebba, *Three Centuries of American Poetry and Prose* (Chicago: Scott, Foresman, 1917), 600.
2. Alister McGrath, *C. S. Lewis: A Life* (Carol Stream, IL: Tyndale House, 2013), 19. See also 131–40 for a helpful understanding of Lewis's increasingly Christian imagination. Much more needs to be written on this subject, particularly in an age that is starved for transcendence.

we profess that there is no metatruth. Such language describing ultimate reality that grapples with the cosmos and our own infinitesimal place in it simply does not fit in our time.

Ours is a posttheological age. At least this is the way the secular academy, the institution that more than any other shapes public thought, commonly views things. This was not always so. In the Middle Ages, when the Catholic Church created the university, theology held sway over all other disciplines. This was true for centuries, even into the American experiment. It was not merely that theology was first among equals; most schools founded in this country in the eighteenth and nineteenth centuries were expressly religious and aimed at educating clergy. Theology was not *part of* the curriculum; theology *was* the curriculum.[3]

In the twenty-first century, most schools have grouped all such instruction in religion departments. The treatment of religions in the academy is generally sociological. The truth claims and ethics of different religious traditions are of some interest, but primary attention revolves around the practices, makeup, and motivating socioeconomic influences of these groups. In other words, it is more the religious group that is to be studied than it is the religion. Of course, in a good number of academic settings, certain groups—such as evangelicals—come under close scrutiny and are found wanting on grounds of their nonprogressive takes on gender, sexuality, environmentalism, and pluralism.[4]

All of this has the effect of demystifying the transcendent and decoloring the cosmos. Students learn that there is no ultimate truth, there is no greater coherence to existence, and they can only trust a microscope (and the opinions of their professors). Such a perspective—or random grouping of perspectives—leaves students listless. They don't know what they were made for; they don't know what their humanness and their bodies are for; they know to perform ritual public motions—side with progressive causes

---

3. For more on this shift, see James Tunstead Burtchaell, *The Dying of The Light: The Disengagement of Colleges and Universities from Their Christian Churches* (Grand Rapids: Eerdmans, 1998); and George Marsden, *The Soul of the American University: From Protestant Establishment to Established Nonbelief* (New York: Oxford University Press, 1996).

4. The first to make this shift public was Allan Bloom, *The Closing of the American Mind* (New York: Simon and Schuster, 1987). It is my belief that all students should read this book at some point during their collegiate experience.

and pay lip service to justice and equity—but they have no deeper sense of why they should behave in such ways.[5]

In such times evangelical Christians and evangelical educators have a tremendous task and a tremendous opportunity. In a secularist world gone bleak and gray, we have the chance to "remystify" and recolor the world. We have the opportunity to provide theological education that will make sense of this fallen order and, most importantly, introduce students to the riches of a theocentric life.[6]

In what follows, we examine the three animating tasks of theological education: developing doctrine, worldview, and a biblical approach to cultural engagement.

We Teach Students Doctrine

Not every Christian institution is chartered as a seminary. Most of our schools are colleges and universities. I do not mean to suggest here, then, that schools should only or exclusively teach Christian doctrine. But we must see as a matter of first principles that every school that is meaningfully evangelical has a massive stake in the truth. It is thus sound doctrine that every Christian institution must profess and teach.

We know this from the Scripture, our inerrant and authoritative source. The Scripture is not *a* record of God's will; it is *the* record of the mind and purposes of God. It is "God breathed" and uniquely so (2 Tim 3:16 NIV). It tells us the history of God's dealings with his people and his world, beginning with the creation of earth and ending with the return of Christ the Savior-King (Genesis 1 and Revelation 22). Scripture is many things, in actuality: it is inspired history, telling us of the covenant relationship between God and his often wayward but redeemed people. It is poetry and

---

5. For a consideration of these themes from a nonevangelical perspective, see William Deresiewicz, *Excellent Sheep: The Miseducation of the American Elite and the Way to a Meaningful Life* (New York: Free Press, 2015). See also David Brooks, *The Road to Character* (New York: Random House, 2015). Neither book, as noted, takes the exact tack I do, but both books explore the lack of moral formation in promising American youth in our era. Despite many hand-wringing articles to the contrary, I do not think we can blame millennials for their lack of religious and moral makeup. They have received what they have been given (or not given, in this case). Christian institutions must step into this gap and provide the young what they are lacking. The church is one of the last public groups to see this problem and cannot fail to address it in days ahead.

6. There is overlap between the vision I am unfurling here and the political vision of Oliver O'Donovan, *The Desire of the Nations: Rediscovering the Roots of Political Theology* (Cambridge: Cambridge University Press, 1999).

song, putting the human experience and the things of God into verse. It is prophecy, telling what is to be and how God's people should engage their world. The Bible, composed of sixty-six books, ultimately gives us a multisensory framework for understanding God and the world he has made.[7]

Christians have historically synthesized the teachings of God's Word on certain crucial topics: God himself, creation, providence, sin, salvation, and so on. When we collate Scripture, bringing together select passages to shape our understandings of a given matter, we are doing the first-order work of theology. (So theologian John Frame has said that the work of theology is, in a word, "application."[8]) The apostles who wrote the New Testament understood the necessity of such work: "You are to proclaim things consistent with sound teaching," said the apostle Paul (Titus 2:1). To teach sound doctrine, we must pull together diverse passages from the whole Bible so we can know God's mind on a given matter. All this formation takes place with Jesus Christ as the apex of Scripture. He is the God-man given in the climax of human history as our cruciform Savior and resurrected Lord.[9]

In theological education we have the unspeakable joy of grounding students in this theistic worldview. Not that we ourselves speak perfectly as instructors, but our text is inerrant; it is the only such text of its kind. For some of our students, this is not a new endeavor. They have grown up in solid churches, and they have a basic knowledge of the core beliefs of biblical Christianity. But here we must take note of a common issue: not all churches that believe the Scripture know just how important doctrine is. It's too easy to take sound theology for granted.

Ours is an anti-intellectual age. But Christianity at its core is an elegantly intellectual faith. By this I do not mean that it reduces only to certain ideas. I mean instead that biblical doctrine makes sense of God, the

---

7. The Bible is, as Kevin Vanhoozer has rightly noted, not merely a record but a living "drama," one in which we are swept up and borne along; Vanhoozer, *The Drama of Doctrine: A Canonical Linguistic Approach to Christian Doctrine* (Louisville: Westminster John Knox, 2005).

8. John Frame, *The Doctrine of the Knowledge of God* (Phillipsburg, NJ: P&R, 1987), 81–85.

9. A rich biblical-theological resource that will give students a great sense of the whole narrative of Scripture is Thomas Schreiner, *The King in His Beauty: A Biblical Theology of the Old and New Testaments* (Grand Rapids: Baker, 2013); see also James M. Hamilton, *God's Glory in Salvation Through Judgment: A Biblical Theology* (Wheaton: Crossway, 2010); Geerhardus Vos, *Biblical Theology: Old and New Testaments* (Edinburgh: Banner of Truth, 2014); Stephen Dempster, *Dominion and Dynasty: A Theology of the Hebrew Bible*, New Studies in Biblical Theology (Downers Grove: InterVarsity Press, 2003); and Graeme Goldsworthy, *Christ-Centered Biblical Theology: Hermeneutical Foundations and Principles* (Downers Grove: InterVarsity Academic, 2012).

world he has made, and our human condition. Christianity has immense and often untapped explanatory power. Think about the following:

Christianity explains why everything exists. All of it is made for the glory of God, destined from the beginning to find its fulfillment in the kingship of Jesus Christ (Col 1:15–20). God is the purpose of this world; God is the One who made all things and rules all things. God is the central fact of existence, much as some might think or feel otherwise.

Christianity explains what we are here to do. The biblical doctrine of humanity teaches that every person is made in the image of God, possessing immense dignity and worth regardless of disability or disadvantaged background (Gen 1:26–27). We are made to rule the earth to the glory of God. We know that our bodies, furthermore, are not created for self-invention or sexual spelunking but for either holy matrimony or holy singleness. Too many people today think otherwise, and it ruins them and leaves them hollow.

Christianity explains why the world groans. The biblical doctrine of sin offers desperately needed clarity on why the unborn are destroyed, evil dictators oppress their people, friends slander one another in jealous fits, people desecrate their surroundings for no good reason, fathers ignore their children, and ten thousand other awful effects transferred to every person by Adam. Evil is personal, and evil is embedded in the air we breathe. It pollutes our world and damns each one of us. We were not made for sin; we were made for more.

Christianity explains how things can go right. In Jesus Christ we find hope. Jesus came to us as a King but not a self-serving king. He came to die on a Roman cross to pardon guilty sinners like us. He triumphed over death by his resurrection, and he showed the watching solar system that he was not only alive but reigning in his ascension to the right hand of the Father. Jesus is the source of grace and hope and eternal life. Jesus's zealous desire is to take ruined wrecks such as us and make us trophies of his grace. Christ's mission is primarily individual and ecclesial, as he saves sinners and creates local churches, but the effects of his kindness to this world spill out of the church into the surrounding culture.

Christianity explains where things are headed. Jesus is not here, but he is not far off. He will soon return and judge his enemies, with Satan, his chief foe, facing terrible destruction. Then Christ will rule the world in a kingdom of love. It may not feel at present as if things are heading to a good conclusion; we as believers might feel the exact opposite is true. But sure as the sun comes up in the morning, Jesus will return, and he will end the cruel reign of sin and death and usher in an eternal rest for the people of God.

We have more to say in teaching students doctrine than this but not less. As we see here, Christianity is not a fragmented system of thought rubber-banded together by a salvific prayer. Christianity is a way of comprehension. The faith is grounded in certain core truths. Doctrine is what shows us the world. Doctrine is what introduces us to God. Doctrine is what preserves us when times are chilling. Doctrine is what motivates us to keep working, keep plodding, and keep fighting for holiness one day at a time. We could say it this way: in learning doctrine, we use our ears, hearing from God in order to know the truth.[10]

As we see, theological education offers students the chance to know the world rightly. It puts all things into perspective. Through theological training, it provides answers to the toughest questions the human race faces. These are life-and-death matters. All around us competitors offer students a different understanding of this world. This is true in both religious and less formal senses. Even in a secularist era, there are still numerous religions that offer a different understanding of ultimate things from Christianity. Buddhism, Mormonism, Islam, Judaism, Catholicism—these and other major religions offer fundamentally different doctrine in key areas of the Scripture. The common portrait of such religions in the media is that these religious traditions have faded fast in the face of intellectual secularism. In truth, many belong to these groups, and many thus need to hear biblical truth and be saved through Christ and Christ alone. This is true of billions of people, representing a major missionary task for the global church.

Many people are either irreligious or vaguely spiritual in a blended sense. These individuals are growing in number in the West. Some profess to believe in nothing and no God; others pick and choose what they like

---

10. The best essay on the practicality of doctrine is J. Ligon Duncan III, "Sound Doctrine: Essential to Faithful Pastoral Ministry" in Mark Dever, J. Ligon Duncan III, R. Albert Mohler Jr., C. J. Mahaney, *Proclaiming a Cross-Centered Theology* (Wheaton: Crossway, 2009). A longer resource with a similar perspective is John Piper, *Desiring God: Meditations of a Christian Hedonist* (Portland: Multnomah, 2011). To connect this perspective with the academy, see David S. Dockery, *Renewing Minds: Serving Church and Society Through Christian Higher Education* (Nashville: B&H Academic, 2008).

from a smorgasbord of philosophies and belief systems. A growing number of people, particularly those who grew up in a mainline tradition and have since left it, help themselves to a buffet of belief: some self-help thinking, some prosperity gospel, some Eastern mysticism for morning yoga, a bit of "do what you would have others do to you" out of nostalgia for their childhood Sunday school experience, and a healthy dose of postmodern skepticism so they don't feel hemmed in.[11]

Theological education exists in large part to equip students to reject both formal religion that is not Christ centered and informal spirituality (or atheism) that is self-made. But this is not enough: we wish for students to consider the riches of Christian theology, and we seek to persuade and lovingly compel them to count the cost and then take up their crosses in following Christ as their only Savior and Lord. Our task has two major components in terms of doctrine: first, we must show how every system of doctrine or religious belief falls short; second, we must show the glory and beauty of evangelical doctrine, seeking to win students to Christ who is himself the way, the truth, and the life.

Some are tempted in our age to feel we should soften our truth claims. It may seem odd to teach students a body of truth in a culture that trades so heavily in feelings and skepticism. As noted above, for their part, a good number of our students may have been trained to distrust religious instruction. They may conceive of the Christian faith as either a loose assemblage of spiritual feelings or a call to practical kindness. The challenge of theological education is to show that the faith is at its core about a person, Jesus Christ, who rules the cosmos and offers fallen humanity salvation in him. This Christ-centered faith is not subrational but fully rational, and even suprarational, for the converting and sanctifying Christ floods our capacities with truth, beauty, and goodness.

Teaching Christian doctrine is thus often an exercise in category creation. Yes, the truths we teach overlap in substantial part with reason and logic. Christianity is the most sensible faith there is. But we must also know that in teaching students Christian truth, we are forming new understanding in them, and seeing them transformed by this understanding

---

11. The Catholic writer Joseph Bottum has written discerningly of this kind of mentality. See Bottum, *An Anxious Age: The Post-Protestant Ethic and the Spirit of America* (Colorado Springs: Image, 2013).

(Rom 12:1–2). Many students will be exploring the intellectual dimension of the Christian faith in our classrooms and chapel settings for the first time. They may not, for example, have a full-blown doctrine of God. We educators have the joyful privilege of introducing them to the cognitive infrastructure of the Christian faith—the one God we worship who is three persons, equal and undivided, perfect unity in perfect diversity. There is no existing framework for this glorious piece of doctrine; in teaching it we create a new category, one that God desires to fill to the brim with worship and adoration. As the great Puritan theologian William Perkins said, theology is nothing other than "the science of living blessedly forever."[12] This, and no other, is what doctrine is for—joyful, persevering, fruitful faith.

We Teach Students the Christian Worldview

He was living the young man's dream. Wealthy, connected to the high and mighty, with the whole earth lying at his feet. He could have been anything. As he made his way through young adulthood, he did what members of his social class excelled at. He went to parties, made small talk, and enjoyed lavish vacations. In sum, he was living the dream so many people in history have coveted. He had money, so he did not want for anything. He was good-looking and socially connected. He was on track to take his place among the powerful. What more could he want?

Why, then, did William Wilberforce find himself discontented? It was because of his conscience. Specifically, it was because of the British slave trade. As Wilberforce learned more about this industry of human trafficking, built on the back of greed and fueled by a culture of wickedness, he lost his taste for the things that sparkle. He yearned to invest himself in a meaningful cause. He wanted to do what he could to end the practice of buying, selling, and enslaving his fellow human beings.

Wilberforce's life was turned upside down not because of a moment of moral awakening. It altogether changed because he learned to view the world through a biblical perspective. Through the preaching of faithful pastors and hours spent reading Christian literature, Wilberforce gained what we call a Christian worldview. He came to see every facet of his life

---

12. William Perkins, *The Workers of That Famous and Worthy Minister of Christ in the University of Cambridge* (London: John Legatt, 1612), 1.11.

through the filter of biblical Christianity. He discovered that the Scripture shaped every moment of his existence, not simply his Sunday-morning priorities. Because of this God-given discovery, Wilberforce became the British figure most responsible for the abolition of the slave trade, a quest he successfully championed as a long-term member of parliament. It took blood, sweat, and tears to achieve this goal, but Wilberforce persevered to the end.[13]

William Wilberforce was not exceptional in discovering that Christianity explains and impacts all of life. Any and every believer in the Lord Jesus Christ is offered this vision. Christian doctrine is the truth stated. The Christian worldview is truth applied. In theological education we have the opportunity of helping students, first, to know the truth and then to apply it. Doctrine relates to the core truths of our world; worldview allows us to figure out what doctrine would have us do during our earthly sojourn. Every student can learn biblical truth, and every student can develop and apply a Christian worldview to every area of life.

Doctrine speaks to the core realities of our world—God, man, the church, Jesus Christ, and so on. We use our ears to know doctrine in the sense that we hear from God's Word on core theological matters. Worldview speaks to the core engagements of our lives: work, the public square, money, the family, the dignity of every person, and more. If doctrine involves our ears, then worldview involves our eyes. In building a Christian worldview from Scripture for our students' perusal, we are helping them see the world rightly.

In terms similar to our discussion on doctrinal instruction, many students will arrive on our campuses without knowing a great deal about the Christian worldview. They will have a healthy appreciation for Christianity, and they will know the rudiments of the faith. They should pray to God. They need fellowship with his people. They should read the Bible. They should tell people about Jesus. But they will not necessarily know that all of life, not just their private prayer moments, has been claimed by Jesus. They will know that Christ is their Savior, but they will not necessarily know that he is Lord and that his lordship extends over

---

13. See Eric Metaxas, *Amazing Grace: William Wilberforce and the Heroic Campaign to End Slavery* (New York: HarperCollins, 2007). For a similarly inspiring story of personal transformation and cultural impact, see Owen Strachan, *The Colson Way: Loving Your Neighbor and Living with Faith in a Hostile World* (Nashville: Thomas Nelson, 2015).

every second of the day. As the great apologist Francis Schaeffer once said, "Christianity is not just involved with 'salvation,' but with the total man in the total world."[14]

Christian worldview thinking seeks to bulldoze a privatized faith. Through theological education wise instructors and guides befriend students and help them see the superiority of Christianity in all facets of life. In classes and other venues, mature believers can help students understand that Jesus is not a living fire-insurance policy. He is a Master, a Sovereign, a King. By the grace of Christ, students can live like him and give their heart, soul, mind, and strength to God. This fulfills the first and greatest commandment (Matt 22:34–36). This is the Bible's understanding of a follower of Jesus—someone who lives heart and soul for the glory of God. No one is perfect, but the Scripture never calls us to a kind of middle position where we halfheartedly obey God but derive great joy from evil. There are only two roads, after all. A wholehearted Christian views all of life from the perspective that God owns it all.[15] This means doctrine-loving and truth-believing Christians think and act differently from non-Christians. Theological educators model this truth, but they also teach it in areas that include those listed below.

Work

The world sees work as a bore, or a tool, or a fountain of purpose, or a pain. Christians know that work is subject to the Adamic curse (see Gen 3:16–19) but that God made work for his glory and our good (Genesis 2). Work is part of what gives life form and shape, for it allows us to take dominion of the world around us (Gen 1:26–28). We find purpose for our daily lives to a considerable degree in the labor God sets before us to do. Yet we also know that we can idolize work and treat it as a god that gives us significance. Christians seek to see their daily labors in terms of a calling, or vocation, such that the enterprise of every believer has value.

---

14. Francis Schaeffer, *Art and the Bible*, IVP Classics (Downers Grove: InterVarsity Press, 2006, 1973), 89.

15. For resources on worldview thinking, see Abraham Kuyper, *Lectures on Calvinism* (Peabody, MA: Hendrickson Publishers, 2008); Francis Schaeffer, *The Francis A. Schaeffer Trilogy: The Three Essential Books in One Volume* (Wheaton: Crossway, 1990); and Nancy Pearcey, *Total Truth: Liberating Christianity from its Cultural Captivity* (Wheaton: Crossway, 2008).

Family

The world sees the family as well and good but struggles to know what the family is intended to be and how to help it thrive. In 2017 we think we can remake the family and structure it however we see fit. Christians know that the family is the first institution, made by God for the happiness and stability of all members. Marriage is the lifelong union of a man and a woman who devote themselves to raising and nurturing children. The family must be guarded and protected, for no other natural institution is so fragile yet so involved in human flourishing.

Gender

The world sees gender as flexible and malleable. Christians know that men and women are distinct though equally invested with full dignity and worth. Men and women glorify God by honoring God's design in the home and church (Genesis 2; Ephesians 5; Titus 2; 1 Timothy 2). Sex has a shape and design and is the exclusive possession of marriage. All sexual activity or identity outside of marriage fails to honor God. We do not choose our own gender identity, despite what we may feel, but rather embrace our God-given sex, seeing it as a major part of our own efforts to honor our Maker.

Public Square

Too often the public square in our time is a place of division and bullying. Christians see the public square as a place they must enter in order to be a witness unto life and unto Christ. Becoming a Christian and growing in one's walk does not mean checking out of our world. It means killing sin, but it also means plunging into meaningful involvement in our spheres, whether this means we interact with politics, culture, public policy, our communities, or other areas of life.

Ethnicity

Our world is full of racial strife. Racism is a major problem, and its fundamental catalyst is the inability to see people who appear different from us as a blessing. Christians working off of Scripture are not threatened by those of other ethnicities. We don't wish that diverse peoples would go away. We believe that the end of history is the ingathering of peoples from every tribe and tongue (Revelation 21). Thankfully, this new creation has already begun, as the local church draws born-again believers who have nothing in common in many cases except Jesus. In a hostile world, evangelicals seek to show onlookers that the church is a united kingdom.

We could continue fleshing out what the Christian worldview is, but this sampling suffices to show that the Scripture helps us know how to see the world and our role in it. Of course, there is room for some differences in precisely how Christians understand these different sectors of life. The point for us to consider is this: Christian theological education can help students develop a richly biblical and theological perspective on all of life. In classes, cafeteria conversations, devotional times, and much more, institutions can free students to comprehend the greatness of God in all things and the relevance of Scripture for all of life.

A Christian worldview is not a burden; it is a blessing, a summons to behold the beauty of our great God and to understand his world aright.

We Teach Students to Engage the Culture

When we form in students a Christian worldview, we ready them for on-the-ground engagement. This is the third component of our study. Here we briefly cover how we may get involved in our fallen world, our hands taking on tasks so that we can be witnesses of grace to the glory of God.

Theological education is a lovely term, but we must take care in using it. We believe fully in the value of thinking in its own right. We know that intellection is itself a direct reflection of the action and character of Almighty God. God is pure intelligence, pure wisdom, truth itself. The Trinity is a fellowship of love, but it is also a fellowship of contemplation as the three persons of the Godhead share the joyous ability to commune deeply with one another and understand things rightly.

For Christians, thinking is thus an irreducible good. It needs no justification; it is an end unto itself. We teach students to love God with their minds per the first and greatest commandment. We seek to win them to a life of pondering, of musing, of turning things over in their minds. We unleash them to think and to think well. This is the core of theological education. We declare boldly to the church and the world that we love truth, that it is unspeakably precious to us, and that our campuses afford students the sterling chance to come and be shaped by truth.[16]

The challenge, however, is to avoid making the faith only an intellectual reality. *Theological education* could convey to students that all our institutions are interested in is some classroom debate and a few term papers. In reality, in concert with the local church, we want to release students to be agents of gospel grace all over the world in ten thousand places. Education is good in itself; but it is intended to catalyze students to be spiritual influences in the name of Christ wherever they go. The biblical passage that most calls the church into the world to engage all aspects of a fallen order is Matthew 5:13–16. Here Christ tells his disciples they are both "salt" and "light":

> You are the salt of the earth. But if the salt should lost its taste, how can it be made salty? It's no longer good for anything but to be thrown out and trampled under people's feet.
> You are the light of the world. A city situated on a hill cannot be hidden. No one lights a lamp and puts it under a basket, but rather on a lampstand, and it gives light for all who are in the house. In the same way, let your light shine before others, so that they may see your good works and give glory to your Father in heaven.

The two concepts here speak to the Christian task of cultural engagement. First, the church seeks to be *salt*, meaning a preservative force in its community, its nation. Salt flavors and preserves meat, keeping it from decay. So, as Jesus teaches, Christians should act. We should seek to preserve goodness, truth, and beauty in our environments. We cannot singlehandedly keep the world from going secular, of course; all things are already under the curse of Adam per Genesis 3. Only Jesus can overturn and destroy the curse; the church does not have this mission. We do, however, seek to preserve the order and health we find in our fallen surroundings.

Second, the church seeks to be an illuminating force in its community. We are *light*, signifying that we go into troubled places and lead people by the grace of God out of darkness. Light in Christ's thinking is not a

---

16. For more on this perspective, including a historical take on the modern church's journey back to an intellectual faith, see Owen Strachan, *Awakening the Evangelical Mind: An Intellectual History of Neo-Evangelicalism* (Grand Rapids: Zondervan, 2015).

nighttime device to give a soft, soothing glow; light is designed for "a stand," the entire house. God wants light to flood the world, to "shine before others," to display the transformative effects of saving faith in Christ. Light is intended to be seen; Jesus wants unrepentant sinners to gaze on the "good works" of the church and turn to God the Father from a penitent heart.

These words enfranchise what we call "cultural engagement." The church has historically understood that Jesus is commissioning it to be a force for good in the world by this charter. This means believers do not have the option of heading for the hills when things get tough for us. We do not pull away from a lost world but plunge into it. We wish to be voices for life, means of mercy, witnesses of conscience, a movement of change, and a kingdom of righteousness. This identity manifests first as members of local churches, because the church together exists as a counterculture representing biblical truth, and second as individual Christians work and labor in many different ways to preserve and promote virtue.[17]

Theological education offers up a sumptuous banquet of doctrine and worldview training in order to equip students for full-throated Christian witness in a dying, decaying world. The university, college, or seminary is rightly a kind of retreat, a place where students can tuck away and contemplate ultimate reality and the great questions of life. How glorious this is! But even as students learn to think, institutions are helping them learn to act. Our faith is not a quietist faith. Jesus was crucified publicly, on a Roman cross. His death testified to the principalities and powers that he was gladly if painfully bearing the weight of sin on his shoulders to free the guilty (Romans 4–5). His resurrection was a public resurrection, attested by many witnesses, and his followers who rose with him to life were commissioned to offer public testimony to his saving nature (Matt 28:16–20; Acts 1:9).

The church is a public church. We do not hide out from the world. We engage our surroundings. Accordingly, as theological educators we train students to think thoughtfully through secular reporting; to question the assumptions of atheist doctrinaires respectfully; to craft public policy for our communities, states, and even nation that is borne of the truth; to oppose unbiblical trends; to create beautiful art testifying to the existence

---

17. A classic work on cultural engagement is Chuck Colson and Nancy Pearcey, *How Now Shall We Live?* (Carol Stream, IL: Tyndale House, 2004, 1999). For a different take that is also profitable, see James Davison Hunter, *To Change the World: The Irony, Tragedy, and Possibility of Christianity in the Late Modern World* (Oxford: Oxford University Press, 2010).

and greatness of God; and much else besides. Done rightly, theological education never boxes students in. It frees them to take intellectual and cultural dominion of their world. It helps them see that their faith is a public faith, and this faith is not shy or bashful but desirous of as much influence and virtue creation as is humanly—divinely—possible.[18]

Conclusion

We began by discussing Balder the beautiful and the experience of "pure Northern-ness" that C. S. Lewis had as a boy. Lewis brushed up against transcendence as he studied the great epics of the world. He had little idea what he was discovering then but later learned that his heart was stirring to find the deepest meaning—the greatest Person—in all the cosmos. As theological educators, we have the joyful privilege of seeking to lead student after student to this same epiphany. We do so by teaching students doctrine, so they hear the grand truths of God; by teaching them a Christian worldview, so they learn to see all of life as the Lord's; and by training them to engage the culture, so they move into the world and by the work of their hands preserve and promote virtue and flourishing of a distinctly theocentric kind.

The church may be used to a more chastened task and identity. But in the age of ascendant secularism, we must recognize that the time for small plans and harmless hopes is over. We must not accept the muzzling of our mission. We must plunge back into our work, seeking with the full force of heart, soul, mind, and strength to love God by knowing God and teaching students to do the same.

"Balder the beautiful is dead," as the old poem says. But as Lewis discovered, and as many of our students will soon learn, Jesus the Christ is alive.

Questions for Further Reflection

1. What attitude do you observe that students in your environment have toward biblical doctrine? Do they see it as helpful or as a hindrance to vibrant Christian faith?

---

18. See Carl F. H. Henry, *The Uneasy Conscience of Modern Fundamentalism* (Grand Rapids: Eerdmans, 2003).

2. What can your institution, organization, or church do to stimulate love for the sound theology this chapter praises?
3. How can Christians encourage those undertaking theological education to see all of life through a Christian worldview and not merely the couple of hours on Sunday they spend in church?
4. What shape does faithful Christian cultural engagement take in a culture that views even acts of Christian charity as laced with hostility? How can we be both loving and truthful?
5. Through love of doctrine, worldview, and a salt-and-light status in the world, what role can Christians play in culture and society, particularly during an era that sees us as behind the times?

Sources for Further Study

Dockery, David S. *Renewing Minds: Serving Church and Society Through Christian Higher Education.* Nashville: B&H Academic, 2012.

Hall, Matthew J., and Owen Strachan. *Essential Evangelicalism: The Enduring Influence of Carl F. H. Henry.* Wheaton: Crossway, 2015.

Henry, Carl F. H. *The Uneasy Conscience of Modern Fundamentalism.* Grand Rapids: Eerdmans, 2003.

Kuyper, Abraham. *Lectures on Calvinism: The Stone Lectures of 1898.* Peabody, MA: Hendrickson, 2008.

Marsden, George M. *The Soul of the American University: From Protestant Establishment to Established Nonbelief.* New York: Oxford University Press, 1996.

Metaxas, Eric. *Bonhoeffer: Pastor, Martyr, Prophet, Spy.* Nashville: Thomas Nelson, 2012.

Mouw, Richard. *He Shines in All That's Fair: Culture and Common Grace.* Grand Rapids: Eerdmans, 2001.

Schaeffer, Francis. *He Is There and He Is Not Silent.* Wheaton: Tyndale House, 1972.

Sproul, R. C. *Everyone's a Theologian: An Introduction to Systematic Theology.* Sanford, FL: Reformation Trust, 2014.

Strachan, Owen. *Awakening the Evangelical Mind: An Intellectual History of Neo-Evangelicalism.* Grand Rapids: Zondervan, 2015.

Chapter Twenty

THEOLOGY FOR CHURCH, WORSHIP, AND MINISTRY

DANIEL L. AKIN

God ordained the church and commissioned her to "go, therefore, and make disciples of all nations, baptizing them in the name of the Father and of the Son and of the Holy Spirit, teaching them to observe all that I have commanded you" (Matt 28:19–20).[1] God did not ordain or give this assignment to institutions of theological education. Such institutions are servants to the churches. To the extent that they fulfill that assignment of providing a well-trained and equipped minister, they justify their existence. To the extent that they do not, they forfeit their right to exist. Seminaries, divinity schools, or any other theological education entity that does not serve well the church of the Lord Jesus Christ should rightly go the way of the dinosaur and the dodo bird into extinction. Daniel Aleshire is correct when he notes, "The church could live without the seminary, but the seminary could not live without the church. . . . That is true, both at a very functional level (where students come from and graduates go) and at a theological level (the nature of Christian community and how the work of the Gospel is accomplished)."[2]

However, as someone who has been involved in theological education full-time since 1988, I am convinced that theological schools can be

---

1. Unless otherwise indicated, all Scripture quotations are from the *English Standard Version*.
2. Daniel L. Aleshire, "Why We Need Seminary: How Christian Leaders—and the People They Serve—Benefit from Graduate Theological Education. Interview with Daniel L. Aleshire," Seminary Grad School, 2013, accessed January17, 2017, http://www.seminarygradschool.com/article/Why-We-Need-Seminary.

effective and helpful servants to the churches they serve. Churches need well-trained and educated ministers who will shepherd them (1 Pet 5:1–4). The fact is, seminaries can do certain things more easily and efficiently than even the finest and largest local congregations. When they do their jobs well, theological schools provide an incredibly valuable service.

Now we need to be crystal clear about several issues before moving ahead and making the argument for the value of schools of theological education. First, seminaries and the like cannot be located in the Bible. They are not there in any form or fashion. Second, not every minister has access to or resources for pursuing a theological education. As costs continue to rise, this will become an even greater challenge. Third, it is a joy to acknowledge that untold numbers of faithful gospel ministers around the globe have not received a formal theological education. These are heroes of the faith who have the smile of King Jesus upon them. Having said this, and attempting to weigh all matters carefully and honestly, I am convinced that a robust, orthodox, evangelical seminary can provide a broader, deeper, healthier, and longer-lasting minister for the churches that have every right to expect such a product for their investment in these institutions.

I would like to set forth fifteen axioms for faithful and effective theological schools that will inspire churches to (1) send students, (2) hire graduates, (3) provide financial support, and (4) fervently pray for the school's continued success until the Lord Jesus returns for his bride. This list of axioms is not intended to be exhaustive. Rather, it is intended to set forth the minimal expectations any congregation should have for the minister hired from our schools. What should schools—who do theology for the sake of the church—produce for the local congregations that look to them for effective and trustworthy ministers? Through these axioms I hope to address issues of theological competence, theological curriculum, theological education, and theological formation—issues that will impact the health and life of communities of faith through the ministers they call and receive.

Axiom 1: Theological Schools Can and Should Produce Ministers Who Are Pastor-Theologians

The job description for those who shepherd the local church is found in Acts 20:28–38; 1 Tim 3:1–7; Titus 1:5–9; and 1 Pet 5:1–4. Eph 4:11 refers to the office of those who meet these qualifications as "pastors and teachers" (CSB) or "shepherds and teachers" (ESV). Understanding the office as pastor-theologian would honor the intent of the title.

Every pastor is called to be a teacher, and thus a theologian. The health and protection of the church depends on elders (*presbuteros*) or overseers (*episkopos*) faithfully serving as capable, mature pastor-theologians.[3] This assignment cannot be handed off to a divinity school or seminary. Those on the front lines of ministry must be equipped for this critical assignment.

We would be historically negligent if we were to forget that until recently, our greatest theologians were also pastors. Just consider the following: Athanasius, Irenaeus, Augustine, Calvin, Luther, and Edwards. How often do we cite Spurgeon, not only as a model pastor, but also as a fine theologian? R. Albert Mohler Jr. is right: "The pastoral calling is inherently theological. Given the fact that the pastor is to be the teacher of the Word of God and the teacher of the Gospel, it cannot be otherwise. The idea of the pastorate as a nontheological office is inconceivable in light of the New Testament."[4]

The Pastoral Epistles make this high calling of pastor irrefutable (see especially 1 Tim 3:2; 2 Tim 4:2–5; Titus 1:9). A pastor must teach his people to think well in biblical and theological categories. This is absolutely essential for faithful discipleship and for obedience to "observe all that [the Lord has] commanded" (Matt 28:20). Faithful pastors will recognize that sometimes the difference between heresy (false teaching) and orthodoxy (faithful teaching) can turn on a single sentence, a single word, or even a single syllable. If you doubt this, consider Athanasius and the Church Council at Nicaea in AD 325, where a single syllable was all the difference between a Christ who *was* God and a Christ who *was like* God. Pastor-theologians know that theology matters and that it is their responsibility to teach their people to think well theologically. Faithful seminaries are well equipped to provide this important service.

---

3. Pastor, elder, and overseer (bishop) are interchangeable terms that speak of the same office. New Testament churches had two offices: elders and deacons.

4. R. Albert Mohler, "The Pastor as Theologian, Part One," AlbertMohler.com, April 17, 2006, accessed January 18, 2017, http://www.albertmohler.com/2006/04/17/the-pastor-as-theologian-part-one/.

Axiom 2: *Theological Schools Can and Should Produce Ministers Who Are Missionary-Evangelists*

The church is ground zero for fulfilling the Great Commission. It is the training base for spiritual SEALS who will go into enemy territory with the sword of the Spirit and the gospel of Jesus Christ, which the enemy of souls cannot hold back (Matt 16:18). Pastors train these soldiers of the cross both by equipping them and modeling for them the work of evangelism and missions. Paul admonished Timothy to "do the work of an evangelist" (2 Tim 4:5). Jesus gave his final commission to the whole church (Matt 28:18–20; Luke 24:44–49; Acts 1:8). Those called to lead our churches would certainly be included in his command. The calling of pastor-theologian and missionary-evangelist are complementary. They naturally go together. We should continually remind ourselves that the greatest theologian who ever lived was also the greatest missionary who ever lived. His name was Jesus. And the greatest Christian missionary who ever lived was also the greatest Christian theologian who ever lived. His name was Paul. Faithful theological schools can impress this fourfold assignment biblically, theologically, historically, and practically on their students. And it can and should be woven into the fabric and culture of each institution.

A healthy balance will result from the wedding of this fourfold calling. R. B. Kuiper points out,

> A noteworthy feature of the Great Commission is that it bids the apostles and the church of all ages to teach. In fact, teaching is spoken of as their chief missionary task. They are to go in order to teach. Going is but a means to the end of teaching. And they are to baptize those who accept their teaching. But they must teach, whether or not men give heed. And, significantly, they are told not once, but twice, to teach.[5]

Following the zeal of missionary Jim Elliot, believers need to be infatuated with the kingdom. That infatuation must start at the top. Churches will rise no higher in evangelistic and missionary passion than what they see in

---

5. Rienk Bouke Kuiper, *The Glorious Body of Christ* (Grand Rapids: Eerdmans, 1958), 245.

their leaders. If we are well trained to set the pace, in time, they will follow. If we raise the bar and reach for it ourselves, they will work to reach it too.

Axiom 3: Theological Schools Can and Should Produce Ministers Who Think in Christian Worldview Categories

C. S. Lewis has well said, "God is no fonder of intellectual slackers than any other slackers. If you are thinking of becoming a Christian, I warn you, you are embarking on something, which is going to take the whole of you, brains and all. But fortunately, it works the other way round. Anyone who is honestly trying to be a Christian will soon find his intelligence being sharpened: one of the reasons why it needs no special education to be a Christian is that Christianity is an education itself."[6] Christianity is indeed an education itself. It is an immersion into a particular worldview, which I define as a "comprehensive and coherent view of life through which we think, understand and judge, and which determines our approach to life and meaning."[7] Seminaries teach biblical studies, theology, history, and pastoral ministries. They also, or at least they should, teach apologetics, discipleship, ethics, and philosophy. These latter disciplines are essential to the healthy cultivation of a biblical worldview.

Seminaries can train pastors to well equip the congregations they shepherd and protect. As a starting point, but certainly not the place to stop, faithful seminaries can help pour a foundation of bedrock essentials that are nonnegotiable for authentic Christian confession and conduct.[8]

---

6. C. S. Lewis, *Mere Christianity* (New York: Macmillan, 1984), 75.

7. Other worldview definitions are worth noting. Russ Bush (former dean, Southeastern Baptist Theological Seminary) defined *worldview* as "that basic set of assumptions that gives meaning to one's thoughts. A worldview is the set of assumptions that someone has about the way things are, about what things are, about why things are." James W. Sire said *worldview* is "a set of presuppositions (assumptions which may be true, partially true or entirely false) which we hold (consciously or subconsciously, consistently or inconsistently) about the basic make-up of our world" (James W. Sire, *The Universe Next Door: A Basic Worldview Catalogue*, exp. ed. [Downers Grove: InterVarsity, 1988], 17). And James H. Olthius suggested that "one's Worldview is perhaps best reflected by one's answers to the 'ultimate questions of life': Who am I? Why am I here? Where am I going? What's it all about? Is there a god? How can I live and die happily? What are good and evil?" (James H. Olthius, "On Worldviews," *Christian Scholar's Review* 15, no. 2 [1985]: 153–64).

8. For a list of essential beliefs, see Danny Akin, "Foundational Beliefs of a Christian Worldview" at http://www.danielakin.com/wp-content/uploads/old/Resource_479/Foundational%20Beliefs%20of%20a%20Christian%20Worldview%20(Handout-Answers).pdf, accessed January 18, 2017.

Axiom 4: Theological Schools Can and Should Produce Ministers Who Have Been Mentored on Some Level in a Partnership Between the School and the Local Church

Several years ago D. A. Carson was asked to respond to the question, what one thing would you change about seminary? He concluded his answer by suggesting a closer relationship between the churches and the seminaries in training ministers. He said, "[We need] close integration with an expanding apprenticeship program in our best churches, led by pastors who believe in theological education but who will also train our MDiv. graduates in relationships, spirituality, consistency, hands-on ministry, street smarts." He called such a vision "utopian."[9]

I believe what Carson calls utopian should be a reality in all seminaries. Seminaries are often criticized for what they do not provide in a theological education. Some of those criticisms are, no doubt, legitimate and deserved. Some, however, are not. The fact is, seminaries are not equipped or set up to do everything a minister in training needs. Some things can only be learned in the refining fires of a local church and life-on-life ministry. The things Carson alludes to—relationships, spirituality, consistency, hands-on ministry, street smarts—are best taught and learned in the laboratory of a faith community where a young pastor-theologian is weekly (or even daily) rubbing shoulders with real people in the real world under the guidance of a seasoned minister. A cloistered seminary is a useless seminary that will produce ineffective, yea defective, ministers. Local churches can be served well by faithful, orthodox schools of ministry training. Seminaries, I know, can be served well by local churches as they work together to produce competent ministers. We should not settle for anything less than Carson's utopia. The fact is, we cannot if we want to raise up a generation of pastors who are well prepared for the challenges of twenty-first-century ministry.

---

9. Collin Hansen, "TGC Asks: What One Thing Would You Change About Seminary?" *Gospel Coalition*, August 13, 2010, accessed January 18, 2017, https://www.thegospelcoalition.org/article/tgc-asks-what-one-thing-you-would-change-about-seminary-education.

Axiom 5: Theological Schools Can and Should Produce Ministers Who Have Been Trained in Proper Hermeneutics, the Biblical Languages, Theology, Church History, Leadership, Missions, Evangelism, Discipleship, and Preaching

David Dockery well notes, "All Christians need to grow and mature in thinking deeply about the things of God."[10] This is true for all Christians, and especially for those training for vocational ministry. Seminaries are uniquely designed and structured, as noted earlier, to train ministers who can help their people think well in biblical and theological categories. Such ministers should master (there is a good reason we call our bread-and-butter degree the "master of divinity") a body of knowledge that is both broad and deep. It should be biblical, theological, and practical. It should also have an awareness of our past, our present, and prospects for our future in light of biblical revelation.

In an article entitled, "Welcome to Seminary—Now What? How to Be Faithful as a Seminary Student," Albert Mohler provides a number of suggestions that help the aspiring pastor to navigate his seminary days without drowning in the high water of a theological education. A theological education is designed and intended to produce pastors not eggheads, ministers not ivory tower elites who have lost connection with their callings and become disconnected from the churches they were supposed to be trained to serve. Mohler notes, "Theological education is a stewardship—a very rare stewardship." He then lists five wise encouragers seminary students need as close companions for the journey that is before them. (1) Do not consider your years at seminary as a prelude to ministry—this is ministry. Just as the preacher's time in the study each week is ministry, so is your theological education. You will misunderstand your seminary experience if you see it as an interruption in ministry, or even as a delay. (2) Do not believe you will be more faithful in ministry in the future than you are now. Just as your ministry is now, so is the call to faithfulness. The habits and practices you establish now will foretell the habits and practices of your future ministry. (3) Do not believe you will love the church more in the future than you do now. Love the church. Be infatuated with the bride of Christ. Join a local

---

10. David S. Dockery, "Introduction—Faith and Learning: Foundational Commitments," in *Faith and Learning: A Handbook for Christian Higher Education*, ed. David S. Dockery (Nashville: B&H Academic, 2012), 10.

congregation as soon as possible, and get deeply invested in ministry. (4) Do not believe you will be more evangelistic in the future than you are now. Share the gospel with eagerness. Talk to your neighbors about Christ. Invite non-Christians to dinner in your home. Develop a heart for the nations. Pray for an unreached people group every day. (5) Finally, be morally strong and stay humble. Knowledge does tend to puff us up, so give yourself the ministry of deflation.[11]

Axiom 6: Theological Schools Can and Should Produce Ministers Who Are Passionately Committed to Obeying the Great Commission

Last words are meant to be lasting words—words that last, words that make an impact. Jesus could have addressed a number of important tasks as he prepared to ascend back to heaven (Luke 24; Acts 1), but he chose to address the Great Commission. The church exists to fulfill the Great Commission.

The Great Commission's best known statement is located in Matt 28:18–20. We find the Lukan version in both Luke 24:46–48 and Acts 1:8. The longer ending to Mark contains it (16:15), and there is a brief Johannine statement in John 20:21. In Matthew we are commanded by our Lord to make disciples of all the nations, every *ethne*, teaching them "to obey everything [he has] commanded." In the process, he promises us his presence "always, to the end of the age."

Theological schools must take the final marching orders of our Commander in chief with grave seriousness. We must train ministers who understand that our divine assignment is not to make converts but to make disciples. A vital and essential component of disciple making is plainly stated in Matt 28:20: "Teaching them to observe all that [Christ has] commanded." Now, if ever there was a daunting task for pastors, there it is. If this is an essential part of the minister's task, seminaries must make it an essential component of their training. Faithful seminaries will have as their moniker, "Every classroom a Great Commission classroom. Every professor a Great Commission teacher. Every student a Great Commission

---

11. R. Albert Mohler, "Welcome to Seminary—Now What? How to Be Faithful as a Seminary Student – AlbertMohler.com," AlbertMohler.com, January 17, 2014, accessed January 18, 2017, http://www.albertmohler.com/2014/01/17/welcome-to-seminary-now-what-how-to-be-faithful-as-a-seminary-student.

student. Every graduate a Great Commission graduate who will go out and build and lead Great Commission churches."

The local church is the missional training center and launching pad for getting the gospel to the nations. Mission agencies and seminaries are servants to the churches that send. They don't send. Churches send. However, no church will be more committed to, and passionate for, the Great Commission than its leaders, whom the theological schools have the privilege of helping train. What the pastors believe is important, the church will believe is important. It is that clear. It is that simple.

Axiom 7: *Theological Schools Can and Should Produce Ministers Who Are Convictional in Terms of Theological Integrity*

Theologians too often are masters of what I call "theological gymnastics." If I were to use more harsh terms, I would say they are slick at "playing word games." Harsher still, I would call them out for being guilty of "doublespeak."[12] To say it plainly, they use an orthodox vocabulary but a neoorthodox or liberal dictionary. To quote a self-professed theological moderate, "These are seminary professors who [try to] please everyone and maintain support from all by using doublespeak. They [are] critical scholars who [speak] clearly within a critical tradition when they [are] with other scholars, but in church and convention settings they [sound as] if they [agree] with the least-educated persons present."[13] There is, of course, a tragic trickle-down effect to this. Seminary graduates, who look up to and admire the teachers who taught them, take this theological duplicity into the churches with devastating consequences. The minister no longer believes he has a clear and certain Word from God.[14] Over time Christians' confidence in the Bible erodes and finally vanishes. Vibrant churches become sick and weak. Many eventually die.

Theological schools with orthodox, evangelical convictions must and should be different. They should be clear in their confessional identities and convictions. They should operate in good faith with the churches they serve. Theological equivocation is not an option. It should never be allowed

---

12. See Ralph H. Elliott, *The Genesis Controversy* (Macon: Mercer Press, 1992). Elliott claims his refusal to play the game of doublespeak and his conviction to share honestly his critical views of Scripture got him fired. Evidence would support his claim.
13. Ibid. This quote is by Morris Ashcroft in the foreword (xv).
14. See Fred B. Craddock, *As One Without Authority*, 4th ed. (St. Louis: Chalice Press, 2001).

on the ecclesial playing field. Those who teach in our schools of ministry preparation should without mental reservation or hesitation teach in accordance with and not contrary to the truth of the Bible and the confessional documents that guide the institution. Those who disagree with our doctrinal convictions are free to teach elsewhere where their theological perspectives are welcomed. This is simply a matter of personal integrity. We should expect nothing less from those who teach and train in our schools. James P. Boyce said it well in his inaugural address at Furman University in 1856: "You will infringe the right of no man, and you will secure the rights of those who have established here an instrumentality for the production of a sound ministry. It is no hardship to those who teach here, to be called upon to sign the declaration of their principles, for there are fields of usefulness open elsewhere to every man, and none need accept your call who cannot conscientiously sign your formulary."[15]

Axiom 8: Theological Schools Can and Should Produce Ministers Who Are Committed to and Exhibit the Highest Ethical and Moral Standards as Revealed in Scripture

Throughout my life as a teacher in a theological context, I have repeatedly heard, "It is not fair that ministers live in a glass house." My response to those complaints is always the same: "It may not be fair, but it is reality." People will watch you more closely, hold you to a higher standard, and criticize you more quickly. Charles Spurgeon understood this to be true in actuality for all Christians and addressed it with his typical eloquence:

> The man who makes a profession of religion . . . will be watched by all the world's eyes, and not by very friendly critics, either. . . . We practice no spy system among the members of our church and yet somehow or other . . . it very rarely happens that a gross act of inconsistency is long concealed. Birds of the air tell the matter. The eagle-eyed world acts as policeman for the church and with no good intent becomes a watchdog over the sheep, barking furiously as soon as one goes astray. . . .

---

15. James P. Boyce, "'Three Changes in Theological Education': Inaugural Address Delivered Before the Board of Trustees of the Furman University, the Night Before the Annual Commencement, July 31, 1856," BaptistTheology.org, accessed January 18, 2016, http://www.baptisttheology.org/baptisttheology/assets/File/ThreeChangesinTheologicalInstitutionsJPBoyce.pdf.

> Be careful, be careful of your private lives, my brethren, and I believe your public lives will be sure to be right. Remember that it is upon your public life that the verdict of the world will very much depend, therefore watch every step, action, and word lest you err in any measure from the truth.[16]

So all Christians receive special scrutiny from the world. It comes with the territory. For ministers of the gospel, however, the bar of observation is raised even higher. While the seminary can never be a substitute for the local church in the theological formation of its ministers, it can be a handmaiden coming alongside in service. How? Allow me to offer a few suggestions: (1) Ground prospective ministers in texts that address the spiritual qualifications for church leadership. As previously noted, Acts 20:28–38; 1 Tim 3:1–7; Titus 1:5–9; and 1 Pet 5:1–4 should be foundations in their developing philosophies of ministry. (2) Warn prospective ministers of the common pastoral snares of pride, egotism, exaggeration, shallow theology, and immorality. Pornography viewing is not only pandemic among those in the pew, but it has become pandemic among those in the pulpit. We must see these sins as a ruthless enemy. We must engage in spiritual warfare and destroy them! (3) Provide students with some biblically sound, common sense principles that the world may lampoon but that will ensure the likelihood that they start well, continue well, and finish well.

Another five suggestions best conclude this axiom. (1) Teach them to carefully guard their thought lives. Ultimately, the battle for moral purity is won or lost in the mind (Rom 12:2). Those things that could erode the thought life must be avoided. (2) Teach them to make sure their best time goes to their families. To say one cannot be a great pastor as well as a great spouse and parent is to perpetuate a lie. Indeed, only great husbands and fathers are truly great pastors in the sight of God. (3) Let me offer my personal opinion at this point, an opinion that may not represent all of the authors in this volume. Encourage those in ministry never to be alone personally or to be involved emotionally with a person of the other

---

16. Charles Spurgeon, "The Parent's and Pastor's Joy," Sermon 1148, December 21, 1873, *Metropolitan Tabernacle Pulpit*, accessed January 18, 2017, http://www.spurgeongems.org/vols19-21/chs1148.pdf, 6–7.

sex who is not their spouse or relative. Simply stated, if one avoids these kinds of situations, it will be difficult, yes, impossible, to have an adulterous affair. This principle would include personal counseling and private conversations. One might say this is too restrictive, too legislative, too narrow. So be it! It is better to be accused of legalistic puritanism and maintain marital purity than to be guilty of sexual sin and suffer the embarrassment and disgrace of adultery. (4) Teach them to remember the cost of sin. It is well said, "Sin will take you farther than you want to go, keep you longer than you want to stay, and cost you more than you want to pay." (5) Teach them to recognize their own vulnerabilities. Not one of us is above sexual temptation. Spending time with the wrong person at the wrong place at the wrong time will inevitably result in the wrong action: adultery. The tragic story of David and Bathsheba should never be forgotten. A man after God's own heart lied, committed adultery, and murdered because of his lust for a woman to whom he was not married. Anyone can fall into this temptation. All of us are capable of any sin. Therefore, teach students to beware of themselves and take the necessary steps to prevent adultery. "Flee from sexual immorality" (1 Cor 6:18).

Axiom 9: *Theological Schools Can and Should Produce Ministers Who Will Mentor Others in an Intentional Process of Discipleship*

Seminaries often do an excellent job in biblical and theological studies. The same cannot be said for discipleship and mentoring. One reason is the failure to partner with healthy local churches led by spiritually mature pastors who see mentoring younger ministers in training as a significant aspect of their calling (see axiom 4). This is a remarkable reality in light of passages like Matt 28:18–20; 2 Tim 2:1–2; and Titus 2:1–8. It is remarkable in light of the pattern of Jesus with his disciples displayed throughout the four Gospels.[17]

Evangelical seminaries operate out of a presupposition that the students they teach are regenerate Christ followers. They have experienced conversion through repentance of sin and faith in Jesus and his perfect atonement and resurrection.[18] They should not, and do not, assume that they receive

---

17. The classic treatment remains Robert Coleman's *The Master Plan of Evangelism* (Old Tappan: Revell, 1963).
18. This presupposition in no way denies the reality that unregenerate students get accepted, attend, and even graduate from our schools. It is the hoped-for ideal.

as students well-formed and mature disciples who are already prepared to teach others also what has been entrusted to them (2 Tim 2:2). As a result, theological schools need to be intentional in building faculties that take seriously discipleship, mentoring, and spiritual formation. They need to instruct and train faculty members to understand the massive impact they can make with students outside the classroom in more intimate and personal context.

Conformity to Christ is as much caught as it is taught. A faculty that understands this will not be aloof, unapproachable, and unavailable. They will aggressively seek out particular students to mentor. They will be available to spend time with their disciples. They will open their offices and their homes. They will model good churchmanship and Great Commission passion. They will take advantage of the unique mentoring opportunities provided supervisors in ThM, DMin, EdD, and PhD programs. Schools will provide curriculum that instructs students in the implementation of biblically grounded discipleship making, recognizing that discipleship will always have a strong informal and personal element. Real discipleship cannot be merely programmatic. That is simply not how it works.

Seminaries are not a substitute for the local church in disciple making. Once more, they are servants to the church to aid, equip, and help. John Piper sums up the matter well:

> Every Christian should be helping unbelievers become believers by showing them Christ; that is, making a disciple. And every Christian should be helping other believers grow to more and more maturity. That is making a disciple. And every Christian should be seeking to get help for themselves from others to keep on growing. And that is also our discipleship. And every church should think through how all of these kinds of biblical disciple-making find expression in their corporate life.[19]

---

19. John Piper, "What Is Discipleship and How Is It Done?," DesiringGod.org, January 25, 2016, accessed January 18, 2017, http://www.desiringgod.org/interviews/what-is-discipleship-and-how-is-it-done.

Axiom 10: Theological Schools Can and Should Produce Ministers Who Will Devote Themselves to Faithful Biblical Preaching

There is a basic but important dictum when it comes to preaching: "What you say is more important than how you say it, but how you say it has never been more important." To state it another way, "It's better to say *something* poorly than to say *nothing* cleverly." Of course there need not be any conflict or choosing between the two. Faithful preachers should work hard to hone their skills to say something and say it well.

I believe theological schools are better equipped and positioned to provide this helpful instruction to aspiring preachers than ever before. It is no secret that homileticians in past days were not known for great skill in the pulpit. They might provide solid instruction in the classroom and valuable feedback in the lab, but the fact that they did not perform well themselves in the pulpit often overshadowed what they taught. Why trust a teacher of preaching who can't preach?

Today, by God's grace, things have changed. Today many instructors of preaching are themselves excellent preachers of the Word of God both in content and delivery. Many of them are both pastor and teacher, modeling beautifully faithful, biblical preaching. These people are excellent teachers and excellent preachers. And, because of the Internet and modern technology, their ministries and messages are readily available. The seminary can well serve local congregations by structured pedagogy that will aid the pastors they call to be more effective preachers of the Bible.

Let me propose a helpful analogy. You learn to ride a bicycle by getting on and riding. The more you do it, the better you get. The same, no doubt, is true of preaching. However, someone has to show you how riding a bicycle works. Someone has to help get you on the bicycle. Someone has to be there to encourage and assist you when you fall off. The aspiring preacher's someone is most often found in a seminary. I acknowledge there are some wonderful exceptions to this pattern. However, they *are* exceptions!

Axiom 11: Theological Schools Can and Should Produce Ministers Who Understand the Gospel, the Implications of the Gospel, and the Difference Between the Two

In our current theological context it has become popular to tie virtually everything to gospel-centrism. This is both good and bad. It is good in that it rightly draws attention to the gospel and its centrality in Christianity. It is bad because not everything is the gospel and not every issue is a gospel issue. It is bad because it fails to make a distinction between the essence of the gospel and the implications of the gospel. Clearly the two are related, but they must remain distinct if we are to avoid serious theological confusion.

The issue is so crucial that the apostle Paul would argue that it is better to preach the *right* gospel with the *wrong* motives (Phil 1:15–18) than to preach the *wrong* gospel with the *right* motives (Rom 10:2; Gal 1:8–9). In the former Paul can celebrate. In the latter he calls for a curse! I cannot improve on the insights of J. I. Packer when it comes to the necessity of the true and pure gospel. Packer writes,

> Salvation, said the Reformers, is by faith (man's total trust) only, without our being obliged to work for it; it is by grace (God's free favor) only, without our having to earn or deserve it first; it is by Christ the God-man only, without there being need or room for any other mediatoral agent, whether priest, saint, or virgin; it is by Scripture only, without regard to such unbiblical and unfounded extras as the doctrines of purgatory and of pilgrimages, the relic-cult and papal indulgences as devices for shortening one's stay there; and praise for salvation is due to God only, without any credit for his acceptance of us being taken to ourselves. The Reformers made these points against unreformed Rome, but they were well aware that in making them they were fighting over again Paul's battle in Romans and Galatians against works, and in Colossians against unauthentic traditions, and the battle fought in Hebrews against trust in any priesthood or mediation other than that of Christ. And (note again!) they were equally well aware that the gospel of the five "onlies" would always be contrary to natural human thinking, upsetting to natural human pride, and an object of hostility to Satan, so that destructive interpretations of justification by faith in terms of justification by works (as by the Judaizers of Paul's day, and the Pelagians of Augustine's, and the Church of Rome both before and after

the Reformation, and the Arminians within the Reformed fold, and Bishop Bull among later Anglicans) were only to be expected. So Luther anticipated that after his death the truth of justification would come under fresh attack and theology would develop in a way tending to submerge it once more in error and incomprehension; and throughout the century following Luther's death Reformed theologians, with Socinian and other rationalists in their eye, were constantly stressing how radically opposed to each other are the "gospel mystery" of justification and the religion of the natural man. For justification by works is, in truth, the natural religion of mankind, and has been since the Fall.[20]

Packer's insight does not negate the fact that (1) the gospel is intimately and integrally tied to the Bible's story line (from above) of creation → fall → redemption → new creation; and (2) we are recreated in Christ Jesus for good works that are the (super)natural outgrowth of our new lives in Christ (2 Cor 5:17; Eph 2:8–10). The indicative of the gospel is the basis and grounds for the imperatives of love and obedience that flow from it. I do not obey Christ so that he might accept me; rather, because I am accepted by him, I gladly and joyfully obey. I do not obey to get God to love me. God loves me in Christ; therefore, I gladly and joyfully obey. After all, all that is at stake in this discussion is the gospel and what truly saves.

Axiom 12: *Theological Schools Can and Should Produce Ministers Who Have Committed Themselves to Being Lifelong Learners for a Lifetime of Ministry*

Three (or four or five!) years of seminary training cannot even begin to give a minister everything he or she will need to faithfully and effectively serve the church of the Lord Jesus Christ. What it can do is provide the tools for a lifetime of learning and instill a passion to be a lifelong student. How do we do that?

First, we introduce them to a world of knowledge that, prior to attending our schools, they had little or no awareness of. I remember my

---

20. J. I. Packer, "Sola Fide: The Reformed Doctrine of Justification," *Ligonier Ministries*, accessed January 18, 2017, http://www.ligonier.org/learn/articles/sola-fide-the-reformed-doctrine-of-justification.

introduction to John Calvin. The only Calvin I knew prior to my theological education was *Calvin and Hobbes*. I remember my introduction to the stable of great preachers both ancient and modern. Prior to my entrance into the world of ministry, I only knew my personal pastors (there were two), as well as Billy Graham and Charles Stanley (I grew up in Atlanta, and my mother watched him every Sunday morning).

Second, we train them in specific disciplines they would probably ignore to their detriment. In particular I am thinking of Hebrew, Greek, philosophy, ethics, church history, and theology. A well-trained ministry needs instruction in each of these areas.

Third, we provide them the necessary equipment, tools, and motivation to continue as lifelong learners until their service to Christ comes to an end. We help them understand that building an adequate and sufficient library takes years, even a lifetime. We warn them that if they stop reading books and growing in their knowledge of the things of God, then their ministries and their people will suffer. A minister's education may start in the Bible college or seminary or divinity school, but it must not stop there. Theologian John Frame provides a simple and succinct commentary that nicely concludes the focus of this axiom. He writes,

> Theology is not self-sufficient. It depends on the maturity of your Christian life, as the maturity of your Christian life depends on theology. Growth in grace will make you a better theologian, and becoming a better theologian will help you grow in grace. There is a "spiral" relationship between the two. When you become a Christian, you usually get some elementary theological teaching, a great help in getting started in your walk with the Lord. But then new questions arise, and you go back to Scripture and theology, and you get more advanced answers—sometimes to the same questions you had as a spiritual babe. But your greater maturity enables you to understand and appreciate teaching of greater depth. And that teaching, in turn, helps you to grow more, and so on.[21]

---

21. John Frame, "Studying Theology as a Servant of Jesus," Frame-Poythress.org, June 5, 2012, accessed January 18, 2017, http://frame-poythress.org/studying-theology-as-a-servant-of-jesus.

Axiom 13: Theological Schools Can and Should Produce Ministers Who Will Protect the Sheep by Exposing and Dealing Appropriately with Dogs, Pigs, and Wolves

The Bible uses colorful images to warn us about the dangers of false converts and false teachers in our churches. There are "dogs" who do not deserve what is holy and "pigs" who do not deserve our pearls (Matt 7:6). There are ravenous "wolves" who don sheep's clothing who are nothing less than false prophets committed to our spiritual harm (Matt 7:15).

The Bible repeatedly warns us in text after text concerning spiritual deceivers who worm their way into our communities of faith with destructive and deceptive heresies. Jesus warned us in Matt 7:15–23; 24:11,14. Paul warned us in Acts 20:29–30; 1 Tim 4:1–3; and 2 Tim 3:1–9. Peter warned us in 2 Pet 2:1–3,12–22. Jude warned us throughout his entire twenty-five-verse letter. John warned us in 1 John 2:18–23; 4:1–3; and 2 John 7–11.

God calls pastors to shepherd his flock (1 Pet 5:1–4). An essential characteristic of any faithful shepherd is his protection of God's children under his watchful care. He must be discerning and courageous. He must have the ability to spot error and the intestinal fortitude to expose it. Seminaries that are unapologetically confessional and committed to the full authority and truthfulness of Scripture are perfectly positioned to train ministers in this crucial assignment.[22]

Axiom 14: Theological Schools Can and Should Produce Ministers Who Both Ask and Answer Well Questions in the Candidating Process

The content of this axiom is practical. It is also extremely important when a church is seeking a pastor and when a seminary student or graduate is seeking a pastorate. Far too often conversations and interviews are ineffective. They can be a total waste of time. Several problems arise again and again. First, search committees are ill equipped for this weighty assignment. They often have no training, no experience, and no idea how to do this job. It

---

22. John Piper provides an excellent list of what I call "battleground issues" the contemporary church and seminary must face. See John Piper, "The Earth is the Lord's: The Supremacy of Christ in Christian Learning," November 5, 2008, accessed January 18, 2017, http://www.desiringgod.org/messages/the-earth-is-the-lords-the-supremacy-of-christ-in-christian-learning.

is not their fault; it is simply the way things are. This assignment is not their world. Second, the interview is usually one-sided. The pastor search committee asks all the questions, and the pastoral candidate fields their questions. Once their questions are asked and answered, they pray (hopefully), and everyone goes home and attempts to process the interview.

I believe there are at least two ways a theological school can serve local churches in this context. Both could go a long way in helping churches and pastoral candidates find a good match. One is for churches to invite a respected and wise theologian to serve on their search committee in a bona fide position or as an ex officio member if he or she is not a part of that body of believers. Second, seminaries can train prospective pastors not only to answer questions well, but also to ask good questions themselves. I have been training my students for years to do this. Time and again they have come to my office to inform me that the search committee said they were the first candidates ever to ask those questions![23]

Axiom 15: *Theological Schools Can and Should Produce Ministers Who Inspire Graduates and Constituency to Support Their Continued Existence and Work Until Christ Returns Again*

Skye Jethani addresses an important question for our day: "Do We Still Need Seminaries?"[24] He notes declining enrollments (though there are a number of exceptions), soaring costs, drop in financial support, and a weakened demand—especially among those under 40. From his research he notes, "But what surprised me about many of these younger pastors was their complete lack of interest in seminary. 'Why would I want to go to a cemetery?' one said to me. He was getting all of the ministry training he needed on the job, he argued, and the deep theological stuff he could pick up from books and blogs. Why incur the debt and bother learning languages he'd never use?" While such facile and shallow responses are unimpressive, it cannot be ignored that a growing class of churches and ministers are buying into such a perspective. It is my firm conviction that the burden to counter

---

23. For a list of such questions, see Danny Akin, "Interviewing for a Church Position—Questions to Ask," accessed January 18, 2017, http://www.danielakin.com/wp-content/uploads/old/Resource_284/Interviewing%20for%20a%20Church%20Position.pdf.

24. Skye Jethani, "Do We Still Need Seminaries?," *Leadership Journal*, April 1, 2013, accessed January 18, 2017, http://www.christianitytoday.com/le/2013/april-online-only/do-we-still-need-seminaries.html.

this point of view falls squarely on the shoulders of the administrators and faculties of theological schools, who justify their continued existence by the way they teach and serve their students and the churches that established them and support them. "Just give us the money and trust us" no longer works. It is irresponsible and shameful that it ever did!

Times have changed, and theological schools must change as well if they are to survive and have viable futures. Such changes have nothing to do with adjusting "the faith that was once for all delivered to the saints" (Jude 3). Interestingly, those schools that have maintained their theological fidelity and confessional identity are growing with healthy prospects for the future. No, as we so often hear in our churches, the message must remain the same, but our methods must be open to change.

Now we should not be advocates for methodological change simply because it is trendy. Some methods are tried and proven and have their roots in Scripture and the practices of Jesus. Others, on the other hand, should always be open to critique, evaluation, and change. Further, seminaries no longer have the luxury of functioning like an aircraft carrier that requires a lengthy period of time to change course. No, the model of a PT speedboat is more fitting, and even essential, in a constantly and rapidly changing twenty-first-century world. Will this challenge our comfort zones? Certainly. Faculty, in particular, is notorious for resisting change—a tendency they must overcome. Only their survival is at stake!

Administration and faculty alike must constantly keep their ears to the ground of the real world, listening well to the voice of their churches as they call out to us. We may not always give them what they want. After all, we are called by God to give them what they need. Still, we will always be ready and willing to listen because we serve them. Such openness, receptivity, and willingness to dialogue will encourage greater support, not less. It will not be easy. And yet we must do it or fail in the high and noble calling of training ministers. David Dockery states it well:

> Our task will be intellectually challenging. The work is not easy, but it is faithful to the calling upon Christ-followers. There is no room for anti-intellectualism in Christian higher education. We are to have the mind of Christ, a concept that certainly requires us to think and wrestle with the challenging

ideas of history and the issues of our day. To do otherwise would result in another generation of God's people becoming ill equipped for faithful thinking and service in this still-new century. A Christian worldview is needed to help interpret an ever-changing culture. Instead of allowing our thoughts to be captivated by culture, we must take every thought captive to Jesus Christ.[25]

Conclusion

Martin Luther understood the benefits, as well as the dangers, of theological education. He knew it could bless or curse, build up or tear down. His words are a haunting reminder of what is at stake when we send our brightest and best off to school. That especially includes those who have "Christian" in their name or tradition. Luther warns, "I am very much afraid that schools will prove to be the great gates of hell unless they diligently labor in explaining the Holy Scriptures, engraving them in the hearts of youth. I advise no one to place his child where the Scriptures do not reign paramount."[26]

Here, then, is a major responsibility of the churches. Know where you are sending your children. Know what they will be taught. Pray and work that they come back or go to serve elsewhere—better, brighter, godlier, and wiser. Pray and hope they go forth more fervent and passionate for Christ and the nations than when they left you. As David Mathis admonishes, "Our prayer is that serious students of the Bible not only avoid spiritual shipwreck, but experience what it is to thrive in the disciplined study of the Scriptures, whether at seminary or in the local church."[27]

Questions for Further Reflection

1. Is there an axiom in this chapter that you see as unnecessary? Is an essential axiom missing?

---

25. David S. Dockery, *Renewing Minds: Serving Church and Society Through Christian Higher Education*, rev. ed. (Nashville: B&H Academic, 2008), 45–46.
26. Martin Luther, *What Luther Says: An Anthology*, ed. Ewald M. Plass (Saint Louis: Concordia, 1959), 449.
27. David Mathis, "Seminary: Life or Death?" DesiringGod.org, January 17, 2012, accessed January 18, 2017, http://www.desiringgod.org/articles/seminary-life-or-death.

2. Do you think seminary professors should be active in a local church? If so, how? Could there be a variety of ways they serve locally and more broadly?
3. Can seminary administrators and professors truly help the process of searching for a pastor or other staff persons? Explain your answer.
4. Is it helpful, even wise, for pastors to maintain an ongoing relationship with a theological school? If so, in what capacity?
5. Should seminaries and like schools train their graduates to be ministers who work themselves out of a job?
6. What are the top three to five expectations a congregation can rightly have of a well-educated minister of the gospel?
7. Should a theological education focus on biblical and theological studies, counseling, and pastoral ministries, or administration and leadership?

Sources for Further Study

Aleshire, Daniel. *Earthen Vessels: Hopeful Reflections on the Work and Future of Theological Schools.* Grand Rapids: Eerdmans, 2008.

Anthony, Michael J., ed. *Evangelical Dictionary of Christian Education.* Grand Rapids: Baker, 2001.

Clark, Robert, Lin Johnson, and Allyn Slout. *Christian Education: Foundations for the Future.* Chicago: Moody, 1991.

Dockery, David, ed. *Faith and Learning: A Handbook for Christian Higher Education.* Nashville: B&H Academic, 2012.

———, and Gregory Thornbury, ed. *Shaping a Christian Worldview.* Nashville: B&H, 2002.

Holmes, Arthur. *All Truth Is God's Truth.* Downers Grove: IVP, 1977.

———. *The Idea of a Christian College.* Grand Rapids: Eerdmans, 1975.

Packer, J. I. *Knowing God.* Downers Grove: IVP, 1973.

———, and Gary Parrett, *Grounded in the Gospel: Building Believers the Old-Fashioned Way.* Grand Rapids: Baker, 2010.

Schaeffer, Francis. *How Should We Then Live?* Old Tappan: Revell, 1976.

Wells, David. *No Place for Truth; or Whatever Happened to Evangelical Theology.* Grand Rapids: Eerdmans, 1995.

Chapter Twenty-One

THEOLOGY AND THE GLOBAL CHURCH

TIMOTHY C. TENNENT

During the last century the Christian church has undergone a transformation, which is unparalleled since the time of the Reformation. The seismic shift in the center of Christian gravity has been well documented.[1] The growing majority of Christians now live outside the West, and it is there that the church is continuing to experience substantial growth. To drive the point home, we need only see that in 1900 there were more than 380 million Christians in Europe and fewer than 10 million on the entire continent of Africa. Today there are nearly 400 million Christians in Africa, comprising one-fifth of the entire Christian church. The gap between Western Christians and non-Western Christians (now called the Majority World Church)[2] is further exacerbated by the fact that Europe and North America are losing approximately 3,400 Christians per day.

The purpose of this chapter is to explore a less documented theme—namely, how the emergence of global Christianity is influencing and shaping theological discourse. As far back as the nineteenth century, vibrant discussions took place regarding the marks of a truly indigenous church.

---

1. See Dana Robert, "Shifting Southward: Global Christianity Since 1945," *International Bulletin of Missionary Research* 224, no. 2 (April 2000); Lamin Sanneh, *Whose Religion Is Christianity? The Gospel Beyond the West* (Grand Rapids: Eerdmans, 2003); Todd Johnson and Kenneth Ross, ed., *Atlas of Global Christianity* (Edinburgh: University of Edinburgh Press, 2009).

2. Terminology in referring to the church in Asia, Africa, and Latin America is varied. Phrases such as *non-Western*, *Third World*, or *Global South* are frequently found in the literature. I have found the term *Majority World* to be the most useful term. For a full discussion of the pros and cons of each, see Timothy C. Tennent, *Theology in the Context of World Christianity* (Grand Rapids: Zondervan, 2007), xviii–xx.

In 1861, Henry Venn and Rufus Anderson, for example, proposed that the marks of an indigenous church were the three "selfs" of self-propagating, self-supporting, and self-governing.[3] These three marks were widely accepted until the twentieth century when missiologists began to question whether these were sufficient marks of indigeneity. Many different proposals have been offered. For example, J. D. Payne, in his *Discovering Church Planting*, proposed that we must embrace seven selfs: self-governing, self-supporting, self-propagating, self-identifying, self-teaching, self-expressing, and self-theologizing.[4] While all seven of these have found traction in contemporary missiology, none has been more persistent than the recognition that a church cannot be truly indigenous until it becomes self-theologizing. Paul Hiebert, who is widely credited with coining the phrase, "self-theologizing," defines it as the right (and responsibility) of a church "to read and interpret the Scriptures for themselves."[5] This chapter is dedicated to exploring this theme by giving practical examples of how this is now emerging within the changing contours of the global church. Certainly the Western church can no longer assume we are the sole arbiters of Christian orthodoxy. In fact, the evidence is emerging that the global church may, in fact, be helping the church as a whole to rediscover orthodoxy in many new and profound ways.[6]

This theme cannot be properly explored without first examining a number of key issues which serve as the foundation for a proper understanding of the emergence of a global theological discourse. First, we must understand the nature of theology, especially as it finds expression in various expressions of theology such as dogmatic theology, historical theology, systematic theology, biblical theology, and practical theology. Second, we must understand the application of theology with a special reference to

---

3. A whole generation of missionaries during this period were deeply committed to exploring the meaning of *indigeneity*. The key leaders in this movement were Anthony Groves (1795–1853), John Nevius (1829–1893), Hudson Taylor (1832–1905), and Roland Allen (1868–1947).

4. J. D. Payne, *Discovering Church Planting* (Milton Keynes, UK: Paternoster, 2009), 18–24. See Melvin Hodges, *Indigenous Church* (Springfield, MO: Gospel Publishing House, 1976).

5. Paul Hiebert, *Anthropological Insights for Missionaries* (Grand Rapids: Baker, 1985), 196. Hiebert is widely attributed as the one who first coined the term, "self-theologizing." For a more thorough discussion of this theme, see Richard E. Trull Jr., *The Fourth Self* (New York, Berlin: Peter Lang, 2013). Trull's work focuses on the emergence of self-theologizing among local church leaders in Kenya.

6. A wonderful exploration of how this is happening can be found in the collection of essays by Kwame Bediako in his *Christianity in Africa: The Renewal of a Non-Western Religion* (Maryknoll, NY: Orbis Press, 1995).

the inherent tension between universal truths (applicable to all Christians in all times and places) and the particularities of theologizing which may have important local functions in the life of the church but may not be applicable in a universal way to all Christians everywhere. Finally, we need to explore the function of theology as it relates to the gospel and the global mission of the church. This will need to include the increasingly important role of oral theology and the often-understated role it plays in the church's theological task. We will now explore the nature, application, and function of theology in the life and discourse of the church.

Nature of Theology

The biblical revelation, as found in the Old and New Testaments, is not limited to revealing merely what happened. In other words, the Scriptures serve both a descriptive and prescriptive function. The Bible, for example, not only tells us *what* happened, but *why* it happened. Descriptive accounts abound where we learn, for example, that God took the initiative and revealed himself to Abraham (Gen 12:1–3), or the Israelites crossed the Red Sea (Exodus 14), or Jesus Christ died on the cross (Luke 24:46). However, the biblical writers are also intent on telling us why these things happened. In the examples noted, they are all signs of God's redemptive purposes: God calls Abraham so he might enter into a covenant with Abraham's descendants. God brings Israel through the Red Sea as a tangible sign of his covenant-keeping commitment to deliver his people out of slavery. Jesus Christ died on the cross "for our sins." Thousands of such examples could be given. Thus, from the outset we recognize that there is a theological substrate to biblical revelation that drives us to the meaning and purpose of the historical record found in Scripture. Thus, while the Scriptures are not organized and revealed to us primarily as a systematic theology (more on this term later), they are fundamentally theological documents which are both prescriptive and descriptive in their purposes and functions.

It should not surprise us, therefore, that the early church from the outset began to reflect on Scripture and draw out of its pages the underlying purpose of God's revelation and the various historical acts, which are found in Scripture. John's Gospel and the Pauline Epistles, for example, are two obvious examples where the person, life, death, resurrection, and ascension of Christ are reflected on theologically and that form much of the content we read in their writings. This process continued in the centuries following the close of the New Testament in what is called the patristic period.[7]

As the church began to encounter new questions and challenges (both within the church and from the surrounding cultures), more formal theological statements began to emerge which summarized the core theology of the church. One early example that will be familiar to most readers is the Apostles' Creed. While the creed emerged after the apostles, it reflects one of the more ancient summaries of the church's faith in a formal set of statements which was formulated to give a grand overview of the key historic works of God which would then be used as the basis for teaching the church why these events are of particular importance to Christian identity. The twelve affirmations of the Apostles' Creed are significant not so much because they were traditionally regarded as twelve statements from each of the original twelve disciples (which is unlikely) but because they represented the ancient apostolic faith. Each of the statements was drawn directly from Scripture, demonstrating the close and vital relationship between the biblical revelation and the core apostolic faith. Later, as major opponents from outside the church (as in Gnosticism) and within the church (as in Arianism) emerged, it became incumbent upon the church to devise more precisely worded theological summaries which refuted various teachings which were regarded as unapostolic and, therefore, heretical. This is the broad reason the Nicene Creed emerged in AD 325 and, later, the Chalcedonian formulations in AD 451. The Nicene Creed, unlike the Apostles' Creed, moved beyond biblical phrases to more philosophically grounded statements which would make the church's teaching abundantly clear. This is the beginning of what would later become dogmatic theology, i.e., theology that represents the officially approved teaching of the church. The Nicene Creed emerged out of an early ecumenical council, which brought together key leaders from across the church to clarify such important themes as the Trinity, the deity of Christ, the precise relationship between the humanity and deity of Jesus Christ, and so forth. The Scriptures do not explicitly use the term *Trinity*, nor do the Scriptures use technical language (such as *homoousios*)[8] to describe the deity of Christ, or the relationship between the deity and humanity of Christ, or

---

7. The patristic period, broadly speaking, spans between the death of John, the last apostle, and the Council of Chalcedon in AD 451.

8. This is the term used by the Council of Nicea in AD 325 to affirm that God the Father and God the Son share the same "substance" or "essence."

whether the person of the Holy Spirit proceeds from the Father or the Father and the Son, and so forth. This demonstrates that there developed a distinct theological tradition which looked across the whole of Scripture and sought to summarize the overall teaching of Scripture, even if the precise language employed by phrases in the Nicene and Chalcedonian formulations are not explicitly stated. Thus, although the phrase *dogmatic theology* did not appear until after the sixteenth-century Reformation, the church from early on was clearly determined to frame official teachings which would be accepted by all Christians everywhere, regardless of their cultural and linguistic background.

Systematic theology is a corollary to dogmatic theology in that it refers to any systematic attempt to summarize the overall teachings of Scripture. A biblical study of prayer, for example, may find specific passages in the Gospels where Jesus teaches on prayer. This, in turn, may shed light on a specific theology of prayer as found in a given passage of Scripture. However, if a student of the Bible were to systematically survey every single passage on prayer found in the entire Bible, then an overall theology of prayer might emerge which transcends (but does not contradict) any specific passage about prayer. Thus, we are beginning to see the important differences between biblical theology and systematic theology.

Eventually, as the church looked not only across the whole of Scripture but across the reflecting church as a whole, then theology could (and did) take on a historic perspective, looking at the teachings of the church throughout time. This would sometimes be called historical theology. Probably the best summary of historic theology can be found in the five volumes of Jaroslav Pelikan.[9] This survey by Pelikan is not intended to accredit all theologies as biblical or consistent with the apostolic message but merely seeks to understand the changing contours and emphases which have emerged as the church reflected historically in light of Scripture, tradition, and the various challenges they faced in their particular time. This is an important observation. All theological formulation must, in the final analysis, stand or fall on the ground of its faithfulness to the whole teaching of Scripture. This is every bit as true for long-standing Western theological formulations as with the latest theological formulation to emerge from a church body in Latin America or China.

---

9. Jaroslav Pelikan, *The Christian Tradition: A History of the Development of Doctrine*, 5 vols. (Chicago: University of Chicago Press, 1971–1991).

Application of Theology

What is today called *systematic theology* emerged slowly within the life of the church. John of Damascus's *Exposition of the Orthodox Faith* in the eighth century and Peter Lombard's *Sentences* in the twelfth century were early pioneers of what we today call systematic theology. Later magisterial theological works such as Thomas Aquinas's *Summa Theologica* or John Calvin's *Institutes of the Christian Religion* have carried an enormous influence in how the church all over the world has organized and understood the teachings of Scripture. Today there are hundreds of systematic theologies, which have arisen from across the church.

When you go to a theological library and pull one of these large systematic theologies off of the shelf, the assumption which is all too often made is that the volume in your hand is nothing less than a grand, systematic overview of the entire teaching of the Bible. However, a careful analysis of any particular systematic theology reveals that this is a myth. What we actually have in our hand is a careful, systematic overview of particularly selected themes from Scripture. The traditional overview often falls under the rubric of certain widely used categories that follow a certain logical progression. Those categories, traditionally, have been theology proper (doctrine of God and his attributes), bibliology (study of revelation), anthropology (study of human creation), Christology (study of Christ), pneumatology (study of the Holy Spirit), soteriology (study of salvation), ecclesiology (study of the church), and eschatology (study of the last things or end time). There are, of course, a number of variations on this list, but this is a fairly widely accepted sequence of categories. In other words, the author begins with this framework and then seeks to organize the teaching of Scripture beneath these headings.

Any given theology, therefore, is not comprehensive of Scripture's teaching, but it is reflective (at best) of the most crucial questions the church has traditionally posed to the biblical texts within those categories. For example, we want to know more about the attributes of God, or how a sinner can be saved, or what the Scripture teaches about the church, or sacraments, and so forth. While these are important questions, they should not be mistaken as comprehensive regarding all the themes taught in Scripture. More importantly, even if we accept these categories as universal, the particulars of what is covered in these categories are largely driven by particular questions that are asked by the church out of which these theologies arose. Two of the abiding problems with our understanding of theology are that we assume all of the major questions have already been posed to the Scriptures and that whatever questions we pose to the text are always universally valid for the church throughout the world and throughout time. Thus, theology is sometimes seen as more of a closed door rather than as an open invitation for the church to bring new questions to the text of Scripture.

I have spent considerable portions of my teaching career working with and training Christians outside the Western world. I realized early on that they had many questions that were not addressed in any of the systematic theologies traditionally found on the bookshelves of theological libraries in the West. For example, Christians in India have read the traditional theologies on ecclesiology but fail to find there what the Scriptures teach about the church's attitude toward idolatry and, in particular, food sacrificed to idols. It is clearly a theme found in Scripture, but it does not appear in any systematic theologies. Christians in Nigeria, reading the same section, were equally interested in a theology of demon possession and how the church should understand it. Can Christians be demon possessed? If so, how does the church respond? If not, what is the role of the church in demonic deliverance in the wider culture or in an evangelistic context? Korean Christians eagerly read the section on soteriology and appreciated the emphasis on how Christ takes our guilt away through the substitutionary atonement but wondered why there was no mention of Christ's bearing our shame. These are just a few examples of questions that have not been traditionally asked by Western Christians and, therefore, do not normally appear in the pages of systematic theologies.

It is not unusual for new Christian movements to point out weaknesses in previously formulated theologies. For example, the inclusion of the category of pneumatology emerged, in part, because of the rise of Pentecostal Christians who wondered why pneumatology was traditionally a subset of ecclesiology and not a category in its own right. Traditional systematic theologies spent considerable energy demonstrating the deity of the Holy Spirit but were amazingly thin on the work of the Holy Spirit in healing, deliverance, and empowering the church for global witness. This has been more adequately addressed in recent years, but it demonstrates that the emergence of new Christian movements often provide deeper theological awareness in the church and helps mature the overall theology of the church. This is, it seems, a perennial process.

The scholastic theologians of the Middle Ages pointed out inherent problems in previous formulations. The Reformation theologians provided important correctives to traditional Roman Catholic theology. The Pietistic movement and the Wesleyan revivals of the seventeenth and eighteenth centuries revealed important shortcomings in Reformation theology. The Pentecostal movement of the twentieth century, as we have noted, provided still more correctives to the study of theology. There is no reason we should think this process, accredited throughout history, should not continue as we experience the plethora of new, vibrant Christian movements emerging around the world who are eagerly reading the Scriptures within their contexts.

The slow emergence of vibrant global theologizing (or self-theologizing) was impeded, in part, because Western theologies were so dominant and tended to carry a kind of universal validity. Having taught in theological seminaries in the Majority World, I have observed the dominant role of Western curriculum and theological textbooks in these institutions. Even materials that are published in the national languages of vibrant, growing churches are often either written by Westerners or are merely translations of Western textbooks which are received, read, and studied as if they hold some kind of universal status. Even textbooks written by Majority World Christians often came from leaders who were trained and studied in the West. They inadvertently deepened the idea that Western theology carried a kind of universal status and the only real work was to translate these ideas or texts into indigenous languages.

Once new questions begin to be asked of the text of Scripture, we are inevitably faced with the perennial challenge in that not all questions are created equal. Some questions, to be sure, are universal questions applicable to all Christians in all times and places. Those are ideal questions. However, other questions are vitally important to a particular church but may not carry the kind of universal status as other kind of questions. This is the classic tension between the "universal" and the "particular" in theologizing. The universal force in theology transcends all of the particularities of time and culture. People on the planet need to know that Jesus died for their sins. Not every Christian leader in training needs to wrestle with the intricacies of how the church can best respond to the presence of food sacrificed to idols.

The universal end of the theological spectrum emphasizes our common identity in Adam as sinner and our common identity in Christ as our Redeemer. But the other end of the theological spectrum is the particularistic side that seeks to help the church frame and position itself theologically with the issues that are relevant to their particular context. Theology has always served as a handmaiden to the church. Therefore, theology should address whatever questions arise out of the particular cultural challenges the church faces. The early church had to take seriously the Arian challenge. In our own day we are being faced with many new challenges regarding creation care and human sexuality that were not traditionally addressed within the pages of systematic theologies. However, it is clear that the theological foundations necessary for the church to embrace a well-framed theology of creation, or a theology of the human body, are no longer so-called nonessentials for contemporary Christians studying to lead churches in the Western world.

Problems inevitably arise when we seek to produce theologies that are solely universal or ones that are heavily weighted toward the particular. If we emphasize only the former, we become unwilling to listen to the insights of other Christians who are facing crucial issues which might help us see blind spots in our theologies, or, perhaps, help us in days yet unforeseen in our setting. A good example of this is how readily Majority World theologians have been able to address issues related to the Christian interface with non-Christian religions because that was a long-standing reality for them, whereas it is a relatively recent phenomena for Western Christians. Yet, if we overly emphasize only the particularities and seek only "local" theologies, then we can easily miss the shared universal realities of being a Christian regardless of our time or context. We can also become skeptical for any theologian to speak with confidence to those outside their own cultural arena. The truth is, we need the whole church engaged with the whole church to produce good theological reflection. We must always maintain a proper balance between these two principles.

Function of Theology

We have demonstrated that theology is the church's attempt to understand the biblical revelation within the framework of our particular historical and cultural setting. However, even given that this is a shared task of all churches throughout the world, we cannot help but notice that the way theology is formulated remains dependent on deeper presuppositions regarding the function of theology. The Western world has, typically, approached the task with a synchronic aim. This means the overriding interest is to organize Scripture within a fixed structure of reality that is "comprehensive, logically consistent and conceptually coherent."[10] This meant that all of the shifting issues the church faced were developed in separate, discreet theological disciplines such as ethics and pastoral theology.

In contrast the Majority World has typically seen the function of theology in a more missional framework and therefore approaches the theological task with a diachronic approach which assumes that whatever new and pressing issues face the church should be addressed as a part of the central theological work of the church. This means that Majority World theologies tend to be more integrated with the life of the church and less concerned with theoretical constructs. It also means that oral theology that arises from the experiences and struggles of the church are taken more seriously within the larger theological task. The exigency of the emerging churches often means they cannot afford the luxury of a full-time class of professional theologians. In the West, theological reflection usually finds it locus in the seminaries and universities, whereas in the Majority World theological reflection finds it locus in the church. The function of theology in the latter context becomes less theoretical and more inherently missional. Oral theology, popular theology, and "people's theology" have an enormous influence in the theological work of the Majority World.

The challenge we face is that the church is growing dramatically in the Majority World, and yet the center of formal theological reflection remains in the Western world. Thus, as John Mbiti has pointed out, there is not corresponding "mutuality and reciprocity in the theological task facing the universal church."[11] To put it bluntly, a steady stream of the brightest minds in the world have made their pilgrimage to do theological studies in the West. However, the theological learning they acquired from the older churches has not been able "to cope with the new concerns in the new

---

10. Tite Tienou and Paul Hiebert, "From Systematic and Biblical to Missional Theology," *Appropriate Christianity*, ed. Charles H. Kraft (Pasadena: William Carey Library, 2005), 121.

11. John S. Mbiti, "Theological Impotence and the Universality of the Church," in *Mission Trends*, vol. 3, *Third World Theologies*, ed. Gerald Anderson and Thomas F. Stransky (Grand Rapids: Eerdmans, 1976), 6.

churches."[12] Yet these new believers from around the world are bringing many new questions and issues to the text of Scripture that are helping reenergize the whole task of theology. Their theological concerns may be less theoretical and more practical and missiological. But what is emerging is what Andrew Walls has called the "rethinking of the framework of theology" in a way that anchors "Christian scholarship in Christian mission."[13]

Examples of the Emergence of Majority World Self-Theologizing

The purpose of this final section is to highlight three examples of how the growing presence of Majority World Christians is helping reshape our common theological task. I will seek to demonstrate how even within the traditional categories of systematic theology, we are discovering vital reflections that demand our attention. The contribution of the global church is heightened with each passing day given the immigration patterns, which have brought people groups from around the world into the West. It is my conviction that these new voices are, in fact, helping bring vitality and renewal to the Western church.[14]

Theology Proper: Is the Father of Jesus the God of Muhammad?

Despite the depth of reflections on the nature and character of God, it has been a struggle for Western Christians to know precisely how to speak about the god of Muhammad with Muslims. Are the terms *Allah* and *God* interchangeable? Arabic-speaking Christians, long before the advent of Islam, used the Arabic word for God, Allah, in speaking about God. How has the rise of Islam changed how Arabic speakers refer to God within the framework of Christian theology? Even though the word *God* in English has a wide, generic application, when a Christian uses the word *God*, it is normally used in reference to an assumed body of predicates about God as revealed in the Bible. In the same way, when a Muslim speaks of Allah, it can only be understood in reference to a received body of predicates about

---

12. Kwame Bediako, *Christianity in Africa*, 155.
13. Andrew F. Walls, "Christian Scholarship and the Demographic Transformation of the Church," in *Theological Literacy for the Twenty-First Century*, ed. Rodney L. Peterson (Grand Rapids: Eerdmans, 2002), 175, 181.
14. Timothy Tennent, *Theology in the Context of World Christianity: How the Global Church Is Influencing the Way We Think About and Discuss Theology* (Grand Rapids: Zondervan, 2007).

Allah revealed in the Qur'an. Even when Christians and Muslims find apparent agreement on certain predicates such as "God is the Creator" or "God is all powerful," are we referring to the same God which, only when pressed for further details, we part ways because of the differences between the Qur'an and the Bible? Majority World reflection on this vital question has pointed out that the centrality of Christ in the Christian proclamation has transformed even the shared attributes. For example, in the New Testament, God's greatest expression of his power is clearly manifested through "weakness," which God displayed by sending his Son to the cross in order to defeat the powers of Satan. Our doctrine of God, heretofore, articulated within the context of a culture shaped largely by Christian thought, needs more reflection if we are to be equipped for our roles in today's society. This is no longer a marginal question that only a few missionaries have had to grapple with in distant places. This is now a crucial point crying out for deeper theological reflection all over the world. The Majority World has assisted us all in seeing this.

Anthropology: Human Identity in Shame-Based Cultures of the Far East

Anthropologists from Ruth Benedict to the present have long made the distinction between shame-based and guilt-based cultures. The basic difference is that "shame cultures rely on external sanctions for good behavior" whereas guilt-based cultures rely on "an internalized conviction of sin."[15] A culture framed by guilt means that transgressors may feel an internal sense of moral failure, even if no one else knows about the transgression. In contrast, shame leaves us with a sense of humiliation, defeat, and ridicule and is intricately tied to our exposure and loss of honor or status before our peers and those in authority within our social network. Shame is not inherently individualistic or private but corporate and public; it cannot be experienced apart from the larger social context.

While no culture is purely "guilt" based or "shame" based, the cultural emphasis is identifiable.[16] Significant research has determined that the biblical context frequently employs the categories of shame and honor

---

15. Ruth Benedict, *The Chrysanthemum and the Sword* (Cambridge, MA: Riverside, 1946), 223.
16. See, for example, Zuk-Nae Lee, "Korean Culture and Sense of Shame," *Transcultural Psychiatry* 36, no. 2 (June 1999): 181–94.

in describing the human response to sin.[17] Interestingly, in the biblical account of the fall, the language used to describe Adam's response to his sin is shame and fear not guilt. This emphasis continues throughout the biblical record, placing as much emphasis on how we, as sinners, have robbed God of the honor he deserves as the fact that we have broken a list of external commandments. In the Old Testament the term *guilt* and its various derivatives occur 145 times and 10 times in the New Testament, whereas the term *shame* and its derivatives occur nearly 300 times in the Old Testament and 45 times in the New Testament.[18] Both guilt and shame prove equally crucial for a proper understanding of the biblical record.

Despite this evidence, the great stream of Western theologies has focused almost exclusively on how Christ has satisfied our guilt through his substitutionary atonement on the cross. I did a survey of all the leading systematic theologies found in a major theological library. I discovered that while the indexes are filled with references to guilt, the word "shame" appears in only one of these indexes.[19] Because of the forensic emphasis in a guilt-only lens on the death of Christ, then there is no reason Jesus could not have been crucified in private. It also tends to reinforce the idea that we stand before God individually as sinners and bear no weight for the larger structural sins of the human race of which we may not be directly involved. Yet many Majority World cultures often see the larger social sins as having as much weight as sins that are personally committed.

---

17. See, for example, Lyn Bechtel, "The Perception of Shame Within the Divine-Human Relationship in Biblical Israel," 79–92, in *Uncovering Ancient Stones*, ed. Lewis M. Hopfe (Winona Lake, IN: Eisenbrauns, 1994). See also, John L. Pilch and Bruce Malina, ed., *Biblical Social Values and Their Meaning* (Peabody, MA: Hendrickson, 1993). Scholars such as J. G. Peristiany and Bruce Malina have made a convincing case that the first-century Mediterranean world was dyadistic rather than individualistic. Thus, one's identity is formed by the group one belongs to and by the larger social context within which one lives.

18. Bruce Nicholls, "The Role of Shame and Guilt in a Theology of Cross-Cultural Mission," *Evangelical Review of Theology* 25, no. 3 (2001), 235.

19. See, for example, Louis Berkhof's *Systematic Theology* (Grand Rapids: Eerdmans, 1949); Henry Thiessen's *Lectures in Systematic Theology* (Grand Rapids: Eerdmans, revised ed.1989); Alan Gomes, ed., *Dogmatic Theology by William G. T. Shedd*, 3rd ed., (P&R: 2003); Helmut Thielicke's *The Evangelical Faith*, 3 vols, ed. and trans. Geoffrey W. Bromiley (Grand Rapids: Eerdmans, 1974); Wolfhart Pannenberg's *Systematic Theology*, 3 vols.(Grand Rapids: Eerdmans, 1991); Millard J. Erickson's *Christian Theology*, 2nd ed. (Grand Rapids: BakerAcademic, 1998); James Leo Garrett Jr.'s *Systematic Theology: Biblical, Historical and Evangelical* (Grand Rapids: Eerdmans. 1990); and Wayne Grudem's *Systematic Theology*,(Grand Rapids: Zondervan, 1994) The only systematic theology I found which has a reference to shame is a single line in vol. 3 of Norman Geisler's *Systematic Theology* (Minneapolis: BethanyHouse, 2002), which acknowledges that Adam's sin "brought on him guilt, as well as the shame he expressed in view of it" (Gen 3:7).

Even a cursory examination of the biblical account of the death of Christ reveals that the work of God in Christ did not simply take place "beyond the veil of tears" but was walked out publicly as is found, for example, in the public beating (especially the blows to the face and head), the mock coronation with the robe and crown of thorns, and the public scorning Christ received by being displayed publicly naked on the cross. Truly Jesus bore our shame as well as our guilt if one steps back and looks at the passion of Christ from the widest lens.

Despite hundreds of years of Western theological reflection, these insights were not brought forward in the major systematic theological works written by Western Christians. It was the insight of Majority World Christians, who live and work in a context far more similar to the first century than we do, which brought these valuable insights to the attention of the church.

Christology: Christ as Healer and Ancestor in Africa

The traditional Western formulation of Christology (because it started from a synchronic goal) focused on the identity of Christ within the Trinity. Thus, Western Christologies tend to focus on a top-down view of the person of Christ rather than the work of Christ. Majority World Christologies tend to look at the same biblical data from below. Thus African writers are not as much concerned about establishing the ontology of Christ and the relationship of his deity and humanity that consumed (rightfully so) so much of Western reflection. In contrast, African Christology is inherently more holistic in the way it integrates the person and work of Christ. It is a deep concern of African writers that Christ is no stranger to the practical realities of poverty, illiteracy, ethnic tensions, colonialism, dictatorship, illness, disenfranchisement, and suffering—all of which John Pobee and Akintunde Akinade have aptly called, Africa's "multi-headed hydra."[20] They have reminded Western theologians that Jesus's ministry demonstrated that he was not only delivering us from sin, but he was also providing protection during dangerous journeys, was Lord over the crops and harvest, and assists in the safe delivery of a baby.

---

20. Akintunde Akinade, "Who Do You Say that I Am? An Assessment of Some Christological Constructs in Africa," *Africa Journal of Theology* 9, no. 1 (1995): 191. See John S. Pobee, in "In Search of Christology in Africa: Some Considerations for Today," in John S. Pobee, ed., *Exploring Afro-Christology* (Bern, NY: Peter Lang, 1992), 10.

The New Testament is filled with an amazing array of Christological images of Christ as Redeemer, Savior, good Shepherd, Lamb of God, King of the Jews, Suffering Servant, and so forth. Some of these are clearly universal images that are equally applicable to all Christians in all times and places (such as Redeemer or Savior). However, other images are clearly rooted in particular expectations that are rooted in Jewish messianic anticipations. The New Testament embraces the notion of using various cultural paradigms if it would help us understand the full nature and stature of Christ. We see this same practice with the church that is described, variously, as body of Christ, vine, temple, bride, God's field, flock, and so forth.

African theologians have been particularly fruitful in exploring Christology from an African perspective. It is actually one of the richest and most vibrant themes within the broad field of global theologizing.[21] Africans have, for example, developed beautifully biblical Christologies around the theme of Christ as Healer or Life Giver. In these theologies they have demonstrated how the theme of healing is central to Christ's mission. However, their insights are not limited to the ways Christ heals our physical bodies. They also explore how Christ brings spiritual healing to the community and, ultimately, cosmic healing over Satan and the principalities and powers arrayed against the people of God.

The healing work of Christ is a theme that is, at best, only scantily treated in traditional Western theologies. Yet Christians from around the world have found in these African Christologies valuable new insights into the work of Christ and how their development of these themes has provided a new Christological lens to more fully appreciate and understand the revelation of God in Jesus Christ as found in the New Testament. Certainly, Western Christologies, which have been so remarkable at reflecting on the person of Christ, can be beautifully complemented by the equally remarkable work of African writers who are powerfully connecting Christology to many of the pressing and existential realities facing Christians in the Majority World. Indeed, only by combining the insights of Western theologians with Majority World theologians may we finally restore the biblical

---

21. See, for example, Charles Nyamiti, *Christ as Our Ancestor: Christology from an African Perspective* (Gweru, Zimbabwe: Mambo, 1984); John S. Pobee, ed., *Exploring Afro-Christology* (New York: Peter Lang, 1992); Robert J. Schreiter, ed., *Faces of Jesus in Africa* (Maryknoll, NY: Orbis, 2005); and Diane Stinton, *Jesus of Africa: Voices of Contemporary African Christology* (Maryknoll, NY: Orbis, 2004).

integration of the person and work of Christ so powerfully portrayed in the New Testament.

Conclusion

This chapter has sought to demonstrate a few glimpses into how the global church is influencing and shaping the way we think about and discuss theology. While the diversity and richness of global theology is profound, certain themes tend to regularly emerge when looking at the Majority World contribution as a whole. First, these newer theological contributions tend to more fully embrace the authority of Scripture and, by Western standards, hold a theology considered conservative and historically orthodox. This means that global theologizing is, on balance, a positive force in upholding historic orthodoxy.

Second, Majority World theologians are more likely to be morally and ethically conservative. This has already made a vital contribution to many of the Western mainline denominations that have been struggling with how to respond to a wide range of moral and ethical issues.

Third, Majority World theologians are more likely to be sensitive to the Christian responsibility to address issues related to poverty and social justice. As this chapter demonstrated, this is due in large part to the cultural contexts out of which much of this theology arises; and, therefore, this will also serve to strengthen the overall witness of the church.

Fourth, Majority World theologians have shown themselves to be far more experienced in articulating the uniqueness of the gospel in the midst of religious pluralism. The Western church was ill prepared to face the sudden rise in religious pluralism in the West. Yet for the Majority World this is, for many, a long-standing, normative context which has shaped their witness for centuries. Finally, Majority World Christians are more likely to grasp the corporate, not just individualistic, dimensions of the teachings of the New Testament.

As a whole, the contribution of the global church is clearly having a positive impact on the shape and vitality of theology. We all should rejoice that we have been able to live to see this day when thousands of newly emerging Christian movements are rising up and reflecting on the work of God in their midst. Together with all Christians in all times and places, we are moving closer to that day when we will all be ushered into the presence of the triune God, the final goal of all theologizing for all peoples in all times and places.

Questions for Further Reflection

1. What would be the signs that a church has become self-theologizing?
2. What is the right balance between a theology that focuses on universal issues with theoretical consistency and a theology that seeks to practically equip the church to respond to the most pressing issues of the day?
3. How have those Christians who live and work in close proximity with Muslims helped us better articulate our doctrine of God?
4. How have Christians from shame-based cultures helped us better understand the work of Christ?
5. What are your thoughts on the role African theologians have played to help root Christology into the daily struggles of people?

Sources for Further Study

Dyrness, William. *Invitation to Cross-Cultural Theology.* Grand Rapids: Zondervan, 1992.

Escobar, Samuel. *The New Global Mission.* Downers Grove: InterVarsity, 2003.

Hesselgrave, David. *Community Christ Cross-Culturally.* Grand Rapids: Zondervan, 1991.

Hiebert, Paul G. *Anthropological Reflections on Missiological Issues.* Grand Rapids: Baker, 1994.

Ott, Craig, and Harold A. Netland. *Globalizing Theology: Belief and Practice in an Era of World Christianity.* Grand Rapids: Zondervan, 2007.

Tennent, Timothy C. *Theology in the Context of World Christianity.* Grand Rapids: Zondervan, 2007.

Walls, Andrew F. *The Cross-Cultural Process in Christian History.* Maryknoll, NY: Orbis, 2002.

Scripture Index

Genesis
1   *94, 96–97, 375*
1:1   *96, 259*
1:1–31   *100*
1:2   *94*
1–3   *162*
1:3   *94, 96*
1:26–27   *76, 115, 377*
1:26–28   *382*
1:27   *357*
2   *382–83*
2:7   *262*
2:16–17   *358*
2:16–20   *264*
2:24   *325*
2:25–3:11   *54*
3   *385*
3:7   *423*
3:7–24   *358*
3:9   *355*
3:15   *355, 358*
3:16–19   *382*
4   *170*
6:3   *262*
7:22   *262*
9:4   *99*
9:4–6   *325, 329*
10:21–31   *117*
11:1–9   *264*
12:1–3   *60, 100, 261, 359, 413*
12:7   *99*
14:13   *119*
15:5   *213*
15:6   *214*
15:13   *213*
17:6–8   *213*
18:1–2   *99*

19   *325*
22:1   *210*
22:1–12   *214*
22:12   *210*
22:17   *213*
26:4   *213*
29:20   *177*
31:47   *123*
39:14   *119*
41:12   *119*

Exodus
1:15–16   *119*
3:1–4:17   *60*
6:2–8   *213*
8:1–5, 16, 20–23   *100*
9:1–5, 8–9, 13–17   *100*
10:3   *119*
14   *413*
14:25   *359*
15:11   *212*
19:4–6   *213*
19:6   *97*
20:1–3   *319*
20:1–17   *319, 327*
20:2   *292*
20:3–4   *323*
20:13   *170*
20–25   *161*
21:22–25   *325*
24   *154*
34:6   *213*

Leviticus
17:11   *99*
18:22   *325*
19:2   *323*
19:18   *321*

19:18, 34   *207*
20:13   *325*
23:40   *211*
26:40–45   *214*

Deuteronomy
1:1   *208*
1:1–5   *207*
1:3   *209*
1:5   *208*
1:7–8   *212*
1:8, 35   *213*
1:10   *213*
1:31   *212*
1:35   *213*
4:1   *215*
4:1–2   *107*
4:1, 5, 9, 14   *208*
4:1–8   *212*
4:1–14   *208*
4:9–14, 36   *211*
4:9–31   *212–13*
4:10   *208, 210*
4:12, 33, 36   *129*
4:14   *215*
4:21   *213*
4:23   *214*
4:25   *213*
4:26–28   *214*
4:30–31   *214*
4:31   *212, 214*
4:32–40   *199, 208, 212*
4:34   *212*
4:35   *208*
4:37   *212–13*
4:39   *209*
4:44   *208*
4:45   *208*

429

5:1 *208*	12:1–26:19 *208*	28:1–69 *213*
5:1–11:32 *208*	12:7, 12, 18 *211*	28:5 *212*
5:1–22 *212*	12:7, 18 *213*	28:6–9 *213*
5:2–3 *212*	12:23 *99*	28:15–68 *214*
5:2–5 *208*	12:32 *107*	28:58 *210*
5:5, 23–33 *211*	13:3 *207*	28:61 *206*
5:6 *212–13*	13:5 *210*	29:1 *208*
5:22–33 *129*	13:6, 11 *213*	29:11 *213*
5:23–29 *210*	13:12 *211*	29:11, 13, 20 *214*
5:29 *210*	14:1–21, 26 *213*	29:19–27 *214*
6 *260*	14:2 *212*	29:21 *206*
6:1 *208, 215*	14:26 *211*	30:1 *129*
6:1–3 *210*	15:10 *213*	30:1–10 *129, 214*
6:2 *210*	16:11–14 *213*	30:2 *130*
6:4 *346*	16:11, 14–15 *211*	30:2, 10 *129*
6:4–5 *258*	17:13 *210–11*	30:3 *129–30*
6:4–9 *259*	17:14–20 *212*	30:3, 8–9 *129*
6:5 *207, 321*	17:19 *210*	30:6 *207*
6:10–11, 23 *212*	17:19–20 *210*	30:10 *206*
6:12 *214*	17:19–29 *209*	30:11–20 *212–13*
6:12, 21–23 *213*	18:1–8 *212*	31:1 *208*
6:13 *155*	18:9–20 *212*	31:2 *208*
6:16 *155*	18:15 *208*	31:7 *208*
6:20–25 *212*	18:15–22 *101*	31:9–13 *214*
7:6–7 *212*	18:16 *211*	31:9–13, 24–29 *209*
7:8 *213*	18:18 *102*	31:10–13 *209*
7:9 *213*	18:18–19 *104*	31:10, 25 *208*
7:21 *212*	18:22 *104*	31:11–13 *210*
8:1–5 *212*	18:34 *101*	31:12 *210*
8:3 *97, 155*	19:20 *210–11*	31:14–22, 30 *209*
8:6 *210, 323*	21 *154*	31:16–18, 26–29 *214*
8:7–10 *212*	21:5 *212*	31:19–21 *209*
8:11, 14, 19 *214*	21:21 *211*	31:22 *208*
8:14 *213*	23:21 *213*	31:24–26 *107*
9:19, 25–10:5 *212*	25:4 *108*	31:26 *206, 209*
10:5 *107*	26:1–11 *213*	32 *213*
10:8–9 *212*	26:5 *213*	32:1–43 *209*
10:12–13 *210, 214*	26:5–9 *195*	32:3 *212–13*
10:15 *212*	26:6–8 *213*	32:6 *208*
10:17 *212*	26:8 *212, 291*	32:14–14 *212*
10:21 *212*	26:9, 15 *212*	32:36 *212*
10:22 *213*	26:11 *211*	32:36–43 *214*
11:1, 13 *207*	26:16–19 *213*	32:43 *214*
11:2–7 *212*	27:1 *208*	32:44–45 *208*
11:9–12 *212*	27:3 *212*	32:44–47 *209*
11:13–28 *213*	27:9 *208, 213*	33:1 *208*
11:18–25 *213*	28:1–14 *213*	33:8–11 *212*
12:1–14 *213*	28:1–68 *208*	33:9–10 *192*

Scripture Index

33:10 *206*
34 *167*
34:1–12 *208*
34:10 *208*

Joshua
1:1–9 *60*
1:7–8 *107*
24:3 *119*

Judges
2:7–12 *215*
6 *61*
16:3 *161*
19 *325*

1 Samuel
12:24 *294*
16:6 *61*
16:12 *61*
17:26, 36 *99*

2 Samuel
1 *154*

1 Kings
2:2–4 *206*
8:27 *99, 349*
11 *323*
14:19 *163*

2 Kings
14:6 *206*
18 *123*
18:13–20:19 *163*
18:26 *123*
18:26, 28 *119*
20:20 *161*
22 *167, 169*
22:11 *206*
23:25 *206*

1 Chronicles
9:1 *163*
29:14 *99*

2 Chronicles
15:3 *206*
19:8 *206*
28:1–4 *323*
32:18 *119*

Ezra
4:7 *124*
4:8–6:18 *117, 123–24*
4:18 *127*
7:10 *206*
7:12–16 *123*
7:12–26 *117, 124*

Nehemiah
8:1–12 *264*
8:8 *127*

Job
28 *51*
28:28 *214*
35:6, 8 *99*

Psalms
1 *206*
1:1–2 *172*
1:1–3 *97*
2:4 *106*
2:12 *123*
6 *129*
8 *99*
8:5–6 *76*
16:2–3 *99*
19 *99, 271*
19:1 *97*
19:7 *117*
19:7–11 *218*
19:7–14 *206*
19:11–13 *357*
22:1 *156*
23:6 *55*
28:1 *94*
29 *99*
33:6 *96*
46:10 *55, 359*
50:12–14 *99*
51 *129*
51:1 *129*
51:2 *129*
51:6 *47*
62:5 *93*
64 *293*
64:9 *293*
65 *99*
66 *293*

66:16 *293*
67:4 *359*
83:1 *94*
86:15 *213*
103:12 *358*
103:15–16 *96*
104 *99*
104:2 *95*
110 *163*
110:1 *155*
111:10 *214*
119 *206*
119:47 *121*
119:105 *95*
119:130 *95*
139:7–10 *341*
146:6 *99*
148:1–5 *96*

Proverbs
1:4 *117*
1:7 *46, 47, 214*
6:6–8 *327*
6:9–11 *327*
6:23 *95*
9:10 *214*
15:3 *357*
15:23 *95*
15:33 *214*
17:6 *vii*
17:28 *93*

Ecclesiastes
4:12 *335*

Isaiah
1:10 *206*
1–39 *169*
3:24 *119*
5:24 *206*
6 *61, 66, 153*
6:6–7 *61*
6:8 *59, 61*
7 *154*
7:14–16 *45*
8:20 *206*
19:18 *119*
20:2 *154*
30:9 *206*
36:11 *123*

431

36:11, 13 *119*
36–39 *163*
40:6–8 *96*
40:12–31 *212*
40:14–18 *99*
41:4 *96*
42:1 *106*
43:25 *358*
45:12 *96*
46:10 *341*
48:13 *96*
51:7 *206*
52:7–10 *99*
53:1 *340*
55 *271*
55:9 *51*
55:10–11 *96*
55:11 *340, 352*
56:1 *99*
60:19 *95*
65:17–23 *100*
65:24 *341*
66:1–2 *99, 190*

Jeremiah
1:4–5 *61*
1: 5, 9–10 *96*
1:6 *61*
1:7–8 *61*
1:9–10 *100*
9:23–24 *18, 174*
10:11 *123*
18:18 *206*
20:9 *66*
23:9–32 *270*
25:11–12 *107*
28 *270*
29:13 *350*
31:34 *358*
34:7 *161*
34:9 *119*
36 *270*

Ezekiel
2:1–3:27 *96*
4:12 *155*
7:26 *206*
24:16 *155*
40:2 *97*

Daniel
2:1, 19–23, 28–30 *100*
2:4–7:28 *124*
2:4b–7:28 *117, 123*
8–12 *124*
9:2 *107*
9:11–14 *107*

Hosea
4:6 *46*
6:5 *107*
14:2 *159*

Amos
9:6 *96*

Jonah
1–4 *359*
1:9 *119*

Micah
5 *153*

Habakkuk
1:13 *94*
2:14 *359*
3:4 *95*

Zechariah
1:4–6 *107*
4:6 *338*

Malachi
2:6, 9 *206*
4:4 *215*

Matthew
4 *155*
4:1–11 *323*
4:4 *27, 97*
4:19 *61, 242*
4:21–22 *62*
5:1–3, 10, 17–20, 45 *97*
5:8 *267*
5:13 *344*
5:13–16 *385*
5:14 *344*
5:17 *198, 206*
5:17–19 *106*
5:29–30 *56*

7:6 *406*
7:12 *317*
7:15 *344, 406*
7:15–23 *406*
9:9 *62*
10:16 *44*
11:27 *100, 241, 268*
11:29 *241–42*
16:18 *392*
17:2 *31*
17:5 *106*
19:4–6 *325*
19:6 *340*
22:34–36 *382*
22:34–40 *321, 323*
22:36 *55*
22:37 *47, 55, 207, 260*
22:37–39 *17, 55*
22:37–40 *360*
22:41–46 *156, 163*
23:13 *46*
24:11, 14 *406*
24:30 *358*
24:35 *96*
26:41 *44*
27:46 *123, 156*
28:16–20 *386*
28:17 *361*
28:18 *362*
28:18–20 *55, 223, 359, 392, 396, 400*
28:18, 20 *264*
28:19 *52, 55, 264, 356, 360, 362*
28:19–20 *3, 34, 370, 389*
28:20 *360, 361, 365, 391, 396*

Mark
1:15 *358*
2:10–12 *100*
2:23–28 *189*
4:35–5:43 *324*
5:41 *123*
7:34 *123*
9:2 *31*
9:34 *248*

10:18 *267*
12 *260*
12:29 *259*
12:29–30 *258*
12:30 *207, 260*
13:31 *96*
15:7 *359*
15:34 *123*
16:11–13 *361*
16:15 *396*

Luke
1:46–55 *45*
2:11 *358*
2:52 *45*
4:4 *97*
4:14–20 *108*
4:16–21 *101*
6:1–5 *323*
6:6–11 *324*
6:40 *242*
9:35 *106*
10 *328*
10:7 *108*
10:27 *207, 260*
12:11 *300*
12:11–12 *300*
12:16–21 *346*
18:19 *267*
19:10 *371*
21:33 *96*
21:36 *44*
24 *396*
24:4, 27, 32, 45 *107*
24:13–27 *361*
24:30–31 *343*
24:32 *338*
24:36–39 *361*
24:44–45 *155*
24:44–49 *392*
24:45–47 *359*
24:46 *413*
24:46–48 *396*
24:50–51 *358*

John
1:1 *50–51*
1:1–2, 14 *96*
1:1–3 *357*

1:1–4, 14–18 *100*
1:1–5, 9–18 *100*
1:1, 9, 14 *273*
1:1–14 *269*
1:14 *50–51, 340*
1:18 *100, 340*
1:45 *107*
1:48 *337*
3:1–7 *47*
3:16 *358*
4:24 *270*
5:2 *119*
5:42 *47*
7:14–18 *50*
8:26, 28, 38 *102*
10:1–30 *101*
10:3–5, 16, 27 *95*
10:35 *106–7, 155*
12:49–50 *25*
14:6 *48, 51, 239*
14:6, 17 *104*
14:10 *104*
14:10, 24, 26 *102*
14:13–14 *44*
14:24–26 *269*
14:25 *104*
14:26 *55, 104*
15:9–17 *327*
15:11 *55*
15:16 *44*
15:26 *269*
16:4, 12–15 *102*
16:5–12 *277*
16:7–9 *349*
16:8–11 *356*
16:12–14 *265, 269*
16:13 *104*
16:13–15 *104*
16:23–24, 26 *44*
17:3 *174*
17:17 *106*
17:21, 23 *260*
20:19 *361*
20:21 *359, 396*
20:24–25 *361*
20:28–31 *219*
20:30 *101*

Acts
1 *396*
1:6 *361*
1:8 *356, 359, 392, 396*
1:9 *386*
1:11 *358*
2 *265, 342*
2:6, 8, 11 *129*
2:14–40 *300*
2:22–36 *101*
2:30 *101*
2:37 *342, 351*
2:42 *342*
3:1 *343*
4:1–20 *300*
4:31 *343*
5:22–32 *300*
6:1–6 *343*
6:4 *343*
7:1–60 *300*
7:59–60 *343*
8:15 *343*
8:27–39 *155*
9 *62*
9:11 *343*
9:15 *62*
10:4 *343*
10:9 *343*
10:9–17, 34–43 *100*
12:5 *343*
13:1–3 *365*
13:15 *108*
13:43 *300*
13:45–50 *300*
14:14–18 *98*
14:15 *99*
14:16–17 *98*
14:17 *97*
15:39 *345*
16:16–24 *300*
17:1–4 *300*
17:16 *345–46*
17:16–34 *335–36, 344–45*
17:17 *346*
17:18 *346–47*
17:18, 31–32 *346*
17:18, 32 *352*

17:19–20 *347–48*
17:21 *348–49*
17:22–23 *347*
17:22–31 *99*
17:22–32 *300*
17:22–34 *299*
17:24 *349*
17:24–27 *99*
17:25 *349*
17:26 *350*
17:27 *346, 350*
17:28 *260, 350*
17:29 *350*
17:30 *347, 351*
17:30–31 *99*
17:31 *351*
17:32 *351*
17:33 *352*
17:34 *336, 352*
18:4, 13 *300*
18:11 *269*
18:12–17 *300*
19:8, 29 *300*
20:27 *20*
20:28–38 *390, 399*
20:29–30 *406*
21:8–10 *102*
21:40 *119*
22:1 *300*
22:1–22 *300*
22:2 *119*
23:1–10 *300*
24:10–21 *300*
24:25 *351*
25:13–21 *300*
25:16, 24 *300*
26:2–32 *300*
26:18 *361*
26:27–29 *300*
28:23–24 *300*
28:31 *359*

Romans
1 *181*
1:2 *103*
1–11 *319*
1:18–2:16 *277*
1:18–25 *98*
1:18–32 *320*
1:19 *50*
1:20 *97*
1:21–23 *320*
1:24–25 *320*
1:26–27 *325*
3:10–12 *358*
3:22 *148*
3:23 *358*
3:28 *224*
4:3 *103*
4–5 *386*
4:7 *358*
5:5 *260*
5:8 *358*
5:12–19 *321*
6:4 *53*
8:5–9 *178*
8:11 *76, 341*
8:18–25 *328*
8:19–22 *358*
8:19–23 *261*
8:29 *76*
9:17 *103*
10 *271*
10:2 *403*
10:9–14 *355*
10:11 *103*
10:14 *336*
10:14–17 *262*
10:17 *335*
11:12 *103*
11:17 *157*
11:33 *268*
12 *55*
12:1–2 *319–20, 380*
12:2 *31, 47, 76, 261, 399*
12:6 *62*
12:6–7 *46*
12–15 *319*
13:1–7 *321*
13:8–10 *321*
13:12 *303*
16:26 *103*

1 Corinthians
1:9 *51*
1:23 *301*
1:26–29 *55*
2:1–16 *102, 104*
2:5,13 *104*
2:6–16 *178*
2:9–16 *25*
2:10 *25*
2:10–13 *104*
2:11 *25, 268*
2:12 *25*
2:12–13 *103*
2:13–14 *116*
2:14 *25, 178*
2:14–16 *25*
2:16b *278*
3:1–3 *25*
4:1–25 *265*
6:9–11 *325*
6:12–20 *325*
6:18 *400*
7:8–9 *323*
7:10–11 *108*
8:1 *46–47*
8:1–3 *116*
8:2 *46*
8:6 *100*
9:3 *300*
9:16 *66*
10:11 *294*
11:1 *239*
12 *55, 59*
12:9, 27–29 *102*
12:14 *55*
12:17 *135*
12:28 *46*
13:1–2 *102*
13:2 *102*
13:12 *237, 278*
14:3 *102*
14:3, 30 *102*
15 *263, 351*
15:1–8 *261*
15:20–28 *259*
15:22 *321*
15:28 *262*
15:49 *76*
15:54–57 *358*
16:22 *123*

2 Corinthians
3:3 *255*
3:3–6 *265*
3:4–5 *271*
3:18 *31–32, 76*
4:4 *361*
5:17 *404*
5:19 *241, 248*
7:11 *300*
10:5 *242, 278*
10:9 *108*
11:3 *43*
11:13–14 *44*
12:8–9 *271*

Galatians
1:8–9 *403*
2:16 *148*
2:20 *54, 255*
3:8 *103*
3:22 *148*
3:24 *243*
4:4 *100*
4:19 *35, 76, 336*
4:30 *103*
5:16–26 *327*

Ephesians
1:3 *143*
1:3–6 *142–43*
1:7–13 *261*
1:10 *100, 239*
1:18 *274*
1:18–22 *101*
2 *139–41*
2:1–3 *140*
2:1–10 *139–40*
2:2 *139, 361*
2:4–7 *140*
2:5 *140*
2:6 *140*
2:8–10 *140, 404*
2:10 *139*
2:11–12 *140*
2:11–22 *140*
2:13–18 *140*
2:19 *140*
2:19–22 *140*

2:21 *140*
2:22 *140*
3:7–8 *62*
3:9 *251*
3:10 *100*
3:16–17 *31*
3:18 *251*
4 *18, 55*
4:4–6 *55*
4:5–6 *252*
4:7 *62*
4:7, 11–13 *62*
4:10–13 *35*
4:11 *45, 63, 102, 117, 390*
4:12 *63*
4:13 *63, 76*
4:13–16 *18*
4:17–24 *259*
4:20 *241*
4:21 *3, 241*
4:22 *54*
4:23 *47*
4:24 *54*
4:31 *55*
5 *187, 383*
5:2 *358*
5:6 *45*
5:22–6:9 *321*
5:22–33 *325*
5:23 *358*
6:10–17 *361*
6:12 *297*
6:17 *128*
6:18 *44*
11–16 *3*

Philippians
1:7, 16 *300*
1:15–18 *403*
1:27 *241*
2:5 *244*
2:12 *322*
2:13 *322*
3:9 *148*
3:10–14 *18*
4:8 *47*

Colossians
1:13 *361*
1:15 *100*
1:15–17 *357*
1:15–20 *377*
1:17 *349*
1:20 *77, 259*
1:28 *336*
1:28–29 *35, 76*
2:2–3 *254*
2:6–7 *251*
2:8 *44*
2:15 *358, 361*
3:3–4 *54*
3:18–4:1 *321*
4:16 *108*

1 Thessalonians
1:8–10 *320*
2:1–13 *102, 104*
4:1–2 *320*
5:27 *108*

2 Thessalonians
2:15 *5*

1 Timothy
1:5 *35*
1:8–11 *325*
2 *383*
2:6 *358*
3:1–7 *390, 399*
3:2 *46, 391*
3:15 *292*
4:1–3 *406*
4:7 *239*
4:13 *108*
5:18 *103, 108*

2 Timothy
1:11 *63*
1:12 *345*
1:13 *5*
2:1–2 *400*
2:2 *4, 401*
2:15 *4, 69, 135, 237, 339, 344*
2:24 *46*

2:26 *361*
3:1–4:5 *105*
3:1–9 *406*
3–4 *218*
3:7–8 *105*
3:15 *103, 117, 218*
3:16 *25, 103–4, 178, 218–19, 239, 265, 357, 375*
3:16–17 *27, 106, 155, 205, 342*
4:1–2 *155*
4:2 *218*
4:2–5 *391*
4:3–4 *105*
4:4 *218*
4:5 *392*
4:16 *300*

Titus
1:5–9 *390, 399*
1:9 *3–4, 46, 391*
2 *383*
2:1 *376*
2:1–8 *400*

Hebrews
1:1–2 *269, 328*
1:1–4 *100, 226*
1:2 *175*
1:3 *100*
2:10 *76*
4 *271*
4:12 *96, 269*
5:14 *243*
7–8 *137*
8:8, 13 *198*
9:15 *198*
10:1 *175*
10:1–18 *323*
11:6 *50*
12:2 *198*
13:7 *269*

James
1:10–11 *96*
1:17 *51, 267*
2:24 *224*
3:17 *117*
4:3, 6–7 *179*

1 Peter
1:10–12 *250*
1:21–23 *269*
1:24–25 *96*
2:7 *358*
2:9 *240–41*
2:21 *323*
3:15 *18, 300–301, 335, 340*
3:15–16 *277*
3:18–21 *54*
5:1–4 *390, 399, 406*
5:5 *190*
5:8 *360*

2 Peter
1:1–2:3 *106*
1:1–4 *106*
1:4 *55*
1:5–15 *106*
1:12 *46*
1:16 *106*
1:17 *106*
1:19 *106*
1:19–21 *270*
1:19, 21 *104*
1:20 *103–4, 108*
1:20–21 *24, 104, 219, 265*
1:21 *103–4*
2:1–3 *106*
2:1–3, 12–22 *406*
3:1–13 *100*
3:15–16 *104, 108, 269*
3:18 *34, 76*

1 John
1:3 *55*
2:2 *358*
2:4, 9, 11, 18–19, 22 *44*
2:18–23 *406*
2:26 *44*
2:27 *43–44, 117*
2:28–3:2 *261*
3:20 *357*
4 *268*
4:1–3 *406*
4:7–10 *260*
4:7b–9a *268*
4:9 *175*
4:10 *268*
5:12–13 *219*
5:21 *323*

2 John
7–11 *406*

Jude
1–25 *406*
3 *44, 301, 308, 408*
4 *45*

Revelation
1:3 *108*
7 *83*
7:9 *359*
12:11 *283, 292*
13:10–12 *321*
14:6–7 *320*
16:16 *119*
17:14 *359*
19:6 *357*
19:10 *29*
19:11–16 *100*
19:13 *100, 269*
20–22 *262*
21 *383*
21:1–8 *100*
21:10–22:5, 12–13, 16, 20 *97*
21:23 *95*
22 *375*
22:6 *270*
22:13 *100, 357*
22:17 *337*
22:18–19 *270*
22:20 *123*

Name Index

A
Ackoff, Russell L. *235*
Adeney, Miriam *37*
Akinade, Akintunde *424*
Akin, Daniel L. *xvii, 17, 280, 389, 393, 407*
Albin, T. R. *31*
Alcántara, Jared E. *353*
Aleshire, Daniel L. *389*
Aleshire, Daniel O. *17, 34, 36, 41, 75, 410*
Alexander the Great *184*
Allen, Jason *72*
Allen, Roland *412*
Allen, Ronald B. *30–31*
Allison, Gregg R. *5, 251*
Allis, Oswald T. *309*
Ambrose *285*
Anderson, Leith *28, 41*
Anderson, Ray S. *254*
Anderson, Rufus *412*
Andrews, Dale P. *353*
Anselm *8, 303, 305, 345*
Anthony, Michael J. *21, 410*
Antiochus IV *184*
Aquinas, Thomas *xii, 8–9, 266–67, 279, 303, 305, 416*
Aristeas *197*
Aristotle *9, 135, 299–300, 327*
Arminius, Jacob *10*
Arnold, Clinton E. *190*
Arnold, John *298*
Ashcroft, Morris *397*
Athanasius *6, 109, 285, 391*
Augustine *7, 12, 75, 116, 280, 303, 305, 326, 347, 391*
Averroes *9*

B
Bahnsen, Greg L. *105*
Bailey, E. K. *337*
Bailey, Mark L. *xvii, 23*
Bailey, Raymond *353*
Balla, Peter *232*
Bangs, C. *10*
Banks, Robert J. *17, 41*
Barclay, John M. G. *196*
Bar-Efrat, Shimeon *173*
Barnett, Kristopher *59*
Barth, Karl *95, 98, 265–66, 277, 280*
Barth, Markus *241*
Bartholomew, Craig G. *240, 256, 262*
Barton, John *107, 113, 173*
Basil of Caesarea *6*
Batsaikhan, Uuriintuya *40*
Bauckham, Richard *103, 224*
Baur, F. C. *186–87*
Beale, Gregory K. *112, 229, 232*
Beasley-Murray, G. R. *54*
Bebbington, David *298*
Bechtel, Lyn *423*
Beckwith, Roger *108, 113*
Bediako, Kwame *412, 421*
Beegle, Dewey M. *105*
Beilby, James K. *314*
Bendroth, Margaret *298*
Benedict, Ruth *422*
Benson, Warren S. *21*
Bentham, Jeremy *327*
Bentley, J. H. *10*
Berkhof, Louis *423*
Bernard of Clairvau *8*
Bingham, D. Jeffrey *xvii, 93, 109*
Bird, Michael F. *20, 149, 191*
Black, David A. *191*
Blaising, Craig A. *6*
Block, Daniel I. *xvii, 192–93, 206, 208, 210–11, 216*
Bloesch, Donald G. *20*
Blomberg, Craig *365–66*
Bloom, Allan *374*
Bock, Darrell L. *228, 322*
Bockmuehl, Markus *191*
Boice, James Montgomery *348*
Bond, L. Susan *354*
Bonhoeffer, Dietrich *14, 76, 85, 352*
Borror, Gordon *30–31*
Bottum, Joseph *379*
Boulton, Matthew Myer *241, 243, 246, 256*
Boyce, James P. *16, 398*
Brackney, William *16*

Bray, Gerald L.   5–6, 8, 20, 302
Briggs, David   39
Brooks, David   375
Brotzman, Ellis R.   158, 173
Brown, Colin   13
Brown, H. O. J.   50
Brown, Peter   7
Brown, Raymond E.   106
Bruce, F. F.   106, 191, 241–42
Brueggemann, Walter   195, 201
Brunn, Dave   131
Brunner, Emil   265, 267–68
Burns, Bob   81, 89
Burtchaell, James Tunstead   374
Bush, L. Russ   314, 393
Byram, Michael   131

C
Cabal, Ted   303
Calhoun, Adele Ahlberg   89
Calian, Carnegie Samuel   41
Calvin, John   10–11, 98, 116, 201, 240–41, 243, 245–46, 326–27, 336, 342, 351, 391, 405, 416
Campbell, Constantine R.   xvii, 133, 137, 139, 147, 149, 150, 152
Cannell, Linda M.   41, 77–78, 245, 246
Carey, William   116
Carnell, Edward John   310
Carpenter, Joel A.   308
Carson, D. A.   104, 113, 138–39, 152, 217–18, 220–21, 225, 227, 232, 249, 394

Celsus   302
Cetuk, Virginia Samuel   80
Chadwick, Henry   6
Chafer, Lewis Sperry   322
Chandler, Diane J.   89
Chapell, Bryan   354
Chapman, Tasha D.   81, 89
Charry, Ellen T.   75, 256
Cheesman, Graham   37, 41
Childs, Brevard S.   195
Chisholm, Robert B.   173
Christian, C. W.   13
Chrysostom, John   6
Cicero   185
Clark, David K.   233, 237, 248, 256
Clark, Gordon   304, 306
Clark, Robert   410
Clement   6
Cleveland, Christena   83
Clowney, Edmund P.   72
Cole, Graham A.   xvii, 75–76, 81–82, 316
Coleman, Robert   366, 371, 400
Colet, John   9
Collins, John J.   165
Colson, Chuck   386
Colwell, E. C.   148
Comfort, Philip W.   191
Constantine   283, 285
Cook, E. D.   273
Copan, Paul   331
Corwin, Gary R.   34, 372
Cotton, John   xii
Craddock, Fred B.   397
Craigie, P. C.   97
Craig, William Lane   305, 314
Cranmer, Thomas   277
Cribb, Bryan H.   70
Croteau, David   132
Currid, John D.   131
Cushman, Robert E.   7

D
Davids, Peter H.   103
Davis, Vernon   40, 42
Decius   283
Dembski, William A.   314
Dempster, Stephen   376
Deresiewicz, William   375
DeRouchie, Jason S.   116
Descartes, René   269
Dettoni, John M.   76
Dever, Mark   378
Diocletian   283
Dockery, David S.   xvi–xvii, 3–5, 9–10, 12, 16, 18, 20–21, 28–29, 33, 42, 99, 191, 378, 388, 395, 408–10
Dorrien, Gary   13
Dostoyevsky, Fyodor   126
Duduit, Michael   xvii, 59, 338
Dulles, Avery R.   301, 314
Dunbar, David G.   108
Duncan, J. Ligon, III,   378
Dunn, James D. G.   149
Dwyer, Karen Kangas   87
Dyrness, William   427

E
Ebba, Alice   373
Edgar, Brian   23, 42
Edwards, Jonathan   341, 391
Ehrman, Bart D.   112
Eichrodt, Walther   95–97, 195
Eldredge, L.   193
Elias, John L.   12, 21
Eliot, T. S.   234
Elliger, Karl   120
Elliot, Jim   392
Elliott, Ralph H.   397
Ellis, E. Earle   187
Emerson, Matthew Y.   227

Name Index

Emerson, Ralph Waldo 93
Enns, Paul 104
Enyinnaya, John O. 87
Erasmus, Desiderius 9–10
Erickson, Millard J. 18, 423
Escobar, Samuel 427
Eusebius 109
Evans, Craig 191
Evans, G. R. 13

F

Fanning, Buist M. 149
Farley, Edward 42, 57, 78, 234
Fea, John 298
Fee, Gordon D. 191
Feinberg, John S. 330
Feinberg, Paul D. 330
Fields, Lee M. 128
Finley, Thomas J. 132
Finn, Nathan 298
Forest, Benjamin K. 21
Fosdick, Harry Emerson 340
Foster, Richard 76, 85
Foster, Richard J. 77
Fowl, Stephen 242
Fox, Michael V. 162
Frame, John M. 4, 30, 113, 310, 376, 405
France, R. T. 106
Froehlich, Karfried 5
Fuller, Charles E. 310
Fuller, Chuck 66–67
Fuller, Daniel P. 105
Funk, Robert W. 112
Futato, Mark David 173

G

Gabler, J. P. 193–94, 236
Gadamer, Hans-Georg 237–38
Gaffin, Richard B. 147
Gangel, Kenneth O. 89

Garrett, James Leo, Jr. 272, 423
Garrett, Stephen M. 114
Gautama, Siddhartha 350
Geisler, Norman L. 113, 423
George, Timothy xi, xiii, 5, 11, 16, 20–21, 28, 354
Gerrish, B. A. 11
Giese, Ronald L. 171
Gignilliat, Mark 177
Gill, Robin 331
Gilson, Etienne 9, 269, 279
Giussani, Luigi 16
Goheen, Michael W. 262
Goldingay, John 97, 157, 173, 195, 198, 216
Goldsworthy, Graeme 376
Gomes, Alan 423
González, Justo L. 7, 11–12, 21, 83
Graham, Billy 405
Granberg-Michaelson, Wes 37
Grant, Robert M. 6
Graybill, Gregory B. 11
Green, Jay D. 298
Green, Joel B. 182, 191
Greenman, Jeffrey P. 89
Gregory of Nazianzus 6, 279, 280
Gregory of Nyssa 6
Grenz, Stanley J. 18
Griffin, Hayne P., Jr. 69
Grillmeier, Alloys 6
Groothuis, Douglas 314
Groves, Anthony 412
Grudem, Wayne 423
Gruen, Erich S. 197
Grundy, Peter 131
Guinan, Michael D. 120
Guinness, Os 72
Gundlach, Bradley J. 15

Guthrie, Donald 186, 229–30
Guthrie, Donald G. 81, 89

H

Habermas, Gary 305
Habets, Myk 247
Hafemann, Scott J. 229, 232
Hagner, Donald 176, 178
Halbertal, Moshe 108
Hall, Matthew J. 388
Hall, M. Elizabeth Lewis 79, 81
Halstead, Philip 247
Hamilton, James M., Jr. 250, 376
Hancock, Curtis L. 57
Hannah, John D. 20, 27
Hansen, Collin 394
Harris, Dana M. xvii, 74
Harris, James H. 354
Harris, John 78
Harris, Murray J. 148
Harrison, Everett F. 310
Harvey, Dave 73
Hasel, Gerhard 195, 216, 220
Hauerwas, Stanley 57
Hayes, John H. 195
Hays, Richard B. 149
Heber, Reginald 342
Helseth, Paul 15
Hengel, Martin 185
Hengstenberg, Ernst Wilhelm 194
Henry, Carl F. H. 304, 306, 310, 387–88
Herodotus 135
Hesselgrave, David 427
Hess, Mary 36, 42
Hiebert, Paul G. 412, 420, 427
Hillary of Poitiers 177
Hill, Charles E. 112–13, 181, 182

Hill, Jonathan 8
Hill, Michael 316–17, 331
Hinch, Jim 112
Hodge, A. A 15
Hodge, Charles 15, 235, 249
Hodges, Melvin 412
Hoffecker, W. Andrew 15
Hogan, Edward M. 87
Holifield, E. Brooks 14
Holmes, Arthur 410
Homer 181
Hooker, Richard 272
Horner, David A. 303
Horton, Michael S. 25, 147, 322
House, Paul J. 195
House, Paul R. 76, 89, 216, 229, 232, 348
Howard, David M., Jr. 173
Howard, Thomas A. 11, 13, 21
Hughes, R. Kent 62
Hume, David 269
Hunter, James Davison 386
Hus, Jon 9
Hüttl, Pia 40
Hutton, Jeremy 120
Hwang, Jerry 213

I
Iorg, Jeff 73
Irenaeus 6, 109, 302, 391

J
Jacobson, Douglas 37
Jenkins, Philip 37
Jennings, Willie James 83
Jensen, Robert 26
Jerome 108
Jethani, Skye 407
John of Damascus 416
Johnson, Keith L. 256
Johnson, Lin 410

Josephus 108, 185, 197
Julius Caesar 181
Justin Martyr 6, 109, 273–74, 301–2

K
Kaiser, Walter C., Jr. 195, 216
Kalantzis, George 74, 89
Kant, Immanuel 269, 327
Kapic, Kelly M. 267, 280
Keener, Craig S. 4, 191
Keith, R. 194
Kellum, Scott 181
Kelly, J. N. D. 6
Kelsey, David H. 17, 42, 57, 78, 243
Keneally, Thomas 207
Kierkegaard, Søren 306
King, Philip J. 173
Kinlaw, Dennis 176
Kinnaman, David 315
Klink, Edward W., III 220, 227, 232
Köstenberger, Andreas J. 132, 181, 220–21, 227, 232
Kramsch, Claire 115
Kreft, Peter J. 315
Kruger, Michael 181, 182
Kruger, Michael J. 108–9, 112, 114
Kuiper, Rienk Bouke 392
Kuruvilla, Abraham 354
Kuyper, Abraham 382, 388

L
Ladd, G. E. 220, 228, 232
Ladd, George Eldon 310
LaRue, Cleophus James 354
Lawless, Charles E. (Chuck) xvii, 355, 359, 361, 365

Lawrenz, Mel 76
Lea, Thomas D. 69
LeClercq, Jean 74
Lee, Gregory W. 250
Lee, Zuk-Nae 422
Legaspi, Michael C. 236
Leibert, Julius 207
Leiman, Sid Z. 108
Lemke, Werner E. 202
Lessing, Gotthold Ephraim 235–36
Levenson, Jon 196
Levering, Matthew 7
Lewis, C. S. 104, 274, 304, 373, 387, 393
Licinius 283
Liefeld, Walter L. 77
Lindars, Barnabas 5
Lindbeck, George 78
Lindsell, Harold 310
Lipka, Michael 38
Lischer, Richard 354
Litfin, Duane A. 42
Livingston, James C. 14
Lloyd-Jones, David Martyn 354
Lockett, Darian R. 220, 227, 232
Lockridge, S. M. 349
Lombard, Peter 416
Longenecker, Richard N. 5
Longfellow, Henry Wadsworth 373
Longman, Tremper, III 170, 173
Long, Thomas G. 27
Long, V. Philips 173
Lovelace, Richard F. 76
Lowe, Mary L. 86–87
Lowe, Stephen D. 86–87
Luther, Martin 9–10, 116, 126–28, 287, 391, 409
Lutzer, Erwin 65
Lysias 135

Name Index

M
MacArthur, John *271*
MacArthur, John F. *371*
Maccabeus, Judas *108*
MacDonald, Gordon *64, 68*
Machen, J. Gresham *116, 309*
Magary, Dennis *159*
Mahaney, C. J. *378*
Maimonides *9*
Malina, Bruce *423*
Marcion *109, 284, 302*
Marsden, George M. *4, 15, 21, 57, 307, 374, 388*
Marshall, I. Howard *178, 222, 228, 244*
Martens, Elmer A. *195, 201*
Massey, James Earl *354*
Mather, Cotton *xi*
Mathews, Kenneth A. *xvii, 115*
Mathis, David *409*
Mbiti, John S. *420*
McCloughry, Roy *331*
McDonald, Lee M. *182, 191*
McDowell, Josh *305*
McGee, Gary B. *34*
McGee, Gary B. *372*
McGowan, Andrew B. *74*
McGrath, Alister *8, 26, 28–29, 57, 373*
McKenzie, John L. *196*
McKnight, Scot *45*
McQuilken, Robertson *331*
McRay, John *183, 191*
Meadors, Gary T. *256*
Meadowcroft, Timothy *250*
Meister, Chad *315*
Melanchthon, Philip *11, 13, 15*
Merrick, J. *114*
Mesguich, Sophie Kessler *130*
Metaxas, Eric *381, 388*
Metzger, Bruce *180*
Miller, Glenn T. *15–17, 22, 132*
Miller-McLemore, Bonnie J. *254*
Miller, Robert Moats *340*
Millers, Eric *298*
Mitchell, Henry H. *354*
Mohler, R. Albert, Jr. *17, 279, 378, 391, 395–96*
Montgomery, John Warwick *305*
Moreau, A. Scott *34, 372*
Moreland, J. P. *305*
Morgan, Christopher W. *xvii, 148, 217, 225, 227*
Morris, Leon *106*
Mounce, William D. *128*
Mouw, Richard J. *82, 388*
Mulholland, M. Robert, Jr. *77*
Murdock, D. M. (Acharya S) *207*

N
Naidoo, Marilyn *80, 86*
Nash, Ron *306, 310*
Netland, Harold A. *427*
Nettles, Thomas J. *16*
Neusner, J. *185*
Nevin, John Williamson *15*
Nevius, John *412*
Newbigin, Lesslie *xiii*
Newcomer, Alphonso Gerald *373*
Newman, Cardinal *xiii*
Nicholls, Bruce *423*
Niebuhr, Reinhold *xiii*
Noelliste, Diememe *23*
Noll, Mark A. *8, 15, 22, 57*
Nyamiti, Charles *425*

O
O'Brien, Peter *241*
Ockenga, Harold John *310*
O'Connor, Michael Patrick *117*
Oden, Thomas C. *29, 52, 58, 354*
O'Donovan, Oliver *317, 375*
Ollenburger, Ben C. *194*
Olson, Roger E. *14*
Olthius, James H. *393*
O'Malley, John W. *12, 306*
Origen *6, 273, 302*
Osborne, Grant R. *256*
Oswalt, John *176*
Ott, Craig *427*
Outler, Albert C. *272*
Owen, John *116*
Owens, Virginia Stem *5*

P
Packer, J. I. *20, 38–39, 114, 178–79, 372, 403–4, 410*
Palka, John M. *78, 86*
Palmer, Parker *35*
Pannenberg, Wolfhart *423*
Parrett, Gary *410*
Pascal, Blaise *304, 306*
Patterson, Paige *274*
Paulsell, Stephanie *82*
Payne, J. D. *412*
Pearcey, Nancy *382, 386*
Pelikan, Jaroslav *6, 415*
Pellican, Conrad *130–31*
Peristiany, J. G. *423*
Perkins, William *380*
Peterson, Eugene *85*
Peterson, Robert A. *148*
Phillips, J. B. *348*
Philocrates *197*
Piderit, John J. *9*
Pilch, John L. *423*

Piper, John *362, 378, 401, 406*
Placher, William C. *8*
Plantinga, Cornelius *94*
Plant, Stephen *76*
Plato *135, 181, 299, 302*
Pliny the Younger *282*
Plummer, Robert L. *360*
Pobee, John S. *424*
Porter, Stanley *191*
Pratico, Gary *122*
Pratt, Zane *356, 372*
Preuss, Horst Dieter *195*
Provan, Iain *173*
Prussner, Frederick *195*

Q
Quarles, Charles *181*
Quash, Ben *316, 331*

R
Rabil, A. *10*
Reeves, Michael *4, 58*
Reid, Alvin *355, 372*
Reid, Thomas *50*
Reisz, H. Frederick *78*
Renn, Stephen D. *128*
Reuchlin, Johannes *130*
Richards, Jay Wesley *314*
Robert, Dana *411*
Robertson, A. T. *133–34, 136, 151–52, 175*
Robinson, G. *33*
Robinson, Haddon W. *338–39*
Rogerson, John *5*
Routledge, Robin *195, 216*
Rowland, Christopher *5*
Rubin, Aaron D. *120*
Rudolph, Wilhelm *120*
Runge, Steven E. *151*
Russell, Mark L. *369*
Ryken, Leland *170*
Ryken, Philip Graham *112*
Ryle, J. C. *318*

S
S, Acharya (D. M. Murdock) *207*
Sailhammer, John *162*
Saint Anselm *50*
Sanders, E. P. *146*
Sandy, D. Brent *171*
Sandys-Wunsch, J. *193*
Sanneh, Lamin *411*
Sargent, Tony *31*
Sarna, Nahum M. *94, 214*
Saucy, Robert L. *3, 19*
Savonarola, Girolamo *9*
Schaeffer, Francis *310, 382, 388, 410*
Schaff, Philip *15*
Schlatter, Adolf *220–21*
Schleiermacher, Friedrich *xii, 13–14, 186*
Schmidt, J. E. C. *186*
Schreiner, Thomas R. *229, 231–32, 376*
Schreiter, Robert J. *425*
Schwarz, Hans *277*
Schweitzer, Albert *146*
Scobie, Charles H. H. *220*
Scott, David *255*
Scruton, Roger *269*
Seitz, Christopher *179, 191*
Sellers, R. V. *6*
Sharp, Granville *148*
Shaw, Perry *17, 42, 369, 372*
Shutt, R. J. H. *197*
Sills, David M. *356, 372*
Sills, M. David *367*
Simmons, Martha J. *354*
Sire, James W. *82, 393*
Slout, Allyn *410*
Smalley, Beryl *7*
Smith, Gary *173*
Smith, Gordon T. *81–82, 84*
Smith, James B. *85*

Smith, James K. A. *75, 85, 89*
Smith, Robert *354*
Smith, Robert R. *335*
Smith, Robert R., Jr. *xviii*
Smith, Wilbur *310*
Socrates *299, 344*
Spitzer, Peter James *132*
Sprinkle, Preston M. *149*
Sproul, R. C. *388*
Spurgeon, Charles Haddon *65, 398–99*
Stache, Kristine *33–34, 42, 78*
Stackhouse, John G., Jr. *30, 42*
Stackhouse, Max *xiii*
Stager, Lawrence E. *173*
Stanley, Charles *405*
Stanphill, Ira F. *345*
Starling, David *244*
Steinmetz, David C. *9*
Stendahl, Krister *236*
Sternberg, Meir *162*
Stetzer, Ed *28*
Steuernagel, Carl *194*
Stevenson, Robert Louis *94, 113*
Stinton, Diane *425*
Stoddard, Richard Henry *93*
Story, Cullen I. K. *302*
Stott, John R. W. *331, 339*
Strachan, Owen *xviii, 17, 373, 381, 385, 388*
Streett, R. Alan *xviii, 299*
Sumner, Sarah P. *xviii, 43*
Sung, Elizabeth Y. *84*
Svigel, Michael J. *27–28, 42*
Swain, Scott R. *238, 256*
Sweeney, Marvin *196*
Sweetman, Brendan *57*
Sweis, Khaldoun *315*

Name Index

T
Tacelli, Ronald K. *315*
Tanner, Kathryn *280*
Taylor, Barbara Brown *354*
Taylor, Hudson *412*
Taylor, William M. *207*
Tennent, Timothy C. *xviii, 20, 411, 421, 427*
Terry, John Mark *372*
Tertullian *6, 273–74, 326, 344–45*
Theodore of Mopsuestia *6*
Theodosius *285*
Theophilus *301*
Thielicke, Helmut *280, 335, 341, 423*
Thielman, Frank *228, 232*
Thiessen, Henry *423*
Thiselton, Anthony C. *269*
Thoennes, Erik *79, 81*
Thomas, Frank A. *354*
Thomas, Heath A. *240, 256*
Thornbury, Gregory *410*
Thucydides *135*
Tienou, Tite *420*
Torrance, Iain *280*
Tov, Emmanuel *132*
Towns, Elmer L. *21*
Tozer, A. W. *52, 58, 94*
Trajan *282*
Treier, Daniel J. *245, 256*
Trible, Phyllis *171*
Trier, Daniel J. *20*
Trueman, Carl *178*
Truett, George W. *68*
Trull, Richard E., Jr. *412*
Tully, Eric J. *xviii, 153, 158, 173*

V
Valerian *283*
Vanhoozer, Kevin J. *xii, xviii, 17, 19–20, 233, 251, 256, 274, 376*
Van Neste, Ray *xviii, 174, 186*
Van Opstal, Sandra Maria *83, 85, 89*
Van Pelt, Miles *122*
Van Til, Cornelius *306, 309–10*
Van Wolde, Ellen *132*
Venn, Henry *412*
Verhoef, P. A. *11*
Vogt, Peter T. *173*
Volf, Miroslav *19*
Volz, Carl *74*
von Rad, Gerhard *195*
von Schlözer, A. L. *117*
Vos, Geerhardus *223, 376*

W
Wainwright, Geoffrey *277*
Waldo, Peter *9*
Walker, Williston *302*
Wallace, Daniel *180–81*
Wallace, Daniel B. *148–49*
Walls, Andrew F. *421, 427*
Walters, Jeff *356, 372*
Waltke, Bruce *201*
Waltke, Bruce K. *117, 216*
Walton, John *162*
Ward, Matthew *277*
Warfield, B. B. *15, 116*
Webster, Douglas M. *354*
Webster, John *252, 256, 267–68, 275–76, 278, 280*
Wellhausen, Julius *164–65, 203*
Wells, David *410*
Wells, Samuel *316, 331*
Wellum, Stephen J. *251*
Wenham, David *225, 251*
Weninger, Stefan *122*
Wheeler, Barbara G. *75*
Whitney, Donald S. *77*
Wilberforce, William *380–81*
Wilhoit, James C. *89*
Willard, Dallas *77*
Williams, Clifford *82, 89*
Williams, Rowan *29*
Williams, S. N. *270*
Wills, Gregory A. *xviii, 16, 281*
Wilson, Alistair *178*
Wilson, Robert Dick *309*
Witherington, Ben, III, *228*
Wolterstorff, Nicholas *50*
Woodbridge, John *113*
Wood, Charles M. *239, 256*
Wrede, William *222–23*
Wright, Christopher *156*
Wyatt, John *331*
Wycliffe, John *9*

Y
Yarbrough, Robert W. *223, 232*
Yarhouse, Mark A. *316*
Yarnell, Malcolm B., III *xviii, 257–58, 265, 267, 269, 271, 275, 278, 280*
Yieh, John H. *116*
Younger, K. Lawson *162*
Yu, Charles *216*

Z
Zevit, Ziony *196*
Zimmerman, Jens *237*
Zuck, Roy B. *228*
Zwingli, Ulrich *116*

Subject Index

A
abortion *325*
apologetics *299–300*
  early Christian *300–301*
  as interdisciplinary *310–11*
  theological apologists *303–4*
apologetic schools of thought *305–6*
Aramaic *123–24*
Aramaic Targums *124–25*
archaeology *183*
assessment *87*

B
baptism *52, 53–55*
Bible as unity *198, 218*
Bible School movement *308*
biblical interpretation *10, 105n, 179, 188–89, 237–38*
biblical theology *220–21, 248–50*
biblical translation *126–27*

C
calling *59, 63–64, 66*
  confirmation of *67*
canon *107–10*
Christ-centered faith *29–30*
Christian worldview *381–82, 393*

church
  in the fourth century *284–85*
  in the Middle Ages *286–87*
community *82, 85, 263, 343*
comparative literature *161–62, 184–85*
conservative seminaries, birth of *309–10*
creed *52–53*
cultural engagement *385–86*

D
Dead Sea Scrolls *119–20*
diachronic approach to theology *420*
discipleship *365–66, 400–401*
disciplinary fragmentation *234–35*
discourse analysis *150–51*
diversity *83–84*
doctrine *375–76*

E
early American seminaries *14–16, 307–8*
Enlightenment *12–14, 186*
ethnicity *383–84*
evangelism *355–56*
exegesis *170–71, 187–88*

exegetical fallacies *138–39*
explanatory power of Christianity *377–78*
expository preaching *338–40*
extrabiblical ethical theories *327*

F
faith *49–50*
family *383*

G
gender *383*
general revelation *97*
gifting *62*
global church *411–12*
  contributions in *421–26*
global mission *34, 82, 128, 356*
gnostic heresy *284*
God's Word *96*
gospel message *357–59, 402–4*
Great Commission *55–56, 359–60, 392, 396–97*
Greek
  commentaries *144–45*
  syntax *141–43*
  for theology *146–49*
  verbal aspect *149–50*

Subject Index

H
Hebrew
  language *118–19, 120–22*
  vocabulary *122*
hermeneutics (see biblical interpretation)
higher criticism *186–87*
historical theology *250–51, 415*
history, importance of *289–90, 291–93, 294–97*
Holy Spirit *178–79, 361*
human flourishing *75, 97*

I
illumination *95*
individualism *80*
inerrancy *105–7, 112*
inspiration *24–25, 102–5, 219*

J
JEDP theory *164–65*

K
knowledge *404–5*
  theological concept of *46–48*

L
learning Christ *241–42, 244*

M
Masoretic Text *120*
ministry
  challenging nature of *65*
  preparation for *69, 363–64*
missional *18, 33*
morality versus ethics *317*

N
New Testament
  for the church *177–78*
  diversity in *224–25*
  historical background *183–84*
  as revelation *175, 176–77*
New Testament theology *221–22, 226*
  in education *230–31*
  method *227–30*
  nature of *222*

O
Old Testament
  challenges for studying *154–55*
  composition of *196–97*
  geography *161*
  historical background *159–61*
  as Scripture *155–56*
  views of the text *165–67*
Old Testament theology *171, 193, 195, 199–201*
  history of *193–94*
  method *203–6*
  orthodoxy *27–28*

P
pastor-theologian *390–91*
persecuted church *282–83*
practical theology *253–54*
prayer *85, 179, 343–44*
preaching *336–37, 402*
  need for languages in *134–35*
  text to sermon *352–53*
  use of language in the sermon *137*

Protestant Reformation *287–88*
public square *383*

R
reading Scripture theologically *243*
reason *50–51*
redemptive history *97*
relationship of the Old Testament to the New Testament *156–57, 175–76*
rule of faith *6–7*

S
Sabbath rest *85*
same-sex marriage *325*
scriptural authority *24, 25–26, 110–11*
self-theologizing *417–19*
semitic languages *117–18*
service *69*
silence *94–95*
source criticism *163–64*
special revelation *99–102, 269–70*
spiritual disciplines *77n*
spiritual formation *31–32, 76–77, 78–79, 84–85, 130*
  in the curriculum *84*
  online *86–87*
  self-awareness in *81–82*
spiritual warfare *361*
sufficiency of Scripture *271–72*
systematic theology *252–53, 266, 276, 278, 415, 416–17*
  as loving God *260*

T
textual criticism *158–59, 180–82*
theological conviction *397–98*

theological education
  challenges to *16–17,
    36–40, 408–9*
  curriculum and methodology in *11,
    367–70*
  early history of *4–14*
  ethics in *329–30*
  goal of *23, 34–36,
    75, 174*
  importance of language
    in *125–26*
  need for *44–45*
  purpose of *18, 48,
    240, 242, 379,
    395–96*
  relationship to the
    church *19–20,
    33–34, 45–46, 357,
    364–65, 389–90,
    394, 406–7*
  responsibility of *4,
    18–19*
  use of the Bible in
    5–6, 111
  value of *51–56*

theological ethics
  316–17, 327–28
  and relationship
    319–22
theological interpretation
  of Scripture *247–48*
theological programs
  70–72
theology *49–51,
  340–41, 414–15*
Torah *211–14, 216*
Trinity *28–29, 267–68*

U
understanding *239*

W
wisdom *75, 245*
work *382*
world religions *370*
worship *30–31*